Let My Nation Ascend

Let My Nation Ascend

The story of the Jewish people's ascent to Eretz Yisrael, from the Waters of Conflict to the crossing of the Jordan

A compilation of Talmudic and Midrashic sources

YOSEF DEUTSCH

FELDHEIM PUBLISHERS
JERUSALEM NEW YORK

Also by the author:
Let My Nation Go (Jerusalem: Feldheim Publishers, 1998)
Let My Nation Live (Brooklyn: Mesorah Publications, Ltd., 2002)
Let My Nation Serve Me (Brooklyn: Mesorah Publications, Ltd., 2004)
Let My Nation Descend (Jerusalem: Feldheim Publishers, 2008)
Let My Nation Wander (Jerusalem: Feldheim Publishers, 2012)

Series design: DC Design
Cover illustration: Deb Hoeffner
Page layout: E. Chachamtzedek

ISBN 978-1-59826-865-2

FELDHEIM PUBLISHERS
POB 43163/ Jerusalem, Israel
www.feldheim.com

10 9 8 7 6 5 4 3 2 1

Printed in Israel

Approbation for Let My Nation Descend

Rabbi CHAIM P. SCHEINBERG
Rosh Hayeshiva "TORAH ORE"
and Morah Hora'ah of Kiryat Mattersdorf

הרב חיים פינחס שיינברג
ראש ישיבת "תורה אור"
ומורה הוראה דקרית מטרסדורף

בס"ד, אלול תשס"ו

מכתב ברכה

הובאו לפני גליונות של הספר החשוב "Let My Nation Descend" שחברו הרה"ג ר' יוסף דויטש שליט"א, עבור דוברי אנגלית, ובו מברר ומבאר המחבר את הפרשה של יוסף הצדיק עם אחיו לפי מדרשי חז"ל, שלא יחשוב הקורא כאילו הדברים כפשוטם אלא יראה קצת עומק הדברים, ומכוח זה מתגלה הסיפור מלא אמונה ויר"ש בירידת כלל ישראל לגלות מצרים. ויש בזה הרבה חיזוק לאדם באמונה בהשם יתברך בעת צרה. ובודאי יביא הספר תועלת רבה וחזוק גדול לבית ישראל.

על כן אברך את המחבר שליט"א שיזכה לשבת באהלה של תורה, ולחבר חיבורים מועילים ולהפיצם בבית ישראל להגדיל תורה ולהאדירה.

הכו"ח לכבוד התורה ולומדיה,

חיים פינחס שיינברג

Elul 5766

I was shown the manuscript of the important book, *Let My Nation Descend*, written by Rabbi Yosef Deutsch, *shlita*, for the benefit of the English-speaking public.

The author writes in a very clear and comprehensive fashion and helps us understand the disagreement between Yosef haTzaddik and his pious brothers, according to the Midrash and the words of our Sages. One should not, God forbid, take the verses of the Torah at face value and think that is all there is to the episode. Through studying this book, one can glean an even deeper understanding and discover a story full of *emunah* and *yiras Shamayim*, during Klal Yisrael's descent into Egyptian exile. There is much here to strengthen one's *emunah* in difficult times. Certainly this book will bring much benefit and great *chizuk* to the Jewish People.

I therefore offer my blessing to the author, *shlita*, that he merit to continue studying Torah and producing quality *sefarim*, which shall spread throughout the Jewish People and enhance the honor of the Torah.

רחוב פנים מאירות 2, ירושלים, ת.ד. 6979, טל. 537-1513 (02), ישראל
2 Panim Meirot St., Jerusalem, P.O.B. 6979, Tel. (02) 537-1513, Israel

This book is dedicated
as an Aliyah for my father

אברהם בן עזרא ע"ה

lovingly called

Albert Roberts

who dedicated himself to providing for
and protecting his children.

And to my mother,
may she live in good health עמו"ש

Ruth M. Gordon

who continues to be a source of love
and support for my children.

Acknowledgments

FIRST AND FOREMOST is my infinite gratitude to the Ribbono Shel Olam for the *siyata diShmaya* as well as the *zechus* to complete my sixth book in the *Let My Nation* series. I can only pray that He continue to give me the strength and fortitude to write, and to be a source of honor to His holy Name.

Let My Nation Ascend is thus named because it covers the final leg of the Jewish people's wandering in the wilderness, as they ascend toward the Promised Land. As with my other books in this series, *Let My Nation Ascend* draws from *midrashim* and commentaries on the Torah, offering varying viewpoints and opinions on the events that took place. I have included two maps to help the reader get a better understanding of where particular events took place. I am hoping that, as with my previous books, the reader will get a new perspective on or a better understanding of the events in the wilderness, and the proper lessons that should be gleaned from them.

I would like once again to thank the readers who have offered feedback regarding my work. I appreciate their support, and encourage them to offer their guidance in the future as well.

In addition, I wish to show my appreciation toward the following:

Rav Yaakov Yosef Reinman is not only a great friend and editor, but a true *talmid chacham* who has offered me guidance and direction on properly articulating the Torah commentary in the book.

Rav Eliyahu Levine, Rosh Kollel of Kollel Choshen Mishpat, has given me his precious time in assisting me with the complexities of this book's subject.

Rav Kalman Krohn has an uncanny ability to zero in on the lessons learned from the events in the Torah, and has significantly contributed to this book's success.

Rav Yirmiyah Gugenheimer has always been a source of encouragement and guidance throughout the writing process. I truly appreciate all of his help.

Eugene Zaveloff has unselfishly given me his warm support as well as the use of his library.

Without the tireless efforts, patience and expertise of Mrs. Deena Nataf of Feldheim Publishers Jerusalem, I cannot imagine what *Let My Nation Ascend* would look like. She has raised it to a level I never imagined could be attained.

To the rest of the editorial, design and production staff of Feldheim Publishers, my deep and sincere thanks. Your help and professionalism is apparent on every page of this book.

Nothing would nor could be possible without the support of my family. My brothers, my parents and my parents-in-law have all played important roles in giving me support, as well as many helpful suggestions and input.

Finally, my wife is a continuous source of encouragement and help. Everything I have accomplished is to her credit. Without her patience and support for my writing, not even one book could have been produced.

Yosef Deutsch
Lakewood, NJ
Nisan 5772

Contents

PROLOGUE

A New Generation Arises

Our last volume, *Let My Nation Wander*, chronicled the Jewish people's sojourn in the wilderness, from the building of the Mishkan through the Korach Rebellion. Henceforth, life settled down to a set rhythm —the nation encamped around the Mishkan, with the Shechinah visibly resting among them. Their basic needs were provided for. They had abundant food in the form of *mahn*, and Miriam's Well provided them with all the water they needed. They studied the Torah, and they regularly received new commandments regarding the Mishkan and Jewish life in general. They knew that due to their sin, brought about by the Spies, they were condemned to remain in the wilderness for the rest of their lives; they came to terms with their fate and made the best of it.

At the same time, the youth matured in this pristine and rarefied environment of holiness and *deveikus* with the Almighty. Hashem had declared: "And your young children about whom you said, 'They will be left for plunder'—I will bring them [to Eretz Yisrael] and they will experience the land which you have despised" (*Bamidbar* 14:31). After many years of wandering, the time was approaching for the Jewish people to fulfill this divine plan of conquering Eretz Yisrael and settling it. With courage and fortitude, emboldened by a deep trust in Hashem and filled with a sacred purpose forged in the crucible of the wilderness experience, this new generation was ready to meet the challenges that lay ahead. And as we shall see in this volume, challenges there will be...

1 Waters of Conflict

After the incidents of the spies and Korach's rebellion, the Jewish people remained in Kadesh Barnea for a long time. It was a period of adjustment and adaptation to the new realities of life,[1] and Hashem allowed them to stay on for another nineteen years.[2] And then, early one morning, the people were surprised by the

1. Every Tishah b'Av night witnessed the sad spectacle of each man having to lay down in what threatened to become his grave, a painful reminder of past misdeeds and their consequences. See Rashi with *Sifsei Chachamim* and Mizrachi, *Devarim* 1:46; *Seder Olam* 9.

2. Together with the sixteen months they had been in the wilderness until then, the Jews had thus far spent more than twenty years there. Compare *Yalkut Me'or haAfeilah*, Ibn Ezra on *Bamidbar* 20:1. See also Rashi with *Sifsei Chachamim* and Mizrachi, *Devarim* 1:46; *Seder Olam* 9.

blaring of trumpets in the camp of Levi signaling that the encampment was about to relocate.

For the next nineteen years, the encampment moved on the average of once a year.[3] From Chatzeiros, they traveled to Rimon-peretz, named for the abundant pomegranates to be found there.[4] Then they traveled to Livnah, named for its brick (*leveinah*) boundaries,[5] and then on to Risah and then Keheilasah[6] and afterward to Har Shefer, a mountainous region blessed with beautiful fruits.[7] From there they traveled to Charadah and then to Makheilos[8] followed by Tachas.[9] They then traveled to Tarach, followed by a place called Miskah, known for its sweet and fresh water.[10] From Miskah they traveled to Chashmonah,[11] and from there to Moseiros, a place where the Jewish people faced rebuke and chastisement.[12]

---

3. See Rashi, *Devarim* 1:40.

4. *Targum Yonasan, Bamidbar* 33:18–19. Part if not all of the Paran wilderness was also known as Rismah, because—as Rashi notes—there the spies slandered Eretz Yisrael, and *Tehillim* 120:4 compares slander to the coals of *resamim* (broom trees).

5. *Targum Yonasan, Bamidbar* 33:20. All the following explanations are based on *Peirush Yonasan*, a commentary on *Targum Yonasan*.

6. According to Tur, *Bamidbar* 33:22, the name Keheilasah, literally "gathering," alludes to Korach's gathering his supporters against Moshe.

7. *Targum Yonasan, Bamidbar* 33:23.

8. According to *Targum Yonasan, Bamidbar* 33:24, the name Charadah, literally "trembling," indicates a place where they trembled over a plague. As for Makheilos, "gatherings," *Sha'arei Aharon* suggests that there they repented for the sins of Korach's gathering. The words *charadah* and *charatah* (regret) are interchangeable.

9. According to *Targum Yonasan, Bamidbar* 33:26, Tachas, literally "below," connotes the lowlands of Makheilos.

10. *Targum Yonasan, Bamidbar* 33:28.

11. Chashmonah was the twenty-fifth encampment of the Children of Israel in the wilderness, where they rested from their journey. This alludes to the holiday of Chanukah, which commemorates the "resting" of the Chashmonaim (Hasmoneans) from their battles against the Greeks on the twenty-fifth of Kislev (*Sefer haToda'ah*, chap. 11).

12. *Targum Yonasan, Bamidbar* 33:30. Moseiros was named thus for the rebellious actions of the Jewish people upon their future return to this place

They then traveled to Bnei-ya'akan, known for its narrow passageways, or narrow wells or pits,[13] after which they moved to Chur-hagidgad, known for its mountains laced with cracks, crevices and clefts.[14] Then they traveled on to Yotvasah, known for its flowing brook[15] that made it a pleasant place to relax.[16] From there, they traveled to Avronah, which was a river crossing.[17] Afterward, they moved on to Etzion Gever, a city of either chickens or roosters.[18]

Finally, on Rosh Chodesh Nisan of the fortieth year of the Jewish people's sojourn in the wilderness, they arrived and settled in a place called Kadesh, in the wilderness of Tzin.[19] There they would stay for four months.[20]

By the time they arrived in Kadesh, all the people condemned to spend the rest of their lives in the wilderness had passed away.[21] The remaining Jews were righteous, and living in unity and harmony.[22] The latter would not discover that they had merited to enter the Holy Land until Tishah b'Av, when they would lie down

---

following the death of Aharon. ("*Moseirah*" derives from the word *musar*, rebuke. The Jews rejected rebuke, and as a result rebelled.) Malbim, *Bamidbar* 20:29, suggests that Aharon is buried here. See *Devarim* 10:6 and Rashi. See also *Devarim* 10:7.

13. *Targum Yonasan, Bamidbar* 33:31. These pits were dug by the children of Anak (Rokeach, cited by *Torah Sheleimah, Bamidbar* 33:13).

14. Ibid., verse 32.

15. See *Devarim* 10:7.

16. *Targum Yonasan, Bamidbar* 33:33.

17. Ibid., verse 34.

18. Ibid., verse 35. The people there knew all about these fowl and may have even worshiped images of them.

19. See *Seder Olam* 9. According to Rabbeinu Meyuchas and Alshich, this was part of the wilderness located on the edge of Tzin, near the land of Edom.

20. See *Seder Olam* 9; *Chizkuni*, Bamidbar 20:1. Gra, *Seder Olam* 9, suggests that the Jews arrived on 10 Nisan.

21. See Rashi, Ibn Ezra on *Bamidbar* 20:1.

22. *Lekach Tov, Ohr haChaim* on *Bamidbar* 20:1; *Yalkut Shimoni* 763. See also Rashi, *Bamidbar* 20:1, 22.

in their graves and no one would die—but Moshe was already aware of it.[23]

Miriam's Well Runs Dry

The thirty-eight years between Korach's rebellion and the Children of Israel's arrival in Kadesh were uneventful, in both a positive and a negative sense. There were no more eruptions against Moshe and his authority. But there were also no more revelations of the Shechinah or prophecy to Moshe, because the divine anger did not completely subside as long as transgressors still lived.[24]

On 10 Nisan,[25] shortly after the Jewish people's arrival in Kadesh, Miriam passed away at the age of 125. She was the sister of Moshe, a great prophetess in her own right, the charismatic leader of the Jewish women and an inspiration for all the Jewish people to serve Hashem with proper devotion.[26] Because of her supreme righteousness, she died via a divine kiss,[27] so to speak, by which the light of the Shechinah touches the person and painlessly draws out the soul from the body. Moshe and Aharon were the only two other people who passed away in this manner.[28]

Rather than dishonor Miriam by carrying her through the wilderness until the Jewish people reached the Holy Land, she was

---

23. See Malbim, *Bamidbar* 20:1; Rashi, *Bava Basra* 121a. See also Rav Chaim Paltiel; *Chasam Sofer* 101.

24. Rabbeinu Bachya, *Bamidbar* 20:1; *Yevamos* 72a with Tosafos; *Pesikta d'Rav Kehana* 50b. According to Rabbeinu Bachya, *Devarim* 2:16, after Moshe mourned the final deaths on Tishah b'Av, Hashem revealed Himself to him on 16 Av. See *Tehillim* 95:10 with Radak.

25. *Seder Olam* 10; *Targum Yonasan*, *Bamidbar* 20:1.

26. See *Targum Unkelos*, Rashi on *Michah* 6:4; Ralbag, *Bamidbar* 20:1.

27. Rashi, *Bamidbar* 20:1; *Bava Basra* 17a.

28. See *Ben Yehoyada*, *Bava Basra* 17a; *Morech Nevuchim* 3:51. See also *Ohr ha-Chaim*, *Vayikra* 16:1, for his explanation of this "divine kiss."

buried in Kadesh, in a holy place with a holy name among holy people.[29]

Miriam was an extraordinary woman, completely selfless and devoted to others. At great risk to herself, she helped save Jewish infants when Pharaoh decreed that they be cast into the river. When the infant Moshe was set afloat on the river, during that dreadful time, it was Miriam who lingered on the riverbank to insure that he was safe. She was always involved in various community activities and issues. She promoted family purity among the Jewish women, and she led them in song after the splitting of the sea.[30]

It would have been appropriate for the Jewish people to react to Miriam's passing with a flood of tears and a public display of grief and mourning.[31] They should have stood in line to offer their condolences to Moshe and Aharon, the grieving brothers.[32] They should have organized gatherings and delivered glowing eulogies.[33] But they did none of those things. They just murmured their obligatory words of regret, and then they went on with their lives. The consequences of their lackadaisical attitude were not long in coming.

The people's water supply during their forty-year sojourn came from a miraculous well that accompanied them in the merit of Miriam.[34] It had appeared forty years earlier when the Jewish people encamped at Refidim had no water.

---

29. *Sifsei Kohen, Bamidbar* 20:1; *Eliyah Rabbah,* cited by *Torah Sheleimah, Bamidbar* 20:24. Until Moshe's death, this area near Edom was considered a part of Eretz Yisrael belonging to the tribe of Levi. See *Sha'arei Aharon, Bamidbar* 20:1; Malbim, *Bamidbar* 20:14; *Meshech Chochmah.*

30. See *Sifsei Kohen,* Rabbeinu Bachya on *Bamidbar* 20:2.

31. Alshich, ibid.

32. Abarbanel, ibid.

33. *Kli Yakar,* ibid.

34. See *Let My Nation Wander* (Jerusalem: Feldheim Publishers, 2012), p. 66 ff.

"Go to one of the stones," Hashem had said to Moshe,[35] "and strike it with your staff. The very staff that transformed water into blood will now bring forth water from a rock.[36] But do not select the stone yourself. If you do, people might say you were drawing water from a hidden subterranean well, and you wanted to make it look like a miracle. Let the elders choose the stone, and you strike it. I assure you that whichever stone you strike will give forth water."[37]

Moshe struck the stone, and it did indeed give forth water. And from then on it accompanied the Jewish people in the wilderness and provided water for them.[38] Our Sages say that this stone had been prepared for this purpose from the time of Creation, and it gave forth its waters in Miriam's merit.[39]

When she passed away, however, the well ceased to provide water.[40] The Jewish people had failed to shed tears for her, and now the well refused to "shed" water for them.[41] The merit of Moshe or Aharon could have restored the flow of water from the rock, but the Jewish people did not deserve it. And so, millions of Jewish people were left waterless in the barren wilderness.[42]

---

35. Ramban, *Shemos* 17:5.

36. *Targum Yonasan*, Ramban, *Chizkuni*, Seforno on ibid.

37. See *Shemos Rabbah* 26:2 and commentaries.

38. See *Seder Olam* 10; *Ta'anis* 9a with Rashi; Rashi, Maharsha on *Shabbos* 35a; *Yalkut Shimoni* 764.

39. *Pirkei d'Rabbi Eliezer* 19. According to *Pirkei d'Rabbi Eliezer* 3 and Radal, this stone was created on the second day of Creation.

40. See *Shabbos* 35a; *Ta'anis* 9a; *Sifsei Chachamim*, *Bamidbar* 20:2. Miriam had merited this well by tending to the babies Pharaoh sought to kill (*Anaf Yosef*). Maharsha, *Ta'anis* 9a, says that although the well returned in the merit of Moshe and in theory should never have dried up, it ceased temporarily in order to show that the merit was originally Miriam's.

41. *Toldos Yitzchak*, *Minchah Belulah* on *Bamidbar* 20:1–2. Some say there was water, but not for the Jewish people. The well didn't dry up; rather, it was clogged (Alshich, *Bamidbar* 20:2).

42. See Tur, Malbim, *Sifsei Kohen* on *Bamidbar* 20:2.

Renewed Complaints

The people were distraught. They could not understand why the flow of water had ceased.[43] It seemed to them that even if Miriam was no longer alive, the water should continue to flow in the merit of Moshe and Aharon. It did not occur to them that they were responsible because of their failure to give Miriam the proper posthumous honor she deserved.[44] Following their usual practice, they decided to seek out Moshe and demand answers.[45]

As the crowd approached Moshe's tent, Moshe and Aharon were sitting on the ground and mourning their deceased sister. "Look at that crowd, Aharon," said Moshe. "I wonder what they want."[46]

"These are kind and charitable Jewish people," said Aharon, "descendants of Avraham, Yitzchak and Yaakov. They are probably coming to console us."

Moshe shook his head. "It looks more like a mob to me. If they were coming to console us, the chiefs and princes would be leading the way. It looks to me like they're up to no good."[47]

The mob gathered in front of Moshe's tent and called out the names of both Moshe and Aharon, but presently they calmed down a bit and directed their comments to Moshe alone.[48]

"Why are you crying over your sister?" they asked.

"Because she died," replied Moshe. "We mourn the dead. Why shouldn't I cry over her? She was my sister and a great woman."

---

43. *Chizkuni*, ibid.

44. See Tur, Malbim, *Sifsei Kohen* on ibid. The Jews had also failed to emulate Moshe and Aharon. They neither learned Torah nor acted with kindness, through which they would have merited water (*Sifsei Kohen*).

45. *Minchah Belulah*, ibid.

46. *Midrash haGadol*, *Bamidbar* 20:3; *Midrash haBeiur* 20:6.

47. *Yalkut Shimoni* 763. Compare *Yalkut Pisron Torah*.

48. *Lekach Tov*, Tur on *Bamidbar* 20:3. According to *Midrash haGadol* and Seforno, their complaints were directed toward Hashem as well.

"While you sit there crying for one woman," they said, "you will soon be crying over many thousands. There is no water, and we are all dying of thirst."

Moshe and Aharon investigated, and discovered that it was indeed true. The flow of water from the rock had ceased.[49]

"It seems," said Moshe, "that there is no water now that Miriam's merit is no longer with us."

"But what about your merit?" one of the men protested. "And Aharon's merit? The two of you have provided us with the *mahn* and the cloud pillars. Why can't you provide us with water as well?"[50]

"We want you to help us, Moshe," said another man. "We are dying of thirst, and we hold you responsible. It is because of you that we are here so deep in the wilderness.[51] You could have prayed to Hashem to take us to the Holy Land by a shorter route.[52] If you can't provide us with water, why did you bring us here in the first place? Back in Egypt, we at least had abundant water. What good is freedom when you're dying of thirst?"[53]

"You know something," said yet another man, "I'm beginning to envy those who died on Tishah b'Av after lying down in the grave.[54] I'm even beginning to envy Korach and his faction who were swallowed up by the earth,[55] or even those who perished in the plagues.[56] At least they died quickly, while we are condemned

---

49. *Midrash haGadol*, ibid.

50. See Tur, Malbim, *Kli Yakar* on ibid.

51. See *Ohr haChaim*, Alshich, *Akeidas Yitzchak* on *Bamidbar* 20:3–4. Because Aharon loved peace, the Jewish people vented their anger at Moshe alone (*Sifsei Kohen*).

52. See *Lekach Tov*, *Kli Yakar* on *Bamidbar* 20:3.

53. *Ohr haChaim*, Malbim on *Bamidbar* 20:4.

54. See *Lekach Tov*, Rokeach, Ibn Ezra, *Sifsei Kohen* on *Bamidbar* 20:3.

55. *Lekach Tov*, Rokeach on ibid.

56. Rashi, Malbim on ibid.

to a long and agonizing death by thirst.[57] In fact, I think it would have been better to drown in a sea of water, as the Egyptians did, than to die for the lack of even a drop of potable water."[58]

"I don't understand," said the first man. "In the past, when the Jewish people were sinners, the loss of water would have been understandable. But those people are basically gone, and our generation is righteous. Why have we been condemned to die of thirst?"[59]

"Explain to us, Moshe," said the second man who had spoken, "why you brought us out of Egypt to this barren wilderness.[60] When the well was giving water, the soil was irrigated and verdant with vegetation. We even enjoyed pomegranates and other fruits.[61] Now we have nothing; no food, no water. We have been condemned to die."[62]

"Both people and animals are on the verge of death," said a man who had been standing silently on the sidelines. "Are we guilty of something? Are our animals guilty of something?[63] Please enlighten us."

Moshe and Aharon remained silent.[64] They recognized the justice of the complaints, and they were ashamed that they were unable to provide for their flock.[65] They saw the level of anger in

---

57. Rashi, ibid. *Minchah Belulah* adds that the Jews would rather have died at the hands of Hashem, as in the previously mentioned deaths, than due to Moshe's inability to provide water.

58. *Toldos Yitzchak*, *Minchah Belulah* on ibid. According to *Yalkut Shimoni* 763, based on *Mishlei* 18:6, the Jews were foolish to utter this death wish.

59. Tur, *Bamidbar* 20:4; *Yalkut Shimoni* 763.

60. *Targum Unkelos*, *Bamidbar* 20:5.

61. See *Bamidbar Rabbah* 19:26; *Shir haShirim Rabbah* 4:13. See also Tur, Rokeach, *Tzeror haMor* on *Bamidbar* 20:4. And see *Let My Nation Serve Me* (Brooklyn: Mesorah Publications, Ltd., 2004), p. 95.

62. *Lekach Tov*, Rav Saadiah Gaon, Malbim on *Bamidbar* 20:5.

63. Rav Samson Raphael Hirsch, *Bamidbar* 20:4.

64. *Lekach Tov*, *Bamidbar* 20:6.

65. *Sifsei Kohen*, ibid.

the crowd rising and feared the mob might turn violent.[66] Without saying a word, they made their way through the crowd and went to the Ohel Mo'ed,[67] where they prayed[68] for prophetic enlightenment.[69] It came almost immediately.

Speak to the Rock[70]

"You have to serve the people, Moshe," Hashem said to him. "Now is not the time to sit and mourn your sister. The people are suffering, and they cannot be faulted for complaining.[71] Deal with them directly, and do not escape to the safety of the Mishkan. You are to draw water from the rock again."[72]

The previous time, back in Refidim, Hashem had instructed Moshe to have the elders choose the stone and to strike it with his staff. This time, it would be a different process. He was to assemble all the people in front of the stone and command it to resume giving water.[73]

---

66. *Midrash haGadol*, ibid.

67. *Yalkut Shimoni* 763.

68. Rabbeinu Bachya, *Bamidbar* 20:6. Ralbag suggests that Moshe "prayed" to the Jewish people to stop complaining. See *Sefer haIkarim* regarding the results of Moshe's prayer.

69. Ibn Ezra, ibid.

70. This is a difficult story with many views of what took place and how Moshe and Aharon subsequently erred. I have followed primarily Rashi, *Bamidbar Rabbah* and *Yalkut Shimoni*. All text and commentary are to be found in *Bamidbar* 20:8–13 unless otherwise noted.

71. *Midrash haGadol, Bamidbar* 20:3; *Yalkut Shimoni* 763. According to *Minchah Belulah, Bamidbar* 20:6, rather than withdrawing, Moshe should have admonished the Jews and assured them that Hashem could solve their water problem. The ensuing solution would have been a *kiddush Hashem*. Instead, Moshe found himself positioned to transgress Hashem's command by hitting the rock.

72. *Lekach Tov, Tzeror haMor, Sifsei Kohen* on *Bamidbar* 20:6. See Tosafos, *Yoma* 22b, s.v. *veha'amar*. See *Toldos Yitzchak* for a dissenting view.

73. According to *Bechor Shor*, this is nothing more than a more detailed recounting of the incident that took place forty years earlier.

"Take your staff," said Hashem,[74] "and speak to the same stone[75] in My Name. Tell the stone that I command it to give water,[76] and the streams will burst forth from it once again so that the people and their animals[77] can drink their fill. Do this in full view of all the people."

Why did Hashem want Moshe to speak to the stone here, when earlier at Refidim He had instructed Moshe to strike the stone with his staff?[78] First of all, Hashem never repeats a miracle in an identical form. If the first time Moshe struck the stone, there had to be a variation the second time.[79] But there were also deeper reasons.

In those days, before the Jewish people had received the Torah, their faith was weaker. The spectacle of striking the stone and extracting water was a sufficient miracle to impress them and inspire them with awe. But now the people were on a much higher spiritual level, and they would have taken in stride the sight of

---

74. See *Targum Yonasan; Yalkut Shimoni* 763; Zohar 272a; *Lekach Tov.*

75. *Be'er Yitzchak.* According to Malbim, however, this was a different stone altogether. *Shemos* 17:6 refers to a *tzur*, a rock-solid stone that had to be struck to produce water. This stone, a *sela*, was softer, stored rainwater in its cavities, and therefore needed only to be spoken to. Yet releasing water from such a stone simply by addressing it is no less miraculous than producing water from a *tzur*.

Be'er Mayim Chaim mentions that *sela* is spelled *samech, lamed, ayin,* and the middle letters of these words spell *mayim*, water.

76. See *Targum Yonasan; Lekach Tov.* The water was still there, just blocked. Moshe had only to command the stone to unseal itself. See *Yalkut Pisron Torah.*

77. Hashem's concern for the Jews' livestock showed that He cares about Jewish property (*Bamidbar Rabbah* 19:9).

78. *Ha'amek Davar* states that Hashem wanted Moshe to speak to the stone in order to teach the Jewish people the fundamentals of prayer. When there is no rain, one must pray. In the absence of sacrificial offerings, one prays. Now too, lacking water, Moshe was to pray—and the stone would then bring forth water.

79. *Lekach Tov*, Rokeach. Hashem drowned the generation of the flood in rain and the Egyptians in the sea. He sweetened bitter water, then surpassed that by producing drinking water from a rock. By failing to speak to this rock, Moshe lowered the level of the miracle, and that was his sin.

Moshe striking the rock and water gushing forth. They needed a greater miracle to make their eyes open wide with wonder and awe; they needed the stone to produce water with nothing more than an oral command.[80]

Alternatively, before the Jewish people had received the Torah, they were comparable to a child that needs to be disciplined by his parents with an occasional slap. Likewise, the nation in its infancy needed to see the symbolic spectacle of Moshe striking the stone. But once the Jewish people had coalesced into a mature nation, there was no longer any need for such symbolism. Oral guidance was sufficient.[81]

Be that as it may, although Hashem instructed Moshe to speak to the stone, He still wanted him to bring his staff.[82] The staff had wrought miracles in the past, as when the Jewish people had battled Amalek,[83] and its mere presence would also be effective.[84] Furthermore, when the stone saw the same staff that had extracted water from it forty years earlier, it would obey Moshe's command.[85]

According to another view, Moshe was to bring Aharon's staff rather than his own,[86] because the former had sprouted blossoms and almonds. When the stone would see that a dry wooden staff could produce almonds when commanded to do so, the dry stone would give forth water when it was so commanded.[87]

---

80. See *Sefer haIkarim*; *Panim Yafos*.

81. See *Yalkut Shimoni* 763; *Tosefos Rabbeinu Yoel*; *Yalkut Midrash Teiman*; Alshich. See also *HaKesav vehaKabbalah*. See *Chasam Sofer* 103 for a similar insight. According to *Ha'amek Davar*, Moshe was supposed to have taught the Jews a word or two of Torah, then have them pray for water, just as one prays for rain. But he failed to do that.

82. *Lekach Tov*.

83. *Ma'aseh Hashem*. See *Let My Nation Serve Me*, p. 120.

84. Alshich.

85. *Me'am Lo'ez*. The staff signified that the Jewish people deserved to be chastised for their rebelliousness (*Chizkuni*; Rashbam).

86. Rashbam; *Chizkuni*; *Panim Yafos*; *Chasam Sofer*.

87. See *Kli Yakar*; *Panim Yafos*. The words *eitz* (wood) and *sela* (stone) have the

Moshe did as Hashem had instructed. He took the staff and went to the spot where he thought the stone was situated.[88]

More Dissension

Moshe assembled all the people around the stone he had identified as the source of the water. Hashem wanted every Jew to be an eyewitness to the miracle that was about to happen,[89] and therefore, miraculously, every single one of the people was able to stand within four *amos* of the stone[90] with an unobstructed view of the proceedings.[91]

"What is going on here?" one man scoffed. "Are we about to witness a miracle involving a stone that Moshe has chosen? I'm not impressed. The son of Amram is an experienced shepherd. He knows how to find subterranean springs and bring forth their water. This won't be much of a miracle, more like a sleight-of-hand. If he wants to impress us, he should let us select the stone from which he will extract water. After all, if it's a miracle he intends to perform, what difference does it make if it's this stone or another?"[92]

Moshe turned and saw that the people had indeed gone off to find stones of their own. In fact, men from each of the twelve tribes were pointing to stones they had chosen for the miracle.[93]

Moshe was angry. Hashem had specifically instructed him to approach the stone that had served as the original Well of Miriam. Could he really disregard his instructions and go instead to a

---

same numerical value (170). *Panim Yafos* adds that it would have been a greater miracle to use Moshe's dry staff than Aharon's moist, flowering one. According to Rashbam, Moshe took Aharon's staff because its miraculous sprouting of almonds recalled the Jews' previous disputes (i.e., Korach's rebellion).

88. *Lekach Tov*.

89. Ramban; *Bechor Shor*; *Hadar Zekeinim*. The miracle would show that the Shechinah was among them.

90. Alshich. See Rashi, *Vayikra* 8:3.

91. See Rashi; Tur; *Midrash haGadol*; *Bamidbar Rabbah* 19:9; *Tanchuma*, *Chukas* 9.

92. *Yalkut Shimoni* 763; *Bamidbar Rabbah* 19:9.

93. *Yalkut Shimoni* 763; *Midrash haGadol*.

different stone chosen by the people? On the other hand, if he disregarded their wishes, the credibility of the miracle would be undermined. But what would happen if he spoke their stone and it did not respond? That would certainly be an embarrassment. No, the safest course of action was to do exactly as Hashem had instructed regardless of the skepticism of the scoffers.[94]

For forty years, Moshe had assiduously distanced himself from the misdeeds of the people. He had never sinned or otherwise transgressed, and he thought he was protected from the decree that all the Jewish men except for Yehoshua and Kalev were to die in the wilderness. He had worried about the omission of his name in that context, but he was hopeful nonetheless. But the predicament he was now facing was more complicated, and he did not manage to extricate himself safely.[95]

"Listen to me, you rebels,"[96] he called out to the people milling about. "Do you think you're worthy of miracles?[97] Do you really think I'll be able to bring forth water from any of these stones[98]—other than from the one regarding which Hashem commanded me? Do you think you can identify the stone Hashem has chosen? Fools! Only Hashem can bring forth water from a stone, and I swear that the only water brought today from a stone will be the one of my choosing."[99]

---

94. *Bamidbar Rabbah* 19:9.

95. Ibid., with Mahrzu, Radal.

96. Moshe called the Jews rebels because, rather than complain, they should have prayed, knowing that all their needs would then be met (*Bechor Shor*). Alternatively, they were rebels because they slandered Hashem and quarreled about water (*Matnos Kehunah*; Mahrzu). Compare Malbim.

97. Alshich.

98. Some say the Jews misunderstood Moshe. They thought that, rather than posing a rhetorical question, he was stating, "I will bring water from these stones." When he failed to do so, the Jews therefore lost some of their faith in Hashem's powers (*Midrash Aggadah*). See Ibn Ezra.

99. See *Yalkut Shimoni* 763; *Lekach Tov*; *Midrash haGadol*; *Bamidbar Rabbah* 19:9; Rashi; Rokeach; *Da'as Zekeinim*; *Bechor Shor*.

Moshe Hits the Stone

While Moshe was chastising the people, the designated stone rolled away into a field of identical stones.[100] Moshe followed the stone, but by mistake, he settled on the wrong one.

"Give forth water!" he commanded the stone.[101]

No water came forth, because unbeknownst to Moshe, it was not the stone to which Hashem had commanded him to speak. Unaware that he had spoken to the wrong stone, Moshe began to have second thoughts about what he was supposed to do. Perhaps he hadn't been meant to speak to the stone at all. Perhaps he was just supposed to strike it, just as he had done forty years before in Refidim.[102]

Another thought occurred to Moshe. Perhaps the stone had not responded to him because the people had scoffed at him and thereby disqualified themselves from witnessing a miracle of the highest order. Perhaps they did not deserve to witness anything more than water emerging from a stone that had been struck.[103]

---

100. Hashem orchestrated this complication because Moshe had gotten angry and verbally attacked the Jewish people. *Midreshei haTorah* says that because Moshe became angry, he forgot where the correct stone was.

101. Rashi. *Tzeror haMor* adds that only after they saw Moshe searching for the designated rock did the Jews demand that their own rocks be used, as they were thirsty and couldn't wait any longer.

102. Rashi; *Midreshei haTorah*; Riva. Some say Moshe believed that the stone could give water via a verbal command only in the Shechinah's presence. Earlier, among the elders, the Shechinah was present. Now, however, amidst all these rebels, it was absent, so the only way to produce water was to hit the stone. See *Panim Yafos*.

103. Alshich; *HaKesav vehaKabbalah*. According to *Tzeror haMor* and Malbim, Moshe meant that, as rebels, the Jews didn't deserve miracles. Yet Hashem works wonders for the wicked as well, if only to show them His mighty hand and sanctify His Name. Moreover, adds Alshich, the fact that originally the people had all miraculously fit in front of the stone was proof enough that they were worthy of miracles. Perhaps Moshe felt that the Jews had forfeited that merit by arguing further or were worthy of only lesser miracles. Whatever Moshe's rationale, Hashem considered it an error in judgment. See *Chasam Sofer* 107.

But there was no time to speculate. The people needed water.

Moshe lifted his staff and struck the stone.[104] A liquid came forth, but it wasn't water; it was blood. The staff that in Egypt had transformed the waters into blood had now brought forth blood instead of water from the stone.[105]

The people recoiled. "Blood!" they shouted. "Do you expect us to drink blood?!"[106]

Hashem stanched the flow of blood, and instead, a tiny trickle of water emerged from the stone.[107] At this point, Moshe should have suspected that he had addressed the wrong stone, but he did not.[108]

"Moshe," said the scoffers, "do you expect to sustain the people with those few drops of water? This might be enough for an infant or two, but what about the millions of people who are thirsty for water?"[109]

---

104. Moshe thought that both speaking to and hitting the stone were necessary (*Ohr haChaim*). See Rokeach.

105. See *Targum Yonasan; Yalkut Shimoni* 2:819; *Midrash Tehillim* 78. See also *Shemos Rabbah* 3:13. According to *Chupas Eliyahu* and Malbim, after the stone bled, Moshe objected that no water had come out. Then Hashem commanded the stone to produce some. (This interpretation doesn't minimize Moshe's transgression in hitting the rock.)

Shemos Rabbah 3:13 notes that Moshe had come full circle. At the burning bush, he had said the Jews wouldn't have faith in his message, and that necessitated the sign of blood—to be produced through the staff. Now, that same staff had drawn blood from the stone, and this had minimized Jewish faith. Furthermore, this blood portended that Moshe's striking the stone would lead to his death. All this sheds new light on *Tehillim* 114:8, "[Hashem] turned the rock into a pool (*agam*) of water." The word *agam* has the same numerical value (44) as the word *dam*, blood. Thus, the verse can be understood as, "[Hashem saw to it that Moshe] turned the rock into a flow of blood" (Rabbeinu Bachya).

106. *Midrash Tehillim* 105.

107. See *Me'am Lo'ez*.

108. Rashi with Mizrachi; *Chizkuni*; Riva. *Midrash Aggadah* suggests that initially Moshe placed his staff on the stone. "Seeing" Hashem's Name engraved on the staff, the stone began dripping water. Only after Moshe actually hit the stone did water gush forth.

109. *Bamidbar Rabbah* 19:9.

Moshe was humiliated. He was determined to bring forth abundant streams of water from the stone to slake the people's thirst.[110] He raised his staff to strike the stone once again, and at that moment, the designated stone rolled back to where he was standing and resumed its rightful position.[111] Moshe brought the staff down onto it with a sharp blow. Immediately, a river of water erupted from the stone, sweeping away the scoffers who had spoken disrespectfully to Moshe.[112] And then, to the utter amazement of the people, all the stones in the field gave forth heavy streams, providing more than enough water to satisfy one and all.[113]

Moshe and Aharon Are Punished

The incident was over. The people had all the water they needed, but Moshe had failed an important test. Hashem told him to speak to the stone, and he had mistakenly struck it.

How could Moshe have made such an error? He knew the staff was only supposed to have a symbolic presence at the miraculous event, that it was not meant to be the instrument of its execution. So why did he use it?[114]

Moshe's grave error in judgment began well before he hit the rock in anger.[115] Anger causes people to err, and even Moshe fell

---

110. *Midrash haGadol*. See *Chizkuni* regarding how Moshe was to extract water from the stone.

111. Rashi with Mizrachi; *Midrash Aggadah; Midreshei haTorah.*

112. According to *Yalkut Reuveni*, when Moshe hit the rock the first time, he did so with the dry side of the staff. The second time, he used the side bearing Hashem's Name, and then the rock gave water.

113. *Bamidbar Rabbah* 19:9; *Midrash Aggadah*; Rabbeinu Bachya; *Midrash Tehillim* 78; *Yalkut Me'or haAfeilah*. As before, twelve streams spread across the camp, heading toward each tribe's encampment.

114. Mizrachi.

115. See *Gur Aryeh; Midreshei haTorah; Ha'amek Davar*. These suffering, thirsty Jews deserved the benefit of the doubt, not anger. Moshe's wrath thus made him a poor emissary of Hashem. That alone desecrated Hashem's Name and

victim to its consequences. When he allowed himself to become angry, he lost himself momentarily and struck the stone with his staff, and then he compounded his error by striking the stone a second time.[116]

"Because you struck the stone instead of speaking to it," said Hashem, "you have diminished the miracle I performed for the people, and thereby you have reduced the amount of faith the people would have derived from it had it been performed as I intended. If you had drawn water from the stone merely by speaking to it, it would have sanctified My holy Name among the people. They would have said, 'Here is a stone that neither speaks nor hears, that receives no reward or punishment for its actions, and still it obeys Hashem's commandment. Surely we, the living servants of Hashem who constantly need assistance, must fulfill His will and obey His commandments.'[117] Moshe and Aharon, because you failed to sanctify My Name, I swear you will both lose the opportunity to enter the Holy Land.[118] Instead, you will both die in the wilderness because of your transgression."[119]

---

warranted punishment. See *Midrash haGadol;* Rabbeinu Bachya; Rambam, *Shemonah Perakim* 4.

116. Mizrachi.

117. Rashi; *Midrash Aggadah.* Additionally, if Hagar had miraculously received water from a well in the merit of Avraham, surely the Jewish nation was worthy of receiving water through the hand of Hashem in the merit of the patriarchs (*Yalkut Shimoni* 763; *Sifsei Kohen*).

118. While both the spies as well as Moshe and Aharon died in the wilderness, their circumstances were quite different. The spies were punished with death; Moshe and Aharon were punished with not entering Eretz Yisrael and only consequently did they perish in the wilderness. Alternatively, both the generation of the wilderness and Moshe were punished for lacking faith, or causing such a lack (Malbim).

119. Rashi; Rabbeinu Bachya. See *Devarim Rabbah* 11:10. *Imrei Shefer* explains that Moshe couldn't pray his way out of this decree, because someone who desecrates Hashem's Name is denied the ability to repent (*Yoma* 86a). Alternatively, Moshe and Aharon were held to a far stricter standard than the rest of the Jews: Hashem scrutinized their actions meticulously and punished them severely (*Midrash Petiras Moshe,* cited in *Otzar Midrashim* 375).

"If I have sinned," Moshe responded, "what has Aharon done? Why should he lose the opportunity to enter the land? He is not the one who became angry or struck the stone. It was I."

"He should have stopped you," said Hashem. "He should have protested. He is responsible, because he was silent when he should have spoken."[120]

Moshe and Aharon did not sin against Hashem directly: they just failed to bring about a sanctification of His holy Name. Ordinarily, Hashem might forgive such a failing. Nonetheless, He held Moshe and Aharon accountable. This showed the people that everyone must suffer the consequences of their actions, even someone as great as Moshe about whom Hashem said, "He is trusted in My entire House."[121] Moshe's punishment sanctified the Name of Hashem by demonstrating that no one is exempt from responsibility.[122]

Other Views on Moshe's Transgression

The following are a number of other opinions regarding the nature of Moshe's transgression.

- Hashem had only instructed Moshe to assemble the elders as witnesses to the miracle, and on his own accord, Moshe had invited all the people, including the Eirev Rav.[123]
- Moshe should not have insisted on speaking only to the stone he himself had identified. This raised doubts about

120. See *Lekach Tov; Bamidbar Rabbah* 19:9; *Imrei Noam*. Even in punishment, however, Aharon is praised for his silence: rather than defending himself or questioning Hashem's justice, he simply accepted His decree (Mahrzu, *Matnos Kehunah*).

121. *Bamidbar* 12:7.

122. See Rabbeinu Bachya; *Yalkut Shimoni* 764; *Ma'aseh Hashem*. In fact, one reason this place was called Kadesh was that Hashem was sanctified through His judgment of Moshe and Aharon. See Rashbam; *Chizkuni*; Alshich.

123. Tur; Rokeach. See Rabbi Yehudah heChasid for a dissenting view.

the authenticity of the miracle in the minds of the people. In actuality, Hashem would have accommodated Moshe's decision regardless of which stone he chose, just as He had accommodated Moshe's idea of having the earth swallow up Korach and his faction. Had Moshe issued the command to any stone suggested by the people, he would have sanctified the Name of Hashem. His failure to do so was a missed opportunity, and he was held responsible.[124]

- Moshe should not have interrupted his mission in order to reprimand the people. Instead, he should just have spoken to the rock without the slightest delay.[125]
- Moshe was not careful to avoid giving the people the impression that he was going to extract water from the stone by his own power rather than as an agent of Hashem. Aharon should have been sensitive to this possibility as well, and since he did nothing to dispel such a possible impression, he was also held responsible.[126]
- Moshe should not have lost his temper and called the Jewish people rebels and fools, which was unbecoming for some-

---

124. *Midrash haGadol, Lekach Tov, Tzeror haMor*. See *Ohr haChaim, Ma'aseh Hashem*. By asking the people if they believed he would extract water from their stone, Moshe unwittingly created the impression that he couldn't, and that Hashem couldn't either. This question thus diminished the nation's faith and desecrated Hashem's Name. Nonetheless, Malbim writes that Moshe would have been forgiven if he hadn't erred a second time by hitting the rock, in addition to using his own rock instead of one chosen by the people.

125. *Tosefos Rav Ephraim al haTorah*. Compare *Sefer haIkarim*.

126. Rabbeinu Chananel; Rabbeinu Bachya; Rokeach; *Da'as Zekeinim*; *Tosefos Rav Ephraim al haTorah*. This impression was created either because Moshe said, "We [Moshe and Aharon] will bring forth water," or because he and Aharon left Hashem out of their statement. *Tzeror haMor* and Ibn Ezra add that Moshe created the impression that he would produce water from the stone because he knew how, not because Hashem can do anything. This failure to depict Hashem as the source of the miracle was the root of Moshe and Aharon's transgression.

one of his stature.[127] Had he controlled his angry reaction he would have sanctified the Name of Hashem, and therefore, he was held responsible for his failure to do so.[128]

- Moshe was punished for both degrading the level of the miracle and reprimanding the people with harsh language. Had he not spoken harshly to the people, Hashem would have forgiven him for his failure to speak to the stone.[129]
- Moshe should have hit the stone only once. He was held accountable for striking it a second time.[130]
- According to one view, Moshe's period of mourning for Miriam had caused a reduction in Torah among the Jewish people, and therefore, the well had ceased to give forth water. Had Moshe taught some Torah to the Jewish people, the situation would have been rectified, and the water would have begun to flow.[131]

Beginning with the rebellions at the sea and continuing with the bitter waters at Marah, crises involving water had been a recurring feature of the Jewish people's experience in the wilderness. Therefore, regardless of the specifics of his transgression, Moshe should have been more sensitive to the nuance of the situation when a new crisis involving water arose.[132]

---

127. *Pesikta d'Rav Kehana* 14; *Devarim Rabbah* 2:8. See *Devarim Rabbah* 2:2; *HaKesav vehaKabbalah*.

128. See Rambam, *Shemonah Perakim* 4; *Derashos Rav Yehoshua ibn Shu'eib*. See also *Bereishis Rabbah* 99:5. Additionally, the Jews might have presumed that Moshe couldn't have gotten angry unless Hashem was angry too. Since no anger was warranted, it was a desecration of Hashem's Name that they thought Hashem had wrongfully become angry (*Midrash haGadol, Bamidbar* 20:24).

129. See *B'Shem Omro*.

130. Abarbanel. Another view suggests that Moshe was to use the staff only if the stone wouldn't bring forth water. Moshe spoke to the wrong stone, however, so hitting it was a sin. See *Targum Yonasan*.

131. See *Yalkut Shimoni* 763; *Ha'amek Davar*.

132. *Ma'aseh Hashem, Bamidbar* 27:14.

The Impact of the Transgression

Earlier, when the complainers wanted meat, Moshe came close to questioning Hashem's ability to provide for their desires, and yet the Torah does not tell us that he was chastised and punished for his remarks.[133] Why then does the Torah take Moshe to task for his failure to only speak to the stone, a transgression that doesn't seem to rise to the level of his remarks regarding the complainers?

It is because those remarks were made in private, and therefore, Hashem was more tolerant of them. This transgression, however, took place in full public view, and it gave the impression that Hashem could not have drawn water from the stone if Moshe had done no more than speak to it. Therefore, Moshe was punished.[134]

Once Moshe learned that he would not be allowed to enter Eretz Yisrael, he requested from Hashem that the Torah publicize the reason for it. Since he knew he would die in the wilderness, he did not want suspicion to fall on him that he was complicit in the sin of the spies and that he had been punished along with them. Instead, he wanted the reason spelled out clearly in the Torah.[135]

The Torah therefore makes it very clear that Moshe was denied entry into the land for this reason alone. [136] Hashem made sure

---

133. See *Let My Nation Wander*, p. 96 ff. See also *Bamidbar* 11:22.

134. Rashi; *Bamidbar Rabbah* 19:10. In the case of the meat, questioning Hashem's ability was an outright desecration. In the case of hitting the stone, Hashem's Name was still sanctified, just not at its highest level—and yet Moshe was punished. See *Nachalas Yaakov; Maskil l'David*.

135. Rashi; *Bamidbar Rabbah* 19:12, 27:13; *Yoma* 86b.

136. See Rashi with *Be'er Yitzchak, Mesiach Ilmim* on *Bamidbar* 27:13; *Sifrei* 137; *Vayikra Rabbah* 31:4. Moshe's defenders would have said, "Had Moshe been guilty of the same crimes as the spies, he would have died along with them." The cynics would have argued that Moshe was already over the age of sixty and hence excluded from the forty-year decree of death. Thus, while he didn't die with them, he was guilty of the same transgression, and hence not allowed to enter Eretz Yisrael. To avoid this argument, Moshe asked that Hashem publicize his sin.

that Moshe's punishment was limited to this and that there were no other consequences. It would not besmirch his reputation.[137]

According to some views, the incident of the Eigel was a factor in the premature death of Aharon, who had played an indirect part in it, and the incident of the spies was a factor in the premature death of Moshe, who had made the decision to send them. Since the people were doomed to die in the wilderness, Hashem did not want their leaders to enter without them. The Midrash compares this to the king's shepherd who loses his flock. The king does not allow him into the city until the sheep are found.

Similarly, Hashem did not want the leaders of the doomed people to enter the land without them. At the same time, He did not want it to seem as if they were implicated in those crimes. Therefore, He waited until the incident with the stone and used this rather minor transgression as a pretext for barring them from the land, a decision that had already been predetermined almost forty years before. In the future, after the resurrection of the dead, those who were doomed to die in the wilderness will return to life, and Moshe will lead them into the Holy Land.[138]

The place where this incident happened came to be called Mei Merivah, Waters of Conflict. It was where the Jewish people came into conflict with Moshe when they entertained some doubt about the legitimacy of his actions.[139] It was also a conflict with Hashem, because any conflict with Moshe, Hashem's loyal servant, was by

---

137. *Tosefos Rav Ephraim al haTorah; Moshav Zekeinim.*

138. *Bamidbar Rabbah* 19:13 with Mahrzu. See Abarbanel and Malbim here and on *Devarim* 10:6. See also *Shabbos* 55b for an apparently different view.

In fact, this incident involves one of six sins for which Moshe was held accountable while leading the Jewish people (*Tanchuma, Va'eschanan* 6).

According to Rabbeinu Bachya, back in the days of Avraham, Hashem foreshadowed this episode by naming its location Ein Mishpat, "Spring of Judgment," for the justice Hashem was to execute on Moshe. See *Bereishis* 14:7.

139. Malbim.

extension a conflict with Hashem.[140] In another sense, the waters themselves were part of the conflict, since it was unclear which stone would produce the water.[141]

Many years before, Pharaoh's stargazers had foretold that the downfall of the Jewish redeemer would be through water. They believed they could effect this by throwing all male babies into the river, but Moshe survived those waters. His downfall came through the Waters of Conflict, which led to his being denied entry into the Holy Land and his premature death.[142] Nonetheless, although Moshe knew that his time was limited and that he would not accompany the people into Eretz Yisrael, he continued to lead them with undiminished devotion and enthusiasm.[143]

---

140. *Sanhedrin* 110a.
141. *Nachalas Yaakov*; Alshich.
142. Rashi; *Lekach Tov*.
143. Rabbeinu Bachya; *Tanchuma*, *Chukas* 12.

2

The Land of Red

After their four-month stay at Kadesh, the Jewish people were poised to end their travels in the vast wilderness where they had spent the previous forty years. It was now time to make the last push into the land of Canaan. The most direct route into Canaan passed through the land of Edom, which abutted Kadesh.[1]

The land was called Edom, which means red, because it was populated by the descendants of Eisav, who had sold his birthright for a bowl of red lentils. Red was the dominant color of Edom. Its king was red.[2] Its soil was red. The Edomites ate red food, and

1. *Me'am Lo'ez, Bamidbar* 20:14.
2. I.e., the "generic" name of their kings was "Edom."

they wore red clothing. And they saw red when they felt threatened.[3]

Before the Children of Israel approached the Edomite border, Hashem commanded Moshe not to provoke the Edomite nation.[4] As descendants of Yaakov's brother Eisav, the Edomites were blood relatives of the Jewish people. They had received the mountains of Se'ir as their inheritance, and the Jewish people were forbidden to violate their sovereignty by crossing through their land without permission.[5]

Hashem pointed out the patriarchs' burial place to Moshe.

"Tell the people," said Hashem, "that Eisav is still seeking rewards for the exemplary manner in which he honored his father Yitzchak, who is buried there. As part of the reward he has earned, the Jewish people will not be allowed to pass through his descendants' land without permission.[6] Remind them as well that when Yitzchak gave Yaakov his ten blessings, he also gave Eisav a blessing that he would live by the sword. If the people overrun Eisav's land and cause his descendants to lose their one blessing, the Children of Israel will lose the ten blessings they inherited from Yaakov. It is best, therefore, not to antagonize or provoke them."[7]

Hoping that the blood relationship would work in his favor,[8] Moshe decided to make an attempt to receive that permission. He called on certain Edomites living in the Kadesh area[9] and dispatched

---

3. *Lekach Tov, Bamidbar* 20:14. See *Bereishis Rabbah* 75:4.

4. See *Devarim Rabbah* 1:19. According to *Da'as Zekeinim, Devarim* 2:9, the Jews would have been right to war with Se'ir/Edom if not for this divine prohibition.

5. Rashi, *Ohr haChaim* on *Devarim* 2:4–5.

6. *Devarim Rabbah* 1:15, 17.

7. Ibid., 1:18.

8. Abarbanel, *Bamidbar* 20:14.

9. *Ha'amek Davar,* ibid. Knowing Hashem's command not to antagonize Edom, Moshe worried that if he sent Jewish messengers, they might encounter a frightened Edom. The Jewish people would then take advantage of Edom's vulnerability and seek to attack it. Therefore, Moshe sent gentile messengers.

them to the king of Edom with a conciliatory message.[10]

"Your Majesty, glorious king of Edom,"[11] the message began, "we are the descendants of Avraham, your relatives known as the nation Yisrael, the name given by the heavenly minister of your ancestor Eisav to our ancestor Yaakov, his brother.[12] We are presently on your border. The people of Yisrael send you this message: You know full well that the Almighty informed our common ancestor Avraham that his descendants would be sojourners in a strange land for four hundred years, after which they would inherit the Holy Land. We, the descendants of Yaakov, have paid that debt, while Eisav declined to pay a share of it and thereby relinquished all rights to a share in the land. And so he and Yaakov parted ways.[13]

"In fulfillment of the divine decree, we have indeed been outcasts, foreigners and laborers in a strange land for all those years, and afterward, we wandered in the wilderness for another forty years. We suffered enslavement, oppression and terrible privation in Egypt, and we have been through a war with Amalek.[14] The Almighty heard our anguished cries, and He brought us through our ordeal.[15] We have paid our debt,[16] and now we have

---

10. *Moshav Zekeinim* asks an obvious question: Why seek permission to pass through Edom when the cloud pillar might not have even led the Jews there? Perhaps the entire dialogue was simply to teach them not to challenge Edom. Additionally, the encounter was intended to preempt their possible resentment at once again traveling circuitously instead of directly.

11. *Minchah Belulah* suggests that the king of Edom had no official name at the time. Ramban says his identity was subordinate to his stature. *Yalkut Me'or haAfeilah* states that his name was Hadar. See *Bereishis* 36:39.

12. *Panim Yafos*. This introduction was meant to appeal to Edom's sense of brotherhood.

13. See Rashi, *Midrash Aggadah, Mesiach Ilmim* on *Bamidbar* 20:14. We felt brotherly toward Eisav, and still do; it was he who distanced himself (*Lekach Tov; Midrash haGadol*).

14. See *Kli Yakar, Midrash haGadol* on *Bamidbar* 20:14.

15. See Rashi, *Bamidbar* 20:17. The Jews emphasized their use of *Kol Yaakov*, the power of prayer.

16. *Ohr haChaim, Bamidbar* 20:14.

come to claim the land that rightfully belongs to us and no one else.[17]

"We have no designs on your lands. We do not wish to conquer or overrun your cities and fields. We just ask permission to pass through your land and continue on to the land of Canaan.[18] We look upon you as brothers, as our blood relatives,[19] and we would not invade or plunder your land as we would others'.[20]

"We understand that you might have reservations about allowing a nation as large as ours to pass through your land. We understand that you might be concerned that we will trample your fields or otherwise damage your land on our way. But with your cooperation, we will institute measures that guarantee the safety and security of your land.

"We will not pass through your fields and vineyards. We will travel only on the king's highway, the main thoroughfare[21] that leads directly through your land. We will not digress from this highway, neither to the right nor to the left. We will muzzle our animals to insure that they do not eat from the produce at the roadside.[22] We will even pay a toll for the right of passage.[23] You can choose a route for us and send a guide to direct us.[24] You can also send agents to supervise our passage and assure our compliance with the terms of passage.[25] We will put no strain[26]

17. See Rashi, *Midrash Aggadah, Mesiach Ilmim* on ibid.

18. See Abarbanel, *Bechor Shor* on *Bamidbar* 20:17.

19. *Bechor Shor*, ibid.

20. *Bamidbar Rabbah* 19:15.

21. Ibn Ezra, Seforno on *Bamidbar* 20:17. Sixteen *amos* wide, this road offered ample room for the Jewish retinue (*Yalkut Me'or Afeilah*).

22. Rashi, ibid.; *Bamidbar Rabbah* 19:15 with *Eitz Yosef*.

23. *Chizkuni*, *Bamidbar* 20:18.

24. Seforno, *Bamidbar* 20:17.

25. Abarbanel, ibid.

26. *Chizkuni*, ibid.

on your food or water supply,[27] because we have our *mahn* and our own itinerant water supply.[28]

"Please take into consideration all the troubles that we've experienced. Please look into your hearts and find a measure of compassion[29] for your brothers.[30] Please[31] allow us to pass through your lands, and we will be not only brothers but also good neighbors. Let us pass through and claim our inheritance."[32]

The Edomite Response

When the King of Edom received Moshe's message, he presented the question to his privy council.[33]

"I am opposed," said one minister. "These people were hosted by the Egyptians, and then they devastated the country; simply laid it waste. We cannot risk opening our borders to them. Who knows what they will do once they get past our defenses?"

"I couldn't agree more," said a second minister. "We have a long legacy of enmity toward this people. It is our hallowed tradition,[34] and they know it. Can we rely on their mercy—the mercy of an implacable foe?"[35]

The king invited comments from all his ministers. They were unanimous in their opposition to opening the borders to let the Jewish people to pass through their land. The king nodded his agreement. The matter was decided. The borders would remain closed.[36]

---

27. Rashbam, *Ha'amek Davar* on ibid.
28. Rashi, ibid; *Bamidbar Rabbah* 19:15.
29. *Minchah Belulah, Bechor Shor* on *Bamidbar* 20:14.
30. *Minchah Belulah*, ibid.
31. Tur, Rokeach on *Bamidbar* 21:21.
32. Rashi, *Bamidbar* 20:17.
33. *Meshech Chochmah, Bamidbar* 20:18.
34. See Rashi, *Bereishis* 33:4.
35. *Lekach Tov, Bamidbar* 20:21.
36. Ramban, *Bamidbar* 20:18.

The king composed a response to Moshe's message and dispatched it.

"Your request is denied. We give you no permission to take the short route to Canaan through our lands. We consider you thorns in our eyes, and we are not interested in promoting your agenda.[37] Furthermore, we are good neighbors with the Canaanites, and we do not want to stab them in the back by allowing you to pass through and invade their land. We want no part of it.[38]

"You pride yourself that our common ancestor Yitzchak blessed you with 'the voice of Yaakov,' meaning that the Almighty listens to your prayers. Let me remind you that this same ancestor blessed us that 'you shall live by your sword.'[39] We don't seek a confrontation with you, but we want you to know that we are formidable foes, easily provoked. Do not venture onto our lands if you do not want to face our swords."[40]

A Second Attempt

Undaunted by the initial rejection, Moshe composed a second message to the king of Edom.[41]

"Your Majesty, you put so much faith in your sword," he began, "but we put our faith in prayer. I assure you that if it came to a confrontation, your sword would be powerless against our prayers.[42] But you needn't worry, because we do not seek a confrontation. Unclench your fist, because we come unarmed and with only peaceful intentions.[43]

"We understand that you are apprehensive[44] about exposing

---

37. Rokeach, *Tzeror haMor* on ibid.

38. Abarbanel, ibid.

39. Rashi, ibid.

40. See Seforno, *Sifsei Kohen* on ibid.

41. Ralbag, *Bamidbar* 20:17. With Edom's refusal, Moshe had no fear of ambush. On the contrary, he inferred that Edom was afraid (*Sifsei Kohen*).

42. *Midrash haGadol*, *Bamidbar* 20:21.

43. *Meshech Chochmah*, *Bamidbar* 20:19.

44. Tur, *Devarim* 2:4, explains that upon seeing the blessings the Jews had inherited from Yaakov, the Edomites were afraid.

yourselves to possible attack or pillage.[45] And we understand that you are concerned that the Canaanites should not think you are in collusion with us.[46] Therefore, let us travel on a road that passes far from your cities,[47] farms and vineyards, and leads into the uninhabited hills and mountains. You could not be accused of being our ally if that is all you allowed us to do.[48]

"Our passage can also be an economic boon to your land, because although we have ample provisions with us, we will agree to purchase food and water from your people. We will even pay for water we draw from rivers and ponds.[49] And do not be concerned about our ability to pay. We may have been enslaved for hundreds of years, but we left Egypt with great wealth, as indeed the Almighty had promised Avraham.[50] Come see for yourself how rich we are. We are willing to pay, and pay well, for anything you provide us. If you welcome us with compassion and goodwill, our passage will bring you only benefit."[51]

The response from the king of Edom was quick to come.

"Our position is essentially unchanged," he declared. "We are not averse to a bit of profitable business. If you want to buy provisions from us we will be happy to sell them to you, especially because you offer to pay top prices.[52] But we will you not allow

---

45. *Bechor Shor*, *Bamidbar* 20:18.

46. Abarbanel, *Bamidbar* 20:19.

47. Ramban, Seforno on ibid.

48. Rav Samson Raphael Hirsch, ibid.

49. See *Chizkuni*, Ralbag on *Bamidbar* 20:17; Malbim, *Bamidbar* 20:19; Rashi, Ramban on *Devarim* 2:6.

50. *Bamidbar Rabbah* 19:15.

51. Rashi, *Bamidbar* 20:17; *Bamidbar Rabbah* 19:15; Ramban, *Chizkuni* on *Bamidbar* 20:21; Rashi, *Devarim* 2:6. Moshe told the Jews to boast of their wealth, not out of arrogance, but to express appreciation for Hashem's blessing.

52. Rashi with *Gur Aryeh*, *Devarim* 2:29.

you to step foot onto Edomite soil. That is final."[53]

The Edomite rejection was reinforced by a full military mobilization. Large numbers of cavalry, infantry and archers[54] massed at the border, blocking every avenue of ingress.[55] The Edomite forces presented a fearless front, confident in their legacy of living by the sword[56] and in their alliance with their Amalek neighbors.[57]

Moshe reported the response to the disappointed people. "We come to them with an offer of peace," he said, "and they flash their swords at us."[58]

"I don't think we should be intimidated," one man called out. "Behind all that bluster, I think they're afraid of us."[59]

"Let's attack," said another,[60] "and teach them a lesson they'll never forget."

"We cannot do that," said Moshe. "Hashem has forbidden it. We could conquer them with ease, but Hashem has commanded us not to step onto their territory without their permission.[61] We may not even speak to them in a hostile manner.[62] We have no choice but to turn aside and look for a different route."[63]

---

53. Abarbanel, *Bamidbar* 20:21. In the end, fearing attack and the resultant use of their land to destroy their Canaanite neighbors, the Edomites wouldn't allow the Jewish people in.

54. *Sifsei Kohen*, Malbim on *Bamidbar* 20:20–21.

55. Seforno, *Bamidbar* 20:20.

56. Rashi, ibid.

57. *Yalkut Me'or Afeilah*, ibid.

58. *Bamidbar Rabbah* 19:15.

59. See Rashi, *Devarim* 2:4.

60. *Chizkuni*, *Bamidbar* 20:20.

61. Malbim, *Devarim* 2:4.

62. *Midrash haGadol*, *Bamidbar* 21:4.

63. See *Targum Yonasan*, Ramban, *Midrash haGadol* on *Bamidbar* 20:21; *Midrash Aggadah*, Rashi, *Lekach Tov* on *Devarim* 2:5; Rabbeinu Bachya, *Devarim* 2:29. Since Edom was untouchable, Moshe thought the Edomites would grant the Jews passage. Once Edom refused, the Children of Israel moved on. See *Bamidbar Rabbah*, *Sifsei Kohen* on *Bamidbar* 20:17. Rashbam, *Devarim* 2:4, maintains that despite bypassing Edom, the Jews bought food from the Edomites.

Journey of the Jewish People from Mitzrayim to Eretz Yisrael

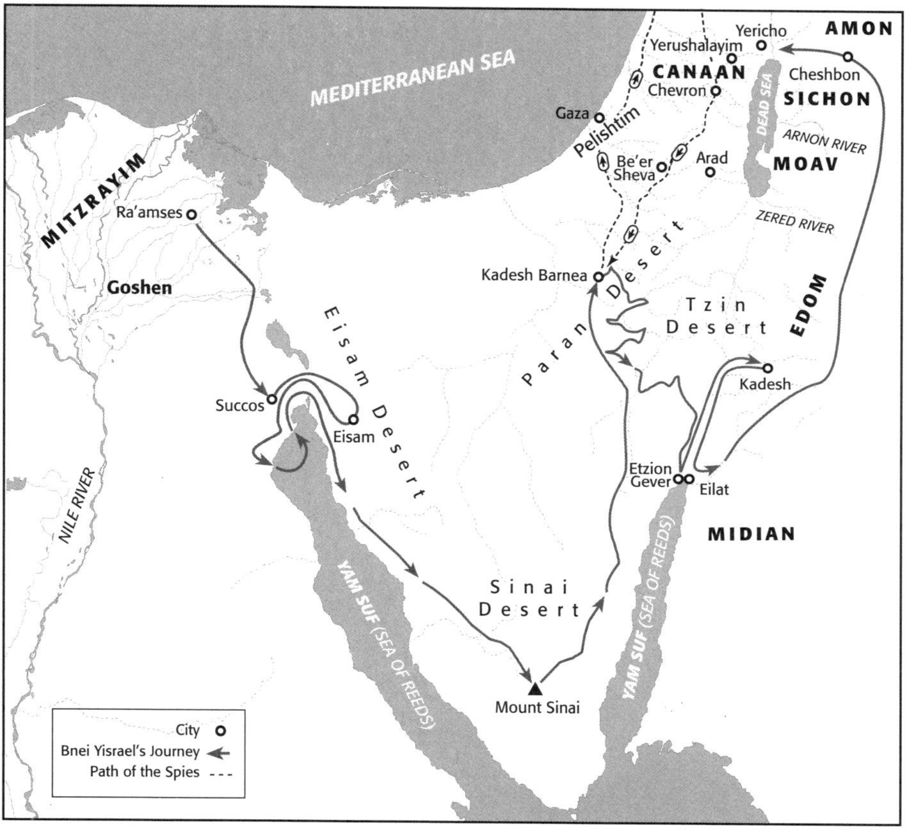

3

Aharon Passes Away

After the king of Edom's refusal to let the Children of Israel pass through his land, the cloud pillar lifted itself, signaling that it was time to travel again.[1] These final stages of the Jewish people's journey took on a new character. No longer were they wandering from place to place in the wilderness. The people were now worthy of entering the Holy Land and of inheriting this world and the next, and the remainder of their travels were pointed directly at Canaan.[2]

Unable to pass through Edom, the people traveled south along the Edomite western

---

1. The Jews had been in Kadesh for four months. *Chizkuni, Bamidbar* 20:1; *Seder Olam* 9.

2. Rashi with *Gur Aryeh, Bamidbar* 20:22.

border.[3] On Rosh Chodesh Av,[4] the cloud pillar came to rest at a place called Har.[5] At the center of this location was a mountain called Hor haHar, which means the mountain of the mountain. The name came from its two-layered appearance, similar to a small apple sitting atop a large apple.[6]

In this place, Aharon would die a premature death. Although the divine decree had barred both Moshe and Aharon from entry into the land, Moshe would die at the threshold of Eretz Yisrael, while Aharon would die considerably earlier.

Hor haHar was one of the three mountains in the path of the Jews' travels, along with Mount Sinai and Mount Nevo, that the cloud pillar did not flatten to ease the Jewish people's journey. Mount Sinai was left standing to serve as the setting for the giving of the Torah. Mount Nevo stayed intact because it would serve as Moshe's burial place. Hor haHar remained unchanged because it would serve as Aharon's burial place,[7] and to remind the Jewish people of the many mountains that had been miraculously flattened during their travels.[8]

Why didn't Aharon die just before the people entered Eretz Yisrael, as Moshe did?

By requesting the right of passage through Edom, Moshe implied that there could be good relations between the Jewish people and the Edomites—the descendants of the evil Eisav—and the people supported him. This was an improper suggestion, and as a consequence, their beloved Kohen Gadol was taken from them.[9]

---

3. Rashi, *Devarim* 2:1.

4. See *Bamidbar* 33:38; *Seder Olam* 9.

5. Rav Saadiah Gaon, *Bamidbar* 20:22.

6. Rashi, ibid.; *Bamidbar Rabbah* 19:16.

7. Ibid.

8. *Bamidbar Rabbah* 19:16.

9. Rashi, *Bamidbar* 20:23; *Bamidbar Rabbah* 19:16. Likewise, Hashem was angered when Yehoshafat, king of Yehudah, sought an alliance with wicked Achav, king of Yisrael (*I Melachim* 22). Moreover, Avraham's covenant with Avimelech

But hadn't Hashem given permission to negotiate a passage with the Edomites? He had only forbidden attacking them, but He had not forbidden peacefully requesting the right of passage. What exactly was the impropriety? Furthermore, how was it connected to the death of Aharon? Where was the measure for measure?[10]

Some suggest that Moshe should not have made a second attempt at reconciliation after the first Edomite rejection. He should have realized that, while there was an advantage to taking a direct route into Canaan, there were also drawbacks to friendly relations with Edom. One rejection was sufficient. He should not have continued to push.[11]

Moreover, by requesting a mountainous route (through Edom), the Jewish people, with Moshe as their messenger, were in essence expressing a willingness to separate from the cloud pillar that had accompanied them for forty years. The cloud pillar flattened all the terrain in their path, but it could not very well change the nature of the mountain ranges of their hosts who had given them permission to pass through. By choosing the mountainous route, therefore, they were turning their backs on the cloud pillar without Hashem's approval. The offer to buy food and drink from the Edomites also involved their stepping out from under the protective umbrella of the cloud pillar to interact with the Edomites, something they were not authorized to do.

Since the Jewish people had enjoyed the accompaniment of the cloud pillar in Aharon's merit, their disregard for it resulted in his death somewhat earlier than Moshe's.[12]

---

delayed Jewish entry into Eretz Yisrael by seven generations. See *Bereishis Rabbah* 54:4, cited in Ramban.

10. Mahrzu, *Bamidbar Rabbah* 19:16, says Aharon should have died after the battle with Sichon.

11. See *Bamidbar Rabbah* 19:16; *Be'er baSadeh, Bamidbar* 20:23. According to *Me'am Lo'ez*, now the nations would see Hashem's people as afraid, and this was a desecration of His Name.

12. *Be'er baSadeh, Bamidbar* 20:23. See *Ha'amek Davar*. Hashem separated the

"The Time Has Come"

On Rosh Chodesh Av,[13] Hashem said to Moshe, "Tell Aharon[14] that the time has come for him to die. He will not enter the Holy Land because he failed to sanctify My holy Name in the incident of Mei Merivah, the Waters of Conflict. I will not inform him of this directly, but I want you to let him know.[15] Speak words of consolation to him.[16] Say, 'How fortunate you are that you can hand over your crown to your son. This is something I will not merit when I die. You will see your son Elazar wearing the mantle of the Kohen Gadol.'"[17]

"But how can I be the one to tell my own brother that he is about to die?" Moshe replied.

"On the contrary," Hashem replied, "it is an honor that he is privileged to be informed of his day of death."[18]

"Hashem, please have mercy on my brother," Moshe prayed. "Please let him live. If You have decreed that he is not to enter the Land, and if that decree cannot be reversed, then let him live out the full term of his life on this side of the Jordan River in the lands designated for the tribes of Gad and Reuven."

---

deaths of Aharon and Moshe in order that Moshe could bury Aharon and in order that the Jewish people could mourn their beloved leaders separately. See Abarbanel for additional reasons.

13. *Seder Olam* 9. *Bamidbar* 33:38 states that Aharon died in the fifth month. Depending on whether the world was created in Nisan or Tishrei, the fifth month was either Av or Shevat. *Minchah Belulah, Bamidbar* 20:24, suggests that Aharon died in Shevat, while *Meshech Chochmah* places this event in Av, which gave Elazar thirty days to mourn and then forty days to prepare for the Yom Kippur service.

14. Alshich, *Bamidbar* 20:23.

15. *Yalkut Shimoni* 764.

16. Rashi, *Midrash haGadol* on *Bamidbar* 20:25.

17. See Rashi, ibid.; *Bamidbar Rabbah* 19:19.

18. *Midrash haGadol, Bamidbar* 20:25. "Fortunate are the righteous, who are informed of their day of death, for they can bequeath their crowns of glory to their sons and die with true happiness." See *Bamidbar Rabbah* 19:17; *Shemos Rabbah* 52:3.

"I will not do that, Moshe," Hashem replied. "Aharon's death is part of the process that will bring the Jewish people into the Holy Land. He must die now."[19]

"But how can I break the news to him? What should I say?"

"Tell him he will not die by the hand of the Angel of Death. When he brought the incense and stopped the plague, I decreed that the Angel of Death would have no power over him. No, I Myself will gather him in to Me."[20]

Hashem then instructed Moshe on all the details of the procedure that would end Aharon's life.[21] Despite his sorrow, Moshe followed Hashem's instructions without hesitation.[22]

Moshe Breaks the News

Every day, the princes of the tribes rose early and came to the tent of Elazar. Together they would make their way to the tent of Aharon, who joined them in walking to the tent of Moshe and beginning the daily regimen. On this day, however, there was a change. Elazar and the princes approached Moshe's tent first, and together they went to Aharon's tent. When Aharon saw this he asked why the change in the normal pattern. Moshe replied that Hashem had commanded them to do so.[23]

On this day as on every day, Aharon performed his regular morning duties which included the daily incense service and lighting of the Menorah.[24] At the conclusion of the morning service, Moshe informed Aharon that he was to join him and Elazar in ascending Hor haHar while still dressed in his priestly vestments.

---

19. *Bamidbar Rabbah* 19:17 with *Matnos Kehunah*. According to Malbim, *Bamidbar* 20:24, since Aharon had fulfilled his purpose in life, and since he didn't merit entrance into Eretz Yisrael, there was no reason for him to remain alive.

20. *Midrash Petiras Aharon* 1:93; *Tanchuma Yashan, Chukas* 2.

21. See Rashi, *Bamidbar* 20:26.

22. See Rashi, *Bamidbar* 20:27; *Bamidbar Rabbah* 19:19.

23. See *Midrash haBeiur*; *Midrash Petiras Aharon* 1:93; *Tanchuma Yashan, Chukas* 2.

24. Ramban, *Bamidbar* 20:26.

Ordinarily, when Moshe walked with Aharon and Elazar, he would walk between them in the place of honor escorted by the other two. On this day, however, Moshe invited Aharon to walk in the middle.

The three men walked together toward the mountain, with the princes and a gathering crowd following closely behind. Observers of the procession were astounded to see Aharon wearing his priestly vestments outside the Mishkan. They also took note of the change in protocol, which placed Aharon in the middle with Moshe and Elazar as his escorts, and wondered if in fact the holy spirit was being transferred from Moshe to Aharon.[25]

When the procession reached the mountain, the three men started up the slope, while the princes and the crowds of followers remained at the foot. Moshe called a halt to their ascent halfway up the mountainside in order to break the news to Aharon that he was going to his final resting place. But he could not bring himself to tell Aharon bluntly that he was about to die. Instead, he broached the subject in a roundabout way.

"Let us review some passages in *Sefer Bereishis,*" Moshe said to Aharon, "that relate to our forefather Avraham. Hashem told him, 'And you will go to your father in peace.'"[26]

Aharon nodded and looked at Moshe quizzically, apparently unaware that he had just been informed that his own death was imminent.

---

25. There is much discussion regarding the permissibility of Aharon's wearing the priestly garments outside the Mishkan. According to *Bamidbar Rabbah* 19:17 with Mahrzu, just as Hashem chose to make Aharon great through his clothing, He now chose to transfer that greatness to Elazar at that particular moment through these same means. *Ha'amek Davar, Bamidbar* 20:26, suggests that Aharon acted according to a *hora'as sha'ah*, a one-time decree, issued for the purposes of transferring the priesthood to his son. *Hadar Zekeinim* theorizes that the Kohen Gadol was forbidden to wear these clothes outside the Mishkan only when he was performing the services. Compare *Sifsei Chachamim*; Malbim. See also Rambam, *Kilayim* 10:32.

26. *Bereishis* 15:15.

"Aharon," Moshe continued, "if Hashem told you that you would die today, what would you say?"

"I would accept His decision without question," Aharon replied, "for His judgment is entirely righteous."

"Aharon, has Hashem entrusted anything to you that He may want you to return to Him?"

"Of course. The entire Mishkan and its vessels. Why do you ask, Moshe? Have I failed in my priestly service in any way?"

"No," said Moshe. "Has Hashem entrusted you with a light?"

"Yes, the light of the Menorah and its seven candles."

"And has Hashem entrusted to you," Moshe continued, "something that resembles a light?"

"Indeed He has," said Aharon. "It is my *neshamah*, my soul, for the light of Hashem is the *neshamah* of a person."[27]

"It is possible," said Moshe, "that Hashem may want to retrieve that which He has entrusted to you."

The light of understanding finally dawned in Aharon's eyes, and they quickly filled with tears.

"My heart weeps within me," he said. "The fear of death has fallen upon me."[28]

"Are you ready to accept your fate?" asked Moshe.

"Yes, I am," Aharon replied.

They continued up the mountainside, with Aharon walking like a sheep to the slaughter, with full acceptance of his fate and absolute servitude to his Creator.

"Look at this," Hashem said to the angels. "You were amazed when Yitzchak allowed himself to be placed on the altar. Look at how the older brother follows his younger brother to meet his fate."[29]

---

27. *Mishlei* 20:7.

28. *Tehillim* 55:5.

29. See *Midrash haBeiur; Yalkut Shimoni* 764, 787; *Midrash haGadol, Bamidbar* 20:26–28; *Midrash Petiras Aharon* 1:93; *Tanchuma Yashan, Chukas* 2.

Aharon's Miraculous Death

It was time for the changing of the guard in the Mishkan. The high office of Kohen Gadol was about to be transferred from Aharon to his son and successor Elazar by removing the priestly vestments from the former and putting them on the latter. But Moshe was in a quandary. How could he accomplish the transfer of the vestments? If he were to remove them from Aharon first, he would be leaving Aharon unclothed; he could not do that. It was also not feasible to transfer the vestments garment by garment from Aharon to Elazar, because he could not reach the inner garments while Aharon was still wearing his outer garments.

"You need not worry," Hashem informed Moshe. "Great miracles will occur. You do yours, and I'll do Mine," Hashem said.

Miraculously, as Moshe proceeded to undress Aharon, Moshe was able to remove his inner garments first despite the outer garments being on top of it. And to add miracle upon miracle, Aharon was not left bare when his garments were removed. A spiritual mist appeared and wrapped itself around his unclothed body, shielding it from the indignity of exposure.[30] According to another view, Moshe dressed Aharon in a burial shroud after he removed his priestly vestments.[31] Others suggest that Moshe only removed Aharon's four outer garments, leaving on him the four inner garments—trousers, shirt, hat and sash—which are common to both the Kohen Gadol and his deputies. Since Elazar was already wearing the four inner garments, he needed only the four outer garments to assume the full raiment of the Kohen Gadol.[32]

Moshe, Aharon and Elazar now entered the cave in which Aharon's soul was to depart from his body. There they found a

---

30. Ramban, Rabbeinu Bachya, *Sifsei Kohen*, Malbim, *Lekach Tov* on *Bamidbar* 20:26, 28; *Yalkut Shimoni* 787.

31. Ramban, Tur, Malbim on *Bamidbar* 20:27.

32. See *Midrash haCheifetz*, *Chupas Eliyahu*, Seforno, *Lekach Tov* on *Bamidbar* 20:26, 28.

bed prepared for Aharon; it was illuminated by glowing candles.

"Go lie down on the bed," Moshe said to Aharon.

Aharon lay down on the bed.

"Stretch out your hands," said Moshe.

Aharon stretched out his hands.

"Close your mouth," said Moshe.

Aharon closed his mouth.

"Close your eyes," said Moshe.

Aharon closed his eyes.[33] The last image he saw in his life was that of his son Elazar fully attired in the priestly vestments of the Kohen Gadol.[34] Aharon was content.[35] The light of the Shechinah touched him and drew out his soul from his body. Miriam had also passed away in this manner.[36]

When Moshe saw the sublime manner in which Aharon had given up his soul, he too yearned for such a death. "Fortunate is the one who dies such a death," he said. "Fortunate is one who dies knowing that his son succeeds him and perpetuates his legacy."[37]

Only Two Descend

The people standing at the foot of the mountain, anxiously awaiting the return of their leaders, suddenly saw Moshe and Elazar appear. Their clothes were rent in mourning, and they had sprinkled ashes on their heads. The sounds of weeping drifted down to the people.

---

33. Rashi, ibid. Aharon's open hands symbolized that he had no more mitzvos to perform; the closed mouth, that he had no further need for speech; and the closed eyes, that he had nothing left to see (*Maskil l'David, Bamidbar* 20:26).

34. Rashi, *Devarim* 32:50.

35. Ibn Ezra, *Bamidbar* 20:26.

36. See *Ben Yehoyada, Bava Basra* 17a; *Moreh Nevuchim* 3:51. According to Malbim, *Bamidbar* 20:24, this death was such that the soul left the earthly, temporal body with the desire to reach its eternal sanctuary.

37. See *Sifrei*, Rashi on *Devarim* 32:50; *Bamidbar* 20:26, 27:13. Although Moshe's son wouldn't replace him, his dedicated student Yehoshua would bring him the same satisfaction (*Be'er baSadeh*).

"Woe is me for your loss, my brother," Moshe lamented. "You carried the prayers of the Jewish people and brought atonement to their sins. The pillar of prayer and the protector of the Jewish people has departed."[38]

The people were bewildered. "Why are there only two of you?" they demanded to know when Moshe and Elazar reached them. "Where is Aharon?"

"I have sad news," said Moshe. "Aharon has passed away."

"Passed away?" shouted a man. "Impossible! How can it be? We just saw him going up the mountain with you, and he looked to be in perfect health.[39] Aharon stopped the Angel of Death when he brought incense during the plague. Are you telling us that he now succumbed to the Angel of Death[40] when there was nothing at all wrong with him?"

"This sounds very suspicious to me as well," said another man. "I suspect that you, Moshe, killed your own brother. He must have done something or said something to offend you, and you did away with him."

A loud murmur rippled through the assembled crowd, and a large group gathered around the man who had accused Moshe, shouting their support for his view.

"I think you have it wrong," declared a third man. "Look at Elazar, all dressed up as the Kohen Gadol. I think he is the culprit."

This view was also greeted with support from a number of people.

Finally, an elderly man stepped forward and signaled for silence.

"You're all wrong," he said. "Moshe and Elazar would never harm a hair on Aharon's head. It is perfectly clear that Hashem

---

38. *Targum Yonasan, Bamidbar* 20:29.

39. *Ha'amek Davar,* ibid.

40. The people made an erroneous assumption because they didn't know that Hashem Himself had orchestrated Aharon's very special death.

decided Aharon's time had come. No one is guilty of anything."

The people were not convinced. They stormed against Moshe and threatened to stone him if he was not more forthcoming. Moshe pleaded with Hashem to convince the people that he was innocent.

Suddenly an angel appeared and tore away a chunk of the mountain, exposing the cave within. The cloud of glory gathered Aharon's body from the cave and bore it aloft to the highest spheres of Heaven. And as it rose up, Hashem eulogized Aharon.

"The Torah of truth was in his mouth," said Hashem. "No iniquity touched his lips. He walked with Me in peace and uprightness, and turned people away from sin."[41]

A pall of sadness descended on the people as they realized what had transpired.[42] They were overcome with grief, and the sounds of anguished wailing reverberated through the entire Jewish encampment. Not only had they lost a spiritual leader, they had lost a man whom they had loved with all their hearts, a man whose passing left a gaping void in all their hearts.

Above all, Aharon was a man who loved his people, a man who loved peace and sought to promote it whenever and wherever he could. When he walked among the people, he always greeted one and all with a smile that radiated genuine love and affection. Every single individual who was rewarded with this smile felt himself elevated and inspired; he walked with a more energetic spring in his step and confidence in his heart. If Aharon feels so kindly toward me, he would think, then I must be a worthy person. And if later, the evil inclination would present this person with an opportunity to sin, he would turn away. How can I sin, he would think, if Aharon has such a high opinion of me?

---

41. See Rashi, *Chupas Eliyahu* on *Bamidbar* 20:29; *Bamidbar Rabbah* 19:20; *Yalkut Shimoni* 764, 787; *Sifrei, Vayeilech* 305. See also *Malachi* 2:6.

42. Seeing Elazar dressed in the garb of the Kohen Gadol, the people understood that Aharon was no longer alive (*Ha'amek Davar*).

Not only would I be letting myself down, I would be letting him down as well.

Whenever Aharon encountered two friends having a quarrel, he would go out of his way to resolve it in an amicable manner. He would approach one of them when the other was not there, and he would say to him, "It is so unfortunate that you and he are having a quarrel. I know that he is very pained by it. He feels so sorry and guilty, but doesn't know how to approach you and make things right again. I think you should forgive him, because he really loves you. He just doesn't know how to express it."

Then Aharon would seek out the second party to the dispute and tell him the same thing. In this way, he would set the stage for the two people to come together in peace and harmony. The next time the two would meet, they would not bother with the old arguments and recriminations. They would just embrace as friends and move on.

Aharon also raised the level of domestic harmony among the people. His door was always open to anyone who needed his help, and his wise and compassionate counseling saved numerous marriages and family relationships. In fact, thousands of children were born to families that Aharon saved from divorce. Three thousand of them were boys, and they were all named Aharon in his honor.

For this reason, the outpouring of love and grief for Aharon upon his passing was universal among the Jewish people, more than Moshe's passing would elicit a few months later. The people respected and admired Moshe, who rebuked and chastised them and always intervened on their behalf. They also knew full well that Moshe's love for them was very deep. But they did not have the same loving, personal relationship with him as they did with Aharon.

After Moshe eulogized Aharon before the weeping multitudes, he was struck by a disturbing thought. When Miriam had passed away, he and Aharon had eulogized her. When Aharon passed away, he had delivered the eulogy. But who would eulogize him?

Who was left of his generation? Who was old enough and wise enough to deliver a proper eulogy? He had no father, no mother, no brother or sister!

"Do not worry," Hashem reassured him. "I will take care of your passing Myself. The Angel of Death will not touch you. I will draw out your soul with My kiss. I will bury you. And I will eulogize you."[43]

43. See Rashi, *Bamidbar* 20:29, 27:13; *Yalkut Shimoni* 764, 787; *Avos d'Rabbi Nasan* 12:4.

4 Confrontation and Retreat

For forty years, the cloud of glory had accompanied the Jewish people in the wilderness, providing a level surface under their feet and a canopy over their heads. The people had enjoyed this extraordinary phenomenon in Aharon's merit, and when he passed away, it came to an end.

Children born in the wilderness had grown up in the shelter of this spiritual cocoon, and now, for the first time ever, they could look up and see the blue sky during the day and the star-studded black velvet of the nighttime sky. For the first time, they could see the blazing sun and the glowing moon. These sights awed and disconcerted them. What were these heavenly bodies? Were they divine beings that demanded worship from mortal men? Not knowing what to do, they prostrated themselves on the ground to the sun and the moon.

"Didn't I warn you," Hashem called out to them, "not to look up to the hosts of the heavens and bow down to them?"

Realizing their error, the people quickly jumped to their feet. Now they knew that the sun, the moon and the stars were nothing more than physical bodies.[1] They had made their first adjustment to life without the cloud pillars, but there were many more to come. The people were now exposed to the elements, to the heat of the day, the cold nights, to the wind and the rain, and they were also exposed to the attacks of their enemies on all sides. Amalek, their archenemy, didn't wait long to take advantage of this vulnerability.[2]

Amalek Devises a Subterfuge

As the Jewish people traveled along the southern part of Edom, the Canaanites and Amalekites on their flank took note of their passage. A group of Amalekite chieftains watched from a high promontory.

"Where are the cloud pillars?" remarked a husky young chieftain.

"I don't know," another young chieftain remarked. "They seem to be gone. Perhaps we should send a scouting party to get a closer look, eh? What do you think?"

"I don't know what you expect them to see close up. Do you think the cloud pillars became transparent? No, they're gone, and good riddance. And according to my intelligence, their high priest

1. *Midrash Petiras Moshe* 1:94.

2. Rashi, Rabbeinu Bachya on *Bamidbar* 21:1; Zohar, *Emor* 102b. *Toldos Tzion* comments on *Bamidbar Rabbah* 19:20 that because the nation sought to stone Moshe over Aharon's whereabouts, it was punished with an attack by Amalek. According to *Tzeror haMor*, Hashem orchestrated this war so the Jews would miss Aharon and the clouds of glory.

is dead. These people are exposed and vulnerable, my friend."[3]

"Where do you think they're headed?"

The first chieftain shrugged. "It's anyone's guess. It looks like they're following the route of the spies they sent back in my grandfather's time.[4] If you ask me, I'd say they're thinking invasion."[5]

"Well, if you ask me, I think they're lost. Either way, now is a good time to attack."[6]

"Not so fast, young fellows," said an old chieftain with a few wisps of white hair on his otherwise bare head. "Weren't you paying attention during your history lessons? I was around in your grandfather's day, and I remember it well. After the Children of Israel came out of Egypt, we organized a raiding party to attack them. I had the honor of being selected to join. But not everything went as planned."

"Really, sir?" said the young chieftain. "What happened? Weren't the descendants of Eisav, among whom we proudly count ourselves, blessed by our ancestor Yitzchak to be indomitable warriors? And hasn't this been the case all through the years? You see, I do know my history."

"Not quite, my boy. This same Yitzchak, the ancestor we share with the Jewish people, blessed them that their prayers would be heard and answered. While we attacked with our swords and spears, they prayed to the Almighty, and miraculously, they were victorious. Believe me, I know. I was one of the lucky survivors."

---

3. Rashi, Rabbi Yehudah heChasid, *Chizkuni* on *Bamidbar* 21:1; *Rosh Hashanah* 3a; *Bamidbar Rabbah* 19:20; *Sifrei Zuta, Pinchas* 27:3; Zohar, *Emor* 102b. Maharil Diskin notes that the Jews had to travel within inhabited areas, because the clouds of glory were no longer around to flatten mountains and straighten routes for them. Thus, the nation was noticed.

4. See *Targum Unkelos*, Rashi on *Bamidbar* 21:1; *Bamidbar Rabbah* 19:20.

5. *Chizkuni*, Ralbag on *Bamidbar* 21:1.

6. *Bamidbar Rabbah* 19:20; *Ma'aseh Hashem*, p. 73; *Ha'amek Davar*, *Bamidbar* 21:1.

"So what do you suggest we do?"

"We have to be clever. We have to undermine the power of their prayers. The more focused and accurate their prayers are, the more power they wield. So we have to introduce errors into their prayers."

"What good will that do? Won't the Almighty know what they want?"

"Yes, of course. But there are rules and guidelines for prayers. Certain formulas are more effective than others. We have to disrupt their formulas."

"So how do you propose we accomplish this?"

"A masquerade."

The husky young chieftain laughed. "What are you saying? That we should invite them to a party?"

"How about showing a little respect, you little whippersnapper? You may be big and brawny, but your elders are wiser than you."

"All right, old-timer. Don't set your tunic on fire. What have you got up your sweaty old sleeve?"

"We masquerade as our Canaanite neighbors.[7] Some of us speak their language quite well. We can dress up in their battle uniforms and learn their battle cries. We can shout slogans about how we'll never give in to the prophecy that gives the Jews the land of Canaan.[8] Yep, we can do a fair masquerade as Canaanite warriors. They'll pray to be saved from the Canaanites, and ..." The old Amalekite paused to cackle. "Sure, the Almighty will know that they're all mixed up, but their prayers will be messed up too. And then, boom, they'll be ours. We'll smash them to bits."

---

7. See *Chizkuni, Bamidbar* 21:1. According to *Midrash Aggadah, Bamidbar* 21:1, even the king wore Canaanite clothing.

8. *Yalkut Shimoni* 764 adds that they dressed up as Canaanites in mourning, dreading the fulfillment of that prophecy.

"Not bad for an old man," said the young chieftain. "Let's do it."[9]

Disguised as Canaanites, then, the Amalekites attacked the Jewish people, immediately capturing a gentile maidservant who had ventured to the outskirts of the encampment.[10]

The Jewish people were startled by the sight of the fierce warriors advancing toward them.

"Who are these attackers?" they called out to each other. "They look and sound like Canaanites, but their complexion is different. Could they be Amalekites?"

Disheartened and terrified, their faith shaken,[11] the Jewish people fled in panic, retreating toward the land of Egypt from which they had come.[12] They retraced their steps, not pausing to catch their breaths until they reached Moseirah, seven campsites back.

Brother versus Brother

Only the tribe of Levi stood in the breach, trying to put a halt to the Jewish retreat. They refused to allow the people to go back to Egypt. But the people were disoriented by their panic and fear. They refused to listen to the exhortations of the Levi'im.

"We are going back with or without your approval," they shouted back. "Try and stop us!"

The tribe of Levi was up to the challenge. They refused to back down, and civil strife broke out between them and the other

---

9. See the *piyut* for *parashas Zachor*; *Chizkuni*, *Bamidbar* 21:1. Those who didn't know the language took a "crash course." See Rashi, *Bamidbar* 21:1.

10. Rashi, *Midrash Aggadah*, Ramban on *Bamidbar* 21:1. Although trivial in the larger scheme of things, this capture served its purpose, for now the Jews would pray for salvation (*Ha'amek Davar*). *Targum Yonasan* and *Lekach Tov* record many prisoners of war.

11. Introduction to *Ruth Rabbah*.

12. See Rashi, *Devarim* 10:6–7; Malbim, *Bamidbar* 21:1–2.

tribes. The latter suffered heavy casualties, with entire clans from Gad, Asher and Shimon completely wiped out. The tribe of Levi also suffered heavy losses; they lost the clan of Shimi, the son of Gershon.[13]

The shock of the battle brought everyone to their senses. What had happened here? Why had they suffered such a terrible calamity? After much thought, the people concluded that they had not eulogized Aharon properly at Hor haHar.[14] They immediately called a great assembly and proceeded to eulogize him at great length.[15] Inspired by the eulogies, their faith was strengthened, and they prayed to Hashem to help them overcome the army that had come out against them.[16]

"If You give us victory over this army," they vowed, "we will consecrate their spoils and plunder and make them holy to You."[17]

---

13. See *Seder Olam* 9; *Bamidbar Rabbah* 19:20. See also *Yalkut Shimoni* 764; *Midrash Aggadah, Bamidbar* 21:1; Rashi, *Bamidbar* 26:13; *Targum Yonasan*, Rashi on *Devarim* 10:6; *Yerushalmi Yoma* 1:1. Regarding the location of Moseirah, see Ramban, *Chizkuni* on *Devarim* 10:6.

14. See *Tzeror haMor, Bamidbar* 21:1. *Ohr HaChaim* suggests that this attack was continued punishment for their complaints about Miriam's Well. See Seforno, *Chizkuni* on *Devarim* 10:6.

15. *Yerushalmi Yoma* 1:1, *Targum Yonasan, Devarim* 10:6. See Ralbag, *Bamidbar* 21:1. There is much discussion regarding *Devarim* 10:6, which says Aharon died and was buried in Moseirah. With the renewed mourning and eulogizing of Aharon, the Torah considers it as though he died and was buried there. Yet others opine that his body didn't remain in Hor haHar. Lest the Edomites idolize him, or the Canaanites desecrate his body, the Jews took Aharon's bier with them and buried him in Moseirah. In fact, nowhere does the Torah say Aharon was buried at Hor haHar. At most, his body was concealed by the mountain but never buried. See *Akeidas Yitzchak*, Malbim, *Sifsei Kohen* on *Bamidbar* 20:29. See also *Ta'anis* 9a; *Mechilta, Beshalach*, s.v. *Vayasa* (*Shemos* 15:22).

16. Moshe didn't pray for the Jews himself since they no longer merited his intercession, having just accused him of killing Aharon and having faithlessly retreated seven stations (*Sifsei Kohen*).

17. Rashi, *Bamidbar* 21:2.

Hashem answered the Jews' prayers in bountiful measure.[18] As they headed back to Hor haHar and beyond,[19] they encountered an amazing scenario. The Amalekites and the Canaanites were engaged in a brutal war that resulted in extremely heavy casualties on both sides.[20] The returning Jewish people attacked the battle-weary Amalekites, killing many of them and sending the rest into a hasty retreat. They even managed to rescue the abducted maidservant.

They plundered the Amalekite cities, capturing livestock and treasure,[21] and they consecrated the spoils as they promised.[22] And they renamed the scene of the battle Chormah,[23] to commemorate their devastating victory.[24]

---

18. In the merit of Moshe, the cloud pillars now returned, and the Jewish nation was once again protected from the elements (*Yalkut Me'or haAfeilah, Bamidbar* 21:3). See *Bamidbar Rabbah* 19:20; *Yerushalmi Sotah* 1:10; Rashi, *Devarim* 10:6; *Shir haShirim Rabbah* 4.

19. *Me'am Lo'ez, Bamidbar* 21:2.

20. Rabbi Yehudah heChasid, *Pa'aneiach Raza* on ibid. Perhaps the Canaanites attacked the Amalekites for imitating them.

21. *Bechor Shor*, Rabbi Yehudah heChasid, *Pa'aneiach Raza* on *Bamidbar* 21:1–2.

22. Rashi, *Bamidbar* 21:3. For an entirely different version of events, see Ibn Ezra, Ramban, Abarbanel. See also Tosafos, *Rosh Hashanah* 3a; *I Shemuel* 15:6. This consecration would be honored when the Jewish people entered Eretz Yisrael. (Achan was among those who disobeyed and took the spoils of war. See *Yehoshua* 7; *Sanhedrin* 43b.)

23. From the Hebrew word *cherem* (consecration).

24. Here too, the brazen rebels (*ma'apilim*) who attempted to enter Eretz Yisrael without authorization fell (*Bechor Shor*; *Sifsei Kohen*).

5

Snake Attack

Adjusting to the new realities of life was not easy for the Jewish people. While they still had *mahn* for food, and while the well returned in Moshe's merit and provided them with their water, the departure of the protective cloud pillars caused great hardship.[1] As they traveled around Edom, toward Tzalmonah,[2] the people were engulfed by a wave of discontent.[3]

---

1. As noted above, *Yalkut Me'or haAfeilah, Bamidbar* 21:3, states that after the Jews prayed, the clouds returned in the merit of Moshe. According to *Ohr ha-Chaim, Bamidbar* 21:12, they returned after the Jewish people's travels through Zered and Arnon.

2. See Ibn Ezra, *Chizkuni* on *Bamidbar* 21:4. The name Tzalmonah derives from the word *tzalmaves*, "shadow of death" (Mahrzu on *Bamidbar Rabbah* 19:24). However, the expression also means darkness (*Metzudos* on *Tehillim* 44:20)—the Jews would enter into dark Gehinnom as a result of their behavior.

3. *Targum Yonasan, Bamidbar* 21:4.

"I cannot bear this heat," said one man to a friend walking alongside him, voicing the unarticulated thoughts of innumerable people. "The sun is beating down on my head so hard that it feels like my brain is being fried."[4]

His companion sighed. "If only we could get the cloud pillars back, how wonderful that would be. The clouds were a floor under our feet that moved by itself and carried us along,[5] and a canopy over our heads to protect us from the scorching sun. It was such luxury, and now, I'm so hot and tired I can hardly breathe."[6]

The Jews' discontent deepened after the panicked retreat all the way to Moseirah, seven stations to the rear.[7] Now they had to recover all of this distance by trudging through the broiling wilderness.

"Look what You've done to us!" they railed against Hashem in their thoughts. "And Moshe, we are upset with you as well. You took us out of Egypt to perish in the wilderness, didn't you? Why else would you have brought us to this miserable state of affairs?[8] All our lives, we hoped and prayed we would be able to enter the Holy Land, the land of our dreams. And we came so, so close. It was right there in front of us. All we had to do was walk through Edom, and we would have been there. But no, you didn't let us do it. We had to take a roundabout route, and who knows how long it will take to get there?[9] So are we going to spend another forty years in the wilderness? It looks like we're going to die.[10]

---

4. See *Tanchuma, Bamidbar* 2; *Chizkuni, Minchah Belulah* on *Bamidbar* 21:4.

5. *Sifsei Kohen, Bamidbar* 21:4. During this trip, the Jewish People temporarily lost the Well of Miriam and the ease with which they ate the *mahn* (*Da'as Zekeinim, Sifsei Kohen* on *Bamidbar* 21:4).

6. Rashi, *Chizkuni* on ibid.

7. *Sifsei Kohen,* Alshich on ibid.

8. Abarbanel, ibid.

9. *Ohr haChaim, Ha'amek Davar,* Malbim on *Bamidbar* 21:4–5.

10. *Da'as Zekeinim, Bamidbar* 21:4. The Jews now despaired of ever entering Eretz Yisrael, believing they would either die first or wander in the wilderness indefinitely. See Abarbanel; *Bamidbar Rabbah* 19:21 with Rashash.

"We were so close, we could almost taste the fruit of Eretz Yisrael.[11] But it was all a mirage. We couldn't even buy fruit from peddlers, let alone pick it off the trees.[12] Hashem, why didn't You let us fight Edom and go directly into Eretz Yisrael?[13] And Moshe, why didn't you intercede with Hashem and plead with Him to let us fight?[14]

"How are we to be expected to live with such uncertainty from day to day? Other nations store reserves of food and water so that they never have to worry from one day to the next, but our lives are always hanging by a thread. If the *mahn* stops falling, we starve. If the stone stops giving water, we die of thirst.[15]

"And can we really be expected to feel satisfied with the *mahn*? It is so light and ephemeral, with no body and bulk.[16] It may provide the nutrients we need, but it cannot still our hunger. And now that we're traveling without the cloud pillars, we need additional nourishment, which the *mahn* doesn't provide. It's a strange food, this *mahn*.[17] It is completely absorbed into the body so that we never need to get rid of waste. That is simply unnatural; that's not how people are made.[18] But at least it keeps us barely alive. If you, Moshe, were to die tomorrow, we would be left without the *mahn* as well. Who knows what will happen to our bodies then?"[19]

---

11. See *Da'as Zekeinim, Bamidbar* 21:4.

12. *Bamidbar Rabbah* 19:21; *Tzeror haMor, Bamidbar* 21:4. Those destined to enter Eretz Yisrael could buy this produce. According to the opinion that more deaths due to the incident of the spies would yet take place this final year, even those Jews hoping just to glimpse this fruit would die upon looking, for Hashem said they would never "see" any portion of Eretz Yisrael—even its fruits.

13. *Minchah Belulah, Sifsei Kohen* on *Bamidbar* 21:4–5.

14. *Ohr haChaim, Bamidbar* 21:5.

15. See *Chizkuni*, Rabbeinu Bachya, *Minchah Belulah* on ibid.

16. *Bamidbar Rabbah* 19:21.

17. See *Ohr haChaim, Bamidbar* 21:5.

18. *Bamidbar Rabbah* 19:21.

19. Rashi, *Bamidbar* 21:5; *Emek haNetziv* on *Sifrei, Bamidbar* 11:6.

Rather than praise Hashem for all He had done for them, the Jewish people were sullen and ungrateful in their attitude. "I prevented them from suffering defeat at the hands of Edom," Hashem said. "I provided them with miraculous bread of the angels to sustain them. I gave them food that would not produce waste so that they would not have to walk long distances away from the camp to relieve themselves. I gave them an inexhaustible source of abundant water in the wilderness. Did they thank Me, or did they complain as the spies did?"[20]

In retribution for their recalcitrance,[21] Hashem decided to withdraw the gift of the *mahn* from them. Let them no longer be like the angels. Let them produce waste, and let them go through the trouble of eliminating it from their bodies.[22]

But that would not be the end of the consequences. They would also have to contend with a snake attack.

The original serpent in Gan Eden sinned with malicious speech. He said to Chavah, "Eat from the very same tree that made Hashem smart. He doesn't want you to eat from it, because He doesn't want you to be His equal."[23] The snake, therefore, symbolizes malicious speech. And now that the Jewish people were guilty of malicious speech, they were appropriately punished with snakes.[24]

There was additional significance to the snakes. The snake, who had enjoyed all the luscious fruits of Gan Eden, had been

---

20. See *Midrash Aggadah*, *Targum Yonasan* on *Bamidbar* 21:4, 6; *Bamidbar Rabbah* 16:24; *Sifrei*, *Devarim* 1; *Mishnas Rav Eliezer* 135–136; *Pesikta d'Rav Kehana* 17; *Avodah Zarah* 5a; Zohar, *Chukas* 183b.

21. Ibid.

22. *Yoma* 75a.

23. *Bereishis Rabbah* 20:1.

24. See Rashi, *Bamidbar* 21:6; *Bamidbar Rabbah* 19:22. Snakes are famous for their slippery tongues, a reminder of the original snake's malicious speech. Hence, one who speaks out of bounds deserves to be bitten by a snake. See Ibn Ezra, *Bamidbar* 21:6; *Bamidbar Rabbah* 19:22; *Ta'anis* 8a; *Koheles* 10:8.

expelled and punished by having all his food taste like dust, and yet he did not complain. In sharp contrast, the Jewish people had been blessed with a heavenly food, but they complained. Now their punishment would be administered by the dust-eating snakes.[25] Favoring food that comes out of the earth, they would be attacked by creatures that crawl with their bellies on the earth and eat it as their food.[26] Finally, a snake strikes with no apparent purpose or gain—a fitting punishment for malicious speech, which brings no reward or gain.[27] The attack was about to begin.

As the Jewish people made their encampment at the next station, a place called Punon,[28] Hashem sent a venomous snake among them.[29] As the snake entered the encampment, it metastasized into numerous slithering duplicates of itself.[30] The cloud pillars had protected the Children of Israel by obliterating the snakes in their path, and now these selfsame snakes returned to plague the nation.[31] They sank their fangs into the flesh of numerous people and injected them with their deadly venom, burning their innards and ultimately killing them.[32]

---

25. *Targum Yonasan*, Rashi, *Midreshei haTorah* on *Bamidbar* 21:6; *Bamidbar Rabbah* 19:22.

26. Malbim, *Bamidbar* 21:6. See also *Ohr haChaim*, *Bamidbar* 21:8.

27. *Ta'anis* 8a; *Koheles* 10:11. See Abarbanel, *Bamidbar* 21:6.

28. *Targum Yonasan*, Bamidbar 33:41; *Bechor Shor*, *Bamidbar* 21:10. Named either because Punon is similar to a Greek word meaning "death," or because the Jews removed (*pinu*) Hashem from their hearts (*Lekach Tov*, Rokeach on *Bamidbar* 21:10).

29. Ramban, *Bamidbar* 21:9, describes this snake as having red eyes, a wide head and copperlike neck features.

30. *Bamidbar Rabbah* 19:23 with Mahrzu. See *Ha'amek Davar*, *Bamidbar* 21:6.

31. See *Chizkuni*, Rabbeinu Bachya, *Toldos Yitzchak* on *Bamidbar* 21:6; *Bamidbar Rabbah* 19:22. The return of this scourge thus reminded the Jews about the miracles of the cloud pillars, for which they were ungrateful. Rabbi Yehudah heChasid adds that the snakes returned after the Jews rejected the *mahn* and attempted to leave the safety of the cloud in order to buy food.

32. See Rashi, *Bechor Shor* on *Bamidbar* 21:6; Zohar, *Chukas* 183b. According to Zohar, *Balak* 205b, Tzelofchad was among the victims.

In the wake of the snakes, wild dogs, scorpions and other predators invaded the Jewish encampment and bit the people as well, but they did not kill anyone. That task was reserved for the snakes.[33]

Moshe heard the screams of pain of those who lay mortally wounded[34] and the panicked cries of those who cowered in fear. He came running to see what had happened.

"Moshe, we have committed a twofold sin," the people cried out. "We engaged in malicious speech among ourselves against you and Hashem, and in doing so, we treated Hashem as your equal.[35] We all recognize that we have sinned, and we are saddened that those who have perished did not have the opportunity to repent.[36] But those of us who are alive do indeed repent with all our hearts.[37] We realize that with our malicious speech we created a spiritual serpent that advocates against us and empowers terrestrial snakes to kill us,[38] and we beg you to pray to Hashem to destroy that serpent."[39]

"I forgive you for speaking against me," said Moshe with complete humility and forbearance, setting an example for future Jewish leaders throughout generations, "and I will pray to Hashem that He forgive you as well."[40]

---

33. Rokeach, Tur on *Bamidbar* 21:6. Rashi with *Sifsei Chachamim*, *Bamidbar* 21:8; *Bamidbar Rabbah* 19:23.

34. See Rashi, *Bechor Shor* on *Bamidbar* 21:6; Zohar, *Chukas* 183b.

35. *Sifsei Kohen*, *Bamidbar* 21:7. See Alshich. See also Rashi, *Bamidbar* 21:5; *Bamidbar Rabbah* 19:21.

36. Alshich, *Bamidbar* 21:7.

37. *Lekach Tov*, *Minchah Belulah* on ibid.

38. See Rabbeinu Bachya, *Ohr haChaim* on *Bamidbar* 21:6; Zohar, *Pekudei* 264b; *Shemiras haLashon* 2, *Chukas*.

39. Maharil Diskin says the Jews sinned twice. For sinning against Hashem, they were bitten by snakes, but for sinning against Moshe, the snakes were venomous. Hence, aside from removing the snakes, Hashem had to heal their victims.

40. Rashi, *Bamidbar* 21:7; *Bamidbar Rabbah* 19:23.

Hashem answered Moshe's prayer and withdrew the snakes. The danger had passed for those who had thus far escaped being bitten, but critically wounded people needed immediate treatment or they would die.[41]

The Fiery Serpent

"Make a *saraf,* a fiery serpent," Hashem commanded Moshe, "and place it high on a pole[42] in full view of all the people throughout the encampment. Whosoever looks upon this snake shall be immediately healed."[43]

The purpose of the snake was not to serve as some kind of curative amulet. It was to draw the eyes of the people upward toward the heavens and remind them to repent wholeheartedly.[44] Their upward perspective would remind them that they had sinned and inspire within them true remorse and regret. They would remember the terror they had felt when the snakes had invaded the camp, and they would resolve never again to speak maliciously against Hashem. This very repentance and resolve would bring about their healing.[45]

Gazing at a snake would be a powerful reminder of the agents of the people's affliction. Recalling the venomous snakes, they would shudder and repent. Furthermore, this was a miracle within

---

41. See Abarbanel, *Sifsei Kohen* on *Bamidbar* 21:7.

42. See Rashi, *Bamidbar* 21:8.

43. *Chizkuni,* Rokeach on *Bamidbar* 21:9.

44. See *Tzeror haMor, Ohr haChaim* on *Bamidbar* 21:8–9.

45. See *Targum Yonasan,* Rav Saadiah Gaon, Rashi, Seforno, Tur, *Tzeror haMor, Ohr haChaim,* Alshich on *Bamidbar* 21:8–9; *Rosh Hashanah* 29a; *Yerushalmi Rosh Hashanah* 3:9 (18a) with *Korban haEidah*; Zohar, *Shelach* 175. See also *Berachos* 33a; *Ohr haChaim, Vayikra* 26:3, reason 39. The Jews thus resembled a son seeing his father's belt ready and waiting should he misbehave (Zohar).

Realistically speaking, it wasn't even necessary to display a serpent. Hashem was simply showing that the same deadly serpent can heal, but only if one recognizes it as an expression of His will rather than natural circumstance (*Sefas Emes*). See *Me'am Lo'ez.*

a miracle. When the waters were bitter, Hashem instructed Moshe to put a bitter staff into it and thereby, paradoxically, sweeten it. Here too, Hashem wanted the symbol of a serpent to mitigate the damage done by snakes.[46]

Moshe, however, had reservations about making a fiery serpent.[47] If it was to symbolize the malicious speech uttered by the people, they had already been forgiven for that.[48] He was also unsure how to make one.[49]

It would serve just as well, Moshe reasoned, to make a snake out of copper, *nechoshes*, which is related to the word for snake, *nachash*.[50] The coppery color would resemble a snake.[51] Moreover, copper was the metal most easily smelted by fire, and snake venom, like fire, "burns" one's insides.[52]

Moshe made the copper snake and tossed it up into the air toward the top of the pole. Miraculously, it remained suspended in midair high enough for the entire encampment to see it.[53]

---

46. See Rashi with *Sifsei Chachamim, Chizkuni,* Ramban on *Bamidbar* 21:9; *Midrash haGadol*. It is a wonder of Hashem that even today, a snakebite is treated by means of venom.

47. Seforno, *Bamidbar* 21:8. Rabbeinu Bachya and *Tosefos Rav Ephraim al haTorah* suggest that the *saraf* and the *nachash* were one and the same, but Hashem didn't want to call it the latter and remind the people of their sin. *Tosefos Rav Ephraim al haTorah* adds that the *nachash* would remind Moshe of the dangerous snake deployed against him when he delayed circumcising his son Gershom on the way to Mitzrayim. See *Let My Nation Go* (Jerusalem: Feldheim Publishers, 1998), p. 145.

48. See Riva, *Sifsei Kohen*, Alshich, *Ma'aseh Hashem* on *Bamidbar* 21:9. Hashem forgave the Jews for sinning against Him but not for speaking against Moshe. Here Moshe likewise forgives the Jews speaking against him but not for sinning against Hashem (Rabbeinu Bachya).

49. See Ibn Ezra, Ramban on *Bamidbar* 21:8–9.

50. See *Lekach Tov*, Rashi with *Gur Aryeh* on *Bamidbar* 21:9; *Bereishis Rabbah* 31:8 with Radal.

51. Ramban, Abarbanel on *Bamidbar* 21:9.

52. *Midrash haGadol*, *Bamidbar* 21:8.

53. *Bamidbar Rabbah* 19:23 with Mahrzu. Alternatively, the snake miraculously attached itself to the top of the pole (Radal). Thus, this pole was called a *nes*, not just as in "flag" but as in "miracle" (*Sifsei Kohen*).

The people looked up at the airborne snake, anxiously hoping to be healed. Those bitten by any of the other predators were immediately healed. Those who had been bitten by the venomous snakes, however, were not so easily healed. They had to stare at it for a long time, their minds and hearts filled with remorse and regret, before the toxins in their bodies were neutralized.[54] Even some who were so critically wounded that they were at death's door were brought back to vigorous life by staring at the airborne snake.[55]

The Jewish people had this copper snake in their possession until the reign of King Chizkiyahu, close to a thousand years later. During these years, some people saw it as an object of worship, calling it Nechushtan. King Chizkiyahu, however, put a stop to this by pounding the snake into dust until not a single trace of it remained.[56]

---

54. Rashi with *Sifsei Chachamim*, *Bamidbar* 21:8; *Bamidbar Rabbah* 19:23; *Yerushalmi Rosh Hashanah* 3:9 (18a) with *Korban haEidah*. Some say that the way in which people needed to look at the copper serpent depended on whether they were bitten by a poisonous or a nonpoisonous snake. *Meshech Chochmah* adds that even those suffering from other ailments were healed by looking at the snake and repenting.

55. *Yalkut Shimoni* 764.

56. See *II Melachim* 18:4.

6

The Battle of Arnon

Spurned by Edom, the Jewish people now moved northward, seeking a new point of entry into the Holy Land. The most direct route after Edom would have been through the land of Moav, but here again, they were forbidden to cross without permission.[1] They also needed to pass by the land of Amon.

"Do not distress Moav," Hashem commanded them. "Do not provoke war with them. For the land of Moav is an inheritance left for the descendants of Lot." The same injunction was extended to contact with Amon, with one addition. While they could present

1. See Malbim, *Devarim* 2:9. The Jews would have been justified to war with Amon and Moav, but Hashem forbade it (*Da'as Zekeinim*). Despite the respect for the sovereignty of the two nations here, the males would never be allowed full entry into the Jewish nation.

themselves fully armed to the Moabites, as long as they did not actually attack them, they could not even present a belligerent face to the Amonites or intimidate them in any way. Before they could speak with the Amonites, they had to hide their weapons under their cloaks.

As they had done with Edom, the Children of Israel negotiated for safe passage to the Holy Land. They gave assurances of non-belligerence and even offered to purchase provisions from them, but it was all to no avail. Permission was refused.[2] However, unlike the Edomites, the Moabites and Amonites had some justification for their refusal. The Emorites had invaded and defeated them in the recent past, and they were leery of being ravaged again.[3]

Nonetheless, the least they could have done was offer a little water and some bread to the Jewish masses passing right before their doorstep. It would have been the hospitable thing to do. But they did not do it. They just stood there, glaring malevolently, until the last of the nation had vanished from sight.[4]

Spurned once again, the Jewish people were forced to bypass the land of Moav.[5] They also avoided the land of Amon.[6] Hashem directed them northwest to the land of Sichon, king of the Emorites. Should the Emorites refuse them safe passage, Hashem gave them permission to devastate and conquer their lands.[7]

---

2. See Rashi, *Sefas Emes* on *Bamidbar* 21:13; *Shofetim* 11:17 with Radak; Rambam, *Melachim* 6:6; Zohar, *Balak* 188; *Sefer haYashar*. Some suggest that Moav did offer the Jewish people provisions, but it was too little, too late. See Chapter 11.

3. *Sefer haYashar*.

4. See *Sifrei*, Rashi on *Devarim* 23:5. See also Ramban; Abarbanel.

5. See Rashi, *Chizkuni* on *Bamidbar* 21:11, 13.

6. *Ha'amek Davar*, *Devarim* 2:37. See Rashi, Rav Samson Raphael Hirsch on *Devarim* 3:1.

7. *Devarim* 2:24. Some say this was Hashem's first instruction to Moshe since the wilderness generation began dying some thirty-eight years earlier. See Rabbeinu Bachya, *Devarim* 2:17.

The Jewish people broke camp at Punon after 15 Av and camped in Ovos.[8] From there, they skirted Moav on the east[9] and headed north to Iyei haAvarim.[10] Next, they crossed the Zered River,[11] near Divon Gad.[12] Finally, they reached Eiver Arnon,[13] which was on the border between Moav and the land of the Emorites.[14] This particular strip of land had once been in the hands of Moav but had been absorbed into the Emorite territories after the latter's invasion of Moav. The Jewish people pitched camp near the Arnon River in Emorite territory.[15]

The Emorite Ambush

The Emorites received intelligence about the approaching Jewish nation, and they determined to make a stand at the Arnon River and turn them away. The Arnon River flowed through a narrow ravine between two tall mountains. The ravine was so narrow that a person standing on one mountainside could converse easily with someone standing on the opposite mountainside. In order to get into Canaan, the Jewish people would

---

8. *Aderes Eliyahu*, based on *Devarim* 2:14. See also *Bamidbar Rabbah* 19:24; Ibn Ezra, *Chizkuni* on *Bamidbar* 21:10. Ovos was so called because its inhabitants were *oivim*, enemies of Hashem (*Bamidbar Rabbah* 19:24).

According to *Ohr haChaim*, *Bamidbar* 21:12, the Jews weren't traveling with the cloud pillar now. It would return after these two encampments.

9. Rashi, *Bamidbar* 21:11.

10. Ibid. Iyei haAvarim was named for its *iyim*, ruins (Rashbam; Rav Saadiah Gaon) and because Hashem was filled with *evrah*, anger, toward its inhabitants (*Tanchuma*, *Chukas* 19; Rabbeinu Bachya).

11. So called because it was as narrow as the distance from the *zeres*, the little finger, to the thumb (*Tanchuma*, *Chukas* 19).

12. See Tur, Rokeach on *Bamidbar* 21:13. See also Malbim.

13. So called because here, after thirty-eight years, Hashem's anger at the Jews finally *avar*, passed (*Bamidbar Rabbah* 19:24; Rabbeinu Bachya). According to Gra, Eiver Arnon was near Almon Divlasaimah, mentioned in *Bamidbar* 33:46.

14. See Rashi, *Bamidbar* 21:13.

15. See Rashi, *Midrash haGadol*, *Da'as Zekeinim*, *Hadar Zekeinim*, *Bechor Shor* on *Bamidbar* 21:10, 13.

have to cross one mountain, descend into the ravine and then cross the second mountain, a total distance of over four miles[16] across difficult terrain. The ravine would be a perfect spot for an ambush.

The Emorite chieftains gathered to discuss strategy under the shade of a spreading elm to escape the hot summer sun.

"There are multitudes of them," said one chieftain, "so we have to rely on the element of surprise. We must strike them before they even know we are near. If we are successful, we will kill many thousands of them, and the rest will flee in panic. Then we will plunder their possessions."

"Good idea, my friend," said another chieftain, "but how do you propose to surprise them? Should we make ourselves invisible until we are upon them?"

"This is no time for jokes," said the first chieftain. "Save those for the celebration party. Right now, we need to be all seriousness. There are caves and crevices in both mountainsides. I know them well, because I used to play in them when I was a boy. We will hide our warriors inside these caves and crevices,[17] and when the Jewish people cross the ravine—smack!" he pounded his right fist into his open left hand. "We'll rain arrows and boulders onto them from close range. We'll hit them so hard they'll be shattered."

A third chieftain shook his head. "You don't win battles with archers. They're very effective, of course, but you need foot soldiers as well. The Jewish fighters will fall back from the arrows and regroup, and then where will we be?"

"Elementary. We place battalions of warriors at both ends of the ravine to cut off their escape routes. We'll wait for them with swords drawn and spears at the ready."[18]

The strategy was a good one, but Hashem had other plans. As

---

16. The equivalent of seven *mil*, the distance cited in *Bamidbar Rabbah* 19:25 with Radal; *Berachos* 54 with Rashi.

17. On the Moav side of the river.

18. *Bamidbar Rabbah* 19:25.

He had done earlier with the cloud pillars, He smoothed out the terrain for the people by tipping it toward the approaching people as if in greeting. Then He inverted the mountaintop and placed it into the ravine so that the land above the filled ravine and the truncated mountain were flat and even.

The mountain that had been shoved into the ravine was covered with trees and spiky rock formations, and now these protrusions penetrated into the caves and crevices of the lower mountainside and simply pulverized all the concealed Emorites. The sealed caverns became blood-filled sepulchers for the slaughtered Emorite warriors.[19]

Meanwhile, the stone that served as the Well of Miriam rolled down to the river and drew enormous amounts of water into itself. Then it disgorged these waters in the direction of the battalions lying in wait with such force that they swept away the Emorites and drowned them, just as the sea had drowned the pursuing Egyptians.[20]

The Jewish people, walking across flat terrain halfway up the mountainside, were oblivious to the dramatic and miraculous events taking place right below their feet. But Hashem made sure that they would discover the great deeds He had performed for them and that they would be inspired.

After the people crossed to the other side, Hashem withdrew the inverted mountain and exposed the ravine below.[21] The Well of Miriam went from cavern to cavern and inundated each one with water, thereby flushing out the bloodied corpses piled within. A river of blood emerged and flowed toward the Jewish

---

19. Rashi, *Bamidbar* 21:15; *Bamidbar Rabbah* 19:25 with Mahrzu; *Berachos* 54. Alternatively, as the Jews traveled, the *Aron Kodesh* leveled the ground, eliminating obstacles and bringing the mountains together.

20. *Bamidbar Rabbah* 19:25.

21. Rashi with *Gur Aryeh*, *Bamidbar* 21:15; *Bamidbar Rabbah* 19:33.

people, carrying along the detached limbs of the dead warriors.[22]

According to another opinion, two Jewish men by the names of Ess and Heiv were afflicted with *tzara'as* at the time and had to be sequestered outside the encampment. They were the ones who witnessed the great miracles and informed the people about them.[23]

After the destruction of the Emorite attackers, the Jewish people collected the rich booty, a treasure far greater than the one they recovered from the Egyptians at the sea.[24]

Ode to the Well

In future years, when the astounding stories of early Jewish nationhood would be retold, people would talk about the great miracles that Hashem performed for the people at the sea right after the Exodus, and at the Arnon River at the end of their forty-year sojourn in the wilderness.[25] And in the annals of wars in Hashem's honor, it would be told that He destroyed the border city[26] of Vaheiv[27] in Sufah at

22. *Targum Yonasan*, Rashi with *Sifsei Chachamim* on *Bamidbar* 21:14, 17; *Bamidbar Rabbah* 19:25. During this miraculous event, Moshe stopped the sun, as he did on four other occasions (Rabbeinu Bachya, *Shemos* 19:17).

23. *Targum Yonasan*, *Lekach Tov* on *Bamidbar* 21:14; *Berachos* 54.

24. Rokeach, *Bamidbar* 21:14. Moav did not take part in this conspiracy, and therefore no Moabites were harmed (*Targum Yonasan*). One wonders why these ambushing Emorites brought so many valuables with them.

25. In this context, the Torah refers to a *sefer*, which some interpret not as an actual book but as a *sipur*, a storytelling (Rashi, *Bamidbar* 21:14; *Bamidbar Rabbah* 19:25). Others posit that it's a book of wars, recording all the Jews' battles along with the miracles Hashem performed since the days of Avraham (Ibn Ezra; Ramban; Rabbeinu Bachya). Alternatively, the *sefer* is *Shemos*, which retells the miracles performed in Egypt and immediately thereafter (*Midrash Aggadah*).

26. *Chizkuni*, *Bamidbar* 21:14. According to *Midrash haGadol*, *Bamidbar* 21:14–19, Vaheiv, Sufah, Eshed haNechalim, Matanah and Nachliel were all places near the new Moabite-Emorite borders (i.e., Emor's expanded territory). *Lekach Tov* equates Nachliel with Divon Gad. Ibn Ezra refers to Matanah as Almon Divlasaimah. And Gra identifies Vaheiv as Nachal Zered.

27. Rabbeinu Bachya, *Bamidbar* 21:15.

the Arnon River[28] where the Emorites perished.[29]

These great miracles inspired the people to sing Shirah to Hashem.[30] "Arise, O well," they sang, "come up from the valley, and bring up the scattered and broken limbs of the dead Emorites."[31]

They went on to sing about the virtues of the well,[32] of the rivers it disgorged and sent cascading from the high peaks to the wilderness below.[33] Moshe's name is not mentioned, however, in this ode to the well, because it had been the instrument of his downfall; it was because of the well that he was forbidden to enter the Holy Land, that he would die in the wilderness. Since Moshe's name was omitted, Hashem decreed that His be omitted as well in deference to Moshe.[34]

Although the well ceased to provide water to the Jewish people after the death of Moshe, it still continued to accompany them. If a person were to ascend Mount Yeshimon and gaze at the lake of Teveriah (the Kinneret), he would see a sieve-like boulder in the water. That boulder is the Well of Miriam.[35]

---

28. *Midrash haGadol, Bamidbar* 21:14.

29. *Ha'amek Davar,* ibid., states that as a precursor to the Jewish victory over Sichon, this destruction was entered in the book of wars.

30. Rashi, *Lekach Tov, Bechor Shor* on *Bamidbar* 21:15–16; *Berachos* 54; *Bamidbar Rabbah* 19:25. Alternatively, the Jewish people sang when, after Miriam's death and the disappearance of her well, water returned in Moshe's merit. See *Targum Yonasan, Bechor Shor,* Rav Samson Raphael Hirsch on *Bamidbar* 21:17–18.

31. See Rashi with *Sifsei Chachamim, Bamidbar* 21:17.

32. See Rashi, *Bamidbar* 21:18.

33. See *Bamidbar Rabbah* 19:26; *Bechor Shor, Bamidbar* 21:20. For more on the well, see *Bamidbar Rabbah,* ibid., with Mahrzu, *Yedei Moshe; Tosefta Sukkah* 3:3; commentaries on *Tehillim* 105:41. Some suggest that the Jews could even sail to the Mediterranean and discover great treasures there.

34. *Bamidbar Rabbah* 19:26; *Midrash Aggadah, Bamidbar* 21:17.

35. Ibid.; Rashi, *Bamidbar* 21:20.

7

Sichon and Og

Four years before the Jewish people appeared on the scene, the kingdom of Moav had fought a desperate war with the Emorites. Under the leadership of the giant Sichon, their king, the Emorites had besieged Cheshbon, the strategically located capital of Moav, but they had failed to conquer it.[1] According to one view, the city of Cheshbon and its suburbs were actually Emorite possessions that had been leased to Moav at a very high rate. Eventually, Moav fell behind in its payments, and this prompted the war.[2]

Frustrated by his military failures, Sichon called on the supernatural to secure victory

1. *Sefer haYashar*. See Ramban, *Bamidbar* 21:26.
2. Rokeach, Tur on *Bamidbar* 21:23. See Zohar, *Chukas* 185a.

for him. He turned to two Arameans, Be'or and his son Bilam, both of whom were wizards. Bilam had attained considerable international fame through his services to Pharaoh in Egypt many years earlier.[3] Sichon hired this father-and-son team to place a curse on the Moabites and render them helpless before the swords of the Emorites.[4] Be'or and Bilam accepted Sichon's commission. They assured him that he would defeat the Moabites and that the city of Cheshbon would be renamed in his honor.[5]

Meanwhile, all was not well on the Moav home front. The Moabite king,[6] a proud, arrogant ruler, alienated many of his subjects with his high-handedness and abrasive personality. He disregarded the gathering clouds of war with Sichon, so confident in his military prowess[7] that he didn't even bother to fortify his capital city of Cheshbon against attack—against the advice of the Emorite governors who had leased the city to him.[8] The king assumed that his superior knowledge of the city would allow him to mount a defense and a counteroffensive even without high ramparts to protect the city. But he did not take into account the disgruntled courtiers who were fed up with the king's rash policies. Rather than perish in ignominious defeat, these courtiers went over to Sichon, bringing with them detailed maps and charts of the city.[9]

With the city unprotected and vulnerable to Sichon's invading army,[10] the insidious incantations of the Aramean wizards

3. I.e., as an advisor. The two ideas he influenced Pharaoh to implement were the enslavement of the Jews and throwing the Jewish male newborns into the river.

4. Rashi, *Bamidbar* 21:27; *Bamidbar Rabbah* 20:7. *Sefer haYashar* identifies this Bilam as a great-grandson of the Bilam of Egypt.

5. Rabbeinu Bachya, *Bamidbar* 21:27.

6. This was the king preceding Balak.

7. Rokeach, *Bamidbar* 21:30.

8. See Rokeach, Tur on ibid.

9. Ibn Ezra, *Chizkuni*, *Ha'amek Davar* on *Bamidbar* 21:28. See *Yahel Ohr* on Rabbeinu Bachya.

10. Malbim, *Bamidbar* 21:27.

providing an umbrella of protective cover and Sichon and his Emorite warriors descending on the city of Cheshbon,[11] the city was soon in flames.[12] The leading members of Moabite society and the priests of its temples all perished in the inferno.[13] The roaring fires spread to the neighboring city of Ar, causing havoc and extensive damage.[14] The Emorites pressed on throughout the land of Moav and even penetrated into the lands of Amon, Moav's closest neighbor and ally.

When the smoke of battle cleared, Cheshbon lay devastated, reduced to bloodstained ashes and trampled into oblivion.[15] The young Moabite men who had gone out to do battle with the Emorites[16] fled for their lives and hid in the mountains, while the young women of Moav were taken captive by the Emorites.[17]

Sichon was now master of the strategic city of Cheshbon, and he had wrested territory from Moav as far south as Divon and the Arnon River valley, beyond which strong winds and raging waterfalls impeded his further progress.[18] He also captured land from Amon as far north as the Yabok River valley, but stiff Amonite resistance arrested his advance.[19]

With the ravaged Cheshbon firmly in his control, Sichon rebuilt it from the ground up and surrounded it with massive fortifications. He then made it his capital city and renamed it Sichon after

---

11. See Ramban, *Bamidbar* 21:14.
12. Rashi, Malbim on *Bamidbar* 21:28.
13. *Targum Unkelos, Me'am Lo'ez* on ibid.
14. Rashi, Malbim on ibid. See *Lekach Tov, Bamidbar* 21:15.
15. *Chizkuni*, Rabbeinu Bachya on *Bamidbar* 21:30.
16. Rokeach, *Bamidbar* 21:29.
17. Rashi, Ramban, *Chizkuni*, Radak on *Bamidbar* 21:28–29.
18. See *Yerushalmi Gittin* 8:1; Ramban, *Chizkuni* on *Bamidbar* 21:26–27; Rashi, Rokeach, Malbim on *Bamidbar* 21:30; Seforno, *Bamidbar* 21:14.
19. See *Da'as Zekeinim*, *Chizkuni*, Ibn Ezra, Rav Saadiah Gaon, *Bechor Shor* on *Bamidbar* 21:24.

himself.[20] Convinced that the efforts of Be'or and Bilam had been instrumental in his decisive victory, Sichon sent them lavish gifts.[21]

Sichon's victory over the Moabites was so stunning and complete that it would earn a place in the annals of history for all time.[22] The troubadours and bards sang of the great victories and the conquest of the city of Vaheiv in Sufah.[23] Bilam took the lead among the vilifying versifiers, mocking and scoffing at the Moabites with his sardonic lyrics.[24]

"Woe to you, O Moav," he chortled. "Your identity is lost.[25] The servants of the god Kemosh[26] are lost. For you have been delivered into the hands of Sichon.[27] Your deity has abandoned your children in their time of need."[28]

Back in Time: A Tale of Two Brothers

Sichon had a half-brother named Og, who reigned over the land of Bashan to the north. The two brothers were the sons of Achia, the son of Shamchazai and Azael, two angels (known as *nefilim*) who descended from heaven and took on an earthly existence in the days of Enosh. This family populated

20. See Rashi with *Maskil l'David*, Seforno, Ramban, *Ha'amek Davar* on *Bamidbar* 21:26–27.

21. *Sefer haYashar*.

22. Ramban, *Bamidbar* 21:14. The historians of the time actually attributed the victory to an act of God.

23. Ramban, ibid.

24. See Rashi with Mizrachi, *Bamidbar* 21:27; Ramban, *Bamidbar* 21:14.

25. *Sifsei Kohen*, *Bamidbar* 21:29.

26. This idol, a female form made of black rocks, had supposedly stood since the beginning of time. Strangely, one out of every thousand people who knelt before it never returned from whence they came (*Lekach Tov*, *Pa'aneiach Raza*, *Yalkut Reuveni* on *Bamidbar* 21:29). *Midrash haGadol*, *Shemos* 20:5, says worshipers shaved their heads before it.

27. Rashi, *Bamidbar* 21:29.

28. Ramban, Rabbeinu Bachya on ibid.

the land with giants, such as Sichon and Og. The spies had caught sight of them in Canaan thirty-eight years earlier, and had taken fright.[29]

Og and Sichon were among the punier members of this stalwart family, but they were exceedingly mighty and self-reliant kings nonetheless. They were the two kings whom Moshe would have to defeat before the Jewish people could enter Canaan.[30]

Og was widely reputed to be the strongest man in the world.[31] He was an invincible warrior, swatting away his enemies like flies. Even as an infant in his wooden cradle, he had been so strong and violent that he had smashed it to bits. After that, his parents confined him to an iron, armor-plated cradle, which offered a little more deterrence.[32] This actually saved his life. An Emorite raiding party attacked the camp of the giants and slaughtered everyone in it, except for Og. They did indeed send a shower of deadly arrows toward his cradle, but its heavy armor stopped the arrows from penetrating and causing any damage. Og survived and flourished, and eventually became king of the entire land of Bashan.[33]

Og was a veteran survivor. He was actually known as the "Palit," the survivor. During the Mabul, the Great Flood, he managed to sit on one of the wooden rungs of an exterior ladder of the Ark.[34] He begged Noach to help him and save his life. "Save

---

29. *Yalkut Shimoni* 6:44. See also *Niddah* 61a with Rashi; Tur, *Bereishis* 6:4.

30. See *Torah Sheleimah, Bamidbar* 21:205; Rashi, *Devarim* 2:32.

31. *Bamidbar Rabbah* 19:32.

32. See Rashbam, Malbim on *Devarim* 3:11. This crib was nine *amos* long and four *amos* wide, so that the most conservative opinion would make Og over five feet tall as an infant. According to Rashi, he was much taller than this.

33. See Rabbi Yehudah heChasid, Rokeach on ibid. According to *Yalkut Me'or haAfeilah,* Og had one of Hashem's Names etched on his bed to protect him.

34. See *Pirkei d'Rabbi Eliezer* 23; *Zevachim* 113b. See also *Devarim Rabbah* 1:25; *Midrash haCheifetz* 3:11; Rashi, *Bereishis* 14:13. This scenario presumes that the entire world was flooded, so Og had no choice but to cling to the Ark. (And how did Og survive the boiling floodwater? Some say that around the Ark

me," he cried, "and I swear that I will be your servant forever." Noach understood that it was Hashem's will that Og survive, and he fed him through a hole in the side of the Ark.[35] Sichon, who was much younger than Og, had not yet been born.[36]

According to another opinion, Noach's wife, Na'amah, died before the Mabul, and he then married the mother of Og, who was already pregnant. Her child, born in the Ark, was Sichon.[37] Others suggest that Noach's son Cham married the mother of Og and that she gave birth to Sichon in the Ark.[38] Still others are of the opinion that Og's father violated the wife of Cham, who then gave birth to Sichon.[39]

More is known about Og than about Sichon. All we know about Sichon, aside from his military victories, is that he was as tall as a cedar tree, towering above all other people.[40] His prowess was widely reported and discussed. In fact, his name was not Sichon at all; it was Canaani.[41] But he was called Sichon, based on the word *sichah*, which means conversation, because he was such a popular topic of conversation. He had only one son, a warrior even mightier than he.[42]

---

the water was cool.) According to the view that the flood never reached Eretz Yisrael, however, Og escaped to there. See Rashi, Maharsha on *Niddah* 61a, *Zevachim* 113b; *Rav Ovadiah Bartenura al haTorah, Bereishis* 14:13; *Pirkei d'Rabbi Eliezer* 23.

35. See *Pirkei d'Rabbi Eliezer* 23; *Niddah* 61a; *Midrash haCheifetz* 3:11.

36. See Tosafos, *Niddah* 61a; *Da'as Zekeinim, Bamidbar* 21:34.

37. *Moshav Zekeinim, Bamidbar* 21:34.

38. *Da'as Zekeinim*, ibid.

39. Maharsha, *Niddah* 61a; Rabbeinu Bachya, *Bamidbar* 21:34. Opinions differ as to whether Sichon and Og shared a mother or a father, but all agree that they had only one parent in common.

40. *Midrash Shocher Tov* 136.

41. *Midrash Aggadah, Bamidbar* 21:23.

42. Rabbeinu Bachya, *Bamidbar* 21:24; Rashi, *Tosefos Rabbeinu Yoel* on *Devarim* 2:33. See *Torah Sheleimah, Bamidbar* 21:163.

Og was a more colorful, flamboyant and malevolent figure. He had a penchant for survival, which he demonstrated during the Mabul and for which he was named the Palit, as mentioned above. Many years later, he had an experience that only reinforced his nickname.

At that time, the four mighty kings of Bavel, led by King Chedarlaomer, invaded Canaan and defeated the five local kings on the battlefield.[43] They captured the cities of the plain, including Sodom, and took Avraham's nephew Lot captive. Og managed to escape without being injured or captured—the perennial survivor with the perfect moniker.[44] He immediately ran to Avraham to inform him that Lot had been taken captive.

This would seem to have been a noble gesture, but it was far from it. Unchastened by his second brush with death, Og persisted in his arrogant attitude, his actions motivated by his own evil designs. Og had set his eyes on Avraham's wife Sarah, and he hoped that Avraham would pursue the Babylonian kings and be killed in the process. Sarah would then be free to marry him. To Og's utter chagrin, Avraham was victorious, and Sarah remained beyond his reach.[45]

When Og arrived to report the abduction of Lot, Avraham was baking matzah for Pesach. Og tasted a matzah and rudely ridiculed it. Because of his effrontery toward Avraham, people began to call him Ugah, which means cake, in reference to the matzah.[46]

Because of Og's exalted status in the firmament of the local potentates, Avraham invited him to attend Yitzchak's weaning

---

43. *Bereishis* 14.

44. See *Bereishis* 14:13.

45. *Niddah* 61a with Tosafos; *Bamidbar Rabbah* 19:32; *Devarim Rabbah* 1:25.

46. *Bereishis Rabbah* 42:8 with *Yefeh To'ar*; *Devarim Rabbah* 1:25; Tosafos, *Niddah* 61a; *Maseches Sofrim* 21:9; *Midrash Shocher Tov* 136; *Midrash Aggadah*, *Me'am Lo'ez* on *Bamidbar* 21:33.

celebration. A great deal of food and wine was served, and the kings and warlords were in high spirits.[47]

"Og, it's strange to see you here," said one warlord, waving his tankard about in the air. "I distinctly remember your calling Avraham a barren mule. Does my memory serve me correctly?"

Og guffawed. "You may very well be right, my friend."

"Weren't you saying that he could not have children?" continued the warlord.

"You could have interpreted my words that way," said Og.

The warlord grew red in the face. "You disgraced Avraham. But now the joke's on you. Right over there you can see the child of Avraham."

"You can't be serious," Og retorted. "That scrawny child? You call that progeny? Why, if I would touch my finger to his belly, he would die on the spot. But I don't have to do anything to put him out of his misery. With two doddering old parents taking care of him, he doesn't stand a chance of survival. And you can take it from me, the quintessential survivor. Who knows better than I do?"

Instead of marveling at the miracle Hashem had wrought by granting a child to Avraham and Sarah in their old age, Og had made a mockery of it. "You've disgraced My gift," Hashem declared, "but you will be the one disgraced. Avraham will be the patriarch of thousands upon thousands of descendants. As for you, when the time comes and your measure has reached its limit, Avraham's descendant Moshe will kill you."[48]

---

47. The kings included the thirty-one who ruled Eretz Yisrael.

48. See *Bereishis Rabbah* 53:10; *Devarim Rabbah* 1:25; *Targum Yonasan, Bamidbar* 21:34. Indeed, all thirty-one kings mentioned in the previous note would live to witness their descendants' demise at the hand of "sickly" Yitzchak's progeny (*Me'am Lo'ez, Yehoshua* 12). According to Rabbeinu Bachya, *Bamidbar* 21:34, the Og Moshe killed wasn't this one but a descendant.

Back to the Wilderness: An Overture of Peace

Toward the end of the month of Elul,[49] the Jewish people were moving in a northwesterly direction toward the Jordan River, beyond which lay Eretz Yisrael. But between them and the river stood the powerful and belligerent Emorite kingdom of Sichon. The people encamped in sukkahs (booths), and prepared to do battle with the Emorites.[50]

The Emorites were long aware of the relentless approach of the Jewish people. Convinced that they faced an imminent invasion, they called a war council to plan strategy.

Sichon pointed to his minister of intelligence. "You will speak first," he said. "All good planning begins with good intelligence. Tell us what you know about these people. Are they one homogenous group or are they a hodgepodge of different groups?"

"According to my information," said the minister, "there are three groups: Kohanim, Levi'im and Yisraelim. We're still awaiting confirmation from independent sources before we can declare this to be hard intelligence, but that is the common wisdom."

"Hmm, three groups," mused Sichon. "That shouldn't pose too great a problem. What about size: how big are they? And how strong?"

"Well, they're not particularly tall," said the minister. "According to my intelligence, they average three *amos* in height."

Sichon laughed. "Three *amos*? What are they — a nation of midgets? They don't sound like much of a threat to us, do they?

---

49. *Bamidbar Rabbah* 19:32; *Yalkut Reuveni, Bamidbar* 22:6; *Panim Yafos, Bamidbar* 21:22; *Seder Olam* 9 with *Yemos Olam*. Aharon died in Av, and the Jewish people mourned him for one month, resuming their travel toward Eretz Yisrael in Elul.

50. *Eliyah Rabbah, Orach Chaim* 625, quotes the Rokeach's view that we celebrate Sukkos because the Jews lived in sukkahs while besieging Sichon and Og. See *Chasam Sofer, Orach Chaim* 185.

All right, this council is adjourned. We'll just attack them and crush them like bugs."

The Emorites mobilized their renowned military forces for war. The sight of the massed warriors and the fearsome chariots struck terror in the hearts of the Jewish people.

"Tell the people not to be afraid," Hashem said to Moshe. "I have delivered Sichon into your hands. He will not be able to stand in your way. You will defeat him and inherit his land."[51]

Moshe conveyed the divine message to the people, and they felt reassured. They girded themselves for battle and prepared to go. But before Moshe gave the order to invade, he made an overture of peace to Sichon.[52] Hashem had not required him to do this, but because Moshe was a peace-loving man, as was his brother Aharon, his first inclination was to seek peaceful solutions.[53]

Earlier, he had made peace overtures to Edom and Moav when requesting right of passage through their lands, and had turned away when his overtures were rejected. However, with Sichon, the overture would actually be an ultimatum. He was giving Sichon a chance to accept a peaceful solution. The alternative was war and destruction.

"Why did you make peace overtures to Sichon?" Hashem asked Moshe. "I told you to go to war with him. I did not command you to offer him peace."

"I learned this from You," said Moshe. "When You wanted to take the Jewish people out of Egypt, You could have destroyed

---

51. *Devarim Rabbah* 1:24. See Ramban, *Minchah Belulah* on *Devarim* 2:24.

52. See Rashi, *Bamidbar* 21:22. See also Mizrachi and Ramban.

53. Abarbanel, ibid. Moshe learned this attribute from Hashem, Who offered the other nations the Torah (Riva). This approach was also pragmatic: If the Emorites humbly accepted Moshe's peaceful overtures, the Canaanites, a weaker nation, would follow suit when the Jews sought to settle Canaan. If instead the Emorites fought, and lost, it was hoped that the Canaanites would fearfully avoid conflict with the Jews (Abarbanel).

Pharaoh with a single bolt of lightning, but You didn't. You sent me to ask him for his consent. You gave him the opportunity to release us peacefully. Only after he refused did You afflict him and his nation with plagues. I have done the same by giving Sichon the opportunity to let us pass in peace."[54]

"You have learned My ways well," said Hashem. "In the future, the Jewish people shall indeed make overtures of peace before going to battle."[55]

Accordingly, Moshe sent Sichon a letter laying out the terms of a formal offer of peace.[56] The letter contained no request for permission, only a declarative statement of the determination of the Jewish people to pass through Sichon's lands and of their peaceful intentions. The implication was that if Sichon tried to stop them there would be a war.[57]

"To the honorable Sichon, king of the Emorites, as a courtesy and in the spirit of peace, the Jewish people would like to inform you that we intend to pass through your territory on the way to Canaan. Our intentions are completely peaceful. We realize that we will be guests in your realm, and intend to act accordingly. We will avoid your fields and vineyards and travel only along the king's highway, the main thoroughfare that crosses your land. Although we have plenty of provisions, we offer, as a gesture of friendship, to purchase food and water from your people and thus boost your economy."[58]

---

54. *Yalkut Shimoni* 764; *Lekach Tov*, Rashi, Abarbanel on *Devarim* 2:26. See also *Chasam Sofer*, *Bamidbar* 21:21.

55. *Devarim Rabbah* 5:13. And indeed, Yehoshua did. See *Devarim Rabbah* 5:14; Ramban, *Devarim* 20:10.

56. See Rashi, *Bamidbar* 21:21. Some say Moshe sent a letter of peace, while the Jews themselves sent a letter threatening war (*Chizkuni*, *Bamidbar* 21:2; Rosh, *Devarim* 2:26). According to *Yalkut Mechiri* 37:8, Moshe's letter began on a peaceful note and ended by threatening war. Compare Malbim.

57. See Tur, Rokeach, *Ha'amek Davar* on *Bamidbar* 21:22.

58. See Rokeach, *Bechor Shor*, *Hadar Zekeinim* on ibid.; *Devarim* 2:26–28; *Bamidbar Rabbah* 19:29; *Sefer haYashar*.

Sichon laughed derisively when he read the letter. He was running a powerful kingdom indeed. He and Og, king of Bashan,[59] were the most powerful monarchs in the entire region; more powerful than Egypt, more powerful than all the Canaanite kingdoms combined.[60] They were so strong and powerful that no enemy could vanquish them, but even had they been weak as flies they could not have been vanquished in their cities because they were protected by impregnable fortifications. How could an upstart nation dare threaten the invincible Emorites?[61] It could only be, reasoned Sichon, that they did not realize with whom they were dealing.

"We are not impressed by your bluster," he wrote back to Moshe. "We know that you are weak and meek. Everyone has heard how the Edomites and the Moabites brushed you aside when you asked for safe passage through their lands. How then can you dare to threaten the mighty Emorite nation?[62] Can you possibly think we fear you, a nation of stragglers wandering in the wilderness? Why should we allow you to pass through our land? That is a courtesy we give only to our equals, not to you.[63] Besides, even if your intentions are entirely peaceful, you are headed for Canaan, which you intend to conquer. And we cannot allow you to attack the Canaanites, because we are the guardians

---

59. *Niddah* 61a. Sichon and Og were both roughly 800 years old.

60. *Bamidbar Rabbah* 19:29; *Midrash Shocher Tov* 136.

61. Rashi, *Bamidbar* 21:23; *Bamidbar Rabbah* 19:29.

62. *Minchah Belulah, Sifsei Kohen* on *Bamidbar* 20:14; *Chizkuni, Devarim* 2:25. See *Yalkut Midreshei Teiman, Bamidbar* 21:23.

63. See *Imrei Shefer, Bamidbar* 21:23. Sichon's logic doesn't add up. If he wasn't afraid, he should have let the Jews pass through his territory. Yet Hashem put this convoluted reasoning in Sichon's head so he would go to war with the Jews and eventually be annihilated (*Ohr haChaim, Devarim* 2:30). The Torah later recounts how Sichon refused the Jews entry, whereupon Hashem *imetz es levavo lema'an tito veyadcha*, "hardened his heart in order to deliver him into your hand" (*Devarim* 2:30).

of their safety. They pay us well for that service.[64]

"Furthermore, I found your message insolent and rude. You didn't even have the decency to ask me politely for permission. You just informed me that you are coming through. We'll see about that."[65]

Total Destruction

Sichon was not aware that he was doomed from the start. Hashem had endorsed Moshe's decision to make an overture of peace, but Sichon really did not have the free will to consent to safe passage. The time had come for the Emorites to be punished, and nothing would prevent their destruction. Hashem hardened Sichon's heart, as he had done with Pharaoh, and it was a foregone conclusion that he would reject Moshe's overture.[66]

Furthermore, Hashem made sure that the Jewish people's victory would come with as little effort as possible. The Jews were preparing to lay siege to the fortified Emorite cities, which promised to be a difficult task, but Hashem inspired the enemy to come out with arrogant confidence and face the invaders in the open field of battle.[67] Moreover, the families they left behind in the cities,[68] equally arrogant, disdained to close the gates of the cities behind the warriors, leaving the Emorite women and children vulnerable to attack.

Sichon led his Emorite army to a place called Yahatz, where he

---

64. Rashi, *Bamidbar* 21:23.

65. See Tur, Rokeach, *Ha'amek Davar* on *Bamidbar* 21:22.

66. See *Midrash haGadol, Bamidbar* 21:23; Seforno, *Devarim* 2:30; Rambam, *Teshuvah* 6:3. In fact, the moment he rebuffed Moshe's gesture of peace, Sichon was considered a fallen man, destined to lose to the Jews (Abarbanel, *Devarim* 2:31).

67. Rashi, *Bamidbar* 21:25.

68. *Imrei Shefer,* ibid. Malbim comments on *Devarim* 2:34 that men unfit for war also remained behind.

chose to make his stand. Utterly confident, he didn't even bother asking his brother Og for military assistance. He had never needed it before, and he certainly didn't think he'd need it now.[69]

As the battle lines formed, Moshe miraculously stopped the sun in its path so that there would be enough time to destroy the Emorites before nightfall.[70] As He had done with the Egyptians, Hashem bound the ministering angel of the Emorites, so to speak, and deposited him, weak and debilitated, at Moshe's feet. Moshe placed his foot on the angel's neck, completely immobilizing him. Without their ministering angel, the Emorites were left defenseless before the Jewish fighters.[71]

Uttering the Name of Hashem (*Hashem haMeforash*) as they brandished their swords,[72] and assisted by swarms of buzzing

---

69. See Rashi, *Devarim* 2:32.

70. See *Avodah Zarah* 25a with Rashi. See also *Targum Yonasan*, Rashi on *Devarim* 2:25, 31. Rashi on the abovementioned *Avodah Zarah* writes that Moshe stopped the sun during the war with Sichon. Rabbeinu Bachya, *Devarim* 2:25, cites another version of Rashi, according to which Moshe did so during the war with Og.

In this miracle, destined since creation, the other heavenly bodies were also halted, forcing the nations of the world to acknowledge a greater power than all the constellations they worshiped.

The sun praises Hashem throughout its cycle around the earth in order to show those who worship it that its power to light and heat the world and to cause vegetation to grow is rooted in Hashem's command. In fact, the Hebrew word for "sun" is *shemesh*, as in *shimush*, service, for the sun serves Hashem's will. During his war with the Emorites, Yehoshua silenced the sun's praises, so that it automatically lost its power (*Tanchuma, Acharei* 9 with *Eitz Yosef*). It then stood still for six to forty-eight hours (opinions vary).

The book of *Yehoshua* explicitly records this miracle, whereas the Torah merely alludes to Moshe's, because Yehoshua publicly decreed the stopping of the sun, whereas Moshe didn't. See *Me'am Lo'ez, Yehoshua* 10:12–14.

71. *Yalkut Shimoni* 764; *Midrash Shocher Tov* 136; Rashi, *Rav Ovadiah Bartenura al haTorah* on *Devarim* 2:31; *Devarim Rabbah* 1:22–23.

72. See Rashi, *Sanhedrin* 67a; *Targum Yonasan, Bamidbar* 21:24. The Jews needed to use Hashem's Name as their source of strength, for Eisav is known as the man of the sword, while the Jews' weapon is prayer.

hornets (or wasps),[73] the Jewish people achieved victory in one fell swoop. They killed Sichon and his son and annihilated his entire army, leaving no survivors.[74] They rushed from the battlefield, surged through the open gates of the cities, wiped out their entire populations and collected mountains of booty.[75]

The Jewish people then took possession[76] of the cities Sichon had captured from Amon and Moav between the Arnon and Yabok rivers.[77] They couldn't push farther south or east because they would be entering the lands of Amon and Moav, which Hashem had forbidden them to attack.[78]

The news of the stunning and miraculous victory reached far and wide and struck fear into the hearts of all the surrounding kingdoms. The only exception was Og, king of Bashan, but he too would soon meet his destiny.

The hostile gentile nations are compared to the sea, while the Jewish people are compared to the sand on the seashore. The waves crash against the shore, but the sand robs them of their power. Wave after wave is stymied and driven back, but the waves continue to come. They never learn their lesson. The Egyptians attacked the Jewish people, and they were destroyed. The Amalekites attacked the Jewish people, and they were destroyed. And still, the Emorites did not learn their lesson. They too attacked the Jewish people, and they too were destroyed.[79]

---

73. *Kli Yakar*, based on *Yehoshua* 24:12. See *Sotah* 36a.

74. *Lekach Tov*, Rabbeinu Bachya on *Bamidbar* 21:24, *Devarim* 2:34.

75. *HaKesav vehaKabbalah*, *Devarim* 2:34. The Jews kept the thin animals for themselves, designating the plump ones as offerings to Hashem (Tur).

76. Rashi, *Devarim* 2:34; Seforno, *Bamidbar* 21:30.

77. *Sefer haYashar*, *Lekach Tov* on *Bamidbar* 21:31. Sichon thus "purified" these cities for Jewish settlement. Had they remained part of Amon or Moav, the Jews would not have been allowed to conquer or settle them (Rashi, Rabbeinu Bachya on *Bamidbar* 21:24, 26; *Chullin* 60b; *Bamidbar Rabbah* 19:30).

78. Rashi, *Chizkuni* on *Bamidbar* 21:21; Seforno, *Bamidbar* 21:31.

79. *Yalkut Shimoni* 765.

Moshe Sends Spies to Ya'azer

With the lands of Sichon conquered and occupied, the Jewish people were on the borders of Amon to the east and Bashan to the north.[80] Nearby stood the Emorite city of Ya'azer, which the Jews needed to conquer before turning their attention to the land of Canaan.[81] Before they began the assault, however, Moshe sent the righteous Pinchas and Kalev on a reconnaissance mission to the city.[82]

Although the first mission of the spies had ended in disaster, Moshe did not hesitate to send Pinchas and Kalev on a similar mission, because he knew they were men of deep faith and righteousness who would carry Moshe's prayers with them.[83] His confidence was well-placed. Pinchas and Kalev scouted out the city and brought back important strategic information. The Jewish people then attacked Ya'azer and conquered it and its suburbs, driving out the remaining Emorites and inheriting their land.[84]

The Jewish people were now just a few miles from the Jordan River, and their entire attention was focused on the long-awaited crossing into the Promised Land. They had no intention of warring with Bashan. But Og would change their plans.[85]

---

80. *Sefer haYashar.*

81. See Rav Aryeh Kaplan, *The Living Torah* (New York: Moznaim, 1981), p. 448; *Ha'amek Davar, Bamidbar* 21:32.

82. *Targum Yonasan*, Abarbanel on *Bamidbar* 21:32. Yehoshua later chose these very spies to scout out Canaan via Yericho.

According to *Yalkut haEizovi, Bamidbar* 21:32, Moshe sent surveyors to see what boundaries bordered which lands, and where they were allowed to travel and camp outside Moav and Amon. See *Sifsei Kohen* regarding why Moshe chose to conquer Ya'azer.

83. Rashi, *Bamidbar* 21:32. See Abarbanel, *Sefer haYashar.*

84. Rashi with *Be'er Yitzchak*, Seforno, Abarbanel on ibid. According to Rokeach, the inhabitants fled without a fight. Abarbanel writes that all the men had already perished in battle, so only women and children remained in the city.

According to *Sefer haYashar*, the Jews captured sixty cities in this battle.

85. See *Ha'amek Davar, Bamidbar* 21:34. Compare *Chizkuni.*

Moshe Battles Og

Og was distraught by the defeat and demise of his brother Sichon.[86] Reports of spies just beyond his border incensed him even further.[87] Supremely confident in his own abilities,[88] he decided to take matters into his hands and prevent the imminent establishment of a Jewish state in Canaan.[89] Although the Jewish people had not sent him any messages or made any move toward him, he mobilized his armies and marched to the city of Edre'i.[90]

Moshe was concerned by this new development. He had not planned on engaging Bashan, which was far to the north and not in the path of the invasion.[91] He did not want to contend with the pugnacious Og, neither to offer him peace overtures nor to war with him.[92] But it seemed that a clash could not be avoided, and Moshe was afraid.

It was not Og's size or prowess that frightened him. Og was certainly no more intimidating than his brother Sichon, whom Moshe had not feared at all. Rather, Moshe feared that Og had merits that could assist him in battle.[93] In fact, Og had survived the Mabul, which made him over eight hundred years old. A man did not live that long without some merits to his advantage.[94] Og had gained these merits when he informed Avraham

---

86. Abarbanel, *Bamidbar* 21:33.

87. *Ha'amek Davar*, ibid. *Chizkuni*, *Bamidbar* 21:34, suggests that Moshe and his men were heading straight toward Og.

88. *Sifsei Kohen*, *Bamidbar* 21:34.

89. Abarbanel, *Bamidbar* 21:33.

90. *Tosefos Rabbeinu Yoel* states that this was where Og worshiped his idols.

91. Ramban, *Bamidbar* 21:21.

92. Ramban, *Ha'amek Davar* on *Devarim* 2:34.

93. Ramban, *Bamidbar* 21:34; Rashi, *Devarim* 3:2; *Niddah* 61a with Tosafos.
According to *Chasam Sofer*, *Bamidbar* 21:34, p. 11, Hashem assured Moshe that minimal effort/merit would be needed to kill Og.

94. *Bamidbar Rabbah* 19:32. The Flood occurred in year 1656 from creation. It was now year 2488, making it 832 years between the two dates. Although the

that Chedarlaomer and the other Babylonian kings had abducted Lot and his family.[95] According to some opinions, Og had gained his merits when he joined Avraham in *bris milah*.[96] There is also an opinion that Og and Avraham's servant Eliezer were one and the same, which means that Og had the great merit of serving Avraham for many years.[97]

Furthermore, Moshe was also afraid that the Jewish people might have been too greedy in collecting the spoils of war after they defeated Sichon, which could possibly work against them.[98]

"Do not fear Og," Hashem informed Moshe. "I have delivered him into your hands.[99] And do not be concerned about the Jewish people. They are without sin.[100] Og may have informed Avraham about Lot's abduction, but his intentions were malicious. He was hoping that Avraham would go to war and be killed, but it didn't happen. And now, Avraham's descendant will kill him."[101]

Midrash states that Og was only 500 years old, Mahrzu detects a printing error here, in which a *ches*, representing the number eight, was mistaken for a *hei*, representing the number five.

95. Rashi, *Bamidbar* 21:34; *Bamidbar Rabbah* 19:32.

96. See Zohar, *Chukas* 184a; *Minchah Belulah, Bamidbar* 21:34. Hashem later told Moshe not to fear *oso*, meaning "him" but also "his *os*," his sign—referring to his *bris milah* (Zohar).

97. *Yalkut Me'or haAfeilah*, Rokeach on *Bamidbar* 21:34; *Pirkei d'Rabbi Eliezer* 16. Moshe worried that the merit of having brought together Yitzchak and Rivkah would protect Og/Eliezer.

98. *Bamidbar Rabbah* 19:32. Moshe's fear was not unreasonable considering the incident with Achan. See *Yehoshua* 7. See also Chapter 4, note 22.

99. Ramban, *Bamidbar* 21:34; *Devarim Rabbah* 1:24.

100. *Bamidbar Rabbah* 19:32.

101. Yet Og was rewarded with long life because his actions proved beneficial despite his intentions. See *Da'as Zekeinim, Kli Yakar, Sifsei Chachamim* on *Bamidbar* 21:34; *Moshav Zekeinim, Bereishis* 14:13; *Bamidbar Rabbah* 19:32; *Bereishis Rabbah* 42:8; *Devarim Rabbah* 1:25. From here we learn that Hashem rewards even the slightest positive action. Similarly, though Balak offered sacrifices as a means of destroying the Jewish people, these offerings were rewarded in the person of Ruth, the daughter of King Eglon, Balak's grandson (*Da'as Zekeinim, Chizkuni* on *Bamidbar* 21:34).

Reassured, the Jewish people prepared for battle.[102] The next day, 23 Tishrei, was an auspicious day for them as it was the last week of a month of prayer[103] and, according to one opinion, the date on which the world was created.[104]

At dawn, Moshe noticed that a second wall seemed to have appeared overnight in front of the walls of the city. Hashem informed him that Og was sitting on the wall and that his dangling feet, which were eighteen *amos* long, gave the appearance of a second wall. "But do not fear him," Hashem said. "I will topple him for you."

When he caught sight of the Jewish fighters, Og snickered and thought, "Why should I exert myself across the Jewish camp spread out over three parasangs,[105] striking at them with swords and arrows? Let me uproot a mountain of that size and throw it on them and crush them."

Og uprooted a huge mountain of three parasangs and balanced it over his head, prepared to hurl it at the Jewish encampment. Moshe immediately uttered Hashem's Name (*Hashem haMeforash*), and the Jewish people were protected from Og's mountain.[106]

"Cursed are the hands," the Jews proclaimed, "that sought to throw the giant mountain at us."

"Blessed (a euphemism for cursed) are the hands," Og retorted, "that hold it back."[107]

As he stood there holding the mountain over his head, Hashem sent an army of ants—or a swarm of locusts according to another view—to gnaw a vertical hole through its center. The hollowed-out mountain fell down over Og and settled on his shoulders, trapping

---

102. *Lekach Tov, Bamidbar* 21:33.

103. *Bamidbar Rabbah* 19:32; *Panim Yafos, Sifsei Kohen* on *Bamidbar* 21:22, 33; *Seder Olam* 9 with *Yemos Olam*.

104. Tosafos, *Bamidbar* 21:23.

105. Seven to nine miles.

106. Rokeach, *Bamidbar* 21:34; *Devarim Rabbah* 1:24; *Midrash Shocher Tov* 136.

107. *Devarim Rabbah* 1:24.

his head inside. As he tried to wriggle out of the mountain, his teeth got caught in the inner mountain walls and anchored him even more tightly to the mountain.

The massive giant stood immobilized in the center of the field, his head ensconced in the hollow mountain. Moshe, who was ten *amos* tall, took hold of an axe that was ten *amos* long and approached the trapped giant. He leaped ten *amos* into the air and struck Og in the ankle, killing him instantly.[108] In the ensuing battle, Og's son and all the rest of the population of Bashan perished.[109] There were no survivors.[110]

The Jewish people took possession of all sixty fortified cities in Bashan under Og's control.[111] All the former lands of Sichon and Og, from the Arnon River in the south to Mount Chermon all the way in the north, now belonged to the Jewish people.[112] These lands would eventually be apportioned to the tribes of Reuven and Gad and the half-tribe of Menashe.[113]

After the glut of booty from the war with Sichon, the Jewish people were not eager to collect all Bashan's booty. They just took the gold and silver and left all the livestock and other property behind.[114]

---

108. See *Berachos* 54b with Rashi; *Bamidbar* 21:35; *Torah Sheleimah, Bamidbar* 21:21; *Devarim Rabbah* 1:24. Og's feet alone may have been eighteen *amos* long. Perhaps from his feet to his ankles were another twelve *amos*, totaling thirty.

According to *Sefer haYashar*, an angel bore a hole into a boulder above Og's head. When this boulder fell on his head, he fell to the ground. Only then did Moshe deliver the fatal ankle blow. See below in the text for how this neutralized Og's merit, allowing the giant to be killed by a mere blow to a limb.

109. See *Lekach Tov, Hadar Zekeinim* on *Bamidbar* 21:35; *Sefer haYashar*; *Bamidbar Rabbah* 19:32.

110. *Devarim* 3:3.

111. Rashi, *Devarim* 3:4–5. The Jews conquered additional, unfortified cities as well.

112. See *Devarim* 3:8–12. This was the northernmost land Moshe conquered. It lay east of Lebanon, in the westernmost portion of present-day Syria.

113. See *Devarim* 3:12–16. See Ramban.

114. Rashi, *Devarim* 2:34. Compare *Panim Yafos*.

According to many views, the descriptions of the battle with Og portrayed in the Midrash are not to be taken literally. The elements are viewed as allegorical symbols. The huge mountain Og wielded against the Jewish people symbolized the merit he had accumulated by his service to Avraham, who was great like a mountain. The army of ants (or the swarm of locusts) symbolizes Moshe's prayers that counteracted Og's merit. Moshe, the axe and the leap that killed Og symbolize the merits of Moshe, the patriarchs and the Jewish people. They struck at Og's ankle, which he had used in Avraham's service, and neutralized its merit.[115]

Following the victory over Og, the Jewish people returned to their encampment to gather their wives and children. Unimpeded, they traveled on toward Canaan and pitched their camp in the western plains of Moav in an area known as Shittim. It was directly across the Jordan River from Jericho.[116]

The victories over Sichon and Og were great miracles worthy of paeans to Hashem, but it was King David, in *Tehillim* 136, who would eventually sing praises to Hashem for this victory.[117]

Give thanks to Hashem, for He is good,	for His kindness endures forever.
To the One Who smote great kings,	for His kindness endures forever.
He slew mighty kings,	for His kindness endures forever.
Sichon, king of Emorites,	for His kindness endures forever.
And Og, king of Bashan,	for His kindness endures forever.
Give thanks to the God of the heavens	for His kindness endures forever.

115. Rashba, *Berachos* 54b. For more on the allegoric dimensions of this battle, see *Gur Aryeh*, Rabbeinu Bachya on *Bamidbar* 21:35; Maharsha, *Tzelach* on *Berachos* 54b.

116. *Chizkuni*, *Lekach Tov* on *Bamidbar* 22:1. See Ibn Ezra, *Bamidbar* 25:1; *Yehoshua* 2:1. The Jews would remain here until Moshe's death (Riva).

117. *Midrash Shocher Tov* 136.

8

Enemies Join Forces

Moab had been defeated and conquered by Sichon's Emorite forces, but in the war between the Jewish people and the Emorites, the Moabites wanted Sichon to win. At least, Sichon provided them with protection. If the Jewish people were victorious, however, the protective shield would be removed, and Moav would face annihilation at the hands of the Jews.

Although the Jewish people were proscribed from attacking Moav, they did nothing to allay the fears of the Moabites, who had just witnessed the annihilation of the kingdoms of Sichon and Og. Bristling with weapons, the Jewish fighters massed at the Moabite border and struck terror into the hearts[1]

---

1. *Midrash haGadol*, Rashi on *Bamidbar* 22:1–2; *Bamidbar Rabbah* 20:2–3. See Rashi, *Devarim* 2:9.

of the inhabitants.[2] Many fled for their lives. The Jewish fighters plundered the possessions they left behind, because Hashem did not forbid them to take the abandoned booty.[3] He only forbade fighting with the Moabites themselves.

At this time, Moav was a land without a strong king. It was governed by a council of elders and warriors, most of whom were confounded by the prospect of a Jewish invasion. As the Jews conquered the lands of the Emorites to the north, the council met in emergency session.

"Gentlemen, I believe we are in trouble," said one of the elders. "The Jewish fighters have obliterated the kingdoms of Sichon and Og, and now they are massed outside our borders. I am not ashamed to admit that I fear for my life and the lives of my family."[4]

"I'm not convinced that they are such a threat," a burly warrior responded. "My intelligence analysts are offering conflicting conclusions. Some are saying that the Jewish fighters massed at our borders indicate an impending invasion, which is a very worrisome prospect. But others have a different prediction. They point out that when the Jewish people asked for permission to pass through the lands of Edom they were refused. And what did they do? Did they attack them as they attacked Sichon? No, they did not. And when we refused them permission, what did they do? The same thing. They just turned away like meek little lambs and continued on their way. What does that tell you?"[5]

"They fear the Edomites and us more than they fear the Emorites?" said the elder.

"More frightening than Sichon and Og?" said the warrior. "I think not. My analysts are convinced that the Jewish Deity forbids

---

2. Zohar, *Balak* 185a; Rokeach, *HaKesav vehaKabbalah* on *Bamidbar* 22:2.

3. *Midrash Aggadah, Bamidbar* 22:4.

4. Rashi, *Da'as Zekeinim* on *Bamidbar* 22:1–2; *Bamidbar Rabbah* 20:2.

5. See Rashi, *Shofetim* 11:17. Regarding Edom's willingness to sell food to the Jews, see *Sifsei Chachamim, Devarim* 2:29. See Ramban.

them to take hostile action against their relatives. We and the Edomites are their cousins, and the Emorites are not. They will not attack us."

"That's a nice theory, young fellow,"[6] said an ancient elder with sunken eyes. "But I don't want to hear about your newfangled analysts. I believe in making decisions the old-fashioned way." He tapped his forehead and his belly. "With good old common sense and my old reliable gut feelings."

"I agree," said another elder. "We can't make policy based on theories. I have my doubts about your theory anyway. Maybe the Jews felt the time was not yet ripe to attack us. You know, if they were so concerned about doing no harm to their cousins, why didn't they return the land Sichon took from us and what they took from Sichon?[7] Maybe they consider our land to be Emorite territory and ripe for invasion.[8] And how about the converts who travel with them? They are not descended from our great-uncle Avraham; what's to stop them from attacking us?[9] Or maybe they only steer clear of cities, and have no qualms about taking the suburbs."[10]

"That's right," said the ancient elder. "My gut tells me that they are coming after us. They are going to devour our fields and pastures like an ox that eats everything he sees, leaving nothing behind when he is done.[11] They will take all our crops and starve

---

6. *Tzeror haMor, Mesiach Ilmim* on *Bamidbar* 22:4.

7. *Chizkuni, Bamidbar* 22:3.

8. *Bamidbar Rabbah* 20:3.

9. *Sifsei Kohen, Bamidbar* 22:2.

10. Seforno, *Bamidbar* 22:4.

11. See Rashi, Ramban, *Lekach Tov, Midrash HaBeiur* on ibid.; *Bamidbar Rabbah* 20:4. *Yalkut haEizovi* notes that the ox figures in Moshe's blessing of Yosef (*Devarim* 33:17). Thus, comparing the latter's descendants to an ox spelled doom for the surrounding nations.

Sichon and Og were compared to the grass that the Jews, the "oxen," devoured. *Yalkut Midreshei Teiman, Bamidbar* 22:4. See *Tehillim* 92:8.

us to death.[12] We are nothing but insignificant thorns in their eyes."

"So what do you suggest we do?" said the burly warrior. "If we fight them, they'll destroy us. If we do nothing, they may destroy us anyway, and in the best-case scenario, we starve to death. We need more options. Do you have any more in your gut, my ancient friends?"[13]

"I may have another idea," said a youngish elder. "I want to tell you a story about two dogs."

"A story?" said the burly warrior. "Have you lost your mind? We face annihilation, and you want to tell stories?"

"Hear me out, my impatient young friend. Two dogs were fighting, and then they saw a wolf coming. 'I think we should stop fighting right now,' one of them barked to the other. 'That wolf is going to kill us both unless we join forces against him.' That's the story."

"So what happened?" said the warrior. "What's the end of the story? You never finished it."

"Oh, everything worked out just fine. The two dogs fought side by side and killed the wolf, and then they went back to fighting each other. The story has a happy ending. And our story can also have a happy ending if we join forces with the Midianites to the south."[14]

"The Midianites?" spluttered the warrior. "We hate them!"

"Exactly. But we'll have to make a temporary truce with them, because we have to fight the wolf."

"What wolf?" said the warrior.

The elder sighed. "The Jewish people. They are our wolf."[15]

---

12. *Pa'aneiach Raza*, *Bamidbar* 22:4.

13. *Ma'aseh Hashem*, *HaKesav vehaKabbalah* on ibid.

14. *Chizkuni*, ibid. Rabbeinu Meyuchas says that Midian was a part of Moav, east of Eretz Yisrael.

15. *Bamidbar Rabbah* 20:4; *Sanhedrin* 105a; *Ohr haChaim*, *Bamidbar* 22:2; Rashi, *Bamidbar* 22:4, *Bereishis* 36:35; *Sifrei* 157.

"If we're looking for allies," said the warrior, "why do we need the Midianites? There are thirty-one powerful Canaanite kings just across the river. Why can't we join forces with some or all of them?"

"Aha! Now you're asking good questions. So, have you noticed that the Jewish people win their victories in a strange and unusual manner? I would almost call their victories miraculous. How do they do it? It's all because of their leader, this man called Moshe. The key to defeating the Jewish people is to figure out how to defeat him."

"So how do we figure this out?" said the ancient elder. "Do you have any ideas? My gut isn't telling me anything about it."

"In my opinion," said the younger man, "we have to turn to the Midianites. This Moshe spent many years among them, and I'm sure they know his strengths and weaknesses better than anyone else. If we join with the Midianites, we have a fighting chance against the Jewish people."[16]

"How do we join with them?" asked the warrior. "What's the strategy?"

"It's all about leadership," his interlocutor answered. "We need a strong king. The Midianites have some quality leader types. Let's call on one of them to be our king, and take it from there."

"Do you have anyone in mind?" asked another member of the council.

"No one in particular," said the junior elder. "Let's send a delegation to confer with their elders.[17] I'm sure we'll come up with a good candidate."[18]

---

16. See Rashi with *Sifsei Chachamim, Bamidbar* 22:4; *Ohr haChaim, Bamidbar* 22:2; *Bamidbar Rabbah* 20:4.

17. *Rav Ovadiah Bartenura al haTorah, Bamidbar* 22:4; Zohar, *Balak* 189b.

18. *Tanchuma, Balak* 3.

Advice from Midian

A few days later, a delegation of young Moabite warriors appeared at the Midianite border and requested an immediate audience with the Midianite council of elders.[19] The message was quickly delivered to the council, and although the elders were puzzled by this unexpected request, they granted it. They sat stony-faced as the young Moabites entered the council chamber.

"Speak," said the senior-most member of the council.

"We are facing a Jewish invasion," said the Moabite spokesman. "Unlike other enemies, the Jews kill everyone, like an ox that devours all vegetation. We are concerned."[20]

"As well you should be," said the senior elder. "What do you want from us?"

"We need your help. You see, this is a problem for both of us. If they swallow us, you can be sure that your lands, south of our border, will serve as the next meal."[21]

"But why come to us, your sworn enemies? You've got plenty of other neighbors."

"It's because of their leader, a man named Moshe."

The Midianite elder's eyes opened wide.

"I see you're familiar with the name," said the Moabite. "I'm not surprised; he lived a good part of his life among your people.

"Anyway, as I was saying," the spokesperson continued, "we need your help. In particular, we need a strong king right away. Can you deliver?"

The Midianite elder nodded. "The enemy of my enemy is my friend. So temporarily, you will be our friends. Afterward, we can go back to our traditional relationship. We have been concerned

19. *Tzeror haMor*, *Mesiach Ilmim* on *Bamidbar* 22:4.

20. Rashi with *Sifsei Chachamim*, *Lekach Tov on Bamidbar* 22:2–4; Zohar, *Balak* 185a.

21. *Akeidas Yitzchak*, *Bamidbar* 22:2.

about Moshe and his people for a long time. Many years ago, we had a high-ranking priest named Yisro, a prestigious man who also served as an advisor to Pharaoh in Egypt. Moshe came to our land as a fugitive from Egypt, and Yisro took him into his home and gave him his daughter in marriage. But Moshe was ungrateful. He refused to accept and honor Yisro's gods. He left his wife and children in Midian. And using sorcery and Yisro's money, he went back to Egypt and brought out all those millions of Jewish people. Even worse, Moshe convinced Yisro to abandon his gods and embrace the Jewish religion. We had to defrock Yisro and remove him from the Midianite priesthood."[22]

"Scandalous," commented the Moabite.

"Indeed," agreed his new friend. "This Moshe may be great and clever, but we have a rising young star, one of our five ruling governors.[23] He will be a worthy adversary to Moshe. He is wise beyond his years—they say he can see the future—and a warrior without equal.[24] He was an Emorite prince in Sichon's realm, but he managed to escape the slaughter."[25]

"Who is this fellow?"

"His name is Balak."

"Balak who?" said the Moabite. "Doesn't he have a patronymic? Isn't he known as Balak the son of someone? What's with the one name? Is he a peasant, or some sort of poster boy?"

"He doesn't like to be called by his father's name."

"Why not?" probed the Moabite.

"That's his private business. You don't need to know."

"I disagree. If this Balak is to be our king, we need to know everything."

---

22. See Zohar, *Balak* 189b, 196b.

23. See Ibn Ezra, Ramban on *Bamidbar* 22:4.

24. See Ramban, Seforno, *Tzeror haMor*, Rokeach, *Ohr haChaim* on *Bamidbar* 22:2, 4.

25. See Rashi with *Sifsei Chachamim*, Ramban, Rabbi Yehudah heChasid on ibid.; *Bamidbar Rabbah* 20:4; *Yalkut Shimoni* 765; Radak, *Yehoshua* 13:21.

There was a pause. Then the Midianite elder sighed. "You're right," he conceded. "Very well, this is the reason. Balak is descended from Yisro, but he is embarrassed by this. He doesn't want the association publicized. His father's name would immediately identify him as one of Yisro's progeny."[26]

"All right, we can handle being a little discrete. But what makes you think he would be a good king? Smart and strong are not enough. Does any royal blood flow in his veins?"

"We are convinced he would be excellent. He has charisma and leadership. He has a command of sorcery, and he is devoted to our gods. He comes equipped with potent spiritual weapons. Trust me, he will be a good king."[27]

"At this point, we don't have much choice, do we? All right, let's meet him."[28]

"Stay right here," said the elder. "We'll bring him in."

Balak Becomes King

When Balak entered the room, the members of the Moabite delegation were impressed with his personality and charisma.

"Balak," said the elder, "these gentlemen are from Moav. They've come to arrange an alliance between our two nations against the Jewish people. And on our recommendation, they are willing to invite you to serve as their king. But they want to ask you a few questions first."

"Of course," said Balak.

The Moabite spokesman got right to the point. "Do you have any thoughts about how to defeat the Jews?"

---

26. Zohar, *Balak* 196b.

27. See Rashi with *Sifsei Chachamim, Bamidbar* 22:4; *Bamidbar Rabbah* 20:4; Zohar, *Balak* 196b, 200a. According to *Targum Yonasan*, Midian and Moav temporarily agreed to take turns ruling each other. It was now Midian's turn, and Balak was chosen to be king.

28. *Sifsei Kohen, Bamidbar* 22:2.

"A few things come to mind," Balak replied. "My grandfather used to tell me that the weasel and the cat, who are old enemies, joined forces and celebrated a wedding feast on the fat of their victim.[29] Therefore, it is appropriate that in these perilous times we should make a pact and join forces. After all, we do have a certain family relationship. The Moabites are descended from Lot, Avraham's nephew, and the Midianites are descended from Avraham through his concubine Keturah.[30] It makes sense that we should unite to destroy the enemy."

"Any concrete ideas?" prompted the Moabite spokesman.

"It won't be easy," Balak answered. "The royal chronicles tell of miraculous victories for the Jewish people.[31] Their ancestor Yaakov went down to Egypt to buy food during a famine. His family eventually settled there and grew vast in number. They practically took over the country. In the nick of time, Pharaoh managed to enslave them and save himself from complete domination. But Moshe and their Deity pulled them out with many miracles, and He split the sea for them.[32] We saw their miracles in action in the victories over Sichon and Og.[33] Did you know that they suffered no casualties in those wars? Can you imagine? No casualties![34] Moshe even stopped the sun in its path.[35] That's a trick even I can't do, and you can ask around. Everyone knows that I'm tops in sorcery. And then there's the food that falls for them every day from the heavens, and the water they've been drawing from a traveling spring for forty years."[36]

---

29. *Sanhedrin* 105a.

30. *Sifsei Kohen, Bamidbar* 22:4.

31. *Kli Yakar, Bamidbar* 22:2.

32. Tur, *Ma'aseh Hashem, HaKesav vehaKabbalah, Alshich, Me'am Lo'ez* on *Bamidbar* 22:2–4.

33. Tur, *Ohr haChaim* on *Bamidbar* 22:2; *Bamidbar Rabbah* 20:2–3. See *Shemos* 15:15.

34. Malbim, *Bamidbar* 22:3.

35. Tur, Rokeach on *Bamidbar* 22:2.

36. *Yalkut Pisron Torah*, ibid.

"We know the problem," said the Moabite, beginning to lose patience at this long-winded *shvitzer*. "But what's the solution?"

Balak consulted his astrological charts.[37] "We cannot defeat these people by conventional means on the battlefield. They are too numerous, and they have too many supernatural powers.[38] We cannot seek peace with them, because they are too despicable. We can never coexist.[39]

"The bottom line," concluded Balak, "is that we can only defeat them through speech. That is their power: they pray. We have to turn the power of speech against them."[40]

"So you think we can defeat them?" asked the Moabite representative.

"We'll know in a minute," said Balak. "I am well-versed in the annals of the past, and I can also use my powers of sorcery to see the future.[41] Here is a *yedua* bird I carry with me. It helps me see the future."

He burnt incense before the bird, and it began to speak.[42] Balak bent over and listened closely. Then he nodded his head and straightened up.

"Good news, my friends," he declared. "I see good fortune in our future. I see the Jewish people falling."[43]

"Tell us more."

"I'm afraid the details are unclear to me," he admitted. "The

---

37. Zohar, *Balak* 184b. See *Akeidas Yitzchak*, *Bamidbar* 22:2.

38. Ramban, Rokeach, *Kli Yakar* on *Bamidbar* 22:2–3. Balak also emphasized that Sichon and Og were mistaken in gathering their armies together, leaving them vulnerable to attack all at once (*Sifsei Kohen*).

39. Malbim, *Bamidbar* 22:3.

40. *Midrash haGadol*, Rashi with *Sifsei Chachamim* on *Bamidbar* 22:1–2; *Bamidbar Rabbah* 20:2, 4.

41. See *Ohr haChaim*, *Tzeror haMor* on *Bamidbar* 22:2, 4.

42. See Zohar, *Balak* 184b; *Sanhedrin* 65b; Rambam, *Avodas Kochavim* 6:2; Rashi, *Moshav Zekeinim* on *Vayikra* 19:31; *Yeshayahu* 8:19; *Kav haYashar* 28:3.

43. *Bamidbar Rabbah* 20:2; Zohar, *Balak* 196b. In this vision, Balak sees himself falling to the Jews as well.

vision is cloudy. We will be victorious, but I do not know how. But how is not so important. The main thing is that we will win when I am your king."[44]

"We accept you as our king," said the Moabite spokesman, and the rest of the delegation murmured their assent.[45] "We are eager to hear your acceptance remarks. We want to share your vision."

The arrogant Balak drew himself to his full height. Fear of the Jewish people reverberated inside his heart,[46] but he struggled to maintain a façade of confidence and bravado.[47]

"Honorable delegates of Moav," Balak began his speech, "this is indeed a historic moment. Our two peoples have joined forces against our common enemy, and we all hope that our willingness to be open-minded will save us from this awful menace that we face.

"First of all, I want to point out that your selection of me as your king is somewhat of a risk. Although the Jewish people are not supposed to attack Moav, they did not hesitate to take Moabite lands previously conquered by Sichon. They may now consider all your lands to be Midianite because I am your king;[48] that's how devious they are. But we will deal with them. We will avenge the deaths of Sichon and Og. Oh, I know that they conquered us, but at least they made us their vassals and protected us from the Jewish enemy. We have been left to fend for ourselves, but we will be successful. We will call upon the wizard Bilam, who helped Sichon defeat your nation. With his powers of sorcery joined to mine, we will be victorious!"[49]

The Torah identifies the new king as Balak the son of Tzipor. He was called Balak, because "he came to lap up" (*ba lak*) the

---

44. *Bamidbar Rabbah* 20:7.
45. *Sifsei Kohen, Bamidbar* 22:2.
46. *Tzeror haMor,* ibid.
47. *Minchah Belulah, Bamidbar* 22:3.
48. *Kli Yakar, Bamidbar* 22:4.
49. See *Bamidbar Rabbah* 20:7; Ramban, *Bamidbar* 22:2; Zohar, *Balak* 189b.

blood of the Jewish people.[50] He was called the son of Tzipor, because he used a bird (*tzipor*) to do his incantations.[51] Like a bird hovering overhead, he sought to hang curses over the Jewish people in order to destroy them.[52]

Balak, like Sichon and Og before him, didn't learn the lessons of history. The "waves" Sichon and Og threw at the Jewish people were stymied by the Jewish "sands." Balak and Bilam would be stymied as well.[53]

Bilam, the Son of Be'or

In the End of Days, the nations of the world will try to defend their immoral behavior. "You deprived us of the chance to serve You," they will argue to Hashem. "You gave the Jewish people a prophet, but we didn't have one. Had You given us a prophet, we would have repented and served You."

This argument is, of course, a spurious one. The non-Jews simply did not want to repent and serve Hashem. They preferred their immoral lifestyles. But Hashem did not want to give them a chance even to open their mouths, so He gave them a king and a prophet.

The results were not unexpected. The Jewish king Shlomo built the Beis haMikdash, while the non-Jewish King Nebuchadnezzar destroyed it. The Jewish people were given prophets like Moshe and Yirmeyahu, while the nations were given a great man of

---

50. Tur, *Lekach Tov* on *Bamidbar* 22:2. The name Balak also refers to his interest in creating a breach and destroying the Jewish people (*Midrash Aggadah*): it has the same numerical value as the word *parutz*, "breach" (*Sifsei Kohen*, end *Balak*).

51. See *Ohr haChaim*, ibid.

52. See Tur, ibid. *Lekach Tov* holds that Tzipor comes from the word *tzafra*, "morning," a reference to Balak's eagerness to destroy the Jewish people as early as possible.

53. *Yalkut Shimoni* 765.

wisdom and ability named Bilam. While Moshe and Yirmeyahu steered the Jewish people away from sin, Bilam did the opposite. The Jewish prophets were compassionate, while Bilam was cruel and subversive. The nations had embraced standards of decency and rejected promiscuity, but through Bilam's counsel they violated their own standards. Such was the great prophet of the gentile nations.[54]

Who exactly was this Bilam, son of Be'or?

The name Bilam is a composite of the words *belo am*, "without a nation"—without a place to call his own. It can also be a composite of *bala am*, the one who intended to devour the Jewish people with his evil counsel, or to confound them by drawing them into sin.[55]

Most sources place Bilam's roots in Aram. Some say he was the original Lavan from Aram, the man who sought to swindle his son-in-law Yaakov. Others suggest he was Lavan's son.[56] Some,

---

54. *Bamidbar Rabbah* 20:1; Rashi, *Bamidbar* 22:5.

55. *Sanhedrin* 105a; *Targum Yonasan, Bamidbar* 22:5. Bilam was also called the son of Be'or because he had relations with his animal (*be'ir*), a she-donkey. See *Yalkut Midreshei Teiman* for an allusion to Bilam in *Devarim* 27:21, "Cursed is he who lies with any animal."

The letters in the names Balak and Bilam can be rearranged to spell *bal emek*, for Hashem mixed up (*bilbel*) the depth (*emek*) of Bilam's words and turned into a blessing his and Balak's evil intentions to curse the Jews (Zohar, *Balak* 199b; *Tzeror haMor, Bamidbar* 22:7).

56. *Sanhedrin* 105a; *Targum Yonasan, Bamidbar* 22:5; *Tanchuma, Vayeitzei* 13. Ibn Ezra, *Bereishis* 36:32, writes that Bilam couldn't have been Lavan, but he acted like him. Abarbanel says Bilam descended from Lavan. *Eitz Yosef* states that Bilam was a reincarnation of Lavan. Alternatively, Bilam was Kemuel, the son of Sarah's sister, Milkah. This would make him Avraham's nephew! He was given the name Kemuel because he "stood up" (*kam*) against the nation of E-l, Hashem (*Bereishis Rabbah* 57:4; *Yalkut Shimoni* 766; *Da'as Zekeinim, Bereishis* 22:21 and *Shemos* 1:10).

If Bilam was indeed Lavan himself, how had this evil man been blessed with living from Yaakov's time all the way to Moshe's? Some say he merited this longevity by marrying off his daughter to a scholar, Yaakov. Additionally, by hosting Yaakov, he merited *ruach hakodesh* (*Peirush l'Targum Yonasan*).

however, suggest that he was originally the king of Edom. He made his way to Egypt, and after escaping death during one of its wars, he returned to his old stomping grounds as the Edomite king.[57]

Bilam began his career as a common interpreter of dreams, but he was a diligent and clever fellow. Eventually, he became a soothsayer and an astrologer, and then a fortune-teller. He mastered the arts of divination, sorcery, wizardry and witchcraft. Finally, having learned all the secrets of the occult, he reached the height of his expertise when he became a prophet endowed with the holy spirit, the recipient of divine visions and messages.[58] At the height of his powers, he was sixty times greater than his father in the spiritual realm, while Balak was sixty times greater than his father in governance.[59]

Arrogant and conceited, Bilam was obsessed with his prophetic abilities. Like an ignorant fool, he also praised himself immensely, trying to convince people that there was none like him.[60] He was a promiscuous and greedy man, a malicious rogue who cast spells with his evil eye.[61]

Bilam's popularity increased in direct proportion to the increase in his spiritual powers. Just as everyone seeks out a money changer, kings and potentates would seek him out and pay him lavishly for his services.[62] He would sit behind tables laden with refreshments and his tools of sorcery close at hand. People would line up to ask their questions, and they would partake of the food and drink while they waited their turn.[63]

Balak's fame spread and far and wide, and before long, he was

---

57. See *Pa'aneiach Raza*, Rokeach on *Bamidbar* 22:5. According to *Sefer haYashar*, cited in *Let My Nation Go*, p. 36, Bilam warred alongside Eisav's grandson Tzefo.
58. See *Sanhedrin* 106a; *Bamidbar Rabbah* 20:7; *Tanchuma, Balak* 4.
59. See Rashi, Riva on *Bamidbar* 24:3; *Sanhedrin* 105a; *Nachalas Yaakov*.
60. Zohar, *Balak* 193b.
61. Rashi, *Bamidbar* 24:2; *Tanchuma, Balak* 6; Rambam, *Avos* 5:19.
62. Rashi with *Gur Aryeh, Bamidbar* 22:5; *Bamidbar Rabbah* 20:7.
63. Zohar, *Balak* 192a.

invited to join Pharaoh's council of advisors. He also became the palace wizard. He was the one who told Pharaoh that the stars had foretold the imminent birth of a Jewish male savior. Bilam, jealous of the success of the Jewish people in Egypt and full of hatred for them, advised Pharaoh to have all the male children thrown into the river.[64] Yisro, who was also an advisor to Pharaoh, protested Bilam's advice. A third advisor, Iyov, remained silent. Hashem repaid each advisor accordingly. Bilam would perish by the sword. Iyov was condemned to a life full of suffering. Yisro merited that his descendants would serve on the Sanhedrin.[65]

This was the man whose help Balak wanted to enlist against the Jewish people.

Moshe, the Superior Prophet

When he was at the height of his powers, Bilam discerned certain aspects of the Shechinah that even Moshe didn't know.[66] Indeed, some of his admirers contended that Bilam was on a higher plane than Moshe, for Moshe had to go to Hashem for his revelations, while Hashem came to Bilam. This was, of course, nonsense.[67]

---

64. According to the view that Bilam was Lavan, his hatred dated back to when Yaakov took his possessions and fled (Zohar, *Balak* 106).

65. *Sotah* 11a.

66. *Eliyah Rabbah* 28. Yet Bilam's knowledge came entirely from sources of *tum'ah*, whereas Moshe's was completely pure. Additionally, knowledge doesn't equal greatness, leadership or righteousness. See *Akeidas Yitzchak; Yeshuos Yaakov; Me'orei Eish; Tuvei Chaim*. Indeed, knowledge without good deeds never lasts (*Avos* 3:12), and hence all of Bilam's intellect proved useless. Eventually, as will be noted, Bilam became a fool and lost the gift of prophecy. See also *Me'am Lo'ez, Devarim* 34:10.

Bilam's potential for greatness rested on his ability to bring the nations of the world closer to serving Hashem through the Noachide Laws. Not only did he fail to do this, but when the nations were offered the Torah, he dissuaded them. Greatness in leadership is judged by one's ability to elevate his constituents by example. While Bilam failed miserably, Moshe excelled like no other. See *Oznaim laTorah*, end *Vezos haBerachah*. See also *Let My Nation Serve Me*, p. 200.

67. According to *Shemos Rabbah* 16:4, Hashem came to Shemuel but not to

Moshe was superior in his prophecy to Bilam in every way. He received his prophecies standing upright, while Bilam had to fall on his face. Moshe spoke to Hashem face-to-face, in the manner of one friend to another, while Bilam received his messages through parables. Moshe could receive a prophecy at any time without prior notification, while Bilam was always informed beforehand so that he could make preparations. Moshe saw with perfect clarity, above and beyond that which anyone ever had or would have, in a state of full consciousness, while Bilam prophesied only when he was so deeply asleep that he was virtually lifeless.[68]

Why did Hashem come to Bilam while Moshe had to come to Hashem? It can be explained with a parable. A king was informed that a leper had come to see him. "Don't allow him to enter and defile my palace," the king responded. "I'll go meet him outside." Then the king was informed that his close friend had come to see him. "Invite him into my palace," he replied. Bilam was like the leper that Hashem wanted to keep at arm's length, so to speak, while Moshe was like the close friend who was invited into the holy abode of the Mishkan.[69]

It can also be explained with a second parable. A king invited his highest minister to a great feast without giving him any of the details of what would be served. Then he summoned the cook and told him precisely what he wanted him to prepare. The officer didn't need to know the details, but the cook did. Would anyone venture to suggest that the cook, being told more details, enjoys a higher status than the minister? The same can be said about Moshe and Bilam. Moshe was given only the prophecies that pertained to the immediate needs of the Jewish people. Bilam, however, who

---

Moshe, because Moshe stationed himself in court, whereas Shemuel went to disputants' homes to adjudicate.

68. See *Sifrei*, *Vezos haBerachah* 357; *Sifrei Zuta*, *Naso* 7:89; Zohar, *Vayishlach* 170b; *Eliyah Rabbah* 26; Ramban, Rabbeinu Bachya, *Sifsei Kohen*, *Ha'amek Davar* on *Bamidbar* 24:1, 4; Ramban, *HaKesav vehaKabbalah* on *Devarim* 34:10.

69. See Zohar, *Balak* 200a; *Tzeror haMor*, *Bamidbar* 22:10.

prophesied in honor of the Jewish people, was given detailed information about their future so that the entire world would recognize the greatness of Hashem and His chosen nation.[70]

An Invitation to Bilam

Balak knew how much Bilam hated the Jews and how much he loved honor, prestige and money, so he decided to play on these feelings in his letter of invitation.[71] He wrote:

> To my good friend Bilam, the son of Be'or,
>
> I hope this letter finds you in good health, fully recovered from your eye and ear ailments. And I hope your lame leg is not giving you too much trouble.[72] It's been a while since the days we were together in Aram.[73]
>
> I am writing to you regarding this nation that has left Egypt.[74] Since its days there, it has exhibited growth unlike anything seen in another place or people.[75] Like the locusts that carpeted the Egyptian soil, these people have carpeted the land with their multitude. They are a vast nation.[76]
>
> They've been the beneficiaries of countless miracles, from the splitting of the sea to the victory over Amalek and the recent victories over Sichon and Og.[77]
>
> Sichon and Og, who were our eyes, watching over our land,

---

70. Ramban, *Sha'arei Aharon* on *Bamidbar* 24:1, *Sifrei*, *Vezos haBerachah* 357. See *Sifsei Kohen*, *Bamidbar* 24:4.

71. Zohar, *Balak* 192a.

72. See ibid., 199b. Other sources suggest that these injuries took place only when Bilam tried to curse the Jewish people. See below in text; *Midrash haGadol*, *Bamidbar* 24:3.

73. Rashi, *Midrash haGadol* on *Bamidbar* 22:5; *Bamidbar Rabbah* 20:7.

74. Rashi, *Bamidbar* 22:5.

75. See *Shemos* 1:7.

76. *Ohr haChaim*, *Ha'amek Davar* on *Bamidbar* 22:5.

77. *Lekach Tov*, ibid.

had their eyes shut forever by these people.[78] And now, rather than being protected by Sichon and Og, we find ourselves surrounded by these Jews. They've taken over the neighboring towns, and I'm afraid they're looking to cut us off next.[79]

This nation is an eyesore to us, and they need to be destroyed.[80] If that's impossible, we should diminish their numbers.[81] But at the very least, we need to drive them away.[82]

It isn't their physical strength or their size that makes them so powerful. They have this uncanny ability to defeat us with their mouths by using the Name of their Deity. That is what makes them strong, and that is why we need you.[83]

You know, back in the days of Aram, when you and I were being schooled in the occult arts, there was a healthy rivalry between us. Eventually, I turned out to be the better diviner,[84] but that has never stopped me from respecting your stellar abilities. After all, your prediction that I would be king one day has come true.[85]

And this is the very reason I am writing to you. You see, technically I have the knowledge and ability to put a spell on the Jewish people. But despite all my expertise, none of my potions or witchcraft has affected them in any way. They are far too strong for me to do this alone.[86] In fact, if you recall, none of your spells worked on them in Egypt either. You attempted to prevent

---

78. See Rashi, ibid.; *Bamidbar Rabbah* 20:7 with Mahrzu; *Tanchuma, Balak* 4.

79. Rashi, *Bamidbar* 22:5; *Bamidbar Rabbah* 20:7.

80. Rashi, *Bamidbar* 22:6.

81. Rashi, *Sifsei Kohen* on ibid.; *Bamidbar Rabbah* 20:7. Indeed, twenty-four thousand Jews would be slain for sinning with the daughters of Moav.

82. *Toldos Yitzchak, Bamidbar* 22:6.

83. *Lekach Tov, Bamidbar* 22:5; *Bamidbar Rabbah* 20:7.

84. *Yalkut Reuveni, Bamidbar* 22:5. Balak knew more, but Bilam did more with what he knew. See *Sha'arei Aharon*, ibid.

85. Rashi, ibid.; *Bamidbar Rabbah* 20:7.

86. See Rashi, *Bamidbar* 22:6; *Kav haYashar* 28:3. Balak tried twenty-eight different spells and charms to weaken the *koach* (which has a numerical value of twenty-eight), strength, of the constellations through which Hashem protected the Jews (*Yalkut Reuveni*).

their growth, kill their leader Moshe and prevent their exodus, and yet they were able to leave Egypt despite your efforts.[87]

Past failures notwithstanding, you have developed two great talents that I must admit I don't have: your ability to utter incantations to curse and your ability to know the exact moment their Deity gets angry so that you can facilitate that curse.[88] I am writing to invite you to come here[89] and curse these people for me.[90] For you have proven in the past that those you bless get blessed—as you blessed me with rulership;[91] and those you curse become cursed—as you did for Sichon against Moav.[92]

From my professional knowledge in this field, I know that the Jewish nation's downfall is imminent. It just isn't clear to me how and when this will come about. That's why we need you. You and I are like a slaughterer and a butcher, each with specific skills. One knows to remove life with the knife, while the other knows how to slice the meat.[93] Together, you and I have the letters of Amalek

---

87. *Ohr haChaim, Bamidbar* 22:5.

88. See *Berachos* 7a; Tur, *Lekach Tov* on *Bamidbar* 22:6; Zohar, *Bechukosai* 112b. See also *Tehillim* 7:12. Malbim differentiates among the Torah's various synonyms for "curse."

89. See *Ohr haChaim, Ha'amek Davar* on *Bamidbar* 22:5–6.

90. In a "Freudian slip," instead of telling Bilam, "Curse *for* me," Balak said, "Curse *me*." And eventually that is what happened (Tur, *Lekach Tov* on *Bamidbar* 22:6). According to *Hadar Zekeinim*, Balak was willing to be cursed himself as long as the Jews went down with him. *Chomas Anach* on Chida adds that Balak was willing to be cursed so Ruth wouldn't live to be the ancestor of David. (Sadly, today as well, Jew-haters are willing to die just to kill Jews.)

91. *Ohr haChaim*, Abarbanel on *Bamidbar* 22:6. Truth be told, Bilam couldn't bless or curse anyone. Rather, through the stars he foretold people's successes or failures, then "blessed" or "cursed" them accordingly. In fact, his blessings were no better than a donkey's. See Ibn Ezra, *Bamidbar* 22:28; Abarbanel, *Tzeror haMor*, *Ha'amek Davar* on *Bamidbar* 22:6; *Moshav Zekeinim*; Abarbanel.

92. Rashi, *Bamidbar* 22:6; *Bamidbar Rabbah* 20:7. The builders of the Tower of Bavel failed because Hashem confused their language. Yet Balak didn't realize that Hashem controls speech and therefore Bilam was useless without His assistance. See *Iyov* 12:20 (Zohar, *Balak* 199b). See also Malbim regarding why Bilam would help the king of Moav after having cursed that nation years earlier.

93. *Midrash haGadol, Bamidbar* 22:6.

in our name (*am* from you and *lak* from me). Together we can prevail over them. I will smite them and you will curse them.[94]

I am also trying to avoid great shame that is destined to come my way. The alignment of the stars tells me that they will have a great king named David who will be a descendant of Ruth the Moabitess. He will destroy Moav, of all places. My nation! I must prevent the birth of Ruth at any cost.[95]

You are undoubtedly wondering why I need you to inconvenience yourself and come here, as opposed to cursing them from where you are. It is because your curse will be effective only if you are looking at them while you are performing it. The power of your evil eye will be necessary for your curse to succeed.[96]

Another problem. This nation can see me, but I cannot see them behind this cloud of glory of theirs. I don't know what they are up to.[97] How can I see their demise if they aren't visible? I need you to fix that.[98]

Know this, my dear friend: If you succeed, you won't be just doing a favor for me, you will benefit immensely as well. I have sent with the bearers of this letter a large sum of money that will compensate you handsomely.[99] Included in it are your expenses. I have also sent all the tools of the trade available in case you don't have them,[100] including books of magic and sorcery.[101]

Now close that one eye of yours and think of the fame and

94. Zohar, *Balak* 193b.

95. Ibid., 198a.

96. *Ohr haChaim*, *Ha'amek Davar* on *Bamidbar* 22:5–6.

97. Tur, *Midrash haGadol*, *Bamidbar* 22:5.

98. *Sifsei Kohen*, *Bamidbar* 22:6.

99. Rashi, Rabbeinu Bachya on *Bamidbar* 22:5; *Bamidbar Rabbah* 20:7.

100. Rashi, *Midreshei haTorah* on *Bamidbar* 22:7; *Bamidbar Rabbah* 20:8. Some add that this was nothing more than a sign of honor for Bilam (*Ma'aseh Hashem*; *HaKesav vehaKabbalah*).

101. *Chizkuni*, *Midreshei haTorah*, *Da'as Zekeinim*, *Bechor Shor* on *Bamidbar* 22:7. Balak also sent sorcerers to confirm that it was indeed an auspicious time to curse the Jews, lest Bilam claim otherwise (Ibn Ezra; *Midreshei haTorah*).

fortune that will follow you worldwide. You'll be the guest of honor at the feast celebrating the defeat of the Jewish people. The Canaanites and Amalekites will bow before you and honor you for being the only one to succeed in defeating the Jews. You'll be the toast of the town.[102] I'm well-aware that you share my hatred toward them. It's quite likely and plausible that your hatred alone is motivation enough for you to curse them. But you can have the money nevertheless.[103]

Please, don't waste a second. Now is an auspicious time for the Jewish people to be destroyed.[104] Come immediately, for every moment you delay, I am in danger.[105]

Sincerely and with best wishes,
King Balak

Emissaries to Bilam

Balak appointed a delegation of trusted Midianite sages well-versed in the art of divination who had come with him to Moav. He put his letter to Bilam into an envelope and sealed it. He also sent a group of Moabite officers along with the Midianite sages.

"Take this letter to Bilam, the son of Be'or,[106] in the Pesorah Valley of Aram-Nahara'im,"[107] he said to the sages. "I am also providing you with all the tools of the diviner's craft so that Bilam will not use the lack of such tools as an excuse for declining my invitation. Go immediately."

He turned to the Moabite officers. "As for you gentlemen," he said, "you'll return in all haste with Bilam's reply. Time is of

---

102. Rokeach, *Bamidbar* 22:5; *Bamidbar Rabbah* 20:7.
103. *Ohr haChaim*, *Bamidbar* 22:5.
104. Zohar, *Balak* 198a; *Tzeror haMor*, *Bamidbar* 22:6.
105. *Ohr haChaim*, *Bamidbar* 22:6.
106. Rashi, *Bamidbar* 22:5; *Bamidbar Rabbah* 20:7.
107. Rashi, *Bamidbar* 22:7; *Bamidbar Rabbah* 20:8; *Devarim* 23:5.

the essence, and any delay can prove disastrous for our kingdom."[108]

As they traveled to Aram, the Midianite sages discussed their mission. "Our nations are in great danger," said one sage. "We have to concentrate our efforts where they will bear fruit. There is no point in traveling down a highway to nowhere."

"Are you saying," said a second sage, "that our mission to Bilam is fruitless?"

"No I am not. I'm saying that it may be, and if so, we would be wasting our time of we pursue it diligently when we could be investing our efforts to better effect elsewhere."

"Granted," said the second sage. "But how will we know?"

"We can make a test," said a third sage. "If Bilam accepts the invitation immediately then we know he is up for the task. If he comes up with excuses and delay tactics, we can assume he'll never curse these Jews."[109]

The first sage nodded sagely. "Sounds good to me," he said.

"To me, too," seconded the second sage. "I would add that if he invokes the Name of the Deity of the Jewish people, we can assume he's a fraud. After all, which father would allow his children to be cursed?[110] Besides, if He wanted them to be cursed, why would He have performed all those miracles for them in Egypt and by the Arnon River?"[111]

"And if Bilam utters the Name," said the first sage, "it would be blasphemy, which would make him a fool, a charlatan and a waste of time.[112] In fact, I have another idea. Let's not tell him the

---

108. See *Sifsei Kohen*, Malbim on *Bamidbar* 22:7. According to *Tzeror haMor*, Balak sent actual angels to help Bilam curse the Jews at the proper time.

109. Rashi, *Bamidbar* 22:7; *Bamidbar Rabbah* 20:8.

110. *Sanhedrin* 105a.

111. *Lekach Tov*, *Bamidbar* 22:8.

112. Alshich, *Bamidbar* 22:7. According to Gra in *Divrei Eliyahu*, the Midianites reasoned that if Bilam agreed immediately, he was greater than Moshe. If he had to consult Hashem first, he was equal to Moshe. However, if he had to wait

purpose of our visit right away. If he knows why we came, we may be onto something, but if he does not, we can assume that he is useless."[113]

Delays and More Delays

The Midianite sages with their Moabite military escort arrived at Bilam's humble abode in Aram. When they failed to state the purpose of their visit, Bilam just looked at them in puzzlement. He had failed his first test.[114]

After a few minutes of awkward silence as the sages waited fruitlessly for Bilam to divine the purpose of their visit, they handed him Balak's letter. Bilam squinted down at the cramped handwriting and took a long time reading it.

"Pardon me, gentlemen, for taking so long," he said. "My eyes aren't what they used to be. Ahem, Balak seems to be in trouble. And to tell you the truth, I would love to come to his assistance right away, but I must answer to a Higher Power.[115] I've been promoted, you know. I'm not your everyday soothsayer, sorcerer and diviner; I'm a prophet now.[116] If I help Balak, it has to come to me through prophecy, and that will take me a little time. I have to get into the right frame of mind and such.[117] Then the holy spirit will come over me at night, and I will receive my divine guidance. Perhaps I should go with you. Perhaps I shouldn't. Perhaps I should demand a more suitable escort.[118] Hopefully, we will

---

until nighttime to speak with Hashem, he was inferior to Moshe and incapable of cursing the Jews.

113. *Sifsei Kohen*, ibid.

114. Ibid.

115. Rashi, *Sefer Zikaron* on *Bamidbar* 22:8.

116. Abarbanel, Malbim on ibid.

117. Seforno, ibid.

118. Rashi, ibid.; *Bamidbar Rabbah* 20:8. As a prophet, Bilam's honor was in essence Hashem's.

know by tomorrow.[119] But tonight, you will be my guests."[120]

This whole speech was just subterfuge. Bilam knew that he couldn't curse the Jewish people without Hashem's approval and permission, but he wouldn't admit it to his visitors.[121]

After they settled in their quarters, the sages reviewed Bilam's words.

"I'm completely unimpressed," said the first sage. "He wants us to stay overnight while he talks to the Deity of the Jewish people? He needs to wait for the spirit of prophecy? This must be some kind of joke."

"His eyes have grown old," said the second sage, "and I suspect that the same has happened to his brain. Well, we've fulfilled our mission by delivering the letter. I'm getting out of here."

"So am I," said the first sage.

"Me too," said the third sage.[122]

Without further delay, the Midianite sages left, but the Moabite officers remained. They had been commanded to return with Bilam's reply, and they had no choice but to wait for it.[123]

Meanwhile, in Bilam's room, strong emotions were emerging. The embers of his hatred for the Jewish people were being fanned into roaring flames. He had trouble falling asleep, his

---

119. Rashi, ibid.; *Bamidbar Rabbah* 20:8. Hashem reveals Himself to non-Jews (such as Lavan) only at night. He spoke with Bilam by day only for the sake of the Jewish people (*Rav Ovadiah Bartenura al haTorah*).

120. *Tosefos Rav Ephraim al haTorah*, ibid. Because the Midianite delegation came with expense money for Bilam, he had no problem hosting this entourage that night. Once he discovered that he wouldn't be able to curse the Jewish people, however, he housed his visitors no longer.

121. Mizrachi, ibid. According to Alshich, Bilam was actually stalling for their benefit, waiting and hoping for permission to curse the Jews. According to Rokeach, Bilam never sought Hashem's approval, just His advice.

122. Rashi, Alshich, Malbim on *Bamidbar* 22:7–8; *Bamidbar Rabbah* 20:8. Some say the Midianites were rewarded for dissociating from Bilam and his curse. Others say they were punished for doing so, since they knew everything depended on Hashem and not on Bilam's magic. See Zohar, *Balak* 200a.

123. *Sifsei Kohen*, Malbim on *Bamidbar* 22:7.

mind consumed with a deep desire to curse them, but he knew he could do nothing before Hashem spoke to him.[124]

Hashem Speaks to Bilam

Bilam was the lowest of low, the dregs at the bottom of the barrel even among evildoers. Indeed, his eventual recommendation to draw the Jewish people into harlotry was abhorrent even to the other nations. Why then would Hashem even bother revealing Himself to Bilam? He did it out of respect and love for the Jewish people, as we shall see.[125]

After nightfall, Hashem appeared to Bilam in a dream.[126]

"Who are these people that came to you today?" Hashem said to him.[127] "Why have you hosted these lowly enemies of the Jews?[128] You're a prophet now and should not be keeping company with such people."[129]

Bilam was stunned and excited. Hashem seemed to be asking a question to which He didn't know the answer. Could there be moments when Hashem didn't know everything? If so, he would be able to curse the Jewish people during those moments.

Bilam's assumption revealed his primitive understanding of divinity. In his arrogance, he didn't realize that Hashem was setting a trap for him. Just as Bilam intended to lead the Jewish people into error, Hashem was leading Bilam into error. Instead of responding to Hashem by reaffirming that He knows everything, Bilam responded to Him as he would have responded to a human being.[130]

---

124. *Eliyah Rabbah* 28.

125. Rabbeinu Bachya, *Bamidbar* 22:9.

126. *Midrash haGadol*, ibid.

127. *Ma'aseh Hashem*, ibid.

128. Alshich, ibid.

129. *Ohr haChaim*, Abarbanel on ibid.

130. See Rashi, *Yalkut Pisron Torah* on ibid.; *Bamidbar Rabbah* 20:9; *Tanchuma, Balak* 5. Rather than startle him, Hashem began His revelation with a question, hoping that an innocent conversation would make Bilam reconsider. When he didn't, Hashem posed a question that would make Bilam err in judgment. See

"You want me to tell You who they are?" Bilam replied.[131] "All right, I'll tell You. These men are important people sent by Balak the son of Tzipor, king of Moav. Even if You do not hold me in high esteem, the king of Moav does.[132] Concerned that the Jewish people are approaching his borders, he wants me to direct a curse at them that will debilitate them and allow him to make war on them and drive them away.[133] In my opinion, I am permitted to do so, because the nation of Israel is harassing Moav in violation of Your command.[134] I am entitled to direct a higher-level curse against this people that will drive them from this world and the next."[135]

The conniving Bilam had distorted Balak's request. Balak had never asked for more than a lower-level curse that would turn the Jewish people away from his borders, but Bilam was requesting permission for a stronger curse.[136] He was hoping he could "fool" Hashem into forbidding the higher-level curse and by implication allowing the lower-level curse.

"No," Hashem replied. "Do not go with these people."

Bilam considered the possibility that Hashem simply did not want him, an extremely old man, to exert himself with a long journey to Moav.[137]

"I understand," replied Bilam. "I'll just curse them here."

Gur Aryeh. See also Rashi, *Bereishis* 3:9. Hashem adopted a similar approach in His dialogue with Kayin. See Zohar, *Balak* 200b.

131. Seforno, *Bamidbar* 22:9; *Bamidbar Rabbah* 20:6.

132. Zohar, *Balak* 200a; Rashi, *Ohr haChaim* on *Bamidbar* 22:10; *Bamidbar Rabbah* 20:9. Once again, Bilam emerges as a two-faced deceiver whose word can't be trusted. To justify the presence of his guests, he respectfully refers to them as emissaries of the *king* of Moav. Yet when addressing Balak, he omits that title and calls him by his first name, showing no respect whatsoever (*Ma'aseh Hashem*, *Bamidbar* 22:9).

133. See Rashi, *Bamidbar* 22:11; *Bamidbar Rabbah* 20:9.

134. Alshich, *Bamidbar* 22:10.

135. Rashi with Mizrachi, Alshich on *Bamidbar* 22:11; *Bamidbar Rabbah* 20:9.

136. Rashi, *Sifsei Kohen* on *Bamidbar* 22:11; *Bamidbar Rabbah* 20:9.

137. *Midrash Shocher Tov* 1.

"No, you won't curse them here or anywhere," Hashem told him. "No curses whatsoever."[138]

"May I go to Moav without cursing the Jewish people?"

"No. You may not even look at them and risk giving them an evil eye."[139]

"Can I at least bless them?"[140]

"No, don't bless them either. I have already blessed them over other nations.[141] They certainly don't need a blessing from you. That would be like the hornet providing honey but ready to sting the beekeeper. They don't need your honey or your sting."[142]

Bilam really did not have the power to bless or to curse. If he could have given blessings, then all he would have had to do was bless Balak to become immune and impervious to any threat to his kingdom. He also could have blessed himself to become a rich and powerful king instead of an ancient cripple selling his divinations to customers. But he did know the exact split second of daily divine rage.[143] That was the cornerstone of his career.[144]

Although Bilam's curses could not have affected the blessed Jewish people, Hashem did not want him to utter any curses at all. Someday, the Jewish people would sin and be punished, and Hashem did not want the world to attribute their misfortune to

---

138. Rashi with Mizrachi, Tur on *Bamidbar* 22:11; *Bamidbar Rabbah* 20:9. Hashem gave Bilam no room to maneuver. Regarding the twists and turns of Bilam's request to curse the Jews, see *Maskil l'David*.

139. Seforno, *Bamidbar* 22:12. Zohar, *Balak* 304a, locates Bilam's power in his mouth and eyes.

140. By blessing the Jews, Bilam knew the nations of the world would become jealous and give them an evil eye (*Yalkut Reuveni*).

141. Rashi, Ibn Ezra, *Lekach Tov* on *Bamidbar* 22:12; *Bamidbar Rabbah* 20:10. See *Devarim* 7:14.

142. Rashi, *Bamidbar* 22:12; *Bamidbar Rabbah* 20:9.

143. I.e., when the idol worshipers worship the sun. See also Chapter 10, note 1, and accompanying text.

144. See *Toldos Yitzchak*, *Bamidbar* 22:9; Rabbeinu Bachya, *Bamidbar* 22:20.

Bilam's curses.[145] He also didn't want Bilam's curses, as ineffectual as they might have been, to offer encouragement and solace to the Canaanite kings as they braced for the Jewish invasion.[146]

In his desperate desire to go to Moav, Bilam decided to interpret Hashem's instructions in the most literal sense. Hashem had told him not to go with the people who had come for him. Bilam reasoned that he was only forbidden to go with these particular people. He would demand a more prestigious delegation and return to Moav with them.[147] In the meantime, he knew he had to word his response to Balak carefully. He could not admit that Hashem had forbidden him to curse or even bless the Jewish people, because then he could forget about all the honors and riches within his grasp. He would have to stall until he could find an opportunity to deliver the curses.[148]

A Message to Balak

Early in the morning, Bilam delivered his response to the Moabite officers, and then, as stingy as he was arrogant, he sent them on their way without even serving them breakfast.[149]

"Go back to your land," he said to them. "Hashem allows me to curse, but refuses to let me go with you people. Hashem is an august Deity, and He demands a more prestigious delegation to invite me. Now go!"[150]

The Moabite officers scorned Bilam's statement. They did not believe he was in contact with any deity. They suspected that this

---

145. See Ibn Ezra, *Chizkuni*, *Toldos Yitzchak*, Rabbeinu Bachya on *Bamidbar* 22:9,12, 20.

146. Abarbanel, *Bamidbar* 22:12.

147. Malbim, ibid.

148. See Rashi, *Ohr haChaim*, Ralbag on *Bamidbar* 22:13. Bilam would also exploit the request for a more distinguished and prestigious delegation to extract more money from Balak. Tur, Rabbeinu Bachya on ibid.

149. *Ohr haChaim*, ibid. But see Rokeach.

150. See Rashi, *Minchah Belulah*, Ralbag on ibid.; *Bamidbar Rabbah* 20:10.

man who was too miserly to offer them breakfast was nothing more than a simple sorcerer trying to extort more money from Balak.[151]

The officers returned to Moav and reported to Balak. "Your Majesty, Bilam refuses to come with us. He wants a more prestigious delegation to deliver the invitation."

"What else did he say?"

"Nothing more, Your Majesty."

Balak stroked his beard. "Hmm," he mused to himself, "I can see his game. Bilam loves honor and money more than anything else. And that's exactly what I'll have to give him. In this situation, we can spare no expense."[152]

"Gentlemen," Balak said to the officers, "stay right where you are. I will not allow Bilam to disrespect you like this. If he wants higher-ranking officers, I will send them, but you will return as well. Now he will have both a larger and a more prestigious contingent. That should satisfy him."[153]

"Yes, Your Majesty," they said.

"Give Bilam the following message," Balak directed. "Listen carefully, because I want you to repeat it exactly as I say it.

"Bilam, you wanted more honor, I have given you more honor. You want more money, I'll give you more money. I'll pay you even more than you were paid by Moav to curse Midian.[154] I am confident that with such a high level of compensation you will direct one of your premium curses at the Jewish people whom you hate so much.[155]

"Bilam, I will do anything to have you join me here in Moav. I'll even reveal to you my secret knowledge in the art of sorcery.

---

151. See Abarbanel, Malbim, Alshich, *Ohr haChaim* on *Bamidbar* 22:14.
152. Ramban, *Midrash haGadol*, *Bechor Shor* on *Bamidbar* 22:13,15.
153. See Ibn Ezra, *Ohr haChaim*, Alshich, Malbim on *Bamidbar* 22:15.
154. Rashi, *Bamidbar* 22:17; *Bamidbar Rabbah* 20:10.
155. *Tzeror haMor*, *Bamidbar* 22:17.

This will make you a greater sorcerer than I, an honor you will surely relish, and I am prepared to do it for you.[156] If you don't want to give the Jewish people a large curse, even the smallest one will do.[157] Just come here, that's all I ask.[158] I'll pay you just for coming.[159] Even your mere presence here may frighten the enemy and persuade them to turn away from our territory.[160] It's an auspicious time now. We can't let this opportunity pass.[161]

"Bilam, I need you here. Even if all you can do is identify a sin that we can induce the Jews to commit, I will accept that as a last resort. For this would separate them from their cloud of glory and expose them to attack.[162] No matter what, I want you to come. Do not focus on the bearer of this message but rather on the sender, the king of Moav.[163] Come and we will talk in person."[164]

The Second Delegation

Balak's second delegation delivered his message. It was obvious to Bilam that Balak didn't know Bilam needed permission from Hashem, as all his comments were directed to influence Bilam to decide on his own. Bilam scratched his head. What should he do? How could he respond to Balak's frantic summons? With the new and improved delegation sent to him, he could no longer claim that the emissaries were not prestigious enough. He had no choice but to admit to Balak his subservience to Hashem.[165]

---

156. *Sifsei Kohen*, ibid.
157. Rokeach, Malbim on ibid.
158. Abarbanel, ibid.
159. *Panim Yafos, Bamidbar* 22:20.
160. *Toldos Yitzchak*, ibid.
161. *Tzeror haMor, Bamidbar* 22:15.
162. *Sifsei Kohen, Bamidbar* 22:17.
163. Alshich, *Bamidbar* 22:15.
164. Abarbanel, *Bamidbar* 22:17.
165. See Rashi with Mizrachi, *Ha'amek Davar* on *Bamidbar* 22:18.

"What are you offering me?" he finally said to the Midianite officers. "Do you think it's all about money? Do you think that if you throw more at me, I'll jump up and run to Balak? Believe me, I want to curse the Jewish people more than anything else in the world, but I can't.[166] I told you before that I'm a prophet, and that my actions are directed by Hashem.[167] All the treasuries[168] filled with gold and silver in Balak's palace couldn't get me to curse them without Hashem's approval.[169] Big curse, little curse; it doesn't make a difference. The question before us is how I can prevail on Hashem to allow me to curse the Jewish people.[170] And when I do—hopefully—whatever reward I demand will not be too high. It would undoubtedly cost the Moabite treasury much more to hire armies to fight against the Jewish people, and the result would probably be defeat. But if I can do what I do best, results are guaranteed."

Bilam's words, especially his reference to all the treasuries of gold and silver in Balak's palace,[171] showed him to be a greedy, covetous man. By saying that he could not transgress Hashem's command, he also unwittingly admitted that he did not have the power to nullify the blessings Hashem gave the patriarchs.[172]

"Servants of Balak,[173] don't despair," Bilam continued. "All is not lost. With the arrival of this more prestigious delegation, I can

---

166. *Ohr haChaim*, *Bamidbar* 22:16.

167. Abarbanel, Malbim on *Bamidbar* 22:18.

168. *Targum Yonasan*, ibid.

169. Ramban, Rabbeinu Bachya on *Bamidbar* 22:13; Abarbanel, *Bamidbar* 22:18. By referring to Balak's riches, Bilam implied that he desired money over honor (*Tzeror haMor*).

170. *Toldos Yitzchak*, *Bamidbar* 22:17.

171. Rashi, *Bamidbar* 22:18; *Bamidbar Rabbah* 20:10.

172. Ibid.

173. Rabbeinu Bachya and Tur note that despite his guests' prestigious status within Balak's court, Bilam dismissed them as mere slaves. *Kli Yakar*, however, states that these were Bilam's personal officers, so the term "servants" was actually a tribute to them.

expect a new communication from Hashem—which I hope is not a command to bless the Jewish people.[174] Maybe He had a change of heart. Please stay the night here in Aram.[175] I will help you find appropriate lodgings.[176] We will speak tomorrow."

Once again, Bilam unwittingly prophesied that his plans would fail. By asking them to stay the night, he was saying that they should do as the previous delegation had done and that the results would be the same. And by saying that Hashem might send a new communication, he was unwittingly prophesying that blessings would be added to the Jewish people through him.[177]

But why indeed did Bilam try again to gain permission when he knew good and well that Hashem didn't want him to go? Surely he didn't believe that the more prestigious delegation would persuade Hashem; that was just a bit of nonsense he told the delegation. But perhaps he did suspect deep down that it just might be true, and he wanted to make sure. Moreover, Bilam thought he could challenge Hashem, or "dare" Him, as it were, to let him go, since he couldn't do anything anyway without Hashem's consent. So where was the risk? And once he was in Moav, he would figure out how to proceed.[178]

---

174. Rashi, *Bamidbar* 22:19.

175. *Ohr haChaim*, ibid. Night, especially Pesach night, has been an inauspicious time for enemies of the Jews throughout history (*Bamidbar Rabbah* 20:12). Rokeach writes that this night too was Pesach night. However, according to our chronicle, this incident with Bilam had to have taken place between Tishrei, when the war with Og occurred, and Adar, the month of Moshe's death.

176. *Tosefos Rav Ephraim al haTorah, Nachal haKadmonim* on *Bamidbar* 22:19. Previously Bilam was confident that Hashem would allow him to curse the Jews, and then Balak would reimburse all related expenses. Now considerably less confident, Bilam had his guests pay for their own lodgings rather than risk having to foot the bill for putting them up himself.

177. Rashi, ibid.; *Bamidbar Rabbah* 20:10.

178. *Chizkuni*, Alshich, Malbim on *Bamidbar* 22:19.

Hashem's Second Revelation

That night, Hashem spoke to Bilam again. "Bilam, you are indeed a greedy and conceited man.[179] I will approve your request to join the delegation that has come for you, but only on the following conditions:[180]

"If you are paid simply to accompany these people, I won't begrudge you the reward.[181] If Balak wants you there just to frighten the Jewish people away from his borders, you may go.[182] You may agree to no conditions that require you to curse the Jewish people. If they insist on such conditions, you may not join them.[183] If they just want your advice, you may go—and it would be wise to advise against antagonizing the Jewish people.[184] If you are to be a guest at a feast, you may go.[185] If Balak wants you to go for a leisurely stroll with him, you may go.[186]

"Finally, you are to do nothing without specific instructions from Me.[187] Do not think you can curse other nations and include the Jewish people along with them. Do not think you can bless other nations and include the Jewish people along with them. There is no room here for your own reasoning.[188] If I tell you to bless the Jewish people, then do so, even if Balak reacts

---

179. Rashi, *Bamidbar* 22:20; *Bamidbar Rabbah* 20:10.

180. See below in text for why Hashem "changed His mind," so to speak, after forbidding Bilam to go with the previous delegation.

181. Rashi, *Bechor Shor* on *Bamidbar* 22:20; *Bamidbar Rabbah* 20:10. Abarbanel likens this situation to a doctor's house call: the physician charges once for the visit and once for his expertise. Thus, Hashem allowed Bilam the wages to visit Balak but not to implement his knowledge in cursing the Jews.

182. *Toldos Yitzchak*, *Bamidbar* 22:20.

183. Ramban, *Kli Yakar*, Ralbag on ibid.

184. Seforno, *Imrei Noam* on ibid.

185. *Chizkuni*, ibid.

186. See *Targum Yonasan*, ibid.

187. Rashi with *Mesiach Ilmim*, ibid.

188. Tur, ibid.

negatively.[189] If I tell you to curse, do that too. Even if I tell you just to keep silent, you will do so.[190] Let this be fair warning to you, Bilam. Do only as I say."[191]

Change of Plans

Of course, Hashem doesn't have a change of heart. There is nothing that He does not know. Therefore, if conditions hadn't changed, why did Hashem change His instructions and allow Bilam to go with the second delegation?

Hashem made it crystal clear to Bilam that not only was he forbidden to curse the Jewish people, they were in any case blessed and immune to his curses. Nonetheless, Hashem gives people free will. In His love for mankind, Hashem places obstacles in front of potential sinners to persuade them to turn away from their evil intentions. But if they are persistent, He allows them to sin.

Despite Bilam's wickedness, Hashem sought to prevent him from going lest he cause his own downfall. Yet Bilam, in his arrogant and haughty way, persisted in his attempts to go to Moav, believing that he would find some way to defy Hashem's command. Therefore, Hashem removed all restrictions to the would-be sinner. *Bederech she'adam rotzeh leilech, bah molichin oso*: A person is led along the path he chooses for himself.

While he had waited for Hashem's communication, Bilam had been fantasizing about destroying the Jewish people with his curses. Hashem responded by saying, "You wicked, conceited man! I don't want you to fall, but if you insist, then go ahead. You think you have control over your mouth? I'll let you go, and we will see who controls it."[192]

Hashem had forbidden Bilam to go, but in the face of Bilam's

---

189. Ramban, ibid.
190. Abarbanel, ibid.
191. *Bamidbar Rabbah* 20:12.
192. See *Bamidbar Rabbah* 20:10–12; *Makkos* 10b; *Midrash haGadol, Bamidbar* 22:13, 20.

persistent impudence, He relented and allowed him to go to his own doom.[193] Once Bilam was going, Hashem would use his mission to prove to the nations how much He loved the Children of Israel. No matter how much Bilam, a prophet of the nations, tried to curse the Jewish people, he would only be able to bless them.[194] And if Balak was foolish enough to believe that sending a more prestigious delegation would convince Hashem to let him to curse the Jewish people, Hashem would show him that it was a useless endeavor.[195]

Furthermore, had Bilam not gone, he might have believed that he could have been successful in cursing the Jews if he had been allowed to position himself in their proximity. But now Bilam himself would discover that he could not curse them.[196]

---

193. *Sanhedrin* 105a.
194. Ramban, Abarbanel on *Bamidbar* 22:20, 22.
195. *Chizkuni, Bamidbar* 22:20.
196. *Midrash haGadol, Bamidbar* 22:20.

9

Bilam Joins Balak

Bilam should have realized that Hashem's permission to accompany the Moabite delegation did not constitute permission to cause harm to the Jewish people. He should have understood that Hashem was only giving him the freedom to proceed along the path he chose for himself. And he should have known that he would not be successful if he tried to harm the Jewish people, the descendants of Avraham, Yitzchak and Yaakov, the beloved of Hashem.[1] But his arrogance, greed and hatred[2] were so strong that he was

1. *Eliyah Rabbah* 28.
2. *Midrash haCheifetz, Bamidbar* 22:22.

willing to risk his life by defying the will of Hashem.[3]

Bilam's eagerness manifested itself the following morning when he rose early to prepare for the journey to Moav.[4] He was so enthusiastic that he didn't even wait for the stable boys to saddle his she-donkey.[5] He did it himself just to gain a few minutes.[6]

"Villain," Hashem remarked. "You think you are demonstrating to the world the extent to which a zealous person goes, even saddling his own donkey?[7] That was already done by Avraham, who in his zeal to bring his son Yitzchak as an offering, rose early in the morning and saddled his own donkey. His merits are protecting his children from the harm that your zeal seeks to cause them."[8]

Bilam assembled all his tools of divination[9] and loaded them onto his donkey. Then he signaled his readiness to his two aides,[10] and the three of them followed the Moabite officers onto the road that led to Moav.[11] The Moabites were eager to attack the Jewish

---

3. *Tosefos Rav Ephraim*, ibid.

4. According to *Tosefos Rav Ephraim al haTorah*, Bilam charged ahead on foot while his attendants saddled his donkey. He believed that the sooner he began the mission, the less time Hashem would have to "change His mind," so to speak.

5. Bilam chose a donkey rather than a horse, pretending he was as humble as Avraham. He specifically chose a she-donkey, because, as mentioned earlier, he wanted to have relations with it (*Toldos Yitzchak*). See also Rokeach.

6. *Targum Yonasan*, *Bamidbar* 22:22.

7. See Rashi, *Bamidbar* 22:21; *Bamidbar Rabbah* 20:12.

8. Ibid. The Kotzker Rebbe (cited in *Sha'arei Aharon*) writes that if Avraham woke early and saddled his donkey in order to carry out the Akeidah with alacrity, only to fail in his mission (because Yitzchak was never slaughtered), surely Bilam would fail in his attempt to curse the Jews.

9. Zohar, *Balak* 207b.

10. Dignitaries commonly travel with two aides, as did Avraham en route to the Akeidah. See *Gur Aryeh*. Bilam's attendants were his sons Ianus and Iambrus, two magicians who had joined him in Pharaoh's court (*Targum Yonasan*; *Yalkut Reuveni*). See *Let My Nation Go*, p. 185.

11. *Chizkuni*, Abarbanel on *Bamidbar* 22:21–22. Bilam remained alone, behind

people, whom they saw as a threat to their country. Bilam, who lived in distant Aram, was equally eager, because of his arrogance, greed and hatred.[12] In fact, his hatred was so deep that he would have been glad to curse the Jews even if Balak had not invited him to do so.[13]

Hashem had only given Bilam permission to go and receive payment. He had not given him permission to curse or assault the Jewish people in any way, and yet Bilam had packed his "professional" tools.[14] Bilam had shown total disregard for Hashem's commands. He chose not to tell the Moabite officers what Hashem had said to him, knowing full well that they would have withdrawn the invitation had they known Bilam was not permitted to curse the Jewish people. In fact, he gave them the impression that he was in control of the situation and could curse whomever he chose, whenever he chose.[15]

Deep in his heart, Bilam knew he could do nothing in defiance of Hashem, but he hoped he could persuade Hashem to allow him to curse the Jewish people.[16] He told himself that just as Hashem had relented and allowed him to go to Moav, He could also be persuaded to relent regarding the curses.[17]

---

the Moabite caravan. Hashem then became angry (see below in text), partly because He'd wanted him to join the Moabites rather than travel alone (*Ohr haChaim; Ma'aseh Hashem; Sifsei Kohen*). According to the Zohar, Bilam sought solitude in order to concentrate on and rehearse his occult powers in preparation for cursing the Jews.

12. Rashi, *Bamidbar* 22:21; *Bamidbar Rabbah* 20:12. It was this eagerness that angered Hashem most.

13. *Ohr haChaim, Bamidbar* 22:22.

14. See Rashi with Mizrachi, ibid. Some suggest that money alone couldn't have been Bilam's motive. Had he known he wouldn't curse the Jews, he would never have gone (*Da'as Zekeinim; Bechor Shor; Imrei Shefer*).

15. Ramban, Rosh, Seforno, *Ohr haChaim* on ibid.

16. Rashi, *Bamidbar* 22:20.

17. See *Midrash haGadol, Da'as Zekeinim, Bechor Shor* on *Bamidbar* 22:20–22.

The Donkey Flees

Despite Bilam's headlong rush to sin, Hashem still sought to prevent his downfall. As Bilam rode upon his she-donkey, Hashem sent an angel of mercy, the angel Michael,[18] to block his way with a drawn sword.[19] Michael's mission was to give Bilam a chance to reconsider and to defend the Jewish people from Bilam's machinations. Bilam had foresworn the sword—the traditional weapon of the nations, and planned to attack the Jewish people with his utterances—the traditional Jewish weapon, which the latter employed via prayer. The angel now turned the tables on Bilam and defended the Jewish people with the sword. Moreover, Bilam would eventually perish by the sword.[20]

The donkey immediately saw the angel with his sword and became terrified. It veered off the road to Moav, and bolted into the fields and vineyards. Bilam, however, did not sense the presence of the angel.[21]

Had the donkey really seen the angel? Indeed, can an incorporeal angel be seen with physical vision?

Some say that the donkey only sensed the presence of the angel, but it did see the sword, which frightened it and caused it to flee.[22] Others say that it actually saw a manifestation of the

18. Rokeach identifies this angel first as Michael, then as Gavriel. Perhaps both were present: Michael as an angel of mercy for the Jewish people, and Gavriel as an angel of justice for Bilam (*Sifsei Kohen*). *Midrash haGadol* states that the same angel served both purposes. (Satan, the *yetzer hara* and the Angel of Death are all the same, depending on the task at hand. See *Bava Basra* 16a.)

19. See Rashi, *Mesiach Ilmim*, Rokeach on *Bamidbar* 22:22; *Bamidbar Rabbah* 20:12, 14. This angel was sent not to kill Bilam but, as explained below, to show him Who was controlling the journey.

20. See Rashi, Rabbeinu Bachya, Rokeach on *Bamidbar* 22:22–23; *Bamidbar Rabbah* 20:13.

21. See Ibn Ezra, Ramban on *Bamidbar* 22:23.

22. See Ramban, Abarbanel, *Ma'aseh Hashem* on ibid. See also *Moreh Nevuchim* 2:6, 42. The same power that allowed the donkey to sense the angel enabled the donkey to talk and prevented the lions from mauling Daniel.

angel. Had a person seen this vision, he would have gone mad. An animal, however, because it is not endowed with intelligence, could see this vision and react with fright alone.[23] Still others say that the entire episode described here was nothing more than a prophetic vision—a prophetic nightmare to dissuade him from the evil course he had chosen.[24]

What was the story of this most unusual donkey? It had been destined to exist since the sixth day of Creation. It came into Yaakov's possession, and when he arrived in Egypt, he gave it to Bilam.

"Bilam," he said, "you are an influential advisor to Pharaoh. Please do not advise him to act against my children. I am giving you this gift as a token of my request."

"I accept your gift," Bilam replied. "You have my assurance."

But Bilam had no intention of keeping his word. He advised Pharaoh to enslave the Jewish people.[25]

This was the donkey that Bilam now rode on his journey to Moav. The donkey's flight into the fields had separated them from the rest of the traveling party. The donkey dug in its heels and refused to return to the road. Bilam grew angry[26] and struck the donkey across its legs[27] with the reins,[28] but the donkey did not respond.

Bilam and his donkey were now alone with an angel that only

---

23. See Rashi with *Nachalas Yaakov, Sifsei Kohen* on *Bamidbar* 22:23. According to *Ha'amek Davar* and Abarbanel, the angel appeared as a human holding a sword, just as Avraham's angelic guests seemed human.

24. Rav Yosef Caspi, Ralbag on *Bamidbar* 22:22.

25. *Midrash Aggadah*, ibid. According to *Tosefos Yom Tov, Avos* 5:6, it's unlikely that this donkey was 2,500 years old. Rather, only the decrees regarding its behavior were issued on the sixth day of Creation.

26. *Tosefos Rav Ephraim al haTorah, Bamidbar* 22:29.

27. *Yalkut Me'or haAfeilah, Bamidbar* 22:28. *Ha'amek Davar* states that Bilam originally slapped the donkey simply to redirect it.

28. *Chizkuni, Tosefos Rav Ephraim al haTorah* on *Bamidbar* 22:27.

the donkey could perceive.[29] The angel reappeared in front of the donkey, and the terrified animal veered off again. It plunged into a narrow alleyway between two stone walls.[30] Bilam's leg was crushed between the donkey and the wall, and his hip was dislocated; he would remain lame for the rest of his life.[31]

Bilam cried out in pain and struck the donkey again in an effort to get it to return to the road. The donkey found its way onto a narrow trail alongside a precipitous drop when the angel reappeared,[32] leaving the donkey no room to maneuver. It sank to the ground and refused to budge.[33]

Bilam was humiliated and enraged. Why was the donkey stopping on this spot? And what was he supposed to do? He was too far away from the rest of the traveling party to catch up on foot. The donkey had always been trustworthy.[34] Why was it acting this way now?[35] Refusing to tolerate this new insubordination, he beat it mercilessly with his wooden staff.[36]

Why did Bilam strike the donkey instead of simply cursing it? Bilam only had the power to curse once a day. Since he was looking forward to cursing the Jewish people later on, he reserved his curse and beat the donkey with his staff instead.[37]

---

29. See *Chizkuni*, *Tosefos Rav Ephraim al haTorah*, Seforno, Abarbanel on *Bamidbar* 22:21–22.

30. See Rashi, *Bamidbar* 22:24.

31. See Rashi, Rashbam, *Chizkuni* on *Bamidbar* 22:25; *Sifsei Kohen*, *Bamidbar* 23:20. From the Zohar, in contrast, it appears that Bilam was already lame. According to *Minchah Belulah*, Bilam reinjured his lame foot during this incident.

32. See Rashi with *Gur Aryeh*, *Bamidbar* 22:26.

33. See *Bechor Shor*, *Bamidbar* 22:23, regarding why the donkey couldn't move. It had also endured enough blows and refused to travel any further (*Chizkuni*).

34. *Bamidbar Rabbah* 20:14; *Bechor Shor*, *Bamidbar* 22:23.

35. Malbim, *Bamidbar* 22:23.

36. *Chizkuni*, *Tosefos Rav Ephraim* on *Bamidbar* 22:27. The final Hebrew letters of the names Avraham, Yitzchak, and Yisrael spell the word *makel*, "staff," suggesting that in the merit of the patriarchs, the donkey refused to assist Bilam in cursing the Jews.

37. Tur, *Tosefos Rav Ephraim* on *Bamidbar* 22:22. Additionally, according to

Symbols and Allusions

There are many symbols and allusions in the details of this episode. The angel positioned itself to block the donkey three times, corresponding to the protection of the three patriarchs. Originally, when the donkey fled into the open field, there were two escape routes, one to the right and one to the left. This was sign that Bilam's curses could be directed at the descendants of Yishmael and Keturah, Avraham's peripheral children, but not at the descendants of Yitzchak, his principal successor.

The second time the angel appeared there was just one escape route. This was a sign that if the curse was directed at the descendants of Yitzchak it could affect his lineage only through his son Eisav but not through his son Yaakov.

The third and final time the angel appeared there was no escape route at all. This was a sign that if curses were directed at the descendants of Yaakov, they would be totally ineffective. In other words, should Bilam attempt to curse the Jewish people, he would not succeed.[38]

The stone walls between which Bilam and the donkey passed symbolized the stone mound that memorialized the non-aggression treaty between Yaakov and Lavan, setting boundaries beyond which neither could go in order to harm the other. Bilam violated that covenant and was therefore harmed by the symbols of that treaty. Furthermore, when the treaty between Yaakov and Lavan was finalized, a sword was embedded in the mound as a further memorial. It was this sword that the angel grasped, and the sword that would eventually kill Bilam.[39] The two stone walls

---

Bilam's calculations, the time of day during which cursing is effective hadn't yet arrived (Tur).

38. See Rashi, *Da'as Zekeinim*, Rosh on *Bamidbar* 22:26; *Tanchuma, Balak* 8; *Bamidbar Rabbah* 20:14. See also Malbim regarding the angel's three stations.

39. See *Targum Yonasan, Midrash haGadol, Chizkuni, Mesiach Ilmim* on *Bamidbar* 22:24. See also *Tanchuma, Vayeitzei* 13; *Da'as Zekeinim, Bereishis* 31:51–53. That

also indicated that the Jewish people would be protected through the merit of the Torah, embodied in the two stone tablets — the Luchos — that were given at Mount Sinai.[40]

The Donkey Speaks

As the donkey absorbed Bilam's blows, it wondered why its master was reacting that way. Didn't he see this nebulous figure wielding a sword?[41]

Hashem opened a "spiritual passage" for the donkey's voice to be converted to actual speech, and it began to speak.[42]

"Bilam," it began, "why have you hit me three times? Was there a mystical significance to that number? Was it directed at the people whose progeny will ascend to the Beis haMikdash three times a year to celebrate the three festivals?"[43]

The amazing phenomenon of a talking donkey would have struck anyone speechless. But Bilam was so intent on his evil designs that he took it all in stride, as if it were perfectly normal. All he wanted was to continue the journey to Moav, and if that involved a conversation with his donkey, so be it.[44] The Moabite officers who witnessed this event from afar, however, watched with their mouths agape.[45]

"Are you toying with me?" Bilam said to the donkey. "You

---

this sword killed Bilam is certainly fitting, according to the view that he was actually Lavan.

40. *Bamidbar Rabbah* 20:14.

41. See *Peirush Yonasan, Bamidbar* 22:25.

42. See *Midrash Aggadah, Ohr haChaim* on *Bamidbar* 22:27. According to Malbim, the donkey spoke through the power of a demon. Not coincidentally, this speech and demons were both created on the sixth day of Creation.

43. See Rashi, *Bamidbar* 22:28; Zohar, *Balak* 210a.

44. Rabbeinu Bachya, *Bamidbar* 22:29. Bilam wasn't impressed. He had heard other magicians make birds speak. To him, a talking donkey was just another form of witchcraft (*Midreshei haTorah*).

45. Rabbeinu Bachya, *Bamidbar* 22:29; *Bamidbar Rabbah* 20:14. The officers attributed the donkey's speech to Bilam's witchcraft (*Midreshei haTorah*).

defied and humiliated me not once but three times![46] You turned away from the road, and you crushed my leg against the stone walls. And as if that were not enough, you lay down and refused to continue. Why, if I had a sword, I would cut you to pieces right here and now."[47]

"You would kill me, exalted sorcerer?" the donkey mocked him. "How would that look to the public? Imagine a snake charmer who had to use a stick instead of a charm to remove a snake. He would be a laughingstock."[48]

"What do you mean?" said Bilam.

"You pride yourself on your ability to curse. You think you will be able to curse a huge nation of millions who have merited the World to Come. And yet you have to resort to sticks and swords to control your own donkey. People will laugh at you for generations."[49]

Meanwhile, the Moabite officers had recovered from the initial shock and had come closer to hear the conversation. When they heard the donkey rebuke Bilam, they threw back their heads and roared with laughter.[50]

"That's some donkey, Bilam," they said. "It seems she's smarter than you. She's making a good point. How can you presume to curse this great nation if you can't even curse your own little donkey? Why were you threatening to kill her with a sword?"[51]

"You people just don't understand," said Bilam.

"Don't understand what?" said one of the officers. "Just tell us this: Why aren't you riding a fast horse like we are? Why are you trudging along on a donkey?"

---

46. Rashi, Radak, Rav Saadiah Gaon on *Bamidbar* 22:29.
47. *Akeidas Yitzchak, Me'am Lo'ez* on ibid.
48. *Bamidbar Rabbah* 20:14.
49. *Tanchuma, Balak* 9; *Targum Yonasan, Bamidbar* 22:29.
50. *Midrash haGadol, Bamidbar* 22:29.
51. Rashi, *Midrash haGadol* on ibid.; *Bamidbar Rabbah* 20:14; Zohar, *Balak* 210a.

"My horse is grazing in the meadow," Bilam replied. "I didn't know I'd need it until last night, and by then there wasn't enough time to fetch it."

"Well, maybe," said the officer. "But why didn't you just curse the donkey? Why should someone like you beat it with a stick?"

"The donkey is not mine. I borrowed it from someone else. I can beat it all I want, but if I curse it I will be destroying the owner's property."

The donkey had been silent during this exchange, but it could hold its peace no longer.

"Now wait a minute, Bilam," said the donkey. "What's this about borrowing me? Why are you making up stories? Just tell them the truth."

Bilam gave the donkey a nasty look and sighed. "All right, I admit it. You are my donkey, but I only use you to carry my packages."

"Packages? Enough with the lies. Tell them that you ride me."

"Well, maybe once in a while."

"How can you lie about me like that? You know perfectly well that you ride me day and night. I don't think you want me to elaborate.[52] Bilam, you trained and taught me that you are my master. I know how you like to ride, and I always do what you want. Have I ever behaved as I did today? Have I ever disappointed you?"[53]

"Well, no," Bilam grudgingly admitted.

"I know good and well that you have a terrible temper,"[54] the donkey continued, "and I know good and well that I have to respect your wishes. But don't you think I had a reason for what I

---

52. See *Avodah Zarah* 4b with Maharsha; *Sanhedrin* 105b; *Targum Yonasan*; *Tosefos Rav Ephraim al haTorah*, *Tosefos Rav Avigdor*, *Lekach Tov* on *Bamidbar* 22:29; Zohar, *Balak* 209b; *Bamidbar Rabbah* 20:14.

53. Rashi, *Bamidbar* 22:30; Zohar, *Balak* 210a.

54. *Tosefos Rav Ephraim al haTorah*, *Bamidbar* 22:29.

did? Why didn't you use your powers of sorcery to learn what it was? Did you give it any thought at all? There may have been a snake nearby. Or perhaps I was ill. Did you even stop and think before you started beating me with that stick of yours?"[55]

The high-and-mighty Bilam was forced to admit—by a donkey, no less—that he had behaved shamefully. Indeed, if animals had the power of speech, a great deal of hypocrisy and conceit would be exposed. It was an object lesson for future generations. If a donkey could confront a man such as Bilam and expose his shortcomings, how can we expect to defend ourselves when we face judgment in the heavenly court?

Yet Bilam was a human being, and despite his wicked ways, there was a limit to how much humiliation Hashem would allow him to be subjected to. His dignity had been much diminished in the eyes of the Moabite officers, who had followed avidly the conversation between the donkey and its master, and they would undoubtedly spread the story. If Bilam's donkey and assistants[56] were to survive, therefore, they would be a constant reminder of Bilam's humiliation. "There goes Bilam's donkey," people would say to each other and to their children. "Did you ever hear the story about Bilam and his donkey? You'll never believe this, but I heard it from his own sons, who were there at the time. You see..."

Hashem, therefore, took pity on Bilam and instructed the angel to slaughter his donkey[57] and his two assistants right then

---

55. See *Chizkuni*, Seforno, *Tosefos Rav Ephraim*, *HaKesav vehaKabbalah*, Malbim on *Bamidbar* 22:30; *Sefer Chasidim*, notes 666–668. The donkey was also saying that its very strange behavior should have given Bilam the unequivocal message that he would fail to curse the Jews (Seforno). According to the Zohar (*Balak* 209b–210a), Bilam got the unspoken message that he would not be successful in cursing the Jews. He also realized that if he knew less than an animal, how could he receive divine inspiration?

See Rabbi Yehudah heChasid regarding why the donkey didn't tell Bilam outright that an angel was present.

56. See note 10, above.

57. *Bamidbar Rabbah* 20:14; Rashi, *Bamidbar* 22:33.

and there.[58] Bilam saw his donkey and his sons fall dead to the ground, but he still didn't know what the donkey had seen, nor did he know what had caused the three of them to die.

There was also another reason that the donkey had to die. The nations of the world would be abuzz about this great miracle, and Hashem did not want them to worship this donkey as a god.[59]

In the final analysis, the supernatural phenomenon of the talking donkey was meant to teach Bilam a lesson. Hashem controls all speech in the world. Just as He could imbue a donkey with the power of speech, He could prevent Bilam from using his own power of speech. Unfortunately, Bilam did not learn his lesson.[60]

Bilam Meets the Angel

It was now time for Hashem to reveal to Bilam what had caused the donkey's sudden fright. Here, too, there was a lesson. Just as Hashem comes to the defense of a mere donkey that has been humiliated and maligned (via the angel's rebuke of Bilam), He would certainly defend the Jewish nation, a nation protected by their own merits and those of the patriarchs, from Bilam's evil designs.[61]

Hashem withdrew the veil from Bilam's eyes, and suddenly he saw standing before him a vision of an angel with a sword in his hand. Stunned and overwhelmed, Bilam kneeled and bowed before it.[62] In his heart, this arrogant man felt a new rush of shame.

---

58. See *Lekach Tov, Ma'aseh Hashem* on *Bamidbar* 22:35. Each time the donkey veered off the road, one of these two attendants (i.e., Bilam's sons) died. (The Moabite officers, who also saw Bilam's humiliation, would be killed later. See Rashi, *Bamidbar* 22:35; *Bamidbar Rabbah* 20:15.)

59. *Bamidbar Rabbah* 20:14; Rabbeinu Bachya, *Bamidbar* 22:32. Additionally, the donkey had fulfilled its purpose in life and was no longer needed (Rabbeinu Bachya).

60. See Rabbeinu Bachya, Seforno on *Bamidbar* 22:28.

61. *Bamidbar Rabbah* 20:15; *Midrash Aggadah*, *Bamidbar* 22:31.

62. See *Bamidbar Rabbah* 20:15 with Radal. Bilam bowed in fear and awe as well, thinking the angel was there to kill him (*Midrash Aggadah*).

Clearly, this was what the donkey had seen and what had caused it to bolt in fright. Yet he hadn't seen it until now. The donkey had seen it, but not Bilam. How humiliating.

"Why did you strike your donkey three times?" the angel rebuke Bilam. "Your donkey behaved properly when it saw me. It veered off the road, because it was trying to protect itself from me."[63]

"I know that now," said Bilam.

"Do you know why I am here?" said the angel.

Bilam hung his head in silence.

"I speak in the name of Hashem," said the angel. "You have defied and angered Me. You rushed along with the intent of fulfilling your will rather than Mine. You rebelled against Me.[64] When your donkey saw the vision, it actually fled to protect you as well.[65] If it had not turned away, you would have perished by the sword."[66]

Bilam shuddered.

"I come on a mission of mercy from Hashem," the angel continued. "Your willingness to risk your life in order to curse the Jewish people has called down judgment upon your head. But you still have a chance to abort your journey and turn back at once."[67]

Having delivered his message, the angel fell silent, but the lesson lingered on. Bilam had now been taught that Hashem controls not only the power of speech but also the power of vision. He can empower a donkey to see, and He can draw a veil across the eyes of a man.[68]

---

63. *Bamidbar Rabbah* 20:15; Malbim, *Bamidbar* 22:32.

64. Rashi with *Sefer Zikaron*, *Bamidbar* 22:32.

65. Rashi, ibid.; *Shabbos* 105a.

66. See Rashi, *Da'as Zekeinim*, *Chizkuni*, Abarbanel, *HaKesav vehaKabbalah*, *Aderes Eliyahu* on *Bamidbar* 22:33; *Bamidbar Rabbah* 20:15. See also *Sefer Chasidim*, notes 666–668. See *Moreh Nevuchim* 3:17.

67. Tur, Seforno on *Bamidbar* 22:33. The Tur states that this was indeed Gavriel, an angel of justice. See note 18.

68. Rabbeinu Bachya, *Lekach Tov*, *Ohr haChaim*, Abarbanel, *Sifsei Kohen* on *Bamidbar* 22:22, 23, 27. See *Lekach Tov*, Rokeach on *Bamidbar* 22:31; *Bamidbar Rabbah* 20:15. Bilam would be tested ten times to see if, after all the obstacles

Bilam had been much admired and respected for his knowledge and skills, but now he had been held up to the world as a bumbling fool.[69] He had been honored as a man possessed of prophecy and the holy spirit, but now he had been reduced to a status even lower than that of a donkey. He had boasted that he could read the mind of the Supreme One, but now he had to admit that he hadn't seen an angel when his donkey had.

Eventually, as he continued on his present course, he would be stripped of his prophetic powers and of the holy spirit. He would return to being a lowly sorcerer,[70] collecting a payment of five small coins per session.[71]

Bilam was terrified in the presence of the angel, and he knew full well that only immediate and sincere repentance would guarantee his safety. But he fortified himself in his evil resolve and in his insolence and hostility toward Hashem. He would feign repentance,[72] but it would not be sincere.[73]

"You angels are all alike," he finally replied. "You nullify what Hashem decrees. When Hashem told Avraham to bring his son as an offering at the Akeidah, the angel nullified His words and told Avraham to desist. Hashem told me to go to Balak, and here you are, an angel, nullifying His words.[74]

---

placed before him, he understood not to curse the Jews. Unlike Avraham and his ten tests, Bilam failed every time (Rabbeinu Bachya; *Aderes Eliyahu*).

According to *Me'am Lo'ez, Devarim* 34:10, this episode proved that Bilam achieved prophecy only momentarily, then was left with nothing but cheap witchcraft. Not only did Moshe remain a great prophet until his death, but his prophecy would be transmitted from generation to generation.

69. See *Targum Yonasan, Bamidbar* 22:5, Abarbanel, *Bamidbar* 22:32. According to the view that Bilam was Lavan, it was indeed foolish for him to curse the very descendants of his daughters, Rachel and Leah.

70. *Sanhedrin* 106a with Rashi; *Ohr haChaim, Bamidbar* 22:32.

71. *Yalkut Pisron Torah, Bamidbar* 24:16.

72. *Bamidbar Rabbah* 20:15; *Tzeror haMor, Bamidbar* 22:34.

73. See Rashi, *Bamidbar* 22:34.

74. Ibid.; *Bamidbar Rabbah* 20:15.

"Nonetheless, please forgive me, for I have sinned.[75] I should not have taken this path against you.[76] I was wrong for beating the donkey.[77] I didn't know you were here.[78] I was stubborn.[79] Had I thought about why the donkey was behaving in this bizarre manner, I would have realized that you were standing in the way.[80] I am full of regret. If it is wicked in your eyes that I go,[81] and if you are here to defend the Jewish people, then I will return at once."[82]

"Bilam, you are forgiven," said the angel.[83] "If you want to go, you can go. It is your choice.[84] However, you have no choice in what you will say.[85] Heed the original warning: the original rules still apply.[86] You will tell the people that you can say only what Hashem tells you to say.[87] You are not in control of your own utterances. You will be forced to say things Hashem places in your mouth against your will.[88] Now go with these people; your portion is with them. You will perish together."[89]

---

75. A thief regrets only that he got caught, not that he stole. Bilam was no better (Rav Chaim Kanievsky, *Ta'ama d'Kra*).

76. *Ohr haChaim*, *Bamidbar* 22:34.

77. *Lekach Tov*, *Tosefos Rav Ephraim* on ibid.

78. *Chizkuni*, *Pa'aneiach Raza*, *Ohr haChaim*, Malbim on ibid. How could Bilam blame himself for defying the angel when he hadn't seen it? The text goes on to say that had he looked into the matter, he would have seen. See *Pa'aneiach Raza*.

79. Seforno, *HaKesav vehaKabbalah* on ibid.

80. *Chizkuni*, Seforno, *Ha'amek Davar*, Malbim on ibid.

81. Rav Saadiah Gaon, ibid.

82. Seforno, ibid.

83. Ramban, *Bamidbar* 22:35.

84. See Rashi, *Ha'amek Davar* on ibid.

85. See *Ha'amek Davar*, ibid.

86. See Ramban, Rabbeinu Bachya, Abarbanel on ibid.

87. Ramban, ibid.

88. Rashi with *Gur Aryeh*, Seforno, *HaKesav vehaKabbalah* on ibid. The angel was referring to the blessings Bilam would give the Jews (Alshich).

89. Rashi, ibid.; *Bamidbar Rabbah* 20:15.

Balak Meets Bilam

Bilam, left without transportation, borrowed one of the officers' horses to continue the journey to Moav.[90] As they rode along, unified in their resolve to curse the Jewish people,[91] Bilam asked one of the officers to ride ahead and inform Balak that Bilam was on the way.

"But why?" asked the officer.

Bilam lifted his nose in the air to show his scorn for the question. "What do you think?" he said. "A man of vast importance such as I cannot just ride into a city like an ordinary person. An appropriate welcome has to be arranged. The king will need time to prepare."[92]

The officer gave Bilam an odd look but made no comment. He spurred his horse and galloped off ahead of the traveling party. Arriving in the capital, he went straight to Balak and delivered the message.

"So how was the journey?" Balak asked.

"Strange and a little ridiculous, Your Majesty," said the officer. "The man is an incompetent fool. I cannot imagine how he will be able to curse the Jewish people. He is powerless. You wouldn't believe the scene we witnessed on the road. Bilam was having an argument with his donkey, and the donkey won! We were all laughing so hard we almost fell off our horses."[93]

Balak sighed. "Well, unfortunately, he is our best hope right now."

Balak put on a happy face and went out to welcome his guest.[94]

---

90. *Sifsei Kohen, Bamidbar* 22:35. Rav Chaim Kanievsky writes in *Ta'ama d'Kra* that Bilam joined the Moabites on foot.

91. Rashi, ibid.; *Bamidbar Rabbah* 20:15.

92. See Rashi, *Bamidbar* 22:36; *Bamidbar Rabbah* 20:16 with Radal.

93. See Zohar, *Balak* 209b.

94. *Sifsei Kohen, Bamidbar* 22:36. *Ohr haChaim* states that Balak would not have honored Bilam this way if not for his ulterior motive of showing him the damage the Jews could cause the metropolis (see below in text).

He waited for Bilam at the border, the site of a newly built metropolis with all the latest conveniences. He wanted Bilam to experience the energy of this new city and to recognize that this bastion of progress was being threatened by the Jewish people.[95] He also wanted Bilam to see firsthand that the Children of Israel had violated international law by invading the nearby lands of Sichon, and that they now intended to do the same to Moav.[96]

When Bilam finally reached the Moabite border, he found Balak waiting to greet him.

"Bilam, my good friend," Balak cried out, "welcome to Moav! Why didn't you come the first time I sent for you? Did you think I wouldn't honor you properly?"[97]

Balak's words were unintentionally prophetic. In the end, Bilam would be scorned by Balak and forced to leave in shame and humiliation.[98]

"I came as soon as I could," Bilam replied. "All your inducements of honor and wealth could not bring me here until I received Hashem's permission. Once I had that, I came right away.[99] But I don't understand what you expect from me. I do not have freedom of speech.[100] Hashem controls the utterances that emerge from my mouth. Are you willing to take that risk? Are you willing to pay me and take a chance that instead of curses I will give the Jewish people blessings? If not, I will go home at once."[101]

"I will risk it."

"And what about the money you promised me?"

"Don't worry, I'm good for the money. You'll get all the wealth

---

95. Rashi, *Bamidbar* 22:36; *Bamidbar Rabbah* 20:16; *Tanchuma, Balak* 11.
96. *Bamidbar Rabbah* 20:16. This law dated back to Noach.
97. Malbim, *Bamidbar* 22:37.
98. Rashi, ibid.; *Bamidbar Rabbah* 20:16.
99. Malbim, *Bamidbar* 22:37.
100. Rokeach, Seforno on *Bamidbar* 22:38.
101. *Me'am Lo'ez, Bamidbar* 22:37.

and honor I promised you. All I ask is that you do your best.[102] In the meantime, let me show you around."

Balak took Bilam to the fortified city of Chutzos,[103] a bustling center of commerce and financial services. The streets were teeming with people buying and selling all kinds of products. From the factories emerged the clang of tools and machinery, blending with the raucous cries of street vendors and peddlers.

"Isn't this a wonderful city?" Balak said to Bilam. "We are bringing our society into a modern era of progress and enlightenment. And this is what the Jewish people seek to uproot. Your work here will determine the future course of history for all humankind."[104]

They returned to the capital city as the sun settled into the western sky. Bilam was shown to his quarters and Balak went away. Bilam was hungry, and he waited for dinner to be brought to him. An hour passed, then two, and still no dinner. Perhaps, thought Bilam, they were preparing a royal banquet in his honor. These things could not be done in a few minutes, of course. But Bilam would wait all night, and no dignitaries would appear.

Balak had lost confidence in Bilam. Ordinarily, he would have sent him packing, but his desperate hatred of the Jewish people kept a small spark of hope alive in his heart that perhaps Bilam could do something, despite his procrastination and lame excuses.[105]

Bilam finally did get dinner, but it was paltry and without pomp and honor. A servant brought him some leftovers from the kitchen,[106] a piece of low-grade[107] mutton and a shank bone with

---

102. Ibid.

103. Ibn Ezra, *Bamidbar* 22:39.

104. See Rashi, *Midrash Aggadah* on ibid.; *Bamidbar Rabbah* 20:17; *Tanchuma, Balak* 11.

105. See *Ohr haChaim, Bamidbar* 22:39.

106. *Sifsei Kohen, Mesiach Ilmim* on *Bamidbar* 22:40.

107. *Midrash Aggadah,* ibid.

scraps of meat.[108] The food was a slap in the face. He dined alone.[109]

Bilam was furious. "What an outrage!" he cried out to the silent walls. "Has Balak brought me all the way here to treat me so shabbily? What a parsimonious man he is. Talks big but gives very little. Where is my feast? Where is my honor?[110] Well, I will retaliate. I will curse his possessions, and I will further deplete his treasury by recommending that he slaughter unnecessary offerings and sacrifices."[111]

Balak had indeed shown himself to be the exact opposite of Avraham. When the angels disguised as guests came to Avraham, he invited them in for bread, but when they sat down to eat, he served them a lavish meal of meat and delicacies. He promised little but delivered a lot. Balak, on the other hand, persuaded Bilam to come with promises of great wealth and honor, but when he arrived, he served him a paltry meal of leftovers and table scraps. Balak promised a lot but delivered little.[112]

The following day would demonstrate what Bilam could deliver.

---

108. See Rashi, *Midrash Aggadah, Midrash haGadol* on ibid. Rabbeinu Bachya writes that since Bilam had come on business, Balak didn't want him wasting time eating. *Yalkut Me'or Afeilah* adds that Bilam should have expected nothing, and this snack was intended to placate him for the time being.

109. *Ohr haChaim*, ibid.

110. See *Midrash Aggadah, Ohr haChaim* on *Bamidbar* 22:41; *Bamidbar Rabbah* 20:17.

111. *Bamidbar Rabbah* 20:17; *Sefer Zikaron, Sifsei Chachamim* on *Bamidbar* 22:40.

112. *Bamidbar Rabbah* 20:17. Furthermore, Balak disrespectfully fed Bilam before "feeding" Hashem via offerings (*Aderes Eliyahu*).

10 Blessings and Prophecies

Bil'am saw that it was good in the eyes of the Eternal to bless Yisrael, so he did not go to seek ominous opportunities as on the previous occasions, and he directed his face towards the desert [where Yisrael had sinned with the Golden Calf]. Bil'am looked up and saw Yisrael dwelling according to its tribes, and a spirit of [prophecy from] God [rested] upon him. He proclaimed his parable and said, "[This is] the [prophetic] declaration of Bil'am the son of Be'or, and the [prophetic] declaration of the mighty man with the hollow eye; the [prophetic] declaration of him who hears God's pronouncements, who perceives the vision of the All-sufficing; he lies down and [then it is] revealed to him: How good are your tents, Ya'akov; your encampments, Yisrael! Like streams that extend far, like gardens beside the river; like [fragrant] aloes that the Eternal planted, like cedars by the water. Water will flow from their wells, and their seed will be [planted] in much

water. Their [first] king will triumph over Agag, and their kingdom will be [even further] exalted. God, Who brought them out of Mitzrayim with His soaring strength, will destroy nations that are His adversaries and bare their bones, and drench His arrows [in their blood]. [Yisrael] will rest [and] dwell with power like a lion; and like a lioness, who will [be able to] stir them? Those who bless you are blessed, and those who curse you are cursed." (Bamidbar 24:1–9)

Knowing that the exact moment of Hashem's anger occurs during the first three hours of the day, when the pagans flock to their temples to worship the rising sun,[1] Balak awoke Bilam in the dark hours before the dawn. Balak knew the exact place where the curses would be most effective, and Bilam knew the exact moment of the divine anger.[2] Working as a team, like the slaughterer and the butcher, they hoped to produce the desired results.[3]

Balak took Bilam up to an idyllic spot on the mountain of Ba'al, the chief Moabite idol, located in the Arnon Mountains,[4] a spot dedicated to the worship of the idol Pe'or.[5] Because of his lame leg, Bilam found the climb difficult and painful, and he had to lean on Balak to reach the top.[6] A place such as this was necessary for the curse to be effective, since Bilam foresaw that idol worship would be the downfall of the Jewish people.[7]

---

1. See *Berachos* 7a. Hashem's anger occurs in the early morning, either because that is when the sun is worshiped (Malbim), or because that is when people relieve themselves—an activity used in the worship of Pe'or. See *Ohr haChaim*, Rokeach, *Bamidbar* 22:41.

2. *Ohr haChaim*, *Ha'amek Davar* on *Bamidbar* 22:41. See *Sanhedrin* 105b.

3. *Midrash haGadol*, *Bamidbar* 22:6; *Bamidbar Rabbah* 20:18; *Tzeror haMor*, *Bamidbar* 22:40. See Zohar, *Bechukosai* 112b.

4. Ibn Ezra, *Bamidbar* 22:41. In this border area, Sichon had conquered half of Moav, and the Jews had then conquered Sichon. This location was thus ideal for stirring Bilam's fury and facilitating the curse (*Sifsei Kohen*).

5. See Rashi, Rokeach on ibid. This serene and secluded area lent itself to idol worship (*Yalkut Me'or haAfeilah*, *Bamidbar* 22:39).

6. *Ohr haChaim*, *Bamidbar* 22:41.

7. *Bamidbar Rabbah* 20:18; *Tzeror haMor*, *Bamidbar* 22:41. Bilam proved to be right, as we will see in the next chapter.

Moreover, from this high vantage point he could actually see the entire Jewish encampment[8]—or part of it, according to one opinion[9]—and cast his evil spell upon it.[10] Although the clouds of glory hovered over the encampment, Bilam was able to use his sorcery to see through them.[11] Others suggest that he was only able to see those wicked Jews who were expelled from the cover of the clouds of glory,[12] such as the Eirev Rav[13] and the worshipers of Michah's idol among the tribe of Dan.[14]

At the precise moment when he had calculated that Hashem's anger would flare, Bilam peered into the distance at whatever he could see of the Jewish encampment, and he willed his evil eye to penetrate the ranks of his enemies. He then waited for some effect to manifest itself, but none did. Perhaps, thought Bilam, Hashem's anger had abated. He would have to find another way. Perhaps prayers and offerings would help him gain Hashem's favor.[15]

Bribe Offerings

"Balak, help me out," Bilam said. "Build for me seven altars and prepare for me seven bullocks and seven rams, so that I will be able to sacrifice a bullock and a ram on each altar."[16]

"Why do you want to do this?" said Balak. "And why seven?"

"The Jewish people have a long history of bringing sacrificial

---

8. See Ramban, *Da'as Zekeinim, Lekach Tov* on *Bamidbar* 22:41.

9. See Ibn Ezra, Ramban, Rabbeinu Bachya on ibid.

10. Bilaam's power lay in his ability to divine the moment of Hashem's daily "anger," and place his curse then through his "evil eye." Hashem, in His mercy, changed nature and didn't ignite His anger during this ordeal, rendering Bilam's evil eye harmless (*Ha'amek Davar* on ibid.).

11. *Ohr haChaim*, ibid.

12. *Moshav Zekeinim, Midrash haGadol* on ibid.

13. *Sifsei Kohen*, ibid.

14. *Targum Yonasan, Bamidbar* 22:41. See also *Let My Nation Go*, p. 351.

15. See Ramban, *Ha'amek Davar* on *Bamidbar* 23:1.

16. Rav Saadiah Gaon, Ibn Ezra on *Bamidbar* 23:2.

offerings to Hashem. That is how they have gained His favor. Seven of their most prominent ancestors brought offerings—Adam, Hevel, Noach, Avraham, Yitzchak, Yaakov and Moshe.[17] But I, the incomparable Bilam, will surpass them all.[18] All these ancestors of the Jewish people together built only seven altars; I alone, the champion of the seventy nations, will myself build seven altars.[19] And I will bring a bullock and a ram on each one. Avraham brought only a ram, and look how much favor he gained with Hashem.[20] Imagine how beholden Hashem will be to me after all I will do for Him."

"Money's tight these days, Bilam. Why do you need to be so extravagant? Do you really need bullocks and rams? Surely, goats and sheep will do just as well."

"Don't waste your breath, Balak. It's nice to see that you're trying to be fiscally responsible, but sometimes you can go too far. Goats? Sheep? Not for me, my friend. We have to be respectable, you know. Big people bring big offerings.[21] And you want to know why the number seven? Because Hashem likes that number. Seven Noachide laws. Seven days of Creation. The sabbatical year comes every seventh year.[22] Do you want me to go on?"

"Please don't."

Bilam was trying to bribe Hashem, like a storekeeper who uses inaccurate scales to cheat his customers. When confronted by the municipal inspector, he winks and says, "I've sent a gift to your

---

17. *Chizkuni*, *Minchah Belulah*, Ralbag on *Bamidbar* 23:1; *Bamidbar Rabbah* 20:18.

18. *Midrash haGadol*, *Bamidbar* 23:1.

19. The Jews are one nation with one God, so we sacrifice on one altar. The nations of the world are littered with beliefs and deities. Bilam thus believed that the more altars, the better. *Ha'amek Davar*, ibid. See also *Vayikra Rabbah* 4:6.

20. Rashi, *Bamidbar* 23:4; *Bamidbar Rabbah* 20:18.

21. *Shem miShmuel*, *Bamidbar* 23:2.

22. See *Me'am Lo'ez*, *Bamidbar* 23:1. Bilam sought to curry favor with Hashem through the celestial power of seven. See Ibn Ezra, Ramban, Rabbeinu Bachya, *Sifsei Kohen*, Malbim, Tur, *Yalkut Pisron Torah* on ibid. According to *Midrash haGadol*, *Bamidbar* 23:29, Balak sought to cast a spell on the Jews via the seven entities created during the seven days of Creation.

home, so please make sure you certify my scales as accurate."[23] To his chagrin, however, it would do him no good.

Balak brought the animals Bilam had requested, and Bilam offered them up on the altars. Then he turned to Balak.

"You stay here with the sacrifices."[24]

"Where are you going?"

"I'm going up the mountain," said Bilam. "I need to be alone,[25] and to find a quiet place[26] where I can meditate and get into the right frame of mind for collecting and focusing the dark powers.[27] I need to fine-tune my senses so that I can anticipate that split second of divine anger.[28] And I want to receive a communication from Hashem. Believe me, that will take some doing. Hashem has never spoken to me during the daytime yet,[29] but the first time He spoke to Moshe was during the day at the burning bush.[30] Maybe all the preparations we made will induce Him to have compassion on me,[31] and to speak to me today and show me what will befall our Jewish enemies."[32]

Driven by his deep hatred for the Jews, like a snake in ambush, Bilam dragged himself[33] and his lame leg up the craggy

---

23. See *Bamidbar Rabbah* 20:18.

24. See *Ha'amek Davar*, *Bamidbar* 23:3. See *Ta'anis* 26a, 27a.

25. Rashi, *Aderes Eliyahu* on *Bamidbar* 23:3. As the Beis haMikdash would be built on a mountain, Bilam knew prophecy could be attained at elevations.

26. Rav Saadiah Gaon, Rashi, Malbim on ibid.

27. Zohar, *Vayishlach* 169b. See *Sifsei Kohen*, *Bamidbar* 23:3.

28. *Midrash Aggadah*, Tur on *Bamidbar* 23:3.

29. Rashi, ibid.

30. Seforno, ibid.

31. *Sifsei Kohen*, Alshich on ibid. See Tur, Ramban on *Bamidbar* 23:16.

32. Tur, *Bamidbar* 23:3.

33. See *Targum Yonasan*, ibid.; Zohar, *Vayishlach* 169b. The Torah here describes Bilam's movement as *shefi* (slithering like a snake), an acronym for *seh pezurah Yisrael*, "Israel is a scattered flock." Dispersed among seventy "wolves," the Jews eluded Bilam's evil eye (*Sifsei Kohen*).

mountainside, practically crawling all the way.[34] Then he waited for the divine communication.

Hashem doesn't reveal Himself by day to anyone but the righteous, but in this case, He made an exception. His love for the Jewish people was so strong that He was willing to appear to Bilam during the day in order to force him to bless the Jewish people.[35] Nonetheless, the mode of His appearance was angry and abrupt, a clear sign that it was something He preferred not to do, so to speak.[36] Hashem also waited to appear to Bilam until the latter had already given up hope of receiving a divine message and was preparing to descend from the mountain. At the very last moment, Bilam felt a tug, like an animal on a tight leash,[37] and then he felt a divine revelation. But it was not the kind of pure and holy revelation experienced by righteous prophets. Rather, it was a murky blur of nebulous shadows, reflective of Bilam's personality.[38]

"Hashem, I sense your presence," Bilam cried out. "I have set up seven altars in Your honor,[39] and I have offered up a bullock and a ram on each one, for a total of fourteen expensive animals."

In order to quell Bilam's venomous rage against the Jewish people,[40] Hashem appeared to Bilam with the Attribute of Strict Justice. He reprimanded Bilam and took him to task for his iniquitous behavior.[41]

"You are an evil man, Bilam," said Hashem. "What did you think? That you could persuade Me to abandon the Jewish people with a few animal sacrifices? A simple *pesach*-offering accompanied

---

34. See *Chizkuni*, Rashbam, *Ha'amek Davar* on *Bamidbar* 23:3; Maharsha, *Sotah* 10a.
35. Rashi, *Midrash Aggadah* on *Bamidbar* 23:3.
36. Rashi, Rav Chaim Paltiel on *Bamidbar* 23:3–4.
37. *Tzeror haMor*, *Bamidbar* 23:4.
38. See Rashi, ibid.; *Bereishis Rabbah* 52:5.
39. Balak actually arranged these altars, but Bilam took the credit for himself (Zohar, *Balak* 199b). Compare *Ma'aseh Hashem*.
40. *Tzeror haMor*, *Bamidbar* 23:4.
41. *Sifsei Kohen*, Alshich on *Bamidbar* 23:3.

by bitter herbs is more pleasing to Me than your largest bullocks. A handful of flour brought by a pauper finds more favor in My eyes than all your lavish offerings. A dry crust of bread in an atmosphere of tranquility is far better than a gala feast in an atmosphere of strife. You seek to sow strife among the Jewish people, but I assure you that you will fail.[42] You will receive further communications from Me, but your days as a prophet are over."[43]

Meanwhile, back at the altars, Balak went beyond Bilam's performance. He repeated the process two more times, each time sacrificing the full complement of fourteen animals, for a total of forty-two animals.[44] Balak's intentions were malicious. He wanted to harm the Jewish people. But the very act of bringing an offering to Hashem is pure, holy and meritorious, and because of this deed, he merited that Ruth, the matriarch of the Davidic dynasty, would be among his descendants.[45]

Balak looked up and saw that Bilam was returning.[46] He had a strange look about him, as if a muzzle had been placed over his mouth. And in the figurative sense, there was indeed a muzzle over his mouth. Hashem held it under tight control, either by His own hand, so to speak, or according to another view by the hand of an angel appointed to the task. He prevented Bilam from saying what He wanted to say and caused him to say what he didn't want to say. Bilam could be allowed to say only words Hashem placed in his mouth.[47]

---

42. See Tur, Rokeach, *Me'am Lo'ez* on ibid.; *Bamidbar Rabbah* 20:18; *Midrash Tehillim* 4:1. The initials of the words *mibayis malei zivchei riv* ("a gala feast in an atmosphere of strife" [*Mishlei* 17:1]) spell *mamzer*, for Hashem wanted no part of illegitimate Bilam's offerings.

43. *Lekach Tov, Bamidbar* 23:4; *Bamidbar Rabbah* 20:18.

44. *Lekach Tov, Bamidbar* 23:4; Tosafos, *Nazir* 23b.

45. See *Sotah* 47a, *Horayos* 10b with Maharsha; Tosafos, *Nazir* 23b. This view differs from the tradition that Balak was a Midianite.

46. *Bamidbar Rabbah* 20:18.

47. See Zohar, *Balak* 199b; Tur, *Bamidbar* 23:5. See also *Sanhedrin* 105b; *Bamidbar*

The First Curse Attempt[160]

There had never been any possibility that Hashem would let Bilam curse the Jewish people. He had only allowed Bilam to go to Moav so that this celebrated prophet of the gentile nations would pronounce blessings over the Jewish people, praise their stellar qualities and foretell their glorious future and the ultimate downfall of their enemies.[49]

Balak and his officers saw Bilam coming down the mountain and waited hopefully for the good news that he had persuaded Hashem to relent and allow him to curse the Jewish nation.

"Well, Bilam, what have you got to say for yourself?" asked Balak.

Bilam knew he would not be allowed to express the thoughts he entertained in his mind about the Jewish people. He knew he would probably soon hear himself uttering blessings which would never pass his lips voluntarily.[50] But he consoled himself that the nations of the world would hear him bless the Jewish people and would be so upset that they would bombard the Jewish people with the evil eye from every direction.[51]

Rabbah 20:18; *Yalkut Shimoni* 765. See *Aderes Eliyahu*. Hashem set up an angel as a "partition" of sorts between His holiness and Bilam's defilement (*Ohr ha-Chaim, Bamidbar* 23:5). *Tosefos Rav Avigdor* (*Bamidbar* 24:4) and *Sifsei Kohen* (end *Balak*) identify this angel as Gavriel.

48. Breaks in the Torah, indicated by the Hebrew letters *samech* and *pei*, indicate points at which Moshe was given time to review what he learned. The entire episode of Balak and Bilam's attempt to curse the Jews, however, is one long, uninterrupted passage in the Torah. Thus, the Torah is teaching us that had Balak or Bilam had time to consider what they were doing and its ramifications, they would never have attempted it, and the Jewish people would never have received Bilam's blessing (*Chafetz Chaim*).

49. *Ohr haChaim, Bamidbar* 23:5.

50. See *Midrash haGadol, Me'am Lo'ez* on *Bamidbar* 23:7. The Torah speaks of Bilam's taking up *meshalo*, "his parable," but the same Hebrew letters can be pronounced *mishelo*, "from his own," for Hashem transformed Bilam's words into His own (*Me'am Lo'ez*).

51. *Yalkut Shimoni* 766.

In the meantime, Bilam reluctantly opened his mouth and began to speak the words Hashem had placed there. His voice carried much farther than it ever had before, reaching to every remote corner of the world in which members of the seventy nations resided.[52]

The preamble of his speech was a litany against Balak.[53]

"I used to be among the greatest of the great," he declared. "I sat among patriarchs as a prophet destined for a share in the World to Come. But you, Balak, dragged me down to the depths of purgatory.[54] Once I was such a great prophet that I had access to the heavenly Throne, but now, you have caused me to fall from grace and become an ordinary sorcerer, as I once used to be.[55]

"Balak, you are an ungrateful man, and you've caused me to become the same as you. You come from Lot, whom the Jewish patriarch Avraham saved from the conquerors of Sodom. Is this how you repay Avraham's kindness and gallantry, by cursing his descendants? I am descended from Lavan, who had no male offspring before Yaakov arrived in his household. If not for the blessing engendered by Yaakov's dwelling in Lavan's house, I would never have been born. Should I repay my debt to him by cursing his descendants?[56]

"You brought me up to this mountain so that I would see Shittim, the place where the Jewish people will eventually sin. You thought that this would militate against them. But from that same vantage point I could also see Gilgal, where they will accumulate the enormous merit of *milah*.[57]

---

52. *Tanchuma, Balak* 15; Rashi, Tur on *Bamidbar* 23:7; *Bamidbar Rabbah* 20:20. See *Mishlei* 27:14.
53. *Lekach Tov, Yalkut haEizovi* on *Bamidbar* 23:7.
54. *Bamidbar Rabbah* 20:19.
55. Ibid.
56. Ibid.; Rabbeinu Bachya, *Bamidbar* 23:7. See *Tzeror haMor*.
57. *Me'am Lo'ez, Bamidbar* 23:9.

"You told me that the Jewish people are sometimes called the sons of Yaakov and sometimes the sons of Yisrael. You wanted me to know their authentic name so that my curse would be effective. And since I didn't know which name was the authentic one, I resolved to curse them in both names.[58] But what were you thinking? Could I possibly curse Yisrael, whose letters contain Hashem's Name?"[59]

"Very well," said Balak. "Don't curse their name, just curse the nation."

"Curses are not effective against them," replied Bilam. "There were times when it seemed they would be cursed, but the curses never materialized. Yaakov wanted to curse Shimon and Levi, but in the end, he only cursed their rage, not them. When Yaakov impersonated Eisav and took his father Yitzchak's blessings, it seemed he was in danger of being cursed. But Yitzchak blessed him instead.[60] When the Jewish people scandalously worshiped the golden calf, you might have thought that here finally they would be cursed. But did Hashem curse them? Absolutely not. He did the opposite and they survived. They were given the protection of the clouds of glory. They were fed *mahn* from Heaven and water from a miraculous well. So how do you expect me to curse them when Hashem refused to do so?[61]

"And let's talk for a moment about Hashem. My special skill is identifying the precise moment of divine anger.[62] But in all this time that I've been here, there has been no divine anger at

---

58. Rashi, Tur on *Bamidbar* 23:7.

59. *Lekach Tov*, *Bamidbar* 23:8; *Bamidbar Rabbah* 20:20.

60. *Bamidbar Rabbah* 20:19; Rashi, *Bamidbar* 23:8.

61. *Bamidbar Rabbah* 20:19; Rabbeinu Bachya, *Bamidbar* 23:8.

62. Some suggest that in that moment Bilam could squeeze in only one word: *Kaleim*, "Destroy them." Alternatively, Bilam had only to begin his curse in that moment, and then he could continue afterward. See *Avodah Zarah* 4b with Tosafos; *Yeshayahu* 26:20; *Tehillim* 30:6.

all.[63] Without it, I am powerless to do anything against the Jewish people."[64]

"Can't you find anything in their past?" pressed Balak. "Is there nothing that would arouse divine anger against them?"

"I am looking all the way back to their roots and origins," Bilam answered, "and I see that they are as solid as the rocks and the hills, protected by the merit of important events in their history that took place on mountains: the Akeidah and the giving of the Torah, for example.[65] And they are also protected by their patriarchs and matriarchs.[66] How can I curse a people whose patriarch Avraham was promised that those who curse him will be cursed?"[67]

Balak sighed. "I'm sorry to hear that. I was really counting on you to do the job for us. So listen, if you can't curse them directly, why don't you curse a whole group of nations with them included? That would not really be considered cursing them, now would it? It would be kind of a collective curse."[68]

"Good try, Balak, but the answer is no. I can see that they are a nation that dwells alone,[69] apart from other nations,[70] so I can't very well include them in a collective curse. They do not belong to any collectives.[71] Furthermore, I can see that they have their own individual destiny. While other nations are annihilated, they will

---

63. Rashi, *Bamidbar* 23:9. Bilam added that the Jews are beyond the celestial forces, so even when the stars align for Hashem's moment of anger, the Jewish people is impervious to it (*Yalkut Me'or haAfeilah*).

64. See *Sanhedrin* 105b; *Bechor Shor*, *Bamidbar* 23:8.

65. Rabbeinu Bachya, *Bamidbar* 23:9. See also *Menoras haMaor*, *Bamidbar* 23:8.

66. See *Bamidbar Rabbah* 20:19; Rashi, *Targum Yonasan* on *Bamidbar* 23:9.

67. *Pa'aneiach Raza*, *Bamidbar* 23:7.

68. *Me'am Lo'ez*, *Bamidbar* 23:9.

69. See Rashbam, Ramban on *Bamidbar* 23:9–10.

70. Rashi with *Sifsei Chachamim*, *Bamidbar* 23:9.

71. *Midrash haGadol*, ibid. For even if the Jews chose to mingle, they would never be considered a nation among others. The world will never have seventy-one nations, just seventy and the Jews (Alshich).

survive and prevail. The world belongs to them.[72] So how can I curse them? Their roots are indestructible. Their future is assured. They remain one unified nation under Hashem."[73]

Balak threw up his hands in frustration and groaned.

"I'm not finished yet," said Bilam. "Their young are too numerous to count. Why, even one-quarter of their encampment is too numerous to be counted. Hashem promised multitudinous and sanctified offspring to their patriarch Avraham.[74] Although I do not understand why Hashem, as awesome and holy as He is, should concern Himself with the seed of unborn people."

Bilam paused to catch his breath.

"Hey!" he suddenly cried out. "What's happening? My eye! I can't see. I've gone blind! I think my eye fell out, but I'm afraid to touch it to see if I have an empty socket there. What am I going to do now? How can I give the Jewish people the evil eye if I don't even have one? And how am I going to make a living if I can't give people the evil eye on behalf of my clients?"[75]

Bilam had lost his eyesight because "Provoking the Jewish people is like aggravating the pupil in one's eye."[76] Although he'd just suffered a terrible trauma, he couldn't stop himself from talking; he had no control over his mouth at all.

"It is not only their offspring that are multitudinous," he said. "The commandments they fulfill are also exceedingly multitudinous. They've been given so many commandments regarding every aspect of life. Why, their agricultural mandates alone could fill volumes. They have rules for plowing, for mixing seeds, for

---

72. *Targum Unkelos*, Rashi on ibid. See *Yirmeyahu* 30:11.

73. Rabbeinu Bachya, *Bamidbar* 23:9. See *Devarim* 33:29.

74. Rashi with *Gur Aryeh*, *Da'as Zekeinim* on *Bamidbar* 23:10.

75. See *Niddah* 31 with Tosafos, Maharsha; Rashi, *Bamidbar* 24:3. According to *Midrash haGadol* and *Kli Yakar*, Bilam was blinded in one eye for attempting to cast an evil eye on the Jews. Zohar, *Naso* 147, states that he nonetheless attempted to use his one good eye to cast an evil eye upon them.

76. See *Bamidbar Rabbah* 20:6; *Zecharyah* 2:12; *Gittin* 57a with *Iyun Yaakov*.

holy ashes, for earth mixed with water to test a wife for infidelity[77]—and there are even laws of circumcision related to the land![78] These people observe the commandments connected to the earth meticulously. And just as the earth is the fountainhead of life, so are the Jewish people and their mitzvos the fountainhead of the entire world's existence.[79] Is it any wonder that they proliferate and multiply until they are as innumerable as the dust of the earth?[80] How can I curse a nation so populous?"[81]

As Bilam listened to the words emerging from his mouth, he realized that his plot had resulted in utter failure. There was nothing he could do to harm the Jewish people. Perhaps he had aligned himself with the wrong side, he thought. Perhaps it would be wiser to be an ally than an enemy of the Jewish people. He decided to try that avenue.

"May it be the will of the Almighty Blessed One,"[82] he prayed, "that in the merit of not cursing them my soul will expire among the upright and righteous Jewish people such as the patriarchs, Moshe and Aharon.[83] If I die a natural death like those of the righteous, I will know that there is an afterlife for me.[84] But if I am slain, I know that I am destined for Gehinnom."

---

77. *Bamidbar Rabbah* 20:19; Rashi with *Gur Aryeh, Bamidbar* 23:10; Zohar, *Balak* 210b. From the time the Jews plow the earth until they produce bread, they have completed ten mitzvos: two related to plowing and sowing, three related to harvesting (*leket, shichechah,* and *pe'ah*), muzzling an animal during threshing, *terumah*, the two *ma'aser* tithes, and the separation of *challah*. Then, before eating this bread, the Jew washes his hands, whose ten fingers represent these ten mitzvos (*Yalkut Shimoni* 766).

78. Tur, *Bamidbar* 23:10. The foreskin must be buried and covered with earth.

79. *Midrash haBeiur*, ibid.

80. *Gur Aryeh*, ibid.

81. *Ohr haChaim*, ibid.

82. *Imrei Shefer*, ibid.

83. *Bamidbar Rabbah* 20:19; Rashi with *Nachalas Yaakov, Pa'aneiach Raza* on *Bamidbar* 23:10. See *Eliyah Rabbah* 21; *Avodah Zarah* 25a.

84. Seforno, *Bamidbar* 23:10.

Bilam was thus forecasting his own end. He would indeed die by the sword, Eisav's tool, and he would join Eisav and his cohorts in Gehinnom.[85] According to one opinion, Bilam returned in the afterlife as the donkey of Rabbi Pinchas Ben Yair.[86]

Bilam was finally finished. He had spoken for a long time and said many things, and although he had not cursed the Jewish people, it is possible to infer the things he would have liked to say from the things he actually said. He noted that he wanted to do them harm but he couldn't. He said he wanted to bring them down, but he admitted that it was impossible because they were compared to mountains. He wanted to assimilate them among the nations, but he was unable to because they lived apart from others. He wanted to reduce their numbers, but that was not in his power because they were too numerous. He wanted to keep them from an afterlife, but in the end, he sought to join them.[87]

Balak was enraged. "Are you finished?" he said.

"Yes, I'm finished," said Bilam. "I have nothing more to say."

"I should hope not," said Balak. "I hired you to curse the Jews. That's what you were supposed to do. If you couldn't, then at least you should have had the decency to remain silent. Who asked you to bless them? Where do you get the audacity?"

"Audacity? I'll give you audacity. Here I've been talking and talking for who knows how long, and you've pretty much been standing there like a *golem*. And now you decide to complain?"

"I was waiting until you finished," said Balak. "I know what kind of devious devil you are, and I figured you had something

---

85. See *Sanhedrin* 105a with Rashi; *Targum Yonasan, Bamidbar* 23:10. According to one view, Bilam died at age thirty-three or thirty-four (Tur, *Midrash haGadol* on *Bamidbar* 23:10). See *Sanhedrin* 106b. This opinion, of course, precludes the one that Bilam had advised Pharaoh centuries earlier—not to mention the view that Bilam was Lavan. For a reconciliation of all these opinions, see *Ben Yehoyada, Sanhedrin* 106b.

86. *Ohr haChaim, Bamidbar* 23:10.

87. *Midrash haGadol, Bamidbar* 23:8.

up your sleeve. Well, now that you've finished I can see that your sleeve is empty.[88] And one more thing, buddy. When you decided to offer up a prayer for yourself at the end of your state-of-the-union, why didn't you add a little prayer for me?"[89]

"What do you want from me, Balak? You know this isn't what I wanted to do. I would rather have died than stand there blessing the Jews.[90] But what could I do? Hashem took control of my mouth. You knew I was dependent on Him.[91] And what did you think, that He'd let me curse His people?"[92]

The Second Attempt

Balak took a deep, cleansing breath to calm himself down. He walked around for a while until he felt he was thinking clearly once again.

"Very well, Bilam," he said. "I've considered this matter from all sides in light of my understanding of sorcery and my assumptions about the Jews' vulnerabilities.[93] This is what we'll do. Apparently, giving the evil eye to the entire Jewish people isn't feasible, as there are too many of them and they have the merit of the righteous protecting them. So let's concentrate exclusively on the wicked among them. They have disqualified themselves from that ironclad protection, so we can attack them. Once we've done that we'll have penetrated the Jewish defenses, and who knows where we can go from there?"[94]

"Hmm," said Bilam, "not a bad idea."

---

88. *Ohr haChaim*, Malbim on *Bamidbar* 23:11.

89. *Sifsei Kohen*, ibid.

90. See *Ohr haChaim*, *Bamidbar* 23:12; *Bamidbar Rabbah* 20:19.

91. *Ohr haChaim*, Malbim on *Bamidbar* 23:12.

92. Seforno, ibid.

93. See *Sefer Zikaron*, *Mesiach Ilmim* on *Bamidbar* 23:14.

94. See *Midrash haGadol*, *Lekach Tov*, *Tosefos Rav Avigdor*, *Bechor Shor*, *Sifsei Kohen*, Malbim on *Bamidbar* 23:13. Maharam notes that Bilam couldn't see the entire Jewish encampment, for he was already blind in one eye.

"I also think," said Balak, "that we should find a different location.[95] I would like to go to the peak of the lookout mountain where we can scan the horizon for hostiles."[96]

"What's so special about this mountain peak? And how do you know about it?"

"Well, while you were *fumfering* around, I haven't been sleeping. My powers of wizardry[97] have been strained to the limit to come up with some answers. I can sense a breach in the Jewish defenses—a chink in their armor, if you will. I can sense the imminent death of their leader Moshe, who is comparable to the entire nation. I have a feeling that the time is ripe and that we may be able to launch a curse from that mountain peak.[98] But time is of the essence. We must act quickly before the Jewish sinners repent."[99]

"You're a little too quick, Balak. How do you propose to build seven altars on that mountain peak? We absolutely must have the seven altars and the fourteen animal sacrifices. Otherwise, there will be no curses."

"I'm a few steps ahead of you. My construction crews have been up there for a while already, and they're working at double speed. By the time we arrive, everything will be ready for us."[100]

"Not bad, Balak, not bad at all. But you have to keep to the rules. Remember what I told you before: you can't just set up an altar and burn some animals on it. You have to stand there and keep vigil. Did you do that before, my friend? Or did you go away to take care of royal business?[101] We have to work as a team. You

95. Abarbanel, ibid.
96. Rashi, *Bamidbar* 23:14.
97. See *Sefer Zikaron, Mesiach Ilmim* on ibid.
98. See Rashi, ibid.; *Bamidbar Rabbah* 20:19.
99. *Ohr haChaim, Bamidbar* 23:13.
100. *Meshech Chochmah, Bamidbar* 23:15.
101. See *Tzeror haMor, Tosefos Rav Ephraim al haTorah* on ibid.

keep vigil at the altar, and I'll go off to meditate in solitude and prepare the curses for when the opportunity appears."[102]

But Bilam had not learned his lesson. Even as he climbed to a secluded spot and prepared his curses anew, Hashem converted them into blessings.[103] Finally, Bilam realized the utter futility of his enterprise. All he would accomplish if he persisted in his efforts was to cause more frustration and fury to Balak. Clearly, it was time to admit defeat and retreat. Yes, that was the wisest course of action.

Bilam tried to abort the project, but he couldn't stop. He felt himself driven to continue against his will. And slowly, it dawned on him that Hashem had taken control of him completely. Hashem had ordained that he would utter certain words to Balak about the Jewish people, and there was no escaping it.[104]

Disheartened, Bilam returned to the altar where he had left Balak and his officers. He found Balak standing there virtually alone. The officers had lost faith in Bilam's abilities, and many had already left.[105]

"So how did it go, puppet mouth?" asked Balak. "Is Hashem still pulling all your strings, or have you regained some control over your speech?"[106]

Bilam bristled at the king's mocking words. "Your desperation is causing you to speak like a fool. You can snicker at me all you want, but when Hashem speaks, everyone listens.[107] And I have come down to deliver His latest message. Why are you reclining there on your throne? Show some respect. Stand up and listen!"[108]

---

102. See *Tzeror haMor*, *Minchah Belulah* on ibid.
103. *Midrash haGadol*, *Bamidbar* 23:16.
104. See Rashi, ibid.; *Bamidbar Rabbah* 20:20.
105. Rashi, *Bamidbar* 23:17; *Bamidbar Rabbah* 20:20.
106. See *Bamidbar* 23:17; *Bamidbar Rabbah* 20:20.
107. Abarbanel, *Bamidbar* 23:19.
108. See Rashi, *Midrash haGadol* on *Bamidbar* 23:18; *Bamidbar Rabbah* 20:20.

Taken aback by Bilam's words, Balak rose to his feet and stood silently as Bilam began to utter his parable.

"Listen closely, Balak," he said. "Hashem has decreed that I bless the Jewish people. He has already caused me to bless them before, and He wants me to bless them again. To curse them is out of the question. And it's preposterous to think He will reconsider.[109]

"Hashem is not a human being who can be duplicitous and fickle, changing his mind from one moment to the next.[110] He is not constrained by limitations and dependent on unforeseen events.[111] If He retracts His words, it is not because the situation has changed on Him unexpectedly. It is deliberate and with forethought.[112]

"Hashem's word is not only true, it is solid as a rock and effective from the first moment it is expressed. If He says that the Jewish people shall be blessed, they are already effectively blessed from that very moment. There is no turning back. So understand, Balak, Hashem has blessed them and they can no longer be cursed."[113]

According to some opinions, Bilam was saying, at Hashem's command, that there is a vast chasm between the human and the divine, and any human being who makes claims to divinity is an impostor.[114]

"I can see on your face," Bilam continued, "that you are thinking about evil decrees that Hashem made and retracted on other occasions in history. When Hashem decreed destruction against the Jewish people for the golden calf, for example, He retracted the decree when they repented. There is no comparison. An evil

109. See Rav Saadiah Gaon, Rabbeinu Bachya, Abarbanel on *Bamidbar* 23:20.

110. *Targum Unkelos*, Rashi, *Ohr haChaim* on *Bamidbar* 23:19.

111. See *Bechor Shor*, *Aderes Eliyahu*, Malbim on *Bamidbar* 23:19–20.

112. *Bechor Shor*, *Bamidbar* 23:19.

113. Malbim, *Bamidbar* 23:19–20.

114. See Rabbeinu Bachya, *Bamidbar* 23:19; *Yalkut Shimoni* 766 with footnotes; *Yalkut Midreshei Teiman*; *Midrash Yelamdeinu*. See also *Yerushalmi Ta'anis* 2:1. This is a prophetic denunciation of Christianity.

decree is not immediately executed, and it is issued upon condition that the people do not repent. Only decrees against the seventy nations are never reversed. Moreover, a divine blessing takes effect immediately and cannot be reversed.[115]

"After Hashem has said the Jews would become a sovereign nation, is it possible for me to curse them?[116] After He has sworn to them that they will enter and vanquish the lands of the seven nations, is it possible that they will perish in the wilderness? Would He reconsider the oath He made? Would He not act in accordance with what He said? Would He fail to keep His word?[117] After He promised this land to the Jewish people as an unconditional gift, after He gave it to them even if they would not keep His Torah, would He take back His gift?[118]

"Having heard everything I've just said, do you then expect Hashem to listen to you and withdraw His protection over the Jewish people? Only a frail, fickle and disloyal human being would exchange old friends for new ones. Hashem is Divine. He is not a human being, and He will be forever loyal to the Jewish people and faithful to the oaths He made to the patriarchs."[119]

"Why don't you speak about their sins?" said Balak. "Maybe that will induce Hashem to view them in a new light."

"What sins?" said Bilam. "There's no point in talking about sins that were committed before the blessings I've said, and they haven't sinned since."[120]

---

115. *Bamidbar Rabbah* 20:20; *Midrash haGadol*, Malbim on *Bamidbar* 23:19; *Tanchuma, Vayeira* 13. See Rambam, *Yesodei haTorah* 10:4. Bilam sarcastically questions: If Hashem won't undo his dislodged hip and broken leg, how can he expect Him to undo the blessings He's given the Jews? (*Sifsei Kohen, Bamidbar* 23:20).

116. *Ohr haChaim, Bamidbar* 23:19.

117. Rashi, Rav Saadiah Gaon on ibid. See *Tehillim* 62:10.

118. See *Tanchuma, Vayeira* 13; *Lekach Tov, Shemos* 32:13. See also *Tehillim* 105:44.

119. *Bamidbar Rabbah* 20:20. See *Tanchuma, Vayeira* 13.

120. *Chizkuni*, Rashbam, *Hadar Zekeinim, Ha'amek Davar* on *Bamidbar* 23:20; Ibn Ezra, *Bamidbar* 23:21.

"Why can't you mention their past sins to show their innate wickedness?"

"Because Hashem doesn't see iniquity or deceit within the Jewish nation. There are no duplicitous idolaters among them, and therefore, Hashem is always with them.[121] Even when they seem to have sinned, Hashem doesn't see their missteps as iniquity. And if it should happen that they disobey Him, He does not conduct a painstaking scrutiny of their transgressions.[122] He prefers to look at the positive side and focus on the commandments they do fulfill.[123] And if their sins are so blatant that they cannot be ignored, He doesn't rush to punish them. Instead, He waits patiently for them to repent.[124] His conduct with them depends on the degree to which they observe or violate His commandments. Right now, it seems, they are altogether free of sin, because He is lavishing blessings on them."[125]

"But the Jewish people have committed some very serious sins," insisted Balak. "Are you telling me that all those can be swept under the rug?"

"Not quite," replied Bilam. "Most of those incidents were instigated by the Eirev Rav, the 'mixed multitude' that emerged from Egypt with them. Just take a look down at the Jewish encampment, and you will see that distinction manifested before your very eyes. The Jewish people enjoy the protection of the clouds of glory, while the Eirev Rav is relegated to the exposed periphery."[126]

"Maybe the Eirev Rav were instigators," said Balak, "but the rest of the people allowed themselves to be drawn in. That means they aren't innocent."

---

121. *Targum Unkelos*, Rav Saadiah Gaon, Rashi on *Bamidbar* 23:21.
122. Rashi, ibid.
123. *Bamidbar Rabbah* 20:20; *Yalkut Shimoni* 768.
124. Rashbam, *Bamidbar* 23:21. See *Iyov* 11:11 with Rashi. See also *Mesillas Yesharim* 4.
125. Rabbeinu Bachya, *Bechor Shor* on *Bamidbar* 23:21.
126. *Sifsei Kohen*, ibid. See *Kli Yakar*.

"Point well taken, Balak. But you have to understand that Hashem uses special attributes to conduct His relationship with the Jewish people. Even when they rebel against Him and arouse His anger, He is not quick to abandon them. Why? Because He is not only their King,[127] but also their loving Father. So can I curse them? Would a father let me curse his children?"[128]

"I'm disappointed in you, Bilam. Can't you find any chink in Hashem's protection? Can't you find any point of vulnerability?"

"Think about this, Balak. Imagine an orchard with a security guard day and night. The only way robbers can get in is if the security guard falls asleep. But Hashem never sleeps. He always watches over the Jewish people. Their protection is thus impregnable."[129]

"I think a lot of this has to do with Moshe, their leader. He is an exceedingly great man. Perhaps when Moshe is gone—and according to my prognostications, it won't be long now—we'll have a better chance against his successor."

"That's real wishful thinking, Balak. Moshe's successor will be Yehoshua, who is also great. Even if he's not a 'sun' like Moshe, he's at least a 'moon.' In fact, in some ways, he will be more powerful than Moshe. I foresee that he will sound a blast on the shofar and the walls of Yericho will come tumbling down."[130]

"That's depressing."

"But what's the point of talking about Moshe and Yehoshua?" said Bilam. "The Jews aren't just 'a people that has come out of Egypt,' as you wrote me in your message. They didn't just come out by themselves, you know. Hashem, the Almighty Master of

---

127. The word *kaleim*, "destroy them," has the same letters as *melech*, king. Hashem thus turned Bilam's curse into a blessed affirmation of His Kingship. See *Devarim* 23:6; Tosafos, *Avodah Zarah* 4b.

128. Rashi, *Bamidbar* 23:21.

129. *Bamidbar Rabbah* 20:20.

130. Ibid.

the universe, took them out.[131] And His strength is immeasurable, greater than any power on earth.[132] Believe me, I used all my occult powers to prevent them from leaving Egypt, but it was futile. Nothing can stand in His way."[133]

"But what is His motivation?" asked Balak. "What's so special about the Jewish people that they should deserve such divine protection and support? Why does He perform so many miracles for them?"[134]

"Because He loves them.[135] Because they are a pure people, free of divination or sorcery, and that makes them worthy of His blessing. They trust in Him and Him alone. They do not seek out mediums.[136] They need no diviner or sorcerer to peek into the future. When they need to know their prospects in war, they ask Hashem for guidance and direction through their prophets or the *choshen mishpat*, the priestly breastplate. While we use sorcery to assist us in war, their repentance overwhelms our occult powers and brings them victory.[137]

"Someday, the entire world will see Hashem's manifest love for the Jewish people. In fulfillment of the verse, 'And your eyes shall see your Teacher,' they will sit before Him, more exalted than the ministering angels, and learn Torah directly from His mouth. And the angels will ask them, 'What new Torah insight were you taught today?' And all because they don't divine and practice the occult."[138]

"All right, Bilam. I concede defeat. Cursing them is not feasible.

---

131. Rashi with Mizrachi, *Bamidbar* 23:22; *Bamidbar Rabbah* 20:20.

132. *Chizkuni*, Ramban, Rabbeinu Bachya on *Bamidbar* 23:22.

133. Zohar, *Balak* 212a; *Yalkut Reuveni*, *Bamidbar* 23:22. According to *Sanhedrin* 105a, Bilam performed acts of sorcery with his anatomy. See *Ben Yehoyada*.

134. Seforno, *Bamidbar* 23:23.

135. Rashbam, ibid.

136. Ibn Ezra, ibid. See Rambam, *Avodas Kochavim* 11:16.

137. Rashi, Rashbam on *Bamidbar* 23:23; *Bamidbar Rabbah* 20:20.

138. Rashi, *Bamidbar* 23:23; *Bamidbar Rabbah* 20:20. See *Yeshayahu* 30:20; *Nedarim* 32a.

But what if we use just plain sorcery against them?"

"Balak, I admire your persistence, but it's useless. They have with them a movable temple in which they perform the holy service. Hashem dwells among them in this temple and protects them. So you see, their holy service deflects His anger and prevents any sorcery or incantations from infiltrating among them.[139] They are also immune to the control of the celestial powers, so that avenue is also closed to us. It's a lost cause, my friend."[140]

"Think hard, Bilam. Isn't there *anything* we can do? Isn't there any part of the day in which they are more vulnerable?"

Bilam shook his head. "I'm afraid not. They awaken in the morning like eager lion cubs, and rush with the might of lions to serve Hashem by fulfilling His commandments that pertain to the morning. They put on *tallis* and *tefillin* and say *Shema*, proclaiming Hashem's unbounded sovereignty, and for this, measure for measure, Hashem grants them protection as if they were guarded by lions throughout the day.[141] The entire day—morning, afternoon and evening—they surround themselves with prayer and Torah."[142]

"What about at night?"

"I'm afraid not. At night, they don't retire until they ward off any potentially harmful forces by saying *Shema* again and entrusting their souls for safekeeping in the hands of Hashem. If an army should try to attack them, Hashem stands guard over them and fights their battles until their enemies are destroyed.[143]

"And Hashem stands beside them not only to defend them but also to assist them when they go on the offensive. He causes

---

139. Zohar, *Bechukosai* 112b.

140. Ramban, *Bamidbar* 23:23. See Malbim.

141. Rashi, *Bamidbar* 23:24; *Bamidbar Rabbah* 20:20; Zohar, *Balak* 211a.

142. Zohar, *Balak* 211a.

143. Rashi, *Aderes Eliyahu* on *Bamidbar* 23:24; *Bamidbar Rabbah* 20:20. See *Tehillim* 130:6; Zohar, *Balak* 211a.

them to rise up like awesome lions, and He leads the fight tirelessly until they conquer the land of their enemies.[144] They fought like lions against Amalek, and they will do so again against the Canaanites. They didn't rest in their war against Sichon, and they will practically drink the blood of their fallen Midianite foes."[145]

"Midianites? What's this about Midianites?"

"The Midianites will feel the edge of the Jewish blade. And fairly soon. As you said, Moshe will not live much longer, but before he dies, he will slay the five kings of Midian and yes, I will perish too on that day.[146] But not one Jew will die. Is that normal? Did you ever hear of a war in which the victor does not suffer a single casualty? So how are we supposed to oppose them?[147]

"These people do not mingle with us. They have no truck with demons, angels or the occult. They seek only Hashem. They wake up uttering His Name, and they go to sleep uttering His Name. I cannot penetrate such a defense.[148] It's no use, Balak. We can't stop them or even bring them down a notch or two. Like the lion, the king of all beasts, they just keep getting stronger and stronger."[149]

Bilam's fervent dream was to induce Hashem to break His covenant with the patriarchs, to withdraw His blessings and His Divine Presence from the Jewish people, to abort the future Jewish kingdom, to prevent future miracles like those that led to the Egyptian exodus, to sap the Jews' strength, to deflate the Jews' flourishing economies, to return the Jews to the control of the celestial powers and to deprive them of prophets and the Beis

---

144. *Targum Unkelos, Bamidbar* 23:24. See Zohar, *Balak* 211a.
145. *Aderes Eliyahu, Bamidbar* 23:24.
146. Rashi, ibid.; *Bamidbar Rabbah* 20:20.
147. See Ibn Ezra, Rabbeinu Bachya on *Bamidbar* 23:24.
148. *Midrash Aggadah, Bamidbar* 23:22. See *Shemos Rabbah* 15:7.
149. *Bechor Shor, Bamidbar* 23:24.

haMikdash. On every front, he failed miserably.[150]

Balak finally realized that he would get nowhere with Bilam, and he was furious.[151] "Enough already!" he cried out. "Stop with the blessings.[152] If you want to bless anyone, bless me![153] Don't tell me you intend to curse the Jewish people eventually. It seems that the more you try to curse them, the more you bless them. Just do nothing. Don't try to curse them, and don't bless them."[154]

"The blessings are not connected to my intention to curse them.[155] It's not me talking to you at all. Does it sound like me? Don't even bother to answer. Of course not. Hashem is in complete control of my mouth."[156]

Final Attempt

"Let's give it one last try," said Balak.[157] "Maybe we were doing something wrong. If we review everything we've done before we try again, perhaps we'll find our mistake as well as the solution. So let's go for a third time. If we fail, we'll know we're done.[158] Are you willing?"

"Sure. Why not give it a shot?"

"Okay; let's review every step. Could the problem be in your preparation?"

"No, I prepared properly."[159]

---

150. *Midrash haGadol, Bamidbar* 23:19.

151. See *Lekach Tov, Bamidbar* 23:27.

152. *Lekach Tov, Bamidbar* 23:25.

153. Alshich, ibid.

154. See Rashi with *Sifsei Chachamim*, ibid.

155. *Ohr haChaim, Bamidbar* 23:25–26.

156. See *Tzeror haMor, Lekach Tov*, Malbim on *Bamidbar* 23:26.

157. See *Lekach Tov, Bamidbar* 23:27. "The wicked man shall see [his failures] and grind his teeth in anger...; the desire of the wicked shall perish" (*Tehillim* 112:10). Despite repeatedly failing to curse the Jews, wicked Bilam kept trying, only to be disappointed again and again.

158. Abarbanel, *Bamidbar* 23:28.

159. *Ha'amek Davar, Bamidbar* 23:25–26.

"Perhaps the vantage points we've chosen show us too many merits of the righteous. Should we find a place that shows us mostly wicked Jews? Maybe then the curses will penetrate the Jewish encampment. I believe I've mentioned such an idea before, but let's try it again.[160] Perhaps we'll stir a divine memory that will arouse hatred toward the Jewish people."[161]

"We've tried this already. What exactly do you have in mind?"

"Well, for starters, let's find a place from where we can save Midian. Maybe this will help us defeat the Jewish people, just as Amalek and Canaan defeated them not too long ago after Aharon's death."[162]

"Go on."

"Look, it seems clear we can't activate a conventional curse. Nothing we do will change Hashem's attitude toward them. But rather than curse them outright, let's go to a place from which we can see destruction and desolation, a place where Hashem Himself will cause the Jewish people to fall. Maybe He will allow our curses to take effect in that place."

"Really? Is there such a place? Can you see it?"

"Yes, there is such a place. The vision I'm receiving is murky, but I see that the Jewish people will be smitten. Let's go to the peak of Mount Pe'or overlooking the wasteland in which they are currently encamped. From there we may get Hashem to approve a curse."[163]

"Weren't we there already?"

"No, this is a different place with a different vantage point. I just have a feeling that we may be on to something. I sense a

160. *Ohr haChaim, Bamidbar* 23:27.

161. *Tosefos Rav Ephraim al haTorah, Bamidbar* 23:28.

162. Ramban, *Bamidbar* 23:27.

163. See Rashi, *Midrash haGadol, Ha'amek Davar,* Malbim on *Bamidbar* 23:26–28. Thus far, Balak and Bilam had followed their own will. Now they were looking to suit Hashem's—despite His reiteration that He loves the Jews too much to will their downfall.

connection to the golden calf. Perhaps there is also something else that will arouse the divine wrath."[164]

"It's worth a try," said Bilam.

"Fine," said Balak, "let's go. Right this minute."

"Not so fast, my friend. Aren't you forgetting something?"

"What?"

"The altars, Balak. Send your construction crews to erect the altars. Don't get lazy on me now. Just because they haven't worked yet doesn't mean they aren't important."

"All right," Balak grumbled. "I'll take care of it."

"Good. You concentrate on building the altars; I'll take care of the rest. It might just be that your negativity is interfering with my thoughts. As long as you focus on constructing the altars, I may just be able to get something through the protective shields. And one more thing. This time I'm going to stay with you at the altars, and I will bring the offerings myself. We'll make one last try."[165]

Presently, Bilam found himself standing deep in thought next to the altars on which the offerings were smoldering.[166] He decided to discard for the meantime his tools of sorcery, because they were obviously useless against the Jewish people.[167] Nor would he ask Hashem to curse them. Instead, he would just recall their sins and hope that a curse would automatically devolve on them.[168]

He cast his eye toward the place in the wilderness where the

---

164. See *Midrash haGadol, Midrash Aggadah, Yalkut Pisron Torah* on *Bamidbar* 23:28. Balak was alluding to their future worship of Pe'or.

165. See Tur, ibid.; Ramban, *Bamidbar* 23:1, 27. According to *Tosefos Rav Ephraim al haTorah*, Bilam thought it propitious that the one king of Moav would sacrifice to the one God of the Jews. Compare *Ha'amek Davar*. This view may disagree with the one cited earlier that Balak himself brought forty-two offerings and earned merit thereby.

166. Abarbanel, *Bamidbar* 24:1.

167. Ibn Ezra, *Bamidbar* 23:28; *Chizkuni*, Ramban on *Bamidbar* 24:1; Zohar, *Balak* 211b.

168. *Targum Unkelos*, Rashi, Seforno on *Bamidbar* 24:1.

sin of the Eigel, the golden calf, took place. Nothing happened, however, because Hashem had forgiven the Jewish people. Moreover, in that same place in the wilderness, the Jews had accepted the Torah, which meant that the recollection of their merit in that place far outweighed the recollection of their sin.[169]

As a last resort, Bilam tried again to affix an evil eye to the Jewish people. If not a curse, he reasoned, then at least an evil eye. But what he saw next thwarted his efforts.[170]

Hashem led him to see that the tribes were separated from each other in districts identified by distinctive banners mirroring the arrangement of the angels in Heaven. The nations of the world would praise the Jewish people for the honor and distinction given to each individual part of the national whole.[171] Hashem also led Bilam to observe that the doors of the Jewish family tents did not face each other, insuring privacy and modesty among the people.[172] This combination of tribal identity and family integrity threw Bilam into a jealous rage and spurred on his efforts to cast an evil eye on the Jews, but these Jewish virtues prevented it from penetrating. Hashem's spirit rested on each tribe, blocking Bilam's evil designs and adding to his rage and frustration.[173]

"They are breaking my bones!" Bilam cried out. "These holy abodes, this Torah study and the Divine Presence hovering above them is just too much. I'm stymied at every turn. My evil eye is blinded. I'm helpless!"[174]

---

169. *Lekach Tov, Midrash haGadol* on ibid.

170. Rashi, *Bamidbar* 24:2; Zohar, *Balak* 211b.

171. *Bamidbar Rabbah* 2:4.

172. See *Bava Basra* 60a; Rashi, Ibn Ezra, *Sifsei Kohen* on *Bamidbar* 24:2.

173. See *Minchah Belulah, Ohr haChaim* on ibid.; *Bamidbar Rabbah* 2:4; Zohar, *Noach* 68b, *Balak* 211b. Bilam realized that the Shechinah resides amid modesty, so he couldn't inflict an evil eye on the Jewish people (*Be'er baSadeh; Sha'arei Aharon*).

174. See *Eliyah Rabbah* 21.

Bilam's Third Blessing

Bilam finally accepted defeat and capitulated.[175] He decided to fulfill the will of Hashem of his own volition and bless the Jewish people outright, bestowing on them the blessing that Hashem had converted from his earlier curses.[176] He was still far from a repentant, reformed and righteous person, but as a reward for these few moments of genuine goodwill toward the Jewish people, Hashem rested His spirit upon him as a sign of approval and affection.[177]

Bilam began his parable, "This is the word of Bilam son of Be'or, the word of the man compared to a rooster with an open eye."[178]

Bilam's words confirmed that he had the use of only one eye. Either his attempts at giving the evil eye or his disrespectful comments toward Hashem resulted in his (half-) blindness.[179] He also compared himself to a rooster. Like a rooster, he kept close track of the hours of the day. Like a rooster, he was promiscuous. And like a rooster, he stood on one leg, his other leg being lame.[180]

In contrast to his earlier prophecies, Bilam now enjoyed greatly enhanced clarity of vision, because the spirit of Hashem rested on him.[181] Intoxicated by his new-found prophetic abilities, Bilam

---

175. *Minchah Belulah, Bamidbar* 24:3.

176. See Rashbam, *Chizkuni, Minchah Belulah, Ohr haChaim* on ibid.; Zohar, *Balak* 211b.

177. See Rashi with Mizrachi, Ramban, Rashbam, *Chizkuni* on *Bamidbar* 24:2–3. Bilam's blessings were tinged with curses, but Hashem transformed them into complete blessings. In fact, one way to cast an evil eye is to start with praise, as Bilam did. See Seforno, *Bamidbar* 24:1; Rashi with *Maskil l'David, Sha'arei Aharon* on *Bamidbar* 24:6; *Minchah Belulah*. See *Sanhedrin* 105b; *Ta'anis* 20a; Zohar, *Balak* 211b.

178. *Bamidbar* 24:3.

179. See Rashi, *Midrash haGadol, Kli Yakar* on ibid. Alternatively, Bilam's jealousy led to his being blind in one eye (*Bamidbar Rabbah* 2:4).

180. See Rabbeinu Bachya, Rokeach, Tur on *Bamidbar* 24:3.

181. Abarbanel, *Sifsei Kohen* on *Bamidbar* 24:2, 4.

became conceited and began singing his own praises.[182]

"It is the word of the one who hears Hashem's sayings," he continued, "who sees the vision of the Almighty descending amidst mystical insight."[183]

Bilam prided himself on his outstanding ability to withstand the voice of Hashem, a sound that could move mountains and shatter rocks.[184] Yet it was totally inappropriate for the uncircumcised Bilam to stand upright while receiving a prophetic vision from Hashem. Unlike Moshe or Avraham, who after their *bris milah* were able to receive prophecy standing up, Bilam had always fallen to the ground or, according to another opinion, had always been lying in his bed at night when receiving a vision.[185]

"How good are your tents, Yaakov," Bilam began blessing the Jews, "that their entrances are not aligned with one another.[186] Your modesty began upon your entrance into Egypt and continued out here in the wilderness.[187] Your houses of study and your temples of prayer are beneficial not only to you but to the other nations as well.[188] Your Tabernacle and future Beis haMikdash,[189] in which offerings are brought, provide atonement for you. Even when destroyed, they will serve as your protection, for Hashem will vent His anger on the wood and stones of these dwelling places rather than on the people.[190]

"You and your encampments, Yisrael, are spread out like

---

182. *Midrash haGadol, Sifsei Kohen* on *Bamidbar* 24:2.

183. *Bamidbar* 24:4. *Aderes Eliyahu* states that Bilam heard the conversations between the angels and saw what they saw.

184. *Tosefos Rav Ephraim al haTorah,* ibid. The power of Hashem's voice was evident during the giving of the Torah.

185. Rashi, ibid. See Rashi, *Bereishis* 17:3.

186. Rashi, *Bamidbar* 24:5.

187. *Yalkut Shimoni* 770.

188. Seforno, *Bamidbar* 24:5. See *Sukkah* 55b.

189. All goodness begins with the benefits of the Beis haMikdash (*Tzeror haMor*).

190. Rashi, *Tzeror haMor* on *Bamidbar* 24:5. See *Eichah* 4:11.

streams of running water and like gardens beside a river. Your scholars will nourish others with your rich Torah harvest.[191] You will get stronger and stronger; you will grow in Torah.[192]

"Like streams of running water that flow ceaselessly summer and winter, the Jewish people will endure forever.[193] Like the heavens stretched out like a tent, so is the Jewish encampment; it will endure forever.[194] After you capture the Promised Land, it will yield the best that a garden beside a river can offer.[195] Like the fragrant aloes Hashem planted in Gan Eden, the sweet scent of your existence will never cease.[196]

"Hashem has implanted in you the beauty and stature of a cedar and the best progeny like the fruit of a date palm.[197] As a cedar continues to grow, so will your progeny,[198] and you will be exalted above other nations.[199]

"Water shall flow from your wells;[200] in other words, your future kings, who are anointed near bodies of water,[201] will flourish. Your royal dynasties will continue to rule over many nations.[202] They will succeed and triumph over nations like a seed planted next to water.[203] You will blossom and proliferate continuously,[204]

---

191. Seforno, *Bamidbar* 24:6.
192. *Targum Yonasan*, ibid.
193. *Yalkut Shimoni* 770.
194. See Rashi with *Sha'arei Aharon*, *Bamidbar* 24:6.
195. Ramban, ibid.
196. Rashi, ibid.
197. See *Akeidas Yitzchak*, ibid. See also *Tehillim* 92:13.
198. *Bechor Shor*, Bamidbar 24:6.
199. *Targum Yonasan*, ibid.
200. Rashi, *Bamidbar* 24:7.
201. Tur, ibid.
202. *Targum Unkelos*, ibid.
203. Rashi, ibid.
204. Ibn Ezra, ibid.

even during times of crisis and exile.[205] From the poor among you who have no water, Torah will flow like water.[206] You will produce great scholars and prophets.[207]

"Your first king will be exalted by his might through his conquest of Agag,[208] the Amalekite king. And in the End of Days, your royal dynasty will eradicate Amalek once and for all.[209]

"Who caused your greatness? It was Hashem, Who brought you forth from Egypt. With His power and majesty, He will consume the enemy nations.[210] He will delight in the spoils of their kingdoms.[211] He will devour your enemies and divide the inheritance and spoils that come into your possession.[212] And as He brought you forth from Egypt, He will eventually bring you forth from exile in the End of Days.[213] Hashem's arrows will dip into the blood of His enemies like a foot soaked in the blood of a slain enemy.[214] He shall smash the bones of His enemies and divide up their land.[215]

"You will settle in your land led by Moshe and Yehoshua with the strength and might of lions.[216] You will knock your enemies to the ground like a lion pounces on its prey, and no one will be able to remove you from your territory. So I ask: Who can stand

---

205. *Tzeror haMor*, ibid.

206. See Rabbeinu Bachya, ibid.; *Nedarim* 81a with Maharsha.

207. *Midrash Aggadah, Bamidbar* 24:7.

208. Just as Pharaoh is a generic name for a king of Egypt, Agag refers to any king of Amalek (Ramban).

209. Rashi, Ramban, Rashbam on ibid. See also *Ohr haChaim*. The Mashiach's first order of business will be to eradicate Amalek.

210. *Targum Unkelos*, Rashi on *Bamidbar* 24:8.

211. *Targum Unkelos, Gur Aryeh* on ibid.

212. *Targum Unkelos, Sefer Zikaron, Lekach Tov* on ibid.

213. Tur, ibid.

214. Rashi, ibid.

215. Rashi, Rabbeinu Meyuchas on ibid.

216. *Targum Unkelos*, Rashi on *Bamidbar* 24:9.

up to such a nation?[217] And what exactly is the use of standing up against you? Those who bless you are blessed, and those who curse you are cursed."

Bilam paused. "Well, that's a very good point," he thought to himself. "Why would I be foolish enough to try and curse the Jews?[218] Those who bless will be blessed like Moshe and those who curse will be cursed like me."[219]

Bilam really desired to curse the Jewish people, but Hashem changed his wording so that he ended up uttering blessings. He wanted to remove the Jewish people's houses of study and prayer, but Hashem made him say, "How good are your tents, Yaakov."[220] He sought to prevent Hashem's Presence from dwelling among them, but was forced to say, "Your encampments, Yisrael."[221] He wanted to curse them that their kingdom should not endure, but instead was made to bless, "Like streams of running water."[222]

Bilam wanted the Jews to be deprived of olive orchards and vineyards, but had to utter, "Like gardens beside a river." He wanted their "pleasant fragrance"—i.e., their reputation for doing mitzvos—not to carry far, but he ended up saying, "Like the [fragrant] aloes Hashem planted."

---

217. *Midrash Aggadah*, ibid. Confident and secure as a lion, the Jews will leave their possessions behind to go up to Eretz Yisrael during the three festivals (*Bechor Shor*).

218. *Chizkuni*, ibid. Bilam hoped the blessing would include him and the curse would exclude him (*Ohr haChaim*).

219. *Targum Yonasan*, ibid. Although Bilam ultimately blessed the Jews, the nations of the world are judged by their intentions, and his were to curse the Jews. His blessings were forced, so he received no credit for them (*Sha'arei Aharon*).

220. Cf. *Bereishis* 25:27; *Sanhedrin* 105b with Maharsha.

221. The word *mishkenosecha*, "your encampments," alludes to the word "Shechinah." See Maharsha, *Sanhedrin* 105b, for a different explanation.

222. Bilam sought to liken the Jews to bodies of water that cease to flow at times. Yet Hashem had him refer to ceaseless streams (*Yalkut Shimoni* 770). See Rashi, *Sanhedrin* 106a.

Bilam wanted to curse the Jewish people that their kings would be weak and puny, but Hashem placed in his mouth the words, "Like [mighty] cedars by the water." He did not want them to have royal dynasties, but instead had to say, "Water shall flow from [their] wells."[223]

Bilam didn't want the Jewish kingdom to dominate other nations, but Hashem forced him to say, "Their seed will be [planted] by much water."[224] He wanted to declare that their kingdom should not be strong, but was made to say, "Their king will triumph over Agag." Finally, Bilam sought to curse the Jewish kingdom that it should not instill fear in others, but instead blessed, "And their kingdom will be exalted."[225]

Tragically, these backhanded blessings would be transformed into curses in the future when the Jewish people would transgress. But the implicit wish that the Jewish people would be deprived of their houses of study and prayer would never materialize. In all times and places, the Jews would continue to have these anchors in their lives, allowing them to survive and endure.[226]

Hashem had had enough of Bilam's blessings. Originally, he was meant to bless the Jews seven times, but Hashem stopped him after the third time. And because the Jewish people were given many "blessings" from a mean-spirited man with an evil eye, Hashem therefore instructed Moshe, the man with the ultimate good eye and goodwill toward the Jewish people, to bless them at the end of his life.[227]

---

223. Representing the flow of leadership from father to son.

224. See *Bamidbar Rabbah* 2:16, which explains that "much water" refers to the nations of the world (based on *Yeshayahu* 17:12).

225. *Sanhedrin* 105b with Rashi, Maharsha; Rashi, *Bamidbar* 24:6.

226. *Sanhedrin* 105a; *Me'am Lo'ez, Sifsei Kohen* on *Bamidbar* 24:5. For the Jews, a lack of places of prayer and study is the ultimate curse, rendering the nation most vulnerable (*Sifsei Kohen*).

227. See *Tanchuma, Vezos haBerachah* 1.

Go Home!

As Bilam's lengthy blessing finally came to an end, Balak was beside himself with fury. He banged his hands together in frustration,[228] gnawed his skin and banged at his legs[229] in despair and disgust.[230] "You have to calm down," he told himself. "Calm down right now."[231]

"I wanted curses!" he shouted at Bilam. "Curses, not blessings. Three times you've blessed these people. Is that why I brought you here? Why did you even bother coming? [232] It's over, finished. I give up.[233] You are useless. Once you declare that those who curse these Jews will be cursed, what is there left to do?[234] What's more, not only did you bless the Jewish people, you cursed Moav when you said the Jewish people will consume their enemies.[235] About whom were you talking if not us, you fool?[236] I brought you here with honor and fanfare, and now you must leave in shame and disgrace. Just go, get out."[237]

"Wait a minute, Balak, what about my fee? What about all the honors you promised me?"[238]

"Don't talk drivel. For what should I pay you? Why should I honor you further? Because you came to bless my enemies and curse me? I don't pay appearance fees.[239] I'm not interested in your excuses about Hashem not letting you do this and forcing you to do that."

---

228. See Rashi, *Bamidbar* 24:10.
229. *Midrash haGadol*, ibid.
230. *Targum Yonasan*, Rav Saadiah Gaon on ibid.
231. *Ohr haChaim*, Radak on ibid.
232. Abarbanel, ibid.
233. *Chizkuni*, Seforno, Ramban on ibid.
234. *Midrash Aggadah*, *Bamidbar* 24:9.
235. Alshich, Ramban on *Bamidbar* 24:10–11.
236. See Ramban, *Bamidbar* 24:11.
237. See Abarbanel, ibid.
238. See *Bechor Shor*, ibid.
239. Abarbanel, ibid.

"But it's true! What could I do?"

"Well, Hashem is not letting me pay you, Bilam.[240] And wait! I hear Him talking to me again. I think He's saying I should cut off your head and hand it to you. If you leave right away,[241] I'll cover my ears before He tells me what to do with you. Run as fast as your gimpy leg will carry you.[242] Stop nowhere, and go straight home[243] before my angry Moabite officers come after you."[244]

Bilam was not intimidated. "Look, Balak," he said with a smug look on his face, "let's compromise. Keep your honors. I don't want them anyway. Just give me the money you promised me just for showing up.[245] A deal's a deal. I told you from the beginning that all the money in the world couldn't get me to violate Hashem's will.[246] You knew I could say only what He allowed me to say. That was the agreement, so now you have to pay up."[247]

Bilam's Advice

"Balak, you will not frighten me into fleeing," Bilam continued. "I will leave when I want to leave with my money and my dignity intact. Then I will return to my people, who will honor me as I deserve to be honored.[248] I am not afraid of your silly officers. Don't forget that I am a master sorcerer. If they come after me, I

---

240. Ibid.

241. Rabbeinu Bachya, *Bamidbar* 24:11.

242. *Ohr haChaim*, ibid.

243. Ibid.

244. *Midreshei haTorah*, Alshich, Abarbanel on *Bamidbar* 24:11.

245. *Tzeror haMor*, *Bamidbar* 24:14.

246. Seforno, *Bamidbar* 24:12.

247. See Abarbanel, *Akeidas Yitzchak*, *Ohr haChaim* on *Bamidbar* 24:12–13.

248. Abarbanel, *Tzeror haMor* on *Bamidbar* 24:14. Bilam unknowingly prophecied that he would return to his people and share in their downfall (*Midrash Aggadah*; Rokeach).

will turn them all into field mice. If anyone is in danger, it is you, not me.[249] Balak, our contract is over, right?"

Balak sneered. "Right."

"So now Hashem has returned to me control of my mouth, and I'm free to speak my mind.[250] So let me offer a bit of unsolicited[251] but nevertheless valuable advice before I go.

"Don't worry so much about the Jewish people consuming Moav. That is destined to happen in the End of Days. You'll be long dead by then.[252] Right now, you have nothing to worry about. The Jewish people are forbidden to fight with you in any way, shape or form, so just keep your distance from them and you'll be fine.[253] As to the present, I have some advice for you about that as well."

Balak waited for Bilam to continue, but he remained silent.

"So tell me already," said Balak.

"Not here," Bilam whispered. "It has to be in secret. Come with me."

Balak led him to a secluded spot.[254]

"Listen carefully," said Bilam. "Here's some priceless advice.[255] You want to bring down the Jewish people? You don't need a curse to do that. The way to prevent Moav from destroying the Jewish people is to –"

"What are you talking about?!" interrupted Balak. "Am I trying to prevent Moav from destroying the Jewish people?"

Winking at Balak,[256] Bilam put his finger to his lips. "Haven't you ever heard of euphemisms? How did you ever get to be king?

---

249. *Sifsei Kohen, Bamidbar* 24:14.

250. Malbim, ibid.

251. Zohar, *Balak* 212a.

252. See Rashbam, Seforno, *Bechor Shor, Da'as Zekeinim*, Abarbanel on *Bamidbar* 24:14.

253. *Da'as Zekeinim, Tzeror haMor, Ha'amek Davar* on ibid.

254. Ramban, Rashbam, Malbim on ibid.

255. See Rashi, ibid.

256. *HaKesav vehaKabbalah*, ibid.

Don't say the words, but you know I really mean the opposite. But it's so … belittling to say it."

"Fine. What's the advice?"

"Hashem despises harlotry. So if you can get the Jewish people to violate those laws, He will hate them and punish them severely. In effect, He will be doing your work for you."[257]

Balak smiled. "At last you're starting to earn the money you want. I like it. All right, so what's the plan?"

Bilam went on to explain how he would get the Jewish people to sin and how they would be punished in the process.[258]

"Excellent," said Balak. "But why all the secrecy? Why not publicize your brilliant ideas?"

"Publicity will ruin everything," said Bilam. "Moabite women are known for their modesty,[259] especially since the Great Flood resulted from immorality.[260] If the idea is not presented carefully and properly, they will undoubtedly object with all vehemence. No, we must have secrecy."[261]

"Well, if it's a secret, how will we get our women to entice the Jewish men to sin?"

"It's up to you, Balak. Get your own daughter to start it off. The other women will follow suit."[262]

"You have an answer for everything, don't you? I'll think about it."

---

257. See Rashi, *Chizkuni* on ibid.

258. This crime and its punishment will be discussed in the following chapter. See Ramban, *Bamidbar* 24:14, 25:1.

259. As evidenced by Ruth generations later. And long before her, when the people of Midian refused to provide the Jews with bread and water, only the Midianite men were punished, not the women, for they were too modest to be involved in such public doings (Malbim, *Bamidbar* 25:1).

260. After the Mabul, all nations became far more modest, relatively speaking, than they had once been.

261. *Sifsei Kohen, Bamidbar* 24:14.

262. *Yerushalmi Sanhedrin* 10:2; Zohar, *Balak* 189b.

Bilam's Prophecy

"I think my work here is done," said Bilam, "but before I go, do you want to hear what will befall Moav in the End of Days?"[263]

"Long after I'm gone?"

"Long after your bones have turned to dust."

"All right, tell me."

Bilam began his parable. "This is the word of Bilam son of Be'or, the word of the man with an open eye.[264] It is the word of the one who hears Hashem's pronouncements, who knows the Highest One's will, who sees the vision of the Almighty, descending amidst mystical insight.[265] Yes, I know the will of Hashem. I don't need His guidance any longer.[266] I know why He raises up the Jewish people the way He does.[267] I know what the angels are saying,[268] I know what the future brings,[269] and I know when their Messiah is coming.[270] And let me repeat: I know the precise moment of His anger."[271]

"All right, you've convinced me. So speak already."

"First, I'll tell you the Jewish future," said Bilam. "I see glory and good fortune for the Jewish people. Not right now, but in the future.[272] I see that a star will rise. It will be King David, an

263. See Rashi, Rav Saadiah Gaon, *Lekach Tov* on *Bamidbar* 24:14. See also *Tehillim* 83:3.

264. *Bamidbar* 24:15.

265. Ibid.

266. *Bechor Shor*, *Bamidbar* 24:16.

267. *Ha'amek Davar*, ibid.

268. Rokeach, ibid.

269. Ramban, Malbim on ibid.

270. Tur, *Tzeror haMor* on ibid.

271. Rashi, *Bamidbar* 24:15; *Berachos* 7a. Although Bilam had prided himself on this knowledge earlier, now that he no longer sought to curse the Jews, Hashem's anger would once again come to the forefront. Although this anger was useless to him in cursing the Jews, much of the destruction he foresaw was directly related to his knowing when Hashem becomes angry (*Sha'arei Aharon*).

272. Rashi, *Bamidbar* 24:17.

anointed king, who will lead them.[273] This powerful ruler[274] will dominate[275] and strike down the extremities of Moav,[276] leaving not even a remnant intact.[277] He will go on to overwhelm the people of all nations."[278]

"Sounds very encouraging."

Bilam ignored the remark. "Like a shooting star high in the sky, arching from one end of the earth to another, the great Messiah will gather dispersed Jews from every corner of the earth[279] and slay the heads of the Moabite nation.[280] He will overwhelm all nations of the children of Sheis; in other words, all of mankind,[281] including your Moabite nation.[282]

"Through the hands of David,"[283] Bilam continued, "Edom will be conquered by its arch enemies, the Jewish nation.[284] Through the Messiah,[285] Seir will be driven out by their Jewish enemies.[286] They will never rise again,[287] and the Jewish people will triumphantly attain power and wealth.[288]

---

273. *Targum Unkelos*, Rashi with *Yosef Hallel* on ibid. See Rambam, *Melachim* 11:1.

274. *Da'as Zekeinim*, *Bamidbar* 24:17.

275. *Targum Unkelos*, Rashi on ibid.

276. Rashi, ibid.; Rambam, *Melachim* 11:1.

277. *Ohr haChaim*, *Bamidbar* 24:17.

278. Rashi, ibid.

279. Ramban, Tur on ibid. See Rambam, *Melachim* 11:1; *Sifsei Kohen*; *Aderes Eliyahu*.

280. *Targum Yonasan*, *Bamidbar* 24:17.

281. *Targum Yonasan*, Rashi on ibid.; Rambam, *Melachim* 11:1.

Noach was a descendant of Sheis and the father of all of mankind (Ibn Ezra; Rabbeinu Bachya; Abarbanel).

282. Tur, *Bamidbar* 24:17.

283. Malbim, *Bamidbar* 24:18; Rambam, *Melachim* 11:1.

284. *Targum Unkelos*, Rashi, Ramban on *Bamidbar* 24:18.

285. Malbim, ibid.; Rambam, *Melachim* 11:1.

286. *Targum Yonasan*, ibid.

287. *Ohr haChaim*, *Bamidbar* 24:18.

288. *Tosefos Rav Shemuel d'Rusina*, ibid.

"Yes, there will be yet another ruler from the Jewish people, the Messiah,[289] who will obliterate any remaining remnant of Rome[290]— or any city in the world, for that matter.[291] No one will be able to escape the Messiah's sword."[292]

"Sounds exciting. Are you sure I'll be gone by then?"

Bilam picked up his head. A smile appeared on his lips,[293] and a faraway look came into his eyes. "I see the nation of Amalek. Yes, I am looking at it right now,[294] and I am also seeing a vision of it.[295] Amalek, the greatest, finest and mightiest of nations,[296] was the first to wage war against the Jewish people."[297] A pained look now appeared on Bilam's face.[298] "And so Amalek faces a harsher destiny than that of all the other nations.[299] Amalek will be erased forever,[300] wiped from memory[301] by the very Jewish people it attacked."[302]

Bilam took a deep breath and closed his eyes. "I will now speak to the Kenites, descendants of Yisro and neighbors of Amalek,"[303]

---

289. Rashi, *Bamidbar* 24:19.
290. Rashi, Tur on ibid. See Rabbeinu Bachya, *Bereishis* 36:39.
291. Ramban, *Bamidbar* 24:19.
292. Malbim, ibid.
293. *Midrash haGadol, Bamidbar* 24:20.
294. Ramban, ibid.
295. *Gur Aryeh*, ibid.; *Lekach Tov, Bereishis* 48:8.
296. Ramban, *Bamidbar* 24:20.
297. Rashi, ibid.
298. *Midrash haGadol*, ibid.
299. Ramban, ibid.
300. *Targum Unkelos, Yonason* on ibid.
301. Rav Samson Raphael Hirsch, ibid.
302. Rashi, ibid. "Amalek" is an acronym of Amram, Moshe, Levi and Kehas, for Amalek assumed it could overpower even the most outstanding Jews. Yet the final letters of those same four names spell *misah*, death. Haman made a similar error in using his lottery to destroy the Jews. See *Let My Nation Live* (Brooklyn: Mesorah Publications, Ltd., 2002), pp. 172–176.
303. Rashi, *Bamidbar* 24:21.

he finally said. "I see[304] your greatness. Yisro was with me in the councils of Egypt when we plotted against the Jewish people. And now his descendants dwell in the stronghold of the mighty Jewish people. How is it that they sit alongside the scholars of the Sanhedrin inside the Beis haMikdash? How did they earn this honor?[305]

"It is because Yisro repented, while Amalek and I did not. It is because Yisro fled from Pharaoh's council that you became worthy to sit on the Sanhedrin.[306] Yisro welcomed the Jewish people in the wilderness, while Amalek tried to destroy them. Therefore, you are worthy of coming among them.[307] Yisro advised Moshe regarding the judicial process and established guidelines for the high courts in the Beis haMikdash. Amalek, on the other hand, tried to prevent the Jewish entrance into the Holy Land, which means that had he succeeded, the Beis haMikdash would not have been built. Just as the Jewish people are commanded to eradicate Amalek, so are they required to show appreciation and gratitude to Yisro's descendants.[308]

"Be faithful to the Jewish people, you Kenites," Bilam continued. "You are fortunate to have become associated with this power, and you will never be driven from the world. For even if you are exiled with the ten tribes and uprooted from your homeland by the Assyrians, it will be only a temporary setback. You may wander from place to place, but in the end, you'll return with the rest of the exiles.[309] Amalek, however, will be lost forever.[310] Amalek is a fool who instigated against the Jewish people and who will be wiped

---

304. Ramban, ibid.
305. Rashi on *Bamidbar* 24:21, *Sanhedrin* 106a.
306. Maharsha, *Sanhedrin* 104a. See *Eliyah Rabbah* 5.
307. *Bechor Shor*, *Bamidbar* 24:21.
308. *Tzeror haMor*, *Bamidbar* 24:20.
309. Rashi, Ramban, Tur, *Tzeror haMor* on *Bamidbar* 24:22.
310. Ramban, ibid.

from the pages of history, but Yisro, who repented and embraced the Jewish people, remains forever in their good graces.[311]

"As for the Assyrian captivity, who can survive decrees imposed by Hashem? Sancheriv of Assyria will scramble the nations, leaving no people able to identify themselves with their homeland. Following this, the Romans will come with a fleet of warships against the Assyrians and Ishmaelites and will conquer them. They will continue their onslaught in Eretz Yisrael against the Jewish people. But Rome, too, will eventually fall in the End of Days.[312]

"And who will have the will to live when the pangs of the Messianic era arrive? People will suffer so much they will welcome death.[313]

"Woe to the one who proclaims himself a god.[314] Woe to the one who indulges all his pleasures while casting off the yoke of Torah. Woe to the one who will witness the rewards given to the righteous while he shares the punishment for the wicked at the time of redemption. Woe to the one who prevents the Jewish people from connecting with Hashem. His end will be no different from that of the man trying to keep a lion and lioness apart when they are determined to be together. In the end of days, nations will battle one another and be destroyed, leaving only the Jewish nation standing."[315]

Bilam had completed his prophecies, and finished blessing the Jewish people as well; they would gain directly from his words.

---

311. *Bechor Shor*, ibid.; *Shemos Rabbah* 27:6. According to *Midrash Lekach Tov*, Bilam and Yisro were both part of the those who advised Pharaoh to enslave the Jews in Egypt. Yisro later repented and joined the Jewish people. When Bilam foresaw that the Kenites, Yisro's descendants, would eventually be exiled, he declared, "If the righteous Kenites will not be spared, certainly the evil Assyrians will suffer."

312. Rashi, Ramban, *Bechor Shor*, Malbim on *Bamidbar* 24:23–24.

313. *Midrash haCheifetz*, *Sifsei Kohen* on *Bamidbar* 24:23.

314. *Bamidbar* 24:23. This is another prophetic denunciation of Christianity (Rokeach).

315. See *Sanhedrin* 106a with Rashi; *Targum Unkelos*, Rashbam on *Bamidbar* 24:23.

All the material benefits they enjoy in this world are directly attributable to the blessings Hashem bestowed on them through Bilam. However, the spiritual blessings of the patriarchs are kept for their benefit in the future.[316]

Parting of the Ways

Bilam had been lying down all through his prophetic words.[317] When he was finished, he rose and headed straight to Midian.[318] Never again would Bilam experience prophecy. He would return to being a mere sorcerer,[319] as wicked as he was when had set out on this journey. His great prophetic revelations had not inspired him to change at all.[320]

As for Balak, reassured by Bilam that the Jewish people posed no clear and present danger to his nation, he abandoned all plans to go to war against them. The disgruntled Moabites assumed that he had lost his nerve, and they in turn lost confidence in him and dethroned him.[321] Nonetheless, Balak sought to implement Bilam's advice as his last act on behalf of Moav. He began setting up a flea market or bazaar as a ruse, in order to ensnare the Jewish people and lead them into sin. Bilam would join him later.[322]

---

316. *Devarim Rabbah* 3:4.

317. Ibn Ezra, Rabbeinu Bachya on *Bamidbar* 24:25.

318. See Chapter 15, footnote 58. See also *Ohr haChaim, Bamidbar* 24:25; Ramban, *Bamidbar* 25:18.

319. See *Yalkut Shimoni* 771. See also *Sanhedrin* 106a with Rashi; *Ohr haChaim, Bamidbar* 22:32; *Yalkut Pisron Torah, Bamidbar* 24:14.

The Torah describes this return in language similar to its depiction of Lavan's returning home after confronting Yaakov in *Bereishis* 32:1. This parallelism would support the opinion that Bilam was Lavan, or at least somehow connected to him.

320. *Tzeror haMor, Bamidbar* 24:25.

321. See *Minchah Belulah, Tzeror haMor, Ohr haChaim, Be'er baSadeh* on ibid.

322. See *Targum Yonasan, Yalkut Me'or haAfeilah, Sifsei Kohen, Ha'amek Davar* on ibid.

11 Immorality at Shittim

After their victories against Sichon and Og, the Jewish people encamped on the Plains of Moav, a flat terrain directly across the Jordan River from Yericho, near a place known to us as Shittim.[1]

The waters of Shittim were contaminated with the aura of promiscuity. In fact, many years earlier, streams had flowed from Shittim into Sodom, affecting the moral nature of that decadent city. Everyone knew that Shittim was a place in which it was difficult to resist the allures of hedonism.[2]

The name Shittim is derived from the word *shoteh*, meaning fool. It was in Shittim

1. *Emek haNetziv, Sifrei.*
2. *Bamidbar Rabbah* 20:22; *Tanchuma, Balak* 17.

that the Jewish people acted in a foolish manner and inevitably transgressed.[3] The immoral atmosphere of that place was well-known, and even stepping into it was considered foolish.[4]

As Bilam had noted in his blessings, the Jewish people were famous for their modesty, their family values and their scrupulous protection of the integrity and sanctity of the family. This made them a sanctified nation worthy of Hashem's protection. The nations of the world, on the other hand, indulged their base desires—a manner of living perfectly consistent with idol worship.

Bilam, therefore, had given Balak and the Midianite and Moabite officers cunning advice.[5] He had informed them that they were in no immediate danger from the Jewish people, who had been commanded not to war with Moav. And he had also pointed out that their vulnerability would be exposed if they were drawn into sin. Otherwise, no army in the world could defeat them; even the Egyptians with their untold thousands of war chariots were powerless against them. Bilam had said that he saw "no iniquity in Yaakov," implying that the Jewish people were protected by Hashem only as long as they were free of sin.

"But if you get them to cast off the yoke of Heaven through acts of promiscuity," he said, "Hashem will get angry and turn away from them. Only then can you prevail against them."[6]

"But why those sins specifically?" they wanted to know.

"Because Hashem hates harlotry," replied Bilam.[7] "Your only

---

3. See *Targum Yonasan*, Tur on *Bamidbar* 25:1; *Bamidbar Rabbah* 20:22.

4. *Emek haNetziv, Sifrei*. One must wonder if perhaps Shittim was the only entry way from which to cross the Jordan. Even so, considering the dangers inherent in the place, why would the Jews enter a land so predisposed to sin? It is quite plausible that Hashem was seeking to test the Jewish people to see if they could withstand temptation. Most of the Jewish people prevailed.

5. Abarbanel, *Bamidbar* 25:1. According to Malbim, Balak rejected Bilam's advice, but the Midianites accepted it.

6. *Bechor Shor, Bamidbar* 25:17; Rav Samson Raphael Hirsch, Abarbanel on *Bamidbar* 25:1; *Pirkei d'Rabbi Eliezer* 41; *Yalkut Shimoni* 771.

7. Rashi, *Bamidbar* 31:16; *Sanhedrin* 106a.

chance to defeat them is by having your women entice them to sin. The sanctity of their families is their crowning achievement. Undermine that, and they will no longer stand out among the nations. They forfeit Hashem's love."[8]

The officers were doubtful. "Are they really so much better than we are? Our societies have also been known to maintain a level of social decency."

"It's not nearly the same," said Bilam.

"I don't know, Bilam," said Balak. "The men are right. We are basically a moral people. I don't believe I can get the nation to support this."

"Don't stall, Balak," said Bilam. "We've been over this before. As the king of Moav and a prominent former leader among the Midianites, you have to take the lead and set an example. Offer your daughter to the Jewish people for immoral purposes, and the rest of the men of both Moav and Midian will follow suit."[9]

"You really believe that?"

"I do. In fact, I foresee that the episode will cause the downfall of a Jewish leader. I'm assuming that leader is Moshe.[10] Wouldn't that be wonderful?"

"Beyond wonderful," said Balak. "Very well, let's do it."

Balak's hatred for the Jewish people was so intense that he was willing to stoop to an all-time low level. He, the king of a nation, summoned his daughter Kosbi, a royal princess, and presented her with his indecent proposal.[11]

"Father," she replied, "it would give me the greatest pleasure to help crush and slaughter these Jews. I'll be glad to participate in any way I can."

Balak kissed his daughter. "One word of fatherly advice, my dear

---

8. *Yalkut Shimoni* 673. See Zohar, *Shemos* 2b, *Balak* 189b.

9. *Yerushalmi Sanhedrin* 10:2. See Rashi, *Sifsei Kohen* on *Bamidbar* 25:14; *Sha'arei Aharon*, *Bamidbar* 25:15.

10. Zohar, *Balak* 189b.

11. *Sanhedrin* 82a; *Bamidbar Rabbah* 20:24; Rashi, *Bamidbar* 25:14.

daughter," he said. "Don't get carried away by your enthusiasm. Don't give yourself to anyone but their leader. You are a princess, and you should not associate with anyone of a lower status."[12]

In actuality, Bilam's plan would only find traction because the Jewish people had already begun to fall from their high level; they were ripe for a comeuppance. Their glorious victories in the wars against Sichon and Og had gone to their heads. They became overconfident and thought themselves invincible, both physically and spiritually. In their complacency, they let down their guard against sinfulness, and when Bilam and Balak sent temptation their way, they were unable to resist.[13]

After Balak secured a commitment from his daughter that she would participate in his plan, he returned to consult with Bilam.

"All right, Bilam. You said I should recruit my own daughter, and I did. She's in. Now, what's the plan?"

"Listen carefully. We can't go directly to immoral temptations. We have to be more circumspect. Let's think about it. What do the Jewish people really want? What will tempt them in an acceptable way?"

"I give up. What's the answer?"

"Food and clothing," said Bilam. "They've been eating *mahn* for who knows how long. Don't you think they would enjoy a bit of normal food and drink? And to the best of my knowledge, they've had a soft spot for linen ever since they were in Egypt. And all this time they've been in the wilderness, they've never changed their clothes."

"Never?" asked Balak. "Didn't their clothes get dirty and wear out?"

"Nah. Miracle food, miracle clothes; you can get tired of it. I'm sure the Jewish people would like some fresh new garments, especially the women. Can you imagine—forty years without a new dress?"

---

12. *Sanhedrin* 82a–b; *Bamidbar Rabbah* 20:24.

13. *Emek haNetziv*, *Sifrei*.

"Now that's a miracle," said Balak. "All right, so what do we do?"

"We make a bazaar right here in the open fields. I'll use my occult powers to make all the preparations.[14] We'll set up booths and tents along a route from snow-topped Mount Chermon in the north to Beis haYeshimos in the south. We'll sell all kinds of food and garments, and we'll use clever tactics to lure the Jewish people into the marketplace."

"Such as?"

"We'll recruit older and younger women. At first, we'll employ older Moabite women, and eventually the young Midianite princesses will join them.[15] After their evening meal, some Jewish men will take leisurely walks through the marketplace to see what's for sale. The older, professional-looking Moabite women, dressed as proper businesswomen, will hawk their merchandise outside their tents and tell people that the items are to be found inside. The Jews, whose curiosity will have been piqued, will enter the tents and come face-to-face with the young, made-up, perfumed and decorated Midianite princesses, who will offer to sell them the items at rock-bottom prices."

"That's your plan to get the Jews? You want to turn them into shoppers?"

Bilam snickered and shook his head. "Do you really take me for such a fool, Balak? Just listen. Innocently enough, the men will buy the merchandise we're selling. They'll start frequenting our marketplaces to look for bargains. And when they least expect it, we'll make our move."

"Which is?"

"After three days of this innocent shopping, they'll become friendly with our saleswomen, perhaps even on a first-name basis. Trust will be established, and the young damsels will invite them in

---

14. *Ben Yehoyada, Sanhedrin* 106a.

15. See *Pirkei d'Rabbi Eliezer* 41 with Radal.

to talk and perhaps even to dine with them. The young women will serve them a special aromatic wine made by the Amonites, which contains an aphrodisiac. Once the Jewish men drink it, they will feel the urge to sin. They will go so far as to consort with women outside their faith. Once they do that, their God will be furious with them. He'll punish them, while we sit back and enjoy the show."

"Wear 'em down, eh? Not bad, Bilam. Not bad at all."[16]

Moabites and Midianites

Balak executed the plan exactly as Bilam had designed it.[17] And when he took the lead role by offering up his daughter, others followed suit.[18] Convinced that the Jews no longer posed an immediate threat to their nation, the Moabite women befriended those who entered their places of business and eventually invited the Jewish men to dine with them.[19]

And what exactly did the Midianite women do?

Many opinions suggest that the Moabites focused on the spiritually weak Eirev Rav and persuaded them to worship idols, while the Midianites went after the stauncher Jewish faithful and seduced them into sin. The Moabite women were more reticent and passive in their subversive activities, while the Midianite women were more aggressive. In fact, the Midianites themselves were so determined to lead the Jewish people astray that they often disguised themselves as Moabites to attract those who might have been leery of Midianites.

According to others, the Midianites did not come into Moabite territory for any special purpose and played no special role. They

---

16. See Rashi, *Bamidbar* 25:2; *Sanhedrin* 106a with Maharsha, *Ben Yehoyada*; *Yerushalmi Sanhedrin* 52a; *Bamidbar Rabbah* 20:23; *Pirkei d'Rabbi Eliezer* 41 with Radal; *Sifrei*, *Bamidbar* 25:1; *Targum Yonasan*, *Bamidbar* 24:14; *Yalkut Pisron Torah*, *Bamidbar* 25:2–3; *Avos d'Rabbi Nasan* 1:4.

17. Rashi, *Bamidbar* 25:1.

18. *Sifsei Kohen*, *Bamidbar* 25:15.

19. See Ramban, Abarbanel, Malbim on *Bamidbar* 25:1; Alshich, *Bamidbar* 25:17.

had simply accompanied Balak, a former Midianite, when he ascended the throne of Moav.

According to all opinions, however, it was the Moabites who precipitated the downfall of the Jewish people, and it was the more aggressive and sinful Midianites who administered the *coup de grâce*. Together, they caused an enormous breach in Jewish sanctity.[20]

The People Are Corrupted

The Jewish people, in their complacency, believed themselves immune to Bilam's curses and designs.[21] The first chink in their spiritual armor appeared when men of the Eirev Rav and other lowly men[22] ventured away from the encampment to explore the wares in the new bazaar outside the cloud of glory surrounding the camp of the Jewish people.[23]

"Get your linens here," they heard the Moabite women yell. "Get your freshly woven linens here. Steep discounts as high as 80 percent. Why pay a thousand when you can pay two hundred?"[24]

The men came over to inspect the merchandise.

"Check these materials," the Moabite women said. "Important men such as you deserve only the best. Sit down and relax while we bring you more samples. Satisfaction guaranteed."

Soon, an easy camaraderie arose among buyers and sellers.[25] Emboldened, the Moabite women invited their Jewish customers to share a snack with them.

"Why do you despise us?" the women asked as they ate. "We

---

20. See *Me'am Lo'ez, Be'er baSadeh, Gur Aryeh, Sifsei Kohen*, Alshich, Abarbanel, Malbim on *Bamidbar* 25:1; *Pirkei d'Rabbi Eliezer* 41 with Radal; *Emek haNetziv, Sifrei*. According to *Sifsei Kohen, Bamidbar* 25:17, the idol Pe'or originated in Midian (Yisro worshiped it) and was entrusted to Moav.

21. See *Devarim Rabbah* 1:2 with Radal.

22. *Tzeror haMor, Bamidbar* 25:1.

23. *Ohr haChaim*, ibid.

24. *Yalkut Pisron Torah, Bamidbar* 25:2.

25. Rokeach, *Bamidbar* 25:1.

should be friends. We are all descended from Terach, you from Avraham and we from Lot. Why can't we all just get along? Do our cultural differences really matter that much? Here, as a token of our friendship, take this merchandise free of charge. And let's seal our newfound friendship by sharing a lavish meal we will prepare for you. Please don't refuse. It's a harmless meat feast."

The Jewish men politely declined the Moabite offer. They explained that they scrupulously obeyed the dietary laws and would not eat meat unless it was slaughtered properly.

But the women were not so easily deterred. "We'll bring you a live animal," they said. "Slaughter it as you wish, make sure the meat is as kosher as you like. When you're finished, we will prepare the feast."

The men wavered and nodded.

"And when you slaughter the animal," the Moabite women said, "please do it in front of our household gods, the ones that you see here. It's good luck."

"But that's idol worship," the men protested. "No Jew would do that."

"There's no sense getting so worked up over it," countered the Moabite women. "You have to lighten up a little. It's not such a major issue. In fact, it's quite harmless. Whom will it hurt? But no matter. If it makes you uncomfortable, we'll just skip it. We can't let such a trivial matter come between us."

The Jewish men prepared the meat for the feast, making sure it was kosher. They did not know that this was to be a pagan feast in honor of one of the Moabite idols, but their unwitting participation lowered their spiritual level.

The Moabite women plied them with many foods, until they felt they had to relieve themselves.[26] Then the women offered them the Amonite wine, but the men declined.

---

26. See *Ohr haChaim, Bamidbar* 25:2. The Moabite and Midianite women deliberately increased the Jews' food intake to increase their need to relieve themselves.

"Oh, come, don't be such stuffed shirts," the women said. "You're not forbidden to drink with us. Aren't we friends? One drink never hurt anyone. We still have business to conclude. A good cup of wine will clear your heads."[27]

By the end of the hearty meal, the men's bellies and bowels were full, and the spiked wine was coursing through their veins. They were weak and vulnerable, and the idea of sin was difficult to resist.

The women removed statuettes of the god Pe'or from the folds of their clothing.

"We will only submit," they said, "if you bow down to our little god."

"Absolutely not," said the men. "We're going home."

"All right," said the women, "don't bow down, but at least acknowledge our little god. That would be only polite. All right, all right, we're not asking you to worship him. Don't bow down. But what if you relieve yourselves in front of him? That would be an acknowledgment with which you should have no problem. You would be demeaning Pe'or instead of worshiping him. So where's the harm?"

The Jewish men relented and relieved themselves in front of Pe'or. Little did they know that this was the accepted form of worship for this god. They had unknowingly committed an act of idol worship.[28] They should have had a clue from the very name of the idol, Pe'or, which is associated with the word *po'er*, which is to expose or relieve oneself.

The men had stepped off the plateau of righteousness, and their fall was accelerating.

---

27. *Ben Yehoyada*. Alternatively, no drinks were offered, lest the Jews claim they were drunk and therefore not responsible for their actions.

28. Ibn Ezra, *Bamidbar* 25:2, suggests that the Jews also bowed before the idol. According to *Toldos Yitzchak, Bamidbar* 25:17, the Moabite women persuaded the Jews to use this idol to purge themselves of forty years of undigested manna.

"If you want us to submit to you," said the women, "you have to repudiate the Torah of Moshe, which states that a Moabite may not come into the Jewish congregation."[29]

They complied, and the Moabite women finally satisfied their desires. Then these fallen men boasted of their experience to others in the Jewish encampment and urged them to follow their example.[30] More and more men followed this route, and in a matter of days, business was no longer discussed during these visits to the Moabite bazaar. The men who frequented them became so attached to the worship of the Moabite god that they could barely pull themselves away. It was as if they were affixed to the idol with nails.[31] And the Moabite women were so determined to subvert the Jewish men that they even pursued them, throwing themselves at those who were less eager.[32]

What started as "innocent" visits to a "harmless" shopping bazaar ultimately led to idolatry and harlotry, frightful sins that no one would ever expect from a holy, sanctified nation such as the Jewish people were.[33] Driven by lust, they denied Hashem through their idol worship.[34] It was an act of treachery.[35]

---

29. See Rashi, *Bamidbar* 25:2; *Sanhedrin* 106a with Maharsha, *Ben Yehoyada; Yerushalmi Sanhedrin* 52a; *Bamidbar Rabbah* 20:23; *Pirkei d'Rabbi Eliezer* 41 with Radal; *Sifrei, Bamidbar* 25:1; *Targum Yonasan, Bamidbar* 24:14; *Yalkut Pisron Torah, Bamidbar* 25:2–3; *Avos d'Rabbi Nasan* 1:4.

30. *Ohr haChaim, Tzeror haMor,* Malbim on *Bamidbar* 25:1–2. This grassroots campaign alone made their sin worse than that of the golden calf, which was led primarily by the Eirev Rav. Here many distinguished Jews joined in the transgression. Additionally, everyone sinned with much greater attachment and enthusiasm than were shown regarding the golden calf. See Radal, *Matnos Kehunah* on *Bamidbar Rabbah* 20:23.

31. *Targum Yonasan, Lekach Tov* on *Bamidbar* 25:3. See *Sanhedrin* 64.

32. Rokeach, *Bamidbar* 25:1. Other Jews, however, *were* eager to meet with these women. They even bought jewelry to please their new friends (*Tzeror haMor*).

33. *Tzeror haMor*, ibid.

34. Rashi, *Sanhedrin* 106a.

35. Tur, *Bamidbar* 25:1.

Death to the Violators

"While you were connected to Me," Hashem said to the Jews, "Bilam and his curses were powerless against you, but now that our connection has been weakened, your enemies can now affect you."[36]

As Bilam had correctly predicted, Hashem's anger burned furiously, and He sent a plague into the Jewish encampment.[37]

"As long as My wrath burns," Hashem told Moshe, "the deaths will continue. Kill the violators. My wrath will subside, and the plague will end."[38]

"What shall I do?" asked Moshe.

"Assemble Jewish tribal leaders and men in positions of authority and have them stoned and then hanged for standing by and failing to protest and halt this sinful event. They are as guilty as the transgressors themselves.[39] Let the public see that no one is above the law or immune to judgment, no matter how exalted their status.[40] And let their fate atone for the public disgrace.[41] As to the violators, beginning with the Eirev Rav,[42] let the Sanhedrin bring the idolaters of Pe'or to justice[43] and stone them and hang their corpses in full pubic view."[44]

"But what about those who sinned without being warned and without witnesses?" asked Moshe. "How can they be brought to justice?"[45]

---

36. Zohar, *Bechukosai* 112b.

37. Rashi, Rashbam on *Bamidbar* 25:3.

38. See *Sanhedrin* 35a with Rashi.

39. Abarbanel, *Bamidbar* 25:4; *Bamidbar Rabbah* 20:23. See Seforno, *Bamidbar* 25:4.

40. *Ma'aseh Hashem, HaKesav vehaKabbalah* on *Bamidbar* 25:4.

41. Rabbeinu Bachya, ibid. *Tzeror haMor* adds that the Jews tried to hide their sin, but now Hashem would expose them.

42. Zohar, *Balak* 237b.

43. See Rashi with *Sifsei Chachamim, Bamidbar* 25:4. See *Ha'amek Davar* regarding what constituted the worship of Pe'or.

44. See Rashi with *Sifsei Chachamim*, Rashbam, Malbim on ibid.; *Sanhedrin* 35a with Rashi.

45. See *Midrash haGadol, Bamidbar* 25:4.

"I myself will prosecute them. Place these men out in the open. The rays of the sun will identify the ones who are guilty and deserve to die."[46]

Moshe immediately convened a special Sanhedrin, made up of representatives from every tribal judicial council except Shimon's.[47]

"We are in a crisis," he said to the judges. "A plague is raging through the encampment, and it will only cease when we rid ourselves of those who worshiped Pe'or. The faster we bring the sinners to justice the sooner the plague will end.[48] We must stone the sinners and hang their corpses before sundown, for they must be buried after that."[49]

This special Sanhedrin was composed of 78,600 men. Each one was required to kill two violators, for a total of 157,200 sinners.[50]

The Evil of Zimri

A new tragedy of mammoth proportions was developing. While all other tribes complied with Moshe's instructions, the tribe of Shimon took exception. The people of Shimon approached Zimri, their prince. Zimri was descended from Dinah and Shimon. His ancestry had been tainted by the incident with Shechem, and he was predisposed to evil.[51]

"How can you do nothing, Zimri?" the people protested to him. "Members of our tribe are being condemned to death! Don't you realize that a plague has begun and the deaths seem to be

46. See Rashi with *Sifsei Chachamim*, ibid.; *Sifrei* 131; *Bamidbar Rabbah* 20:23. See also *Sanhedrin* 35a with Meiri.

47. Malbim, *Bamidbar* 25:5.

48. *Minchah Belulah*, *Bamidbar* 25:4; *Sanhedrin* 35a with Rashi.

49. *Targum Yonasan*, Rabbeinu Bachya, Malbim on *Bamidbar* 25:4.

50. See Rashi, *Bamidbar* 25:5; *Yerushalmi Sanhedrin* 10:2. See Ramban for his views on the matter and how he resolves this large number of deaths. See also *Sanhedrin* 35a with Meiri.

51. See *Sha'arei Aharon*, *Bamidbar* 1:22; *Sifsei Kohen*, *Bamidbar* 25:6; *Tzeror haMor*, *Bamidbar* 25:11; Zohar, *Balak* 237a.

occurring only among the people of our tribe? Don't you realize that you weren't invited to be among the thousands of judges of the new Sanhedrin? What an insult to your position and status! Will you just stand there and ignore the plight of your tribe?"[52]

This was not Zimri's first exposure to the unfortunate events taking place with the Moabite women. When the whole affair began, he received word that Balak's daughter, Kosbi, had made herself available for immoral purposes. He immediately gathered an escort of twenty-four thousand men and approached her with a proposition.

She looked away demurely. "I'm afraid I must decline, sir," she said. "My father specifically instructed me not to give myself to anyone but the highest, most elite of the Jewish people. I assumed he meant someone like Moshe; his nephew Elazar, the high priest; or his second-in-command, Yehoshua. You, sir, do not qualify. After all, my father is a king, and I too should only consort with men on that level."[53]

Zimri was upset. "You don't consider me the Jewish elite? I'll have you know that I'm a distinguished prince, the leader of my tribe. Besides, I'm even greater than Moshe and Elazar. They are both descendants of Levi, the third of Yaakov's sons, while I am a descendant of Shimon, the second of his sons."[54]

Kosbi batted her eyes. "Indeed?"

"Yes indeed," said Zimri. "I'll show you in public. Watch and learn as I challenge the great Moshe and render him speechless. Watch as they all rise for me when I enter before him.[55] Trust me;

---

52. Rashi, *Imrei Shefer, Me'am Lo'ez* on *Bamidbar* 25:5; *Sanhedrin* 82a; *Sifrei, Bamidbar* 25:5–6.

53. *Sanhedrin* 82a; *Bamidbar Rabbah* 20:24; *Yalkut Pisron Torah, Bamidbar* 25:6. According to Zohar, *Balak* 189b, Kosbi thought she was talking to Moshe, and that's why she consented.

54. *Sanhedrin* 82a; *Bamidbar Rabbah* 20:24; *Sifrei, Bamidbar* 25:5–6.

55. Ibid.; *Midrash haGadol, Yalkut Pisron Torah, Ha'amek Davar* on *Bamidbar* 25:5–6. Zimri arrived as *Shema* was being recited, for which the custom was to rise, but Kosbi thought they were rising for him. See *Targum Yonasan*.

I'm the prince of the generation. I'm immune to harassment. I can't be touched."[56]

Zimri grabbed Kosbi by her braids and brought her before Moshe at the entrance of the Mishkan.[57] The entire congregation was already assembled there to observe the proceedings of the Sanhedrin.[58]

"Moshe, I have a question for you!" Zimri shouted, his voice full of derision. He thrust Kosbi forward. "Is this woman permitted or forbidden?"

"Of course she's forbidden,"[59] Moshe replied.

"Really?" said Zimri. "Are you the man to whom the Torah was entrusted? So let's talk about your wife, Tziporah. Is she permitted? Isn't she the daughter of Yisro the Midianite? Well, this woman is also a Midianite. Why should yours be permitted and this one forbidden?"[60]

Moshe found himself at a loss for words. Hashem had momentarily taken away his ability to refute Zimri's argument. He should have responded that he had married Tziporah before the giving of the Torah, when all people were considered gentiles, and after the giving of the Torah she had converted. Kosbi, however, had not offered to undergo conversion.[61] Furthermore, Zimri was of the opinion that a gentile was forbidden only in the context of a broader practice of idol worship, not in the exclusive context of forbidden relations. And Zimri had no intention of worshiping idols. To prove his position, he pointed out that Moshe had ordered the Sanhedrin to execute the idol worshipers. He had not

---

56. *Tzeror haMor*, *Bamidbar* 25:6.
57. *Sanhedrin* 82a; *Bamidbar Rabbah* 20:24.
58. Ramban, *Bamidbar* 25:5.
59. See Rambam, *Issurei Biah* 12.
60. *Sanhedrin* 82a; *Bamidbar Rabbah* 20:24; *Shemos Rabbah* 33:5; *Sifrei*, Rashi on *Bamidbar* 25:5–6.
61. See *Sanhedrin* 82a with Rashi; *Imrei Noam*, *Bamidbar* 25:6.

ordered the execution of the adulterers.[62]

When the people of Shimon demanded action, Zimri decided to take the next step. He invited Kosbi to his tent, and impressed by his earlier histrionics, she accepted his invitation.[63]

Kosbi's name was really Shevilnai. But she is known to us as Kosbi, which is associated with the Hebrew word for deceit, because at this point, she disobeyed her father and submitted to a Jewish prince rather than the Jewish king-leader.[64]

In an exceedingly brazen act, totally lacking in shame before the scholars, leaders and general congregation, Zimri now joined Kosbi in her tent, and together they sinned.[65]

Once again, Moshe was speechless and immobilized. How should he respond to Zimri's brazen act? What should be done at this moment? He simply forgot the answer.

How could this happen? How could the great leader, who had ruled over a nation of millions of people, who had weathered the crises of the Eigel, the spies and Korach's rebellion—how could such a leader be bested by a single man? How could he forget the simple answers? Why did this happen?[66]

It was because Hashem was preparing the way for Pinchas to take action and perform his heroic act of sanctifying Hashem's holy Name. When Moshe forgot the law, Pinchas had an opportunity to take matters into his own hands.

As this terrible tragedy unfolded in front of their very eyes, the righteous among the Jewish people, who included Moshe, Yehoshua and Pinchas, burst into tears. Some cried because they

---

62. See *Ma'aseh Hashem, Bamidbar* 25:6. See also *Sefer haChinuch* 427; Rambam, *Issurei Biah* 22:8. Those who were lenient about the adultery, thinking they could withstand any temptation of idolatry, were mistaken. Anyone who committed adultery eventually worshiped Pe'or (Seforno, *Devarim* 4:3).

63. *Ha'amek Davar, Bamidbar* 25:6.

64. See *Pirkei d'Rabbi Eliezer* 41 with Radal; *Sanhedrin* 82; *Bamidbar Rabbah* 21:3.

65. *Sanhedrin* 82b states that Zimri sinned either 60 or 424 times that day.

66. *Sanhedrin* 82a; *Bamidbar Rabbah* 20:24; Rashi, *Bamidbar* 25:6.

saw the Angel of Death circulating among the people and delivering the plague. Others cried because, as judges, they were required to execute their own relatives. Yet others cried because no one knew how to respond to this public breach of Jewish sanctity.

This was a heartbreaking tragedy. Like a bride dressed up and ready to enter the matrimonial canopy, the Jewish people were adorned with spiritual beauty, ready to enter the Holy Land.[67] And despite it all, Zimri acted without regard for the Jewish people and the ramifications of his actions.[68]

Moshe was also held responsible for his own delayed reaction in this matter, and he would be punished by not meriting to have the Jewish people attend his burial or even know where he is buried.[69]

Pinchas to the Rescue

As the horrific events were taking place before their eyes, Moshe and the leaders were contemplating what to do. Was this act punishable by judicial execution, or should it be left to divine retribution? No one had a definitive answer.[70] In the meantime, Zimri's transgression was continuing uninhibited. The rest of the people watched silently and expectantly, but Pinchas, who had been asked to serve on the Sanhedrin, could not remain passive.[71]

"Where are the lions, Yehudah and Dan?" he declared. "Where

---

67. *Bamidbar Rabbah* 20:24; *Pirkei d'Rabbi Eliezer* 47; *Chizkuni, Bamidbar* 25:6.

68. Abarbanel, *Ha'amek Davar* on *Bamidbar* 25:6.

69. *Bamidbar Rabbah* 20:25. How could Moshe have been blamed if Hashem had erased his knowledge of what to do? Perhaps Moshe should have taken an immediate stand, but instead he deliberated. Only then did Hashem make him forget the law.

70. According to *Yalkut Pisron Torah*, Moshe knew Zimri deserved death, but didn't know which death penalty he had incurred.

71. See *Sanhedrin* 82a; *Be'er Yitzchak, Bamidbar* 25:7.

is Binyamin the wolf? A transgression of epic proportions is taking place! A plague is devastating the encampment. People are dying left and right. How can I let this continue? My heart aches for the loss of life. I must take a stand at once![72]

"The tribe of Reuven can't lead the way, because others will protest that his involvement in the infamous incident with Bilhah's bed disqualifies him. The tribe of Shimon obviously cannot take a stand against their own leader, whom they goaded into this action. Ironically, their ancestor Shimon defended Dinah's honor against Shechem's immorality, and his descendants are leading the way toward it. Next is the tribe of Levi, my own tribe. Levi took a stand against immorality in Shechem and against idolatry at the Eigel, and now I, Pinchas, from the tribe of Levi, must take a stand here as well."[73]

Having made the decision to act, Pinchas suddenly recalled the ruling regarding a Jew sinning with a non-Jew. He turned to Moshe.

"Didn't you teach me that zealots may kill anyone who sins with a non-Jewish woman in public? Usually, if someone transgresses or violates a law, there is a procedure in which to adjudicate the matter. There has to be prior warning, witnesses and a trial. But if someone sins publicly with a non-Jewish woman, a zealot can come to the defense of Hashem's honor immediately and strike down the offender in the act."[74]

"Yes, I now recall the law," said Moshe. "There is a saying that

---

72. *Sanhedrin* 82a; *Targum Yonasan, Lekach Tov, Tzeror haMor* on *Bamidbar* 25:6–7. "Pinchas" is a contraction of *Panah chas*—he "turned" to "care" for Hashem's honor (*Lekach Tov*; Rokeach; *Tosefos Rav Ephraim al haTorah*).

73. *Lekach Tov, Midrash Aggadah, Yalkut Pisron Torah* on *Bamidbar* 25:7; *Yalkut Reuveni, Bamidbar* 25:11; *Pirkei d'Rabbi Eliezer* 47. Amazingly, Moav owed its very existence to the Jews' distant relatives, Lot's daughters, who had committed incest but with the best intentions. And Shimon himself had honored Hashem in Shechem. Yet here the descendants of both Moav and Shimon abandoned their ancestors' meritorious ways (*Bereishis Rabbah* 51:10).

74. *Bamidbar Rabbah* 20:25; *Sanhedrin* 82a. See Rambam, *Issurei Biah* 12.

the one who reads the king's letter should be the one to execute its order. You are that agent."[75]

According to another view, Pinchas carried out his mission on his own instead of deferring to Moshe because he recalled a verse, which would eventually be written by King Shlomo: "No wisdom, understanding or counsel may stand against the honor of Hashem."[76] If Hashem's Name is being desecrated, it is not a time to stand on formality and protocol. It was not a time to be concerned about giving proper respect to Moshe. Pinchas saw the desecration, recalled what needed to be done and did it instantly.[77]

Fury raging in his heart, Pinchas ran to risk his life for the sake of Hashem's honor, and to put an end to the appalling desecration of His holy Name.[78] It didn't make a difference that he was confronting a tribal leader. It didn't matter that he was confronting the daughter of a king. Pinchas didn't fear them. He was intent on his mission.

He removed the tip of his dagger-like spear,[79] slipped it under his cloak and used the shaft of the spear as a walking stick to hide his intentions. He then approached the tent where Zimri and Kosbi were sinning.[80]

Members of the tribe of Shimon were guarding the tent, but they did not suspect that Pinchas was armed and ready to strike. After all, who would think a member of the scholarly tribe of

---

75. *Sanhedrin* 82a; Rashi, *Bamidbar* 25:6. Unaware that the law had been forgotten, Pinchas couldn't understand why no one was taking action. When Moshe realized that Hashem had made the law known only to Pinchas, he ordered him to proceed with killing Zimri (*Panim Yafos*).

76. *Mishlei* 21:30.

77. *Sanhedrin* 82a. Although Nadav and Avihu were killed for rendering a legal decision in the presence of their mentor, one may issue such a ruling to prevent the desecration of Hashem's Name. Thus, witnessing Zimri's atrocities, Pinchas took action without consulting Moshe.

78. Rabbeinu Bachya, *Bamidbar* 25:6. See Rashi, Ramban, Seforno on *Bamidbar* 25:14.

79. According to *Pirkei d'Rabbi Eliezer* 47, Pinchas took Moshe's spear.

80. *Sanhedrin* 82b; *Bamidbar Rabbah* 20:25.

Levi, known for its service to the Mishkan and the study of Torah, would be skilled with weapons?[81]

"Why are you here?" asked a guard.

"Isn't it obvious?" Pinchas replied, implying that he had come to participate in Zimri's transgression. "As a member of the younger tribe of Levi, I don't consider myself holier or more righteous than you people. I too like Midianites. In fact, I'm a descendant of Midianites myself."[82]

"I suppose it's all right," said the guard. "You may enter."

Pinchas entered the tent[83] and found Zimri and Kosbi in the midst of their offense. He replaced the tip of his spear and drove it into them, impaling both of them together and leaving them mortally wounded.[84] The miraculous nature of this accomplishment[85] proved to all the people that Pinchas had acted with the purest of motives. As a zealot seeking to do the right thing, his intention was only to sanctify Hashem's holy Name, not for any personal vendetta.[86]

It was a miracle that the people of the tribe of Shimon did not kill Pinchas when he left the tent. "You went in with one intention and came out with another. You deceived us!" they shouted. They tried to kill him, but an angel protected him. Although they did

---

81. Abarbanel, *Sifsei Kohen* on *Bamidbar* 25:7.

82. *Sanhedrin* 82b; *Bamidbar Rabbah* 20:25; Rokeach, *Bamidbar* 25:14. Pinchas was descended from Yisro, a Midianite; see note 93 and corresponding text.

83. See Rashi, Rashbam on *Bamidbar* 25:8.

84. *Bamidbar Rabbah* 20:25.

85. There were twelve miraculous aspects to Pinchas' feat. For an enumeration, see *Sanhedrin* 82b; *Bamidbar Rabbah* 20:25; *Sifrei*, *Yalkut Pisron Torah*, *Da'as Zekeinim* on *Bamidbar* 25:5–8; *Shemos Rabbah* 33:5.

86. Ibid. Despite all the miracles performed on his behalf, Pinchas took action without expecting any of them. With Hashem's help, killing Zimri was as easy as swatting at a blade of grass (*Tehillim* 102:5). Pinchas couldn't have done it without divine assistance, yet Hashem rewarded him for his intent, not his (miraculous) ability. So too, all Hashem wants from us is that we try, not necessarily that we succeed (Alshich, *Bamidbar* 25:11).

not harm him, the fear of death caused his soul to depart from him, but the hovering souls of Nadav and Avihu entered his body, and he was revived.[87]

After Pinchas came out of the tent, bearing the two bodies on his spear, he suddenly noticed the extent of the devastation the plague had caused the tribe of Shimon. He dropped the bodies of Zimri and Kosbi to the ground and began praying to Hashem with great urgency to halt the plague immediately and prevent it from spreading to the other tribes.

"Hashem," he prayed, "why should twenty-four thousand people die on account of just these two?"[88]

The angels didn't take kindly to the seemingly impudent words of Pinchas, and they sought to push him away.

"Leave him be," Hashem told them. "He is a zealot, the son of a zealot. He is a descendant of Levi, who avenged Shechem's immoral act against his sister Dinah. He is a deflector of divine wrath. Through the execution of Zimri, Pinchas has restored the sanctity of the Jewish congregation and ended the plague, just as his grandfather Aharon deflected divine wrath during Korach's rebellion."[89]

The breach had been sealed, and the plague came to an end. There was no longer any need for the special Sanhedrin. Those who sinned would remain alive temporarily, but would eventually die before the Jewish people crossed the Jordan River.[90]

There is an opinion that the twenty-four thousand men who perished were all from the tribe of Shimon and guilty of idol

---

87. See *Tzeror haMor; Sifsei Kohen; Shelah. Matnos Kehunah* comments on *Bamidbar Rabbah* 21:3 that Nadav and Avihu themselves resurrected him.

88. *Bamidbar Rabbah* 20:25; *Lekach Tov, Bamidbar* 25:8, 11. Pinchas prayed for the very people who just moments ago had sought to kill him! Since all Jews are responsible for one another, the sin of one affects all. So without Pinchas' prayer, the plague could have continued (*Midrash haGadol*).

89. *Sanhedrin* 82b; *Lekach Tov, Bamidbar* 25:11.

90. See Ramban, Abarbanel on *Bamidbar* 25:5, 8; *Devarim* 4:3.

worship.[91] Another opinion states that all those who perished were from the Eirev Rav, and although they were part of the tribe of Shimon, they were descended from ancestors of the Eirev Rav who had intermarried with members of the tribe of Shimon.[92]

Pinchas Is Rewarded

Following the example of Zimri who had mocked Moshe, members of the other tribes now began to mock Pinchas.

"Look at the son of Puti," they were saying, "the son of a mother whose father fattened calves for idol worship. How dare such a man kill a tribal prince of the Jewish people?[93] He is no zealot. He came to avenge the shame of Moshe, his great uncle, a man who himself married the daughter of Yisro, a Midianite.[94] Pinchas is a murderer. He has blood on his hands."[95]

In defense of Pinchas, whose motives were indeed pure and honorable, Hashem declared Pinchas' lineage as "the son of Elazar, the son of Aharon," connecting Pinchas for all time with his righteous father and grandfather. This was Hashem's unequivocal endorsement of his actions, as was the reward articulated immediately afterward in the Torah.[96]

The Midrash offers the following parable. One of a group of people insulted the king—a very grave offense, but no one in the group protested. The king was understandably furious with the

---

91. See Rabbeinu Bachya, *Minchah Belulah, Midrash Aggadah* on *Bamidbar* 25:9, 11, 14; Rashi with *Sifsei Chachamim, Bamidbar* 26:13.

92. *Tzeror haMor, Bamidbar* 25:8. According to this view, while the plague ceased among the Jews, it continued to ravage the Eirev Rav.

93. *Sanhedrin* 82b; Rashi, *Bamidbar* 25:7, 11. Pinchas' father, Elazar, had married a descendant of Yisro, who worshiped idols before recognizing Hashem. Pinchas also descended from Yosef (*Sotah* 43a; Rashi, *Bamidbar* 25:11), whose fate he now avenged by killing Kosbi, a member of the very Midianite people that had sold him years ago (*Sifsei Kohen*).

94. *Sha'arei Aharon, Bamidbar* 25:13.

95. *Tosefos Rav Ephraim al haTorah*, ibid.

96. *Sanhedrin* 82b; *Bamidbar Rabbah* 20:25; *Bamidbar* 25:7.

offender, but he was also angry at the entire group, which seemed to condone this man's insolent behavior. Consequently, he decided to punish the entire group. Faced with catastrophe, one man arose and killed the offender. The king was appeased, and he pardoned the rest of the group.[97]

Zimri and his twenty-four thousand men had desecrated Hashem's holiness, and as a result, a plague was raging through the encampment, with thousands already dead. Pinchas arose and struck down the principal offender. Hashem's wrath was appeased, and the plague came to an end.[98]

For Pinchas' act of courage, Hashem sent a loud and public message[99] through Moshe to Pinchas[100] and the entire Jewish nation.[101]

"As a show of appreciation to Pinchas for executing My vengeance,[102] assuaging My anger[103] and atoning for the Jewish people," Hashem declared, "I hereby swear[104] to grant him My covenant of peace as a gift. It shall be covenant of everlasting

---

97. *Bamidbar Rabbah* 20:25.

98. Rashi with Mizrachi, Ibn Ezra, Rabbeinu Bachya, *Lekach Tov*, *Toldos Yitzchak* on *Bamidbar* 25:11, 13. Rabbeinu Meyuchas writes that Pinchas "made" Hashem "forget" His anger. *Minchah Belulah* suggests that Pinchas put Hashem's anger to rest.

The vengeance prevented the plague from continuing among those who failed to protest. Those who actually committed idolatry were given a reprieve to repent (*Ma'aseh Hashem*).

99. *Moshav Zekeinim*, *Bamidbar* 25:12; Zohar, *Balak* 220a.

100. Zohar, *Balak* 220a. Moshe himself was to deliver the message, showing that he had no animosity toward Pinchas for issuing a ruling in his presence. See *Sanhedrin* 84b; *Kli Yakar*, *Bamidbar* 25:12.

101. Ramban, *Moshav Zekeinim* on *Bamidbar* 25:12.

102. Rashi, ibid. *HaKesav vehaKabbalah* translates the word *kin'ah* here, often understood to mean "vengeance," as "purification." Pinchas purified the Jewish camp by ridding it of Zimri.

103. *Lekach Tov*, Rabbeinu Bachya on *Bamidbar* 25:11.

104. *Targum Yonasan*, Rokeach, *Ohr haChaim* on *Bamidbar* 25:12.

priesthood for him and his offspring."[105]

Aharon and his sons were anointed as Kohanim at the inauguration of the Mishkan, and thenceforth, all the descendants of the anointed Kohanim were Kohanim by birth. But Pinchas was Aharon's grandson. He was too young to be among those anointed at the time, and he did not become a Kohen through his father, Elazar, because at the time of his birth Elazar had not yet been anointed. All Aharon's descendants who fell into this category, and their descendants for all future generations, would remain Levi'im. Pinchas was, therefore, destined never to become a Kohen.[106]

But by his courageous act, it was as if he had been reborn, and Hashem rewarded this "new" person with special entry into the *kehunah*.[107] Pinchas and his descendants would remain Kohanim forever. He would one day become Kohen Gadol, and every future Kohen Gadol would be descended from him.[108]

This appointment to the *kehunah* was Hashem's ultimate testimony that Pinchas had no blood on his hands, for had his hands been tainted by blood, he would have been disqualified from serving as a Kohen.[109]

---

105. *Be'er Yitzchak*, ibid. The name Zimri has the same numerical value (257) as the word *nezer*, crown, for by killing him Pinchas was crowned with the priesthood (*Sifsei Kohen*, *Bamidbar* 25:7).

106. Rashi, *Bamidbar* 25:13.

107. Alshich, *Bamidbar* 25:11. According to the opinions that Pinchas now possessed the souls of Nadav and Avihu (see *Tzeror haMor*; *Sifsei Kohen*; *Shelah*), he was truly a son of Aharon and thus a Kohen (*Shelah*). See also *Let My Nation Wander*, Prologue, note 107.

108. *Zevachim* 101b with Tosafos and Maharsha; *Chizkuni*, Ibn Ezra, *Pa'aneiach Raza*, *Sifrei* on *Bamidbar* 25:12. This succession of high priests would begin ten generations later, in the time of Shlomo, with Tzadok. Evyasar, Tzadok's predecessor, descended from Isamar, Elazar's brother. See Rabbi Yehudah heChasid, *Tosefos Rav Ephraim al haTorah*, Abarbanel. Maharil Diskin finds an allusion to Hashem's covenant of peace with Pinchas in that 380 high priests descended from him, the numerical value of the Aramaic word *shalim* (peace).

109. See Zohar, *Balak* 213b; *Chizkuni*, *Tosefos Rav Ephraim al haTorah* on *Bamidbar* 25:12–13; *Berachos* 32b. See also Alshich.

What exactly was the "covenant of peace" Hashem had granted Pinchas? How did this peace relate to the priesthood? Pinchas had made peace between Hashem and the Jewish people, as evidenced by the cessation of the plague. As a Kohen offering sacrifices and performing the holy service, he would consistently bring peace between Hashem and the Jewish sinners.[110] Aharon had been famous as a man of peace, and now, his grandson Pinchas had continued that tradition. He was, therefore, Aharon's logical successor.[111]

The gift of the *kehunah* was a covenant of peace in another sense as well. Hashem was promising him that unlike Aharon, whose right to be Kohen Gadol was disputed by Korach, no one would ever dispute his right to the position.[112]

Furthermore, after the incident with Zimri, a rift had arisen between the descendants of Shimon and Levi, who had previously been comrades-in-arms. Hashem assured Pinchas, however, that Zimri's family would not seek to harm him. Instead, they would seek his friendship in peace.[113] And the members of the other tribes who had mocked him would recognize the righteousness of his deed and also seek peaceful relations with him.[114] They would be grateful that he had saved their lives.[115]

Finally, Pinchas would enjoy eternal peace by never dying.[116] Just as he saved the lives of many and gave them generations of continuity, he would live eternally.[117] He would live either as an angel[118] or by eventually becoming Eliyahu the prophet.[119] His soul

---

110. *Ohr haChaim, Minchah Belulah, Be'er Yitzchak* on *Bamidbar* 25:12–13.
111. *Sifsei Kohen, Bamidbar* 25:11.
112. *Lekach Tov, Bamidbar* 25:12.
113. *Chizkuni, Toldos Yitzchak, Bechor Shor, Sifsei Kohen* on *Bamidbar* 25:11–12.
114. Maharsha, *Sanhedrin* 82b.
115. *Chizkuni, Bamidbar* 25:11.
116. *Bamidbar Rabbah* 21:3.
117. Seforno, Rabbeinu Bachya, *Ohr haChaim* on *Bamidbar* 25:13.
118. *Targum Yonasan, Yalkut Midreshei Teiman* on *Bamidbar* 25:12.
119. *Yalkut Shimoni* 771. See Rashi, *Bava Metzia* 114b; *II Melachim* 2:11.

would never depart, in essence making peace between his body and his soul, living simultaneously until eternity.[120]

As Eliyahu, he would avenge Hashem's honor in the days of Achav when the Jewish people worshiped idols and the tribe of Ephraim discontinued *bris milah*. Eliyahu ordered the rain to cease, and a famine ensued.[121] As Eliyahu, he would announce Mashiach's imminent arrival in the end of days, and he would reconcile ancestors and descendants with the unified interest of serving Hashem.[122]

For carrying out Hashem's vengeance and calming his anger,[123] Pinchas merited entry into the World to Come. For saving the Jewish people from death, he was rewarded in this world as well.[124]

In the merit of stopping the twenty-four thousand deaths, Pinchas and all future Kohanim would receive twenty-four special gifts, donations from offerings brought to the Beis haMikdash as well as tithes in the outlying areas. When a person would slaughter cattle, sheep, or goats (not for a sacrifice), the Kohanim would be given the *zeroa* (right foreleg), the *lechayayim* (jaw), and the *keivah* (stomach) of the animal. These were given as a reward for the right hand that slew Zimri, the mouth that prayed to Hashem

---

120. Abarbanel, *Bamidbar* 25:12.

121. See Rabbeinu Bachya, *Ohr haChaim*, *Pa'aneiach Raza* on *Bamidbar* 25:13. See also *I Melachim* 19:10. Eliyahu's zeal regarding *bris milah* earned him his "ringside seat" at all circumcisions and his status as "the angel of the covenant" (*Malachi* 3:1). See *Pirkei d'Rabbi Eliezer* 29; *Sefer Abudirham, Berachos*; *Shibolei haLeket, Bris Milah.*

122. See *Yalkut Shimoni* 771; *Targum Yonasan*, *Bamidbar* 25:13; *Malachi* 3:24 with Rashi. The fact that Pinchas was rewarded with *shalom* indicates, according to *Devarim Rabbah* 5:15, the tremendous value of peace. *Shalom* is so important to Hashem that it concludes our three daily prayers, and is in the blessing following the evening *Shema* and *birkas Kohanim*. See *Bamidbar Rabbah* 11:7, 21:1.

123. Hashem's "anger" was in essence the plague, in which His angels killed anyone in their way, until they were halted, just as the plague following Korach's rebellion was halted by Aharon and the *ketores*. See Tur, Rokeach on *Bamidbar* 25:11.

124. *Meshech Chochmah*, *Ta'ama d'Kra* on *Bamidbar* 25:11.

to end the plague, and for impaling Zimri in the groin — respectively.[125]

The Violators

The following verse can be applied to Zimri: "The boastful man who willfully sins, scoffer is his name."[126] Zimri scoffed and mocked at Moshe and the Jewish people when he willfully sinned with Kosbi.[127]

Zimri is also known as Shlumiel ben Tzurishadai. In addition, he is called Shaul ben haCanaanis,[128] because he disregarded what his ancestor Shimon did in defending Dinah in Shechem.

Most shamefully, not only did he fail to protest against the debauchery as a tribal leader, he himself actually participated.[129] Therefore, Moshe would not bless the tribe of Shimon outright nor would any member of their tribe ever be selected for a leadership position again.[130]

History's Testimony of Amon and Moav

The Torah bars converts from Amon and Moav from marrying into the Jewish nation because of their unacceptable behavior. When the Jewish people left Egypt, tired and weary from their journey, the least the people of Amon and Moav could have done was offer

125. See *Chullin* 134b; *Pirkei d'Rabbi Eliezer* 47; *Sifrei, Midrash haGadol* on *Bamidbar* 25:13.

126. *Mishlei* 21:24.

127. *Bamidbar Rabbah* 20:24.

128. See *Targum Yonasan, Bereishis* 46:10. Ibn Ezra writes that Shimon actually married a Canaanite woman, and Zimri/Shaul was their son. See *Let My Nation Descend* (Jerusalem: Feldheim Publishers, 2008), p. 381.

129. *Pirkei d'Rabbi Eliezer* 41 with Radal; Zohar, *Shemos* 2b; *Sanhedrin* 82b.

130. Rav Chaim Paltiel, *Bamidbar* 24:14. According to *Yalkut Shimoni, Shofetim* 3:42, because of Zimri's transgression, no judges ever came from the tribe of Shimon. See also *Reishis Chochmah* 7.

them food and water.[131] It was customary among nations at that time to sustain people traveling through the wilderness, just as Malkitzedek did when he sustained Avraham after the war with Sodom.[132]

Especially as descendants of Lot, Avraham's nephew, they owed a debt of gratitude to Avraham for saving Lot's life. Moreover, they were well-aware of Avraham's reputation for hospitality and kindness, and they should have acted in kind. Nonetheless, they failed to offer assistance to the Jews.[133]

The people of Moav took it two steps further. They hired Bilam to curse the Jewish people, and through his advice, they lured the Jewish people into sin.[134]

Because of their failure to show kindness to the Jewish people[135] and because of their evil attempts to harm them and draw them into sin,[136] their men who would choose to convert would never be allowed to marry a Jewish woman.[137]

Edom, on the other hand, advanced toward the Jewish people with swords drawn, ready to do battle, but their converts to Judaism can marry Jewish women after the third generation.

---

131. See *Sifrei*, Rashi, *Meshech Chochmah* on *Devarim* 23:5.

132. Mizrachi, ibid.

133. See *Sifrei*, Rashi, Ramban, *Midrash haGadol* on *Devarim* 23:5–7.

134. See *Michah* 6:5; *Sifrei*, Rashi, Tur on *Devarim* 23:5.

135. Some suggest that although Moav did offer the Jewish people provisions for a price (*Devarim* 2:29), it was far too little too late. When the Children of Israel needed them the most—upon their departure from Egypt—the Moabites were nowhere to be found. See Ramban and Abarbanel for their differing views, as well as *Meshech Chochmah*, on *Devarim* 23:5.

136. Ramban, *Devarim* 23:5. Worse than Moav's specific wrongdoings was its ignoring its debt to the Jewish people, dating back to Avraham's kindness toward Lot. More than anything, this ingratitude ignited Hashem's anger and precluded Moabite entry into the Jewish people. See *Midrash haGadol*, *Me'am Lo'ez* on *Devarim* 23:5–7.

137. *Yevamos* 77b; Rambam, *Issurei Biah* 12:17. The women were exempt from this prohibition because it wasn't customary for them to be out in public, so they weren't held accountable for failing to sustain the Jewish people.

Clearly, then, it is far worse to cause spiritual harm than physical harm.[138]

With this tragic event now behind the Jewish people, preparations to enter the Holy Land would begin in earnest.

---

138. *Sifrei*, Rashi on *Devarim* 23:9. Likewise, despite the suffering they caused the Jewish people, the Egyptians did host and feed the Jews. As a result, third-generation Egyptians may enter the Jewish people.

12 Census and Distribution

Following the plague, Hashem commanded Moshe to have Elazar conduct another census.[1] Just as a shepherd counts his beloved flock after it is decimated by a wolf attack, Hashem counted His beloved Jewish people after the devastating plague.[2]

There was also another important aspect to this census. Within a short time, Moshe would pass away, and there would be a new leader for the Jewish people. Just as the owner of a flock who hires a new shepherd instructs the old shepherd to deliver a count of the sheep before he leaves, so did Hashem instruct Moshe to conduct a final tally of the

1. Ibn Ezra, *Bamidbar* 26:1.
2. Rashi, ibid.; *Bamidbar Rabbah* 21:7.

people before he passed away. The people had been counted at the time they were entrusted to Moshe's care,[3] and now they were counted again when his stewardship came to an end.[4]

It would have seemed logical for Yehoshua to be involved in this census, since he was the new shepherd to whom the people were being entrusted. But this would have been a painful reminder to Moshe that his time as leader, as well as his very life, were just about over. In consideration of his feelings, therefore, Hashem instructed Moshe to communicate only with Elazar.[5]

The results of the census were interesting. Forty years after the Children of Israel's emergence from Egypt, the number of adult males between the ages of twenty and sixty had not changed significantly.[6] At that time, there were 603,550, and now there were 601,730—a net decrease of 1,820 Jews. Hashem wanted a slight decrease to underscore that the victory of the Canaanite kingdoms would not be achieved by superiority of numbers but by the hand of Hashem.[7]

The census also served a number of other purposes. When the Jewish people were coming out of Egypt, the nations of the world snickered to each other that the lineage of these former slaves was probably tainted since the women had been under the control of their Egyptian masters. But when Hashem descended onto Mount Sinai and gave the Torah to the Jewish people in a spectacular display of miracles, there could no longer be any question of tainted lineage. This was underscored by the original census,[8] which had

---

3. I.e., when they left Egypt. See *Shemos* 12:37.

4. *Tanchuma, Pinchas* 4; Rashi, *Bamidbar* 26:1.

5. Alshich, *Bamidbar* 26:1.

6. Abarbanel, *Bamidbar* 26:51. Everyone between the ages of twenty and sixty at the time of the spies had died during the past forty years. No one counted here was counted in the original census, yet it was practically identical forty years later!

7. *Chizkuni*, ibid. There were a thousand more Levi'im than in the original count, making the difference between the two censuses just 820 (Rokeach).

8. *Bamidbar* 1, 2. See also *Let My Nation Wander*, p. 52 ff.

attributed all the people to their tribal clans and connected them back to the patriarchs.

After the shameful episode at Shittim, however, the nations claimed that the Jewish people had shown themselves to be a base and common nation no different from all the others. Once again, they raised the question of tainted heritage. Hashem therefore commanded there be a new census by which His holy Name would be associated with the Jewish people and thereby establish that all those who survived the plague were pure and free of taint.[9]

In a more practical sense, the census was needed to establish the relative size of the tribal populations, because this would be the basis on which the land would be apportioned.[10] The census would also provide an exact number of men of military age so that Moshe would know how many fighters would be available for the imminent war with the Canaanite kings.[11]

In this census, as in all previous censuses, only men eligible for military service were counted. There was no count of women, children, old men, the sick and the infirm. Had these been counted, the population would have been in the millions. By contrast, the very first census, which produced a count of seventy Jewish souls who descended to Egypt with Yaakov, included everyone, even the infant Yocheved. But Hashem did not want later censuses to include the full numbers because He wanted to emphasize that the Jewish people, like the stars in the sky and the sand on the seashore, were virtually too numerous to count. Therefore, the censuses were limited to men between the ages of twenty and sixty who could go out to war.[12]

---

9. See *Yalkut Shimoni* 773; *Ohr haChaim*, Alshich on *Bamidbar* 26:1.

10. *Chizkuni*, *Bamidbar* 26:1. As we will see shortly, this view is one of three regarding how the land was divided.

11. *Pa'aneiach Raza*, ibid.

12. Rabbeinu Bachya, ibid.

The Land Is Apportioned

With the census finished, Hashem informed Moshe how the land was to be divided among the twelve tribes after the conquest of Eretz Yisrael was complete. There is a difference of opinion between Rabbi Yonasan and Rabbi Yoshia regarding how this was to be done.

According to Rabbi Yonasan, all those who were twenty or older at this time were included in the apportionment pool. For instance, a father and three sons over the age of twenty were each eligible for individual portions. A fourth son younger than twenty at the time was not included, even if he would reach the age of twenty before the end of the conquest, when the distribution was to take place. He would eventually receive a portion as an inheritance from his father's portion, sharing it with his older brothers who had received portions of their own.[13]

Once the number of inheritors was established, a lottery system was used to determine the portions. First there was a lottery to divide the land among the tribes. Divine providence insured that the lottery gave each tribe its appropriate portion based on size; the larger the tribe, the larger its portion. In essence, therefore, the apportionment was not by a random lottery but by divine guidance.[14]

Twelve lots were to be prepared for the tribes, and twelve others for the land tracts. All the lots were placed together in one box. Then Elazar would consult with the Urim v'Tumim and say, "If such-and-such a tribe comes up, the lot with which it comes up will be for such-and-such a portion."[15] The prince of each tribe

---

13. Rashi, *Bamidbar* 26:53; *Bava Basra* 117a; *Bamidbar Rabbah* 21:8.

14. Rashi, *Bamidbar* 26:54; *Bava Basra* 117a; *Sifrei* 132. See *Yehoshua* 14, 19:9. Had the tribes received equal portions, individuals from a smaller tribe would each have far more land than members of a larger one (Rashbam).

15. The divine nature of the lottery prevented any tribe from requesting a different portion of land, for its allotment was clearly Hashem's will (*Be'er Yitzchak*).

was to draw two lots. Miraculously, he would draw the lot of his own tribe and the lot identifying the portion Elazar had identified as his tribe's; the lot itself would cry out that the portion recorded on it was for that tribal prince. This happened again and again without fail for every tribal prince.[16]

Furthermore, according to Rav Yonasan, the apportionment took into consideration the sizes of families both at the time of the Exodus and at the time of apportionment. For instance, a man had two sons, one of whom had one son and one of whom had three, and only the four grandchildren were alive by the time of apportionment. The four grandsons merited four portions. These four portions were then considered as belonging to the grandfather, and were divided equally between his two sons—i.e., half of the tract to the descendants of one son, and half of the tract to the descendants of the other son.[17]

Rav Yoshia has a differing view. He maintains that the land was apportioned according to the sizes of the families at the time of the Exodus only. Consequently, in our previous example, only the grandfather and his two sons would be entitled to portions, not the grandchildren, even though they were twenty years old at the time of the apportionment. These three portions would then be divided among the four grandsons.[18]

According to another view, the land was divided equally into

---

16. Rashi, *Bamidbar* 26:54, 56; *Bava Basra* 122a; *Bamidbar Rabbah* 21:9. According to the Gemara, there were two boxes: one with the names of the tribes and another with the land allotments. After consulting the Urim v'Tumim, Elazar would announce each tribe's portion of land even before Yehoshua selected it. Yehoshua would then choose lots from the boxes and announce the results of the lottery, confirming Elazar's declaration.

The size of the portion was inversely commensurate with its quality. The poorer the quality, the more land the tribe would receive (*Sifrei* 132).

17. Rashi, *Bamidbar* 26:55; *Bava Basra* 117a; *Sifrei* 132.

18. Ibid. Therefore, Tzelofchad, who left Egypt but was no longer alive, inherited land. Since he had no sons, this inheritance passed to his five daughters.

twelve parts. Proportional division was done only within the respective tribes,[19] by the tribal princes and the trustees of the people.[20]

Yehoshua and Kalev were excluded from the lottery, because their righteous conduct during the incident of the spies had already earned them portions of the land. Kalev received Chevron, and Yehoshua received the city of Timnas Serach, as he had requested.[21] They also received the portions that the spies would have received had the latter not sinned.[22]

Converts and emancipated slaves were also excluded from the lottery, because they had no tribal affiliation.[23]

The tribe of Levi too was excluded from the census and the apportionment. They were not given a separate portion of the land.[24] Their mission was not to be landholders but rather to participate in the holy service. They did receive for their places of residence forty-eight towns in uninhabited tracts of lands belonging to the other tribes.[25]

The Daughters of Tzelofchad

A man named Tzelofchad, who was descended from Yosef's son Menashe, died and left behind five daughters —Machlah, Noa, Choglah, Milkah and Tirtzah. Like Yosef who wanted his remains taken to the Holy Land because he loved it so much, these righteous women held the Land in the highest esteem as well.[26] They had put off getting married,

---

19. Ramban, *Bamidbar* 26:54.
20. Rashi, *Bamidbar* 34:17.
21. Rashi, *Bamidbar* 26:55; *Bava Basra* 122b. See *Yehoshua* 19:50, 21:12. While Chevron was one of the cities of refuge belonging to Levi, Kalev received a province around the city.
22. *Bava Basra* 117b, 118b, 122b with Rashbam.
23. Rashi, *Bamidbar* 26:55; *Sifrei* 132.
24. Rashi, *Bamidbar* 26:62.
25. Rashi, *Bamidbar* 35:1–8. See also Chapter 17, p. 298ff., "The Cities of Refuge."
26. Rashi, *Bamidbar* 27:1. See *Bamidbar Rabbah* 21:10; *Sifrei* 133. As descendants

because they were unsure how it would affect their position regarding the apportionment.

After hearing Moshe's instructions regarding the division of the land, they wondered where they fit in to the scheme of things.[27] They were the only children of Tzelofchad, who had died without leaving a male heir. Without consulting one another, each of them came up with the same question:[28] Were only males eligible for inheritance and participation in the apportionment? If so, did that mean that Tzelofchad's portion was now forfeit?[29]

The young women presented their questions to the lower courts, but no one could give them an authoritative answer. They sought out Moshe and Elazar in the *beis midrash* and made their case.[30]

"Tzelofchad, our father, unfortunately died in the wilderness," said the oldest daughter. "He left no sons to inherit him. If he had left a son, we would remain silent. Our father was not among the sinners who died because they sided with the spies, nor did he join Korach and his assembly in their rebellion. He led no one into his sin of gathering wood on Shabbos, and therefore, he did not forfeit his right to a portion of the land.[31] Why, then, should his

---

of Machir the son of Menashe, the daughters of Tzelofchad could have easily obtained land across the Jordan, which was slated for half their tribe. This is because the east side of the Jordan River was not bound to inheritance and tribal lot. But because they loved Eretz Yisrael, they wanted land in Eretz Yisrael proper. See Malbim. See also *Bamidbar* 32:39; *Bamidbar Rabbah* 21:11; *Emek ha-Netziv, Sifrei* 133.

27. *Bamidbar Rabbah* 21:11.

28. See *Me'am Lo'ez, Yehoshua* 17.

29. *Akeidas Yitzchak, Bamidbar* 27:1.

30. See Rashi, ibid.; Rashbam, *Bava Basra* 119b; *Sifrei* 133.

31. See Rashi, *Bamidbar* 27:3; *Bava Basra* 119b; *Sifrei* 133; *Yalkut Shimoni* 773; *Shabbos* 96b–97a. Some say Tzelofchad was one of the insurgents who had sought to enter Eretz Yisrael prematurely (*Shabbos* 96b–97a). According to Zohar, *Balak* 205b, he died in the plague of the serpents (*Bamidbar* 21:5–6). See also *Bamidbar* 15:32–36 and *Let My Nation Wander*, p. 324ff.

The spies, complainers, and Korach and his men earned no portion of Eretz

name be eradicated from his family just because he left no sons? If we, his daughters, are in place of his sons, then we should share in the inheritance of the land. Otherwise, perhaps our mother should undergo *yibum* by marrying our father's brother and bearing him a male child."

"That is not feasible," said Moshe. "She is ineligible for *yibum*, because your father was not childless. He left five daughters."

"If we are considered his children to disqualify our mother from *yibum*," the young woman said, "should we not be considered his children regarding inheritance as well? Isn't Hashem compassionate to females and males alike?"[32]

The daughters of Tzelofchad had made some good points, and Moshe did not know how to respond to them. He took their case before Hashem and asked Him for enlightenment.[33]

"The arguments of the daughters of Tzelofchad are correct," Hashem told Moshe. "They understood the laws of inheritance properly. You shall give them numerous portions of inheritance:[34] One belonging to Tzelofchad, who is eligible because he left Egypt

---

Yisrael for their children to inherit. Because they not only sinned but caused others to sin, they were punished severely. See *Bava Basra* 118b; *Emek haNetziv, Sifrei* 133.

32. Rashi, *Lekach Tov* on *Bamidbar* 27:4; *Bava Basra* 119b; *Bamidbar Rabbah* 21:11; *Yalkut Shimoni* 773; *Sifrei* 133. See *Tehillim* 145:9.

33. Rashi, *Bamidbar* 27:5; *Bamidbar Rabbah* 21:12. Not knowing the law was Moshe's punishment for having presumptuously said, upon appointing judges, "Anything difficult for you, you shall bring to me" (*Devarim* 1:17). See *Sanhedrin* 8a.

Bamidbar Rabbah 21:12 presents a completely reverse scenario: Because all the lower courts had recused themselves from this case, it eventually reached the "supreme court," i.e., Moshe. He, too, humbly wanted to defer to someone greater, so he turned to Hashem. According to *Bava Basra* 119a and *Sifrei*, Moshe knew the general laws of inheritance but needed Hashem's guidance on certain specifics. According to the Zohar, Moshe humbly recused himself from the case, lest he seem biased by Tzelofchad's refusal to obey Moshe's warnings against violating Shabbos, which had resulted in Tzelofchad's death. See *Tzeror haMor, Bamidbar* 27:5.

34. Rashi, *Bamidbar* 27:7; *Sifrei* 134.

over the age of twenty, and another portion which he inherited from his father, Chefer. They shall also inherit the portion he inherited posthumously from a brother, who also left Egypt but died childless."[35]

Hashem continued to explicate the laws of inheritance to Moshe. All inheritance was to be passed to the son or sons. If a person had a son who died leaving only daughters, those daughters take precedence over any other kin. If the person had only daughters, his inheritance passes to them. If he had no sons or daughters, the inheritance passes to his brother. If he had no brother either, then his inheritance would pass to his uncle, the brother of his father. If he had no paternal uncle, the inheritance would pass to the closest relative.[36]

At this time, the youngest of Tzelofchad's righteous daughters was already forty years old, and they were all unmarried. Nonetheless, they would eventually marry in age order and bear children. Like Yocheved who also married at a late age and bore children, these righteous women were blessed with the same miracle.[37]

---

35. Rashi, *Bamidbar* 27:7; *Bava Basra* 116b, 118b with Rashbam; *Bamidbar Rabbah* 21:12. In fact, Tzelofchad's daughters received four portions altogether, for as a firstborn, their father received a double portion from his father.

36. *Bamidbar* 27:8–11; *Bava Basra* 115a with Rashbam. See Rambam, *Nachalos* 1.

37. See *Bava Basra* 119b with Rashbam; *Bamidbar Rabbah* 21:11. Additionally, Tzelofchad's daughters had delayed their marriages until their inheritance was assured. See *Me'am Lo'ez*; Rashi on *Yehoshua* 17:3–5.

13 Moshe's Prayer

Moshe thought he saw a glimmer of hope. Hashem had just given him instructions on the division of the land, and this included the lands of Sichon and Og on the other side of the Jordan River—lands that he had already entered and that he was poised to disburse. Could this mean that Hashem had rescinded the vow He had made barring Moshe from the land? Hadn't he in effect already entered some of the future Eretz Yisrael?[1]

"Although I told you the laws regarding the distribution of the lands of Eretz Yisrael," Hashem said to Moshe, "you will not be the one to carry them out. The decree has not been annulled.[2] If I were to allow you to enter

1. See Rashi with *Be'er Yitzchak, Bamidbar* 27:12; Rashi with *Gur Aryeh*, Ramban on *Devarim* 3:23; *Bamidbar Rabbah* 21:13; *Sifrei* 134.

2. Rashi, *Bamidbar* 27:12.

the land, it would create the appearance that you are somehow better than Aharon, who died in the wilderness.[3] The decree was issued against both of you for failing to sanctify My holy Name at Mei Merivah.[4] Why should you be allowed to enter when he wasn't?"[5]

Pleading for Mercy[6]

When Hashem had originally issued the decree against Moshe and Aharon, Moshe had felt confident that he could prevail upon Hashem to rescind it. After all, he had prevailed on Him to rescind decrees against the Jewish people

---

3. Rashi, *Bamidbar* 27:13.

4. Ibid.

5. *Minchah Belulah, Bamidbar* 27:12. Some say people would rationalize that Aharon couldn't enter Eretz Yisrael because he was responsible for the sin of the golden calf. See *Toldos Yitzchak* regarding why Aharon didn't pray for clemency as Moshe did.

6. Rashi opines that Moshe prayed now. Ramban and *Tzeror haMor* offer another view (consistent with *Panim Yafos*), that Moshe began praying immediately after the decree was issued. Yet Rashbam says Moshe wouldn't have begun praying when Hashem was angry at him.

Devarim Rabbah 2:5 states that only after Yehoshua was selected did Moshe begin praying to "change Hashem's Mind," as it were. (But when exactly was that? See *Devarim* 31:7–23 with *Tzeror haMor, Ohr haChaim*, Abarbanel; *Sotah* 13b.) This approach accords with *Sotah* 13b and the Zohar.

Midrash haGadol and Rashbam write that after conquering Sichon and Og, Moshe believed it was an auspicious time to pray, so he began. *Devarim Rabbah* 9:2 and *Vayikra Rabbah* 11:6 add that he prayed for seven days, reminiscent of the seven days Hashem had urged him to lead the Jewish people.

According to *Matnos Kehunah* (quoting *Seder Olam* 10) on *Devarim Rabbah* 9:2, Moshe prayed only on the last day of his life. *Me'am Lo'ez* explains that he had waited until then, hoping the Jews would pray on his behalf in return for all the times he had prayed for them. When they didn't, he finally did. See *Devarim Rabbah* 3:11.

Yalkut Reuveni states that after Moshe received the laws pertaining to vows, he thought Hashem Himself would annul His own vow barring him from Eretz Yisrael.

After speaking at length with Rabbi Aharon Roiter (author of *Sha'arei Aharon*), I chose to follow Rashi's view. I have also divided Moshe's prayer in such a way as to minimize contradictions and inconsistencies with its nature and the flow of the book.

a number of times. Certainly He should be able to rescind a divine decree against two supremely righteous men such as Aharon and himself. There was a slight presumptuousness in Moshe's attitude toward the decree. Therefore, Hashem sealed the decree and swore an oath that He would not allow either brother to enter the Holy Land.

Nonetheless, Moshe did not despair. He prayed to Hashem with all his heart and intensity, pleading with Him to have mercy and allow him to enter Eretz Yisrael.[7]

"Hashem, You are the Master of Mercy," he prayed.[8] "You are merciful in judgment.[9] You are exalted because of Your goodness and Your ability to pardon and forgive. Your right hand is extended to all the world's inhabitants as You suppress judgment with Your Attribute of Mercy.[10] I therefore beg You—*va'eschanan*—using a term included in the Thirteen Attributes of Mercy, attributes in which You declared that You offer favors and gifts even to the undeserving.[11]

"You are unlike a mortal king, whose advisors and counselors can persuade him to change his mind after he has decided to be merciful to the undeserving. But who will argue or object if You show kindness to me? No one![12]

"Why should I, the one who praised the Holy Land, be excluded from entry along with the spies who slandered it? Why should I remain outside along with those evildoers, while everyone else enters the land?[13] Let me in so I can prove to everyone

---

7. *Devarim Rabbah* 2:6; *Midrash Petiras Moshe,* cited in *Otzar Midrashim* 362. See *Tiferes Tzion.*

8. Ramban, *Devarim* 3:24. See *Gur Aryeh.*

9. See Rashi, *Midrash haGadol* on *Devarim* 3:24; *Sifrei.*

10. Rashi, *Devarim* 3:24. See also *Sifrei; Me'am Lo'ez.*

11. Rashi, *Devarim* 3:23; *Sifrei; Devarim Rabbah* 2:1. "*Va'eschanan*" (I begged) is one of ten terms/types of prayer.

12. Rashi, *Devarim* 3:24; *Sifrei.*

13. *Tanchuma, Devarim* 1; *Toldos Yitzchak, Devarim* 3:24.

that I was right when I praised the land."[14]

"Moshe, I have issued My decree," Hashem replied, "and it is final."

"Nonetheless, I'm not discouraged," said Moshe. "You taught me during the incident of the Eigel never to give up. You said to me, 'Let Me be,' and from these words I understood that if I persisted long enough You would relent and forgive the Jewish people.[15] I persisted, and You relented. And now I shall persist again until You relent and allow me to enter the land.[16]

"Please, Hashem, I beg of You. Let me come into the land with the people. Please let me see the awesome displays of Your strength in the great battles that will follow our invasion.[17] Please let me see the holy city of Yerushalayim. Please let me see Mount Moriah, the site of the Akeidah, the site of the future Beis haMikdash. Please let me come into the land so that I can pray on behalf of the Jewish people."[18]

"My decree is final."

"Please, Hashem, grant me this. The Jordan River is fifty *amos* across. Please let me go fifty-one *amos* beyond my restriction so that I can stand on a single *amah* of the Holy Land.[19] If You will only allow me just to pass through a tiny corner of the land without stopping there, that will also be something for me.[20] If You will let me enter a subterranean passage without ever stepping onto the surface of the land, it will also be enough."[21]

"It is as I said before. My decree is final."

---

14. Abarbanel, *Devarim* 3:25.
15. See Rashi, *Devarim* 3:24; *Sifrei*. See *Shemos* 32:10 with Rashi.
16. Rashi, *Devarim* 3:23; *Sifrei*. For more examples of Moshe's persistence, see *Shemos* 6:12; *Bamidbar* 12:13, 27:15.
17. Rashi, *Devarim* 3:24; *Sifrei*.
18. Rashi, Abarbanel on *Devarim* 3:25; *Sifrei*.
19. Tur, *Devarim* 3:25.
20. *Ohr haChaim*, ibid.
21. *Midrash haGadol, Devarim* 3:27; *Sifrei, Devarim* 34:4; *Yalkut Shimoni* 965.

"The Jewish people sinned numerous times, and each time, I prayed for them and the decree was rescinded. And I have sinned only once. Isn't it right that the decree against me should be annulled?"

"Great as you are, Moshe, you are only an individual. The Jewish people are a congregation. There is always more leniency toward a congregation."[22]

Moshe was despondent. The man who had once persuaded Hashem to create a new phenomenon—that of the earth's opening its mouth to swallow Korach and his followers—could not persuade Him to rescind His present decree.[23] The man who had once flown like an eagle into Heaven now could not even cross the Jordan River.[24] Throwing himself on Hashem's mercy was not working. Perhaps a more argumentative approach would produce better results.

"During Korach's rebellion, You called the people rebels," he said. "Why then did You consider it a sin when I called them rebels at Mei Merivah? What was the difference?"[25]

"The two situations are vastly different," Hashem replied. "Korach's followers were indeed rebels. But the Jewish people at Mei Merivah were desperate with thirst. They did not deserve your anger and your calling them rebels."[26]

"I understand," said Moshe, "but let me make a different point. At the burning bush, You urged me to lead the Jewish people out of Egypt and into the Promised Land. I tried to decline the mantle of authority. But You insisted, and I consented. Did I consent in order to perform only part of the mission?[27] Did I endure all this

---

22. See *Midrash Petiras Moshe*, cited in *Otzar Midrashim* 362, 375; *Devarim Rabbah* 9:4.
23. *Devarim Rabbah* 2:3, 9:2.
24. *Devarim Rabbah* 9:2.
25. See *Devarim Rabbah* 2:7–8; *Bamidbar* 17:25.
26. *Ohr haChaim*, *Bamidbar* 20:1.
27. See *Sifrei*, *Midrash haGadol*, *Da'as Zekeinim* on *Devarim* 3:26.

pain and suffering for forty long years just to bring them to the threshold of the land and not bring them in? Did I invest so much effort into teaching the Jewish people Torah and mitzvos only to bring them to the place of the Torah's fulfillment but not to participate in it? Shouldn't my struggle to take care of the people in the wilderness for so many years be rewarded with a share in the happiness of coming home to the land of our forefathers?[28] You granted me the privilege of conquering Sichon and Og. Can You not let me finish what I started, by defeating the thirty-one kings of Canaan?[29] The burning bush was a symbol that You shared in the suffering of the Jewish people. Well, now I am suffering. Can't You share in my suffering as well?"[30]

"Moshe, I made an oath, and I cannot annul it."

"I swore an oath to Yisro that I would not leave Midian. Didn't You annul my oath so that I could lead the Jewish people out of Egypt?"

"Yes, I did. A master can annul the vow of a disciple, and that is what I did for you. But who can annul My vow? Who is superior to Me?!"[31]

"But You took an oath to annihilate the Jewish people when they made the Eigel, and yet, somehow, You annulled it. Why can't You annul the decree against me in the same way?[32] And if I cannot enter the land, why can't I at least be buried there? I brought out Yosef's remains from Egypt, and for the past forty years I have transported them with me so that he could be buried in the Holy

---

28. *Devarim Rabbah* 11:10 with *Tiferes Tzion*; *Midrash haGadol*, *Devarim* 3:24.

Hashem replied that Moshe's reward in the next world would far exceed entry into Eretz Yisrael. For the future of the land was not a pleasant one, so by entering it he would only be replacing one distress with another.

29. Abarbanel, *Devarim* 3:24.

30. *Da'as Sofer*, *Devarim* 3:26.

31. See *Sifrei*, *Midrash haGadol*, *Da'as Zekeinim* on ibid. See *Let My Nation Go*, p. 141.

32. *Devarim Rabbah* 2:8; *Sifrei*.

Land as he requested. Shouldn't that earn me the same privilege?"

"No," said Hashem. "There is a difference. When Yosef was in prison, he proudly told the royal cupbearer that he was a Jew who had been abducted and unjustly accused. He took pride in his identity, and therefore he deserves special consideration to be buried in the land of his fathers. As for you, when you met Yisro's daughters at the well in Midian, they thought you were an Egyptian and you did not correct their error. Therefore, you cannot make a plea for special consideration in this respect.[33]

"But there is more. Hundreds of thousands of Jews have died during these past forty years. They are all buried in the wilderness. How would it look if their leader left them there and was buried in the homeland? What would people say? But with you buried among them, your merit will insure that these people will all be resurrected in the End of Days. What price are you prepared to pay in order to cross into the land and be buried there? Are you willing to accept that hundreds of thousands of people will never rise again?"

"No, I am not," said Moshe in a subdued tone. "It would be worthwhile for one hundred people like me to be buried in the wilderness if that would insure that one more Jew will one day be resurrected.[34] But I still will not abandon my pleas.[35] Don't we learn that even if there is a sharp sword against a person's throat he should not abandon hope?[36] I am still hopeful. Isn't there any way that the dead in the wilderness can be resurrected even if I am buried in the Holy Land? And why can't I remain alive on this side of the Jordan River in the lands of Gad and Reuven? Then I

---

33. *Devarim Rabbah* 2:8; *Midrash haGadol, Devarim* 3:27; *Sifrei, Ha'azinu*. See *Bereishis* 40:15 with Ramban; *Shemos* 2:19. See also *Let My Nation Go*, p. 102; *Let My Nation Descend*, p. 115.

34. See *Devarim Rabbah* 2:9, 7:10; *Yalkut Shimoni* 820; Alshich, *Me'am Lo'ez* on *Devarim* 3:24–26.

35. *Devarim Rabbah* 2:6.

36. See *Me'am Lo'ez, Devarim* 3:23; *Berachos* 10a.

would somehow still be together with those who perished before entering the land."[37]

"Do you expect to live forever, Moshe?[38] Avraham survived the fiery furnace, and eventually he died. Yitzchak survived the Akeidah, and eventually he died. Yaakov survived mortal combat with an angel, and eventually he died. They were all human, and all humans die. You must also eventually die.[39] Once a person's time arrives, he must go. Even if he sprouts wings like an angel, they will not prevent him from falling into the hands of the Angel of Death like a sheep to the slaughter."[40]

"But why?"

"Who was your father, Moshe?"

"Amram."

"And his father?"

"Kehas."

"And that traces back to whom?"

"Levi."

"And all the way back to whom?"

"Adam."

"Exactly, Moshe. All humankind descends from Adam, and I already decreed that Adam and all his descendants must die."

"Adam deserved to die," said Moshe, "because he transgressed the one commandment You gave him. Must all others die?"

"Avraham sanctified My holy Name, and yet he died."

"Avraham had a blemish," said Moshe. "He fathered Yishmael and all his wicked offspring who anger You."

"On the other hand," said Hashem, "he fathered Yitzchak who stretched out his neck on the Akeidah and was prepared to die for Me."

---

37. See *Midrash Petiras Moshe*, cited in *Otzar Midrashim* 366.

38. *Tehillim* 89:49.

39. *Devarim Rabbah* 9:4.

40. *Tanchuma, Va'eschanan* 6.

"But Yitzchak fathered Eisav, whose descendants and successors will eventually destroy the Beis haMikdash."

"What can you say about Yaakov, then?" asked Hashem. "He fathered twelve tribes. His descendants are without blemish. He died. Why should you be better?"

"Yaakov never rose to the heavens," Moshe replied. "He never stepped into the upper domain. He never lived as a ministering angel. He never spoke to You face-to-face. He did not receive the Torah. All these things should set me apart from those who died on account of Adam's sin."[41]

Moshe now appealed to the heavens and earth to plead for him.

"Before we seek mercy for you," they said, "seek mercy for us, for it is written, 'The heavens will dissipate like smoke and the earth will wear out like a garment.'"[42]

Moshe appealed to the stars and constellations to plead for him.

"Before we seek mercy for you," they said, "seek mercy for us, for it is written, 'All the hosts of the heavens will dissolve.'"[43]

Moshe appealed to the mountains and hills to plead for him.

"Before we seek mercy for you," they said, "seek mercy for us, for it is written, 'For the mountains will be moved and the hills will falter.'"[44]

Moshe appealed to the great Sea of Reeds to plead for him.

"Why do you come to me?" it said. "You are the one who smote me, who split me into twelve paths."

"'Oh, if I could only be as in the earlier months,' he quoted sadly, 'as in the days when Hashem would watch over me.'[45]

---

41. Ibid. See *Midrash Petiras Moshe,* in *Otzar Midrashim* 362.
42. *Yeshayahu* 51:6.
43. Ibid., 34:4.
44. Ibid., 54:10.
45. *Iyov* 29:2.

When I crossed you, O sea, I was a king in this world. Now I appeal for help, but no one heeds my plea."

Moshe appealed to the minister of the inner sanctum of Heaven. "Moshe, why place this burden upon me?" he said. "I have heard behind the curtain that your prayer regarding this issue will not be accepted."

Moshe placed his head in his hands and wept. "Whom can I find to plead for me?" he cried.[46]

There was no response.

Moshe declared a fast for himself. He donned sackcloth and put ashes on his head. Then he drew a circle around himself and said he wouldn't budge until Hashem abolished the decree. In this state, he began praying with more intensity than ever before. His prayers shook the heavens until the world thought that it was on the verge of disintegration and that a new world was being created.

"Do not allow Moshe's prayers to pass," Hashem said to all the heavenly courts stationed near the twelve heavenly gates, "and do not pray for him."

Moshe persisted. With the uttering of Hashem's Name, Moshe's prayers were like a sword penetrating the heavenly gates leading to the seven heavens.

"Close the gates at once," Hashem commanded the angels, "so that his prayers do not reach the heavenly Throne."

"Stop, Moshe," the heavenly courts proclaimed. "The decree is final. It cannot be rescinded."

Hashem had reissued the decree forbidding Moshe to enter the Holy Land ten times. And now it was sealed with finality.[47]

---

46. *Tanchuma, Va'eschanan* 6.

47. Had Hashem rescinded His sealed decree, it would have paved the way for future annulments. He had to set a standard: Prayer and repentance can reverse a decree only until it's sealed. Therefore, as a precedent for future generations and predicaments, Hashem wouldn't budge (*Tiferes Tzion*).

"It is done," Hashem said. "I decreed you may not enter, and it is final."[48]

Nonetheless, Moshe's prayer continued unabated. He repeated his prayers 515 times.[49]

"Moshe, do not pray anymore," Hashem finally said. "People will not understand what is happening here, and they'll say, 'How harsh is the Master, and how obstinate is the disciple who continues to press Him.'"[50]

"But people will misunderstand my death as well," said Moshe. "They'll think I'm guilty of undisclosed sins."

"I have made sure that they make no such error," Hashem replied. "I've written in the Torah that the only reason you will not step into the land is because you failed to sanctify My holy Name at Mei Merivah."[51]

"Then perhaps You will allow me to utter Your holy Name

---

48. *Devarim Rabbah* 11:10 with *Tiferes Tzion*. Because the Jews sinned ten times in the wilderness, it was decreed ten times that Moshe would die before entering Eretz Yisrael. Thus, he had ten opportunities to pray for the cancellation of the decree. This time was his last. See *Tiferes Tzion, Devarim Rabbah* 11:6. According to *Tiferes Tzion*, the acceptance of Moshe's prayers was built into creation. The only possibility of their rejection was that they not reach their destination.

49. *Devarim Rabbah* 11:10. See *Tiferes Tzion* for why Moshe prayed 515 times.

Panim Yafos points out that if Moshe began praying on 10 Nisan, when Hashem pronounced the decree, and he prayed thrice daily, his 515 prayers concluded during the Ten Days of Repentance. Factoring in the extra Musaf prayers, Moshe concluded his prayers when Sichon and Og were defeated.

According to *Pnei Yehoshua, Berachos* 32a, Moshe began praying on 15 Av, when the death of the wilderness generation concluded. From 15 Av until 7 Adar, there are 200 days. Deducting the twenty-eight Sabbaths during this period leaves 172 days. Three prayers daily times 172 equals 516 prayers in all. Yet the first day Moshe prayed only twice, since Hashem revealed Himself by day, so he missed the previous night. Thus, Moshe prayed 515 times.

Yalkut Reuveni, Devarim 3:23, states that angels offer 515 prayers daily.

Midrash Petiras Moshe, cited in *Otzar Midrashim* 364, reckons that Moshe prayed ninety-five days, from 22 Tishrei to 1 Shevat.

50. *Sifrei; Sotah* 13b; Rashi, *Devarim* 3:25.

51. *Midrash Petiras Moshe*, cited in *Otzar Midrashim* 362.

and fly into the land without actually stepping into it."

"No, that would be considered a violation of My oath.[52]

"Moshe, I know you don't desire to enter the land to enjoy its fruits and its bounty. I know you want to perform the mitzvos that can only be performed in the land: from establishing cities of refuge to the destruction of Amalek to the eventual construction of the Beis haMikdash.[53] You want to tithe fruits, bring offerings and the firstfruits to the Kohen, to perform the mitzvah of sukkah, to observe the festivals, to sanctify the moon and the months of the year, to say one hundred *berachos* daily.

"You want all this so that it will be a merit for you and the Jewish people.[54] I assure you that you will be far better off this way than if you were actually performing mitzvos in the land, because I will judge not by your actions but by your intent. Your intention to perform all those mitzvos will be considered as if you had actually performed them. And you will also earn the merit of all the myriad Jewish people who perform mitzvos. You are their leader, their guide and their teacher, and your prayers have rescued them from disaster time and time again. Therefore, all that they do is to your credit. A great reward indeed awaits you."[55]

"Like the daughters of Tzelofchad," Moshe said, "I too love the Land. Can I at least see it?"[56]

"That I will do for you," said Hashem. "And I will do even more. Not only will I allow you to look at the land, I will show you it in its entirety, including portions that Yehoshua will never see and portions you never would have seen had you actually

52. Ibid., cited in *Otzar Midrashim* 366.

53. See *Tashbatz* 198.

54. Moshe wanted to perform as many of the 613 mitzvos as possible. Indeed, the numerical value of "Moshe Rabbeinu" is 613 (*Me'am Lo'ez*).

55. See *Sifrei*; *Sotah* 14a with Maharsha, *Iyun Yaakov, Anaf Yosef*; Rashi, *Ohr haChaim, Yalkut Reuveni* on *Devarim* 3:25.

56. *Tzeror haMor, Bamidbar* 27:12.

entered it with everyone else.[57] Before you die,[58] I will take you up to Mount Nevo,[59] also called Mount Ha'avarim because it is near the Jordan crossing.[60] From there, you will see all the land, in both the physical sense and the spiritual sense."[61]

This is analogous to a prince who rebelled against his father the king and is banned from the inner chambers of the palace. The son follows his father as he enters the palace's gates and courtyard. He follows him as he enters the palace's foyer. But when his father enters the inner chambers, he turns to his son and says, "This is far enough. You cannot go beyond this point."

The Jordan River was the point beyond which Moshe could not go. It was a heartbreaking disappointment for him, but it did not keep him from continuing to serve the Jewish people faithfully and responsibly until the end of his life.[62]

Moshe's desperate and persistent prayers and Hashem's consistent refusal established an important principle for the Jewish people. They learned that despite Hashem's mercy, there are times when He will not rescind a decree He issued against someone who

---

57. *Sifrei; Yalkut Shimoni* 916; *Midrash haGadol*, Rashi with Mizrachi, and *Sefer Zikaron* on *Devarim* 3:27. See *HaKesav vehaKabbalah, Devarim* 34:4.

58. See Ramban, *Chizkuni, Akeidas Yitzchak, Ha'amek Davar* on *Bamidbar* 27:12–13; *Eitz Yosef, Bamidbar Rabbah* 21:13 (14). According to most authorities, Hashem was telling Moshe that before he died he should ascend the mountain to see Eretz Yisrael, as he'd requested in *Devarim* 3:25. Others equate this statement with the comments made in *Devarim* 32:49, shortly before his death. Following Moshe's supplication, he asked Hashem to provide the Jewish people with a new leader. For more on this subject, see Abarbanel, Malbim and the commentaries mentioned at the beginning of this footnote.

59. Named for its proximity to the graves of three *nevi'im* (prophets): Moshe, Aharon and Miriam (*Sotah* 13b).

60. Ramban, *Bamidbar* 27:12. Compare *Kli Yakar*. See also Rabbeinu Bachya, *Devarim* 32:49.

61. See Ramban, *Chizkuni, Akeidas Yitzchak* on *Bamidbar* 27:12. See also Rabbeinu Bachya, *Devarim* 32:52. Moshe beheld the entire future of Eretz Yisrael, with all its highs and lows. According to Tur, he even saw caves and the treasures hidden therein.

62. See *Bamidbar Rabbah* 21:13; *Sifrei* 134; Rashi, *Bamidbar* 27:12.

sinned. Furthermore, they learned that "according to the camel's strength, so is the load placed on him." Moshe was exceedingly great. Therefore, the standard expected of him was much higher than the standard expected of ordinary people.[63]

63. See *Yalkut Shimoni, Va'eschanan*; *Sotah* 13b with Rashi.

14 Preparing for Transition

Moshe finally bowed to the inevitable. It had become abundantly clear that Hashem would not change His "mind," as it were, and rescind the decree. The end was near, and it was time for final preparations.[1] At this critical point in his life, facing his own imminent death, Moshe was characteristically unconcerned with his personal needs, concentrating instead on his responsibilities as a leader to insure an orderly succession.[2] Like a faithful shepherd who does not walk away from his flock until his replacement has matters under control,

1. Abarbanel, *Bamidbar* 27:15.
2. Rashi, ibid.; *Sifrei* 138.

Moshe sought assurance that the people would be in good hands after he was gone.[3]

"Hashem, now that I am about to die," he pleaded, "please appoint a great man to lead the nation. Otherwise, they will be like sheep without a shepherd, who fall prey to wolves and lions, or even to thirst and hunger, without the supervision and protection a shepherd provides."[4]

"I will," replied Hashem.[5]

"I also ask You not to treat him as You treated me. For seven days I resisted the mantle of leadership, but You pressed me, and I agreed. Then I led the people out of Egypt and through the wilderness for forty years, and now that I stand on the threshold of the land, I am forbidden entry. Please allow my successor to complete my mission and lead the people into the land."[6]

"I will," promised Hashem.

Reassured that the succession would be implemented, Moshe turned his focus on his own family. The daughters of Tzelofchad had just been granted the rights of inheritance, and Moshe felt the time was ripe to secure the inheritance of the mantle of leadership for his own sons.[7]

"I am of a different mind," said Hashem. "Your sons will not succeed you,[8] because they are not as expert in the Torah as the leader I have chosen."[9]

"Perhaps You can infuse one of my sons with a holy spirit,"

---

3. *Midrash haGadol, Bamidbar* 27:17.

4. Rashi, *Lekach Tov* on *Bamidbar* 27:15, 17; *Sifrei* 138. See *Shir haShirim Rabbah* 1:7. Moshe worried that, with the *mahn* ceasing upon his death, who would feed the Jewish people? (*Ha'amek Davar*).

5. Rashi, *Bamidbar* 27:15, 17; *Sifrei* 138.

6. *Bamidbar Rabbah* 21:15.

7. Rashi, *Bamidbar* 27:16; *Sifrei* 138; *Bamidbar Rabbah* 21:14. Moshe's top priority was the public good. His familial aspirations were secondary (*Mesiach Ilmim*).

8. Rashi, *Bamidbar* 27:16; *Sifrei* 138; *Bamidbar Rabbah* 21:14.

9. *Bamidbar Rabbah* 21:14. See *Avos d'Rabbi Nasan* 17.

said Moshe, "so that he will be worthy of being my replacement."

"No, Moshe. The one I have chosen is already filled with the holy spirit of the Torah.[10] That cannot simply be conferred on someone. It must be earned over a long period of dedication."[11]

"Perhaps, then, my sons can share the mantle of leadership. Perhaps they can lead the people into battle and leave the conduct of spiritual affairs to the one who is filled with the holy spirit of the Torah."

"No, that is not possible either."[12]

"Then can it be one of my nephews, the sons of Aharon?"

"No, but you will be pleased with My choice."[13]

"Hashem, You are Lord of the spirits of all creatures. You know the innermost thoughts and feelings of all people. Just as no two faces are exactly alike, so are the personalities and minds of people different from each other.[14] Therefore, I ask You, Hashem, to select a leader who is sensitive to these differences and can lead and direct each and every individual member of this great and populous nation in exactly the way they must be guided.[15] May he be humble, soft-spoken and patient, capable of leading the meek as well as the haughty.[16] May he be selfless and concerned with the welfare of the people.[17]

"The kings of the nations," Moshe continued, "send their armies out to the front to do battle, but they themselves stay behind. May the leader You appoint be at the head of the army as it goes into battle and as it returns from battle,[18] as I was in the

---

10. See *Panim Yafos, Bamidbar* 27:16.
11. See *Avos d'Rabbi Nasan.*
12. *Yalkut Reuveni, Bamidbar* 27:16.
13. *Midrash Petiras Moshe,* cited in *Otzar Midrashim* 377.
14. See *Bamidbar Rabbah* 21:22, 15.
15. See Rashi, Malbim on *Bamidbar* 27:16.
16. Meiri's *Magen Avos.* See Meiri, *Yoma* 22b.
17. See *Ha'amek Davar, Bamidbar* 27:15; *Yalkut Shimoni* 776.
18. Naturally, the leader of the Jewish people should head the army as it goes into

wars with Sichon and Og.[19] May he be a conqueror, warrior and general,[20] whose righteousness and virtue will inspire his followers to triumph in battle and whose blessed fortune will bring back his victorious army safely from battle.[21] May he pray on behalf of the people.[22] May he have the wisdom to govern the nation well in every aspect of public interest.[23] May he be kind and considerate, earning the people's respect, yet strong and resolute in enforcing the laws and maintaining social order."[24]

Hashem's Choice

"I have chosen just such a man," Hashem replied. "It is your disciple, Yehoshua. He has shown himself worthy of the mantle of leadership by never departing from the tent of Torah day or night. He woke early and stayed late to learn Torah from you. He set up benches and mats in the house of study on which students and teachers would sit. He served and honored you faithfully. So let the one who guards the fig tree eat from its fruits.[25]

"I, the Lord of all spirits, attest that he has all the qualities you

---

battle, but why when it returns home? *Avir Yosef* explains that the Jewish king leads the army into battle not to brandish his sword and utter bloodcurdling cries, but to set an example of how a faithful Jew goes to war: with prayers on his lips and his head bowed in humility and supplication. Likewise, a Jewish king must set an example upon his forces' victorious return, eschewing arrogant cries of victory and instead reciting paeans of praise and humble gratitude to Hashem.

19. Rashi, *Sifrei*, Alshich, *Midrash haGadol* on *Bamidbar* 27:17.

20. Abarbanel, Malbim on *Bamidbar* 27:16.

21. Rashi with *Be'er baSadeh*, *Mesiach Ilmim*, Abarbanel, *Tzeror haMor* on *Bamidbar* 27:17.

22. *Midrash haGadol*, ibid.

23. Seforno, Malbim, *Midrash haGadol* on ibid.

24. Malbim, ibid.

25. Rashi, *Bamidbar* 27:16; *Sifrei* 140; *Bamidbar Rabbah* 12:9, 21:14; *Mishlei* 27:18. In fact, there were greater Torah scholars than Yehoshua, but the honor and respect he displayed toward them made him more worthy to lead than any other (*Yalkut Shimoni*, *Mishlei* 959). See *Berachos* 7b.

have enumerated.[26] Therefore, take Yehoshua, select him as the next leader and give him words of encouragement. Say to him, 'Fortunate are you to have merited to lead the Omnipresent's people.' Yehoshua is indeed a man of spirit who can discern the character of each individual. Appoint a *meturgman*, a spokesman to serve him even now, so that people will say he is worthy of leadership even in your lifetime.[27]

"And make sure Yehoshua is forewarned about what is in store for him. Tell him the Jewish people are troublesome, obstinate, burdensome and quarrelsome, and he must be prepared for it. Reassure him that he will not face your fate. He will successfully bring the people into the land.[28]

"Bestow some but not all of the radiance of your face upon him,[29] so that the people will look upon him with reverence and awe, as they looked upon you.[30]

"Yehoshua will be your successor, Moshe, not your sons. But I have heard your plea for a leadership role for your nephews, Aharon's sons. Yehoshua will receive his guidance from your tribe, the tribe of Levi. Elazar, the Kohen Gadol, will wear the Urim v'Tumim on his breastplate, and he, in accord with the Sanhedrin, will advise Yehoshua, despite all his valor and might, on decisions of war and peace.[31] The fate of the people is always in the hands of Heaven rather than in human hands, no matter how capable."[32]

---

26. Abarbanel, *Bamidbar* 27:18.

27. Rashi, *Bamidbar* 27:19; *Sifrei* 92; *Avos d'Rabbi Nasan* 17.

28. Rashi, *Bamidbar* 27:19, *Sifrei* 92; Rashi, *Devarim* 3:28. See *Vayikra Rabbah* 10:2.

29. Rashi, *Bamidbar* 27:20. See *Shemos* 34:29.

30. Alshich, *Bamidbar* 27:20.

31. Rashi, *Bechor Shor, Minchah Belulah* on *Bamidbar* 27:21; *Bamidbar Rabbah* 21:15; *Sanhedrin* 16a. See *Yoma* 73b. Much discussion revolves around Yehoshua's use or non-use of the Urim v'Tumim (Tur). After Moshe passed away, Yehoshua developed his own prophecy and never used them. See *Midrash haGadol, Mattos*; *Eiruvin* 63a; Tosafos, *Sanhedrin* 16a; *Me'am Lo'ez, Yehoshua* 3:7; Abarbanel. According to *Gittin* 59a, Elazar equaled Yehoshua in Torah.

32. *Yerushalmi Shabbos* 2:6; *Midrash haBeiur, Tzeror haMor* on *Bamidbar* 27:21.

Moshe Selects Yehoshua

Hashem did not give Moshe a specific time frame for arranging the succession. Nevertheless, despite his disappointment that his sons would not succeed him, Moshe wasted no time in implementing Yehoshua's induction into his leadership role with the love and joy of a father for his son.[33]

Yehoshua was everything Moshe could possibly have wanted. He had piety,[34] knowledge, intellect, understanding and wisdom,[35] and he was also blessed with divine inspiration, even while he was still only Moshe's disciple.[36] He was as strong as an ox[37] yet soft-spoken. He was even-tempered, objective and completely selfless.[38] He had a gentle, loving manner that inspired people to improve themselves and made him immensely popular.[39] He was truly deserving of the leadership position.[40]

On the first day of the month of Shevat,[41] just thirty-seven days before Moshe was to pass away, Moshe appointed Yehoshua the next leader of the Jewish people.[42] Moshe spoke words of en-

---

33. *Me'am Lo'ez*, *Ohr haChaim* on *Bamidbar* 27:22; *Sifrei* 141 with *Emek haNetziv*.

34. *Bechor Shor*, *Bamidbar* 27:23.

35. Abarbanel, *Bamidbar* 27:18.

36. Rabbeinu Meyuchas, *Bamidbar* 27:23; Abarbanel, *Bamidbar* 27:18. See *Bamidbar Rabbah* 12:9 with *Matnos Kehunah*.

37. Rashi, *Devarim* 33:17.

38. *Ha'amek Davar*, *Bamidbar* 27:18.

39. See *Ma'alos haTorah* 14, "*Ratzon.*" See *Yehoshua* 7:20.

40. Rashi, *I Divrei haYamim* 29:25.

41. *Midrash Petiras Moshe*, cited in *Otzar Midrashim*. According to *Devarim Rabbah* 2:5, Moshe now pleaded with Hashem to allow him into Eretz Yisrael, as recorded in *parashas Va'eschanan*.

42. Yehoshua was now either eighty-two or ninety-six. See Ibn Ezra, *Shemos* 33:11; *Let My Nation Serve Me*, p. 116. According to Rokeach, *Bamidbar* 27:18, and *Seder Olam* 12, he was forty-two when the Jews left Mitzrayim, making him eighty-two now. Tur, *Bamidbar* 27:16, counts twenty-eight words in verses 16–17, representing the twenty-eight years Yehoshua would lead the Jewish people. Yet he lived until 110, so if he was ninety-six now, he led the Jews only during the fourteen years of conquest and division of the land, dying

couragement to him, as Hashem had instructed, telling him that the leaders of the Jewish people would be rewarded in this world and the next.[43]

"Do not be worried that you will fail to bring the people into the Holy Land, as I have failed to do," Moshe told him. "Hashem has assured me that you will be successful. Be patient with the people, even though they can sometimes be difficult. Don't accuse them of rebellion in a moment of anger, as I did."[44]

Moshe formally introduced Yehoshua to the entire congregation of the Jewish people, including Elazar, the elders and the Sanhedrin. He then publicly began teaching Yehoshua the laws and rules regarding his ascension to leadership so that all should witness the legitimacy of the latter's appointment and accept him as their future leader.[45] Moshe also initiated him into additional matters of prophecy[46] and instructed him in the use of Hashem's ineffable Name.[47]

Moshe bestowed some of the radiance of his face on Yehoshua, honoring him and glorifying him before the people so that they too would honor him.[48] And indeed they did. But it was a traumatic transition. While Moshe's face was radiant like the sun, Yehoshua's face was like the moon: a mere reflection of Moshe's

---

immediately thereafter. Therefore, according to Tur, Yehoshua could not be more than eighty-two years old at this time. See *Seder Olam* 12 and its commentaries; Tosafos, *Bava Basra* 117b, s.v. *mikan*.

43. Rashi with *Sifsei Chachamim*, *Bamidbar* 27:22; *Sifrei* 141. See also *Emek ha-Netziv*.

44. *Yalkut Shimoni*, *Vayeilech*.

45. See Ramban, Seforno, Alshich on *Bamidbar* 27:19. This teaching included the rule that even war shouldn't disrupt Torah study and the sacrificial offerings. See *Eiruvin* 63b.

46. *Targum Unkelos*, *Midrash haCheifetz* on *Bamidbar* 27:20. Compare *Sifsei Kohen*.

47. Rokeach, *Bamidbar* 27:23.

48. Seforno, Ibn Ezra, *Bechor Shor* on *Bamidbar* 27:19–20. Moshe wanted the people to treat Yehoshua as their new king. See *Ha'amek Davar*, *Bamidbar* 27:18; Rambam, *Melachim* 1:3; *Bereishis Rabbah* 59:6.

greatness, both regarding the glow of his face and regarding his knowledge. Yehoshua was certainly a man of profound greatness and sanctity, but the stark difference between him and the incomparable Moshe was painful for the generation to behold.[49]

Yehoshua practically swooned with embarrassment while Moshe was honoring him in public, and had to be assisted by others who helped him remain standing upright. All this honor made him uneasy. Moreover, he was concerned that the honors he perceived as undeserved would cause him to die before his time.[50]

Moshe saw his disciple's discomfiture and addressed it. "You need not worry, Yehoshua," he said. "There is no sin in accepting this honor. You have earned it by serving me all these years."[51]

Moshe then placed his hands on Yehoshua's head as a sign that he was transferring his leadership to Yehoshua willingly and lovingly.[52] The hands also served as a conduit for a measured flow of blessing (*shefa*), the secrets of prophecy and segments of his own knowledge.[53] Yehoshua's entire body, all two hundred and forty-eight limbs, was now infused with the spirit of Moshe's knowledge.[54] This transmission also gave him an increased measure of heavenly assistance that would allow him to make proper decisions during crises and to formulate responsa on questions of law.[55]

---

49. Rashi, Rabbeinu Bachya on *Bamidbar* 27:20; *Sifrei* 140; *Bava Basra* 75a with Rashi; Zohar, *Devarim* 283a. See *Anaf Yosef*. *Ben Yehoyada* notes that Moshe's face is compared to the sun, because just as the sun is much larger than it seems from afar, Moshe was far greater than publicly perceived. Abarbanel adds that just as one can't look directly at the sun, the same could be said about Moshe's face. For an in-depth treatment of this subject, see the introduction to *Sefer Hafla'ah*.

50. See Rokeach, *Tosefos Rabbeinu Yoel*, Maharam, Seforno on *Bamidbar* 27:22.

Yehoshua displayed the modesty of his progenitor Ephraim, who too was given leadership (by Yaakov) because of his humility (Rokeach).

51. *Midrash Petiras Moshe*, cited in *Otzar Midrashim* 365.

52. Ibn Ezra, Seforno, *Chizkuni* on *Bamidbar* 27:18.

53. *Chupas Eliyahu*, Malbim on ibid.; Ralbag, *Devarim* 34:9.

54. Rabbi Yehudah heChasid, *Devarim* 34:9.

55. *Ha'amek Davar*, *Bamidbar* 27:18.

Moshe displayed great character during the transferral of leadership. Hashem had instructed him to place only one hand on Yehoshua, yet Moshe, despite his disappointment at his sons' exclusion, placed both hands on his disciple, making sure that he became like a vessel overflowing with abundant wisdom.[56]

Moshe did not forfeit any of his holiness by transferring his powers to Yehoshua. On the contrary, it was like lighting one candle from another. Moshe was igniting a new flame of leadership in Yehoshua, a flame from which the Jewish people would be enlightened.[57]

"There is a new prophet among us," Moshe announced to the great public assembly. "His name is Yehoshua. Come hear him speak."

Moshe then accorded Yehoshua the same treatment Yehoshua had accorded him all those years. Moreover, he then went on to serve and honor Yehoshua in the same manner which Yehoshua himself treated Moshe all the years. He prepared a golden throne on which Yehoshua would sit like a king, wrapped him in his *tallis* and adorned him with pearls around his neck. Moshe also placed a hat upon his head and a royal purple cloak on his shoulders, marking his status as leader and king. He also adorned his tent with royal trappings. He cleaned his shoes, opened the door for him, provided him with weapons and arranged for royal guards to protect him and janitorial people to clean his tent—all in order to show the people that Yehoshua deserved to be treated with reverence.[58]

Yehoshua followed Moshe's lead and began delivering lectures to the Jewish people regarding the observance of mitzvos,

---

56. Rashi, *Bamidbar* 27:21; *Sifrei* 141; *Sanhedrin* 105b; *Bamidbar Rabbah* 21:15.

57. *Bamidbar Rabbah* 21:15. When the formal transfer of leadership to Yehoshua was complete, however, Moshe lost a certain aspect of his spirit. As will be elaborated upon below, this was Hashem's way of showing Moshe that his death would come soon.

58. Rokeach, *Bamidbar* 27:21–23.

learning Torah, following in the ways of Hashem and having faith in Him. Moshe appointed Kalev to assist Yehoshua by repeating the lectures to the broader audience not within earshot of Yehoshua. Moshe himself sat among the audience and listened just as any ordinary student would.[59]

"Be strong and courageous," Moshe told Yehoshua, "and inspire the people to be courageous as well. Just as Hashem assisted me with the conquests of Sichon and Og, He will assist you. And just as I had the fighters from the tribes of Gad and Reuven at my command, you will have them at your command when you do battle with the thirty-one Canaanite kings.[60] But know this: you will conquer the land only if you yourself lead the people into battle. If you stay behind and send the armies out to fight, you will fail."[61]

Moshe went on to teach Yehoshua everything a Jewish leader needed to know, from the importance of the daily sacrifices to the conquest of the Holy Land. Yehoshua reviewed the lessons again and again so that they would be at his fingertips when the time came for him to actualize them.[62]

---

59. *Midrash Petiras Moshe*, cited in *Otzar Midrashim* 362, 365. See Rabbi Yehudah heChasid, Rokeach on *Bamidbar* 27:22. See also Chapter 19.

60. *Midrash haGadol*, Rabbeinu Bachya on *Devarim* 3:21; *Shelah, Devarim* 3:28. The emphasis on Gad and Reuven will be elaborated upon in Chapter 16.

61. Rashi, *Devarim* 3:29; *Sifrei*. See also *Yehoshua* 7.

62. Abarbanel, *Devarim* 32:50.

15 Unfinished Business

The time had come to settle unfinished business with the Midianites, who had been responsible for the disaster at Shittim. Pinchas had already been rewarded for his heroic feat of killing Zimri and ending the plague. It was now time for Midian to suffer the proper retribution.[1]

"Tell the Jewish people," Hashem said to Moshe, "that they are to mount an assault against Midian.[2] Besiege their cities,[3] and wage relentless war against them.[4] Kill

---

1. Malbim, *Bamidbar* 25:17.

2. Rashi, ibid. See Rokeach, *Bamidbar* 31:2. According to Ramban, *Bamidbar* 31:6, Moshe didn't specify whether the assault was to include both men and women.

3. R. Saadiah Gaon, Malbim on *Bamidbar* 25:17; *Sifrei* 157.

4. *Chizkuni*, Ramban, *Tzeror haMor* on *Bamidbar* 25:17. See *Ha'amek Davar*.

the conspirators and perpetrators of the Shittim plot. No one shall escape death. Make sure Bilam is slain as well."[5]

"Shouldn't we offer peace first," asked Moshe, "just as You instructed us to do in the past?"

"Midian is different," said Hashem. "With them, there is no time to waste with gestures of peace when no peace is possible. They seethe with hatred and the desire to avenge Kosbi, and even at this very moment, they are actively plotting to inflict more wounds on the people. There is no coexistence with the Midianites.[6] They are underhanded, and they may come to you with friendly smiles on their faces, but know full well that underneath those false façades they are your implacable enemies.[7] They despise you, and you must despise them in return. They caused the people to sin, which brought on a plague that resulted in twenty-four thousand deaths from one tribe.[8] Show them no mercy. Go fight them."[9]

"But why are You commanding us to attack Midian and not Moav? The Moabites started this whole campaign against the Jewish people. They are the ones who asked Midian for advice and invited their assistance. They are the ones who hired Bilam. It would seem that the principal enemy is Moav and that Midian is nothing more than an accessory. Why then are we ordered to attack Midian and not Moav?"[10]

"Your point is well-taken," Hashem replied. "There are several reasons why I am dealing more harshly with Midian than with Moav. Although Moav instigated the plot, it was the Midianites

---

5. See Ramban, Malbim on *Bamidbar* 25:17; *Sifrei* 157.

6. *Bamidbar Rabbah* 21:4 with Mahrzu; Malbim, *Akeidas Yitzchak*, *Minchah Belulah* on *Bamidbar* 25:17.

7. *Ma'aseh Hashem*, *Bamidbar* 25:17.

8. Rashi, Rav Saadiah Gaon on ibid., 25:18. See also Chapter 11, footnote 50, and corresponding text.

9. *Tzeror haMor*, ibid.

10. See *Bava Kamma* 38 with Rashi. According to Tosafos, Moshe and Hashem never had this dialogue. Hashem preempted Moshe's argument with an answer.

who formulated and executed the actual plans.[11] It was their daughters, with Kosbi showing the way, who seduced the Jewish men and persuaded them to worship the idol Pe'or.[12] As for the Moabite daughters, they merely made themselves available. They did not actively pursue the Jewish men.[13]

"Furthermore, the Moabites were motivated by fear and self-defense, not hatred. They saw the Jewish people as an existential, or at least a territorial, threat.[14] They were not convinced that their lands had been given immunity from being conquered, because the Jewish people had conquered the lands of Sichon, which were part of the ancestral Moabite territory that Sichon had captured from them. Their hostile reaction to the Jewish people could be somewhat excused.

"But Midian was not threatened by the Jewish people in any way. In fact, they should have been better disposed to the Jewish people because you are the son-in-law of Yisro, the most illustrious of the Midianites. And in the end, Midian rather than Moav was the principal cause of the plague.[15] The Midianites hate the Jewish people, because you are a circumcised nation that rejects idols, learns Torah and performs mitzvos. Their attack on the spiritual purity of the people, inflicting spiritual damage as well as causing thousands of casualties, was unprovoked and inexcusable, and they deserve to be punished severely.[16]

"The main reason, however, for the exemption of Moav from

---

11. Rashi, Ibn Ezra on *Bamidbar* 25:18. See Zohar, *Balak* 189b.

12. *Yerushalmi Sanhedrin* 10:2. See *Sifsei Kohen, Ha'amek Davar* on *Bamidbar* 25:14, 17.

13. *Kli Yakar*, Alshich on *Bamidbar* 25:17. Alshich elaborates on how the motives of Midian and Moav differed radically. See *Ha'amek Davar* regarding how differently their sins affected the Jews.

14. Rashi, *Bamidbar* 31:2; *Sifsei Kohen, Bamidbar* 25:17.

15. *Midrash Aggadah, Bamidbar* 25:17.

16. *Chizkuni, Sifsei Kohen* on ibid.; Rashi, *Bamidbar* 31:2; *HaKesav vehaKabbalah*, Alshich, Malbim on *Bamidbar* 31:3; *Bamidbar Rabbah* 22:2.

retaliation is in the merit of Ruth, a future descendant of Moav who will convert and become the ancestress of King David and his royal dynasty. In her merit, the entire nation of Moav is spared.[17]

"But their punishment is only temporarily deferred. Centuries from now, King David will punish the Moabite nation for their sins against the Jewish people.[18] In the meantime, keep your distance from them. Do not attack them, but neither make peace treaties with them. And converts from among the Moabites shall not be allowed to marry freely among the people. Egypt and Edom tried to destroy the physical bodies of the Jewish people, removing them from this world but not from the next. Therefore, the descendants of Egyptian or Edomite converts may marry into the people after three generations. But Moabite converts and their descendants may never marry into the people."[19]

Moshe now returned to his earlier line of questioning. "Hashem, is there any way that I can persuade You to rescind the decree against my entry into the Holy Land? After all, the laws of vows allow for them to be rescinded."

"No, Moshe. The decree remains in force."[20]

"But after all I've done, after I've followed in Your path faithfully, is death really appropriate for me? If You allow me to live, I will be able to proclaim Your holy Name to the entire world."

"If death were really a bad thing," Hashem replied, "would I have allowed the patriarchs ever to taste death?"

Moshe was still not pacified.

"I will make you an offer," Hashem told him. "You can live to be a thousand years old, but if you do, the Jewish people will

---

17. *Bava Kamma* 38; Rashi, *Bamidbar* 25:18, 31:2. Amon was spared in the merit of Na'amah, the wife of King Shlomo.

18. See *Yalkut Shimoni* 785; *II Shemuel* 8:2; Zohar, *Balak* 189b.

19. *Bamidbar Rabbah* 21:4. See *Devarim* 20:10, 23:7.

20. Rabbeinu Bachya, *Bamidbar* 31:2.

not avenge the sin committed against them by Midian in your lifetime."

Moshe was in a quandary. He was faced with a conflict between his personal hopes and the national interest of the Jewish people. Should he choose life for himself, or retribution for the enemies of the people? Ever the faithful shepherd, he chose the good of the people. "Better that I die now," he conceded, "so that the enemies of the Jewish people will be destroyed."[21]

The decree was finally sealed beyond any question. Although Hashem had refused to rescind it, He nonetheless lamented it, so to speak. Moshe had been the one who had advocated for the Jewish people for so many years and saved them from retribution when they were rebellious. And now that his death was imminent, who would defend the people when they strayed from the straight path?[22]

"As one of the last acts of my life," Moshe said to Hashem, "can I exact vengeance on the Midianites? If I don't, people will unjustly accuse me of refusing to attack them because of my ties to Yisro's family and my gratitude to the country that hosted me for so many years."[23]

"Moshe, you will exact vengeance on Midian," Hashem replied.[24] "In fact, you have a special responsibility to do it. At the incident of the Eigel, the tribe of Levi stood against the entire people to defend My honor. At Shittim, however, only the tribe of Shimon was involved, and yet you were not quick to take a stand against them. It was Pinchas who was zealous to defend

---

21. *Yalkut Shimoni* 785.

22. Ibid.

23. See *Sifsei Kohen, Meshech Chochmah* on *Bamidbar* 31:2.

24. *Pirkei d'Rabbi Eliezer* 47; *HaKesav vehaKabbalah, Bamidbar* 31:3. Hashem is more concerned with avenging the deaths of the Jews than with defending His honor. As will be mentioned later, Moshe amended this directive and instructed the Jews to avenge the sins Midian caused the Jews to commit, which desecrated Hashem's Name (Alshich; Malbim).

My honor. You must rectify this failure now by punishing the Midianites for what they did."[25]

Preparations for War

Moshe knew that this would be one of the last missions he would receive before he died. He knew that as soon as he accomplished it, his death would be that much closer. He could have made his preparations with more deliberation so that he could live a little longer. But again, he put the national good before his personal benefit.[26] As soon as he received Hashem's command, he wasted no time in carrying out his mission quickly and joyfully.[27]

Although Moshe was perfectly capable of carrying out the mission himself,[28] he mobilized others to do it. First of all, having lived in Midian for many years, he did not think it appropriate to take a direct role in its destruction: "Do not throw a stone into the well from which you drank."[29] Instead, he chose to send emissaries to act in his stead.[30] Moreover, he wanted to involve all the tribes in the mission in order that their cumulative merit would assure them success.[31]

---

25. See *Yalkut Shimoni* 785; *Ohr haChaim*, Tur, *Pa'aneiach Raza*, Alshich on *Bamidbar* 31:2. Compare Ramban, *Moshav Zekeinim*.

26. Rashi, *Bamidbar* 31:3; *Bamidbar Rabbah* 22:2, 6; *Yalkut Shimoni* 785.

27. According to Radal on *Pirkei d'Rabbi Eliezer* 47, the mission was carried out some time after the original command. After all, Hashem had told Moshe to conduct a census before killing the Midianites.

28. *Yalkut Shimoni* 785.

29. See *Bamidbar Rabbah* 22:4; *Sifsei Kohen, Chizkuni, Da'as Zekeinim* on *Bamidbar* 31:2; *Bava Kamma* 92b.

30. *Ohr haChaim, Ha'amek Davar* on *Bamidbar* 31:6.

31. *Yalkut Shimoni* 785; *Midrash haGadol, Bamidbar* 31:4. This merit included the special virtue of the tribe of Levi (*Ha'amek Davar*).

How could the merits of the twelve tribes exceed that of Moshe, who was compared to the entire nation? Perhaps communal merit played a greater role here.

He summoned all the people and addressed them.

"Those who consider themselves[32] righteous, pious and zealous,"[33] he declared, "gird yourselves with weapons, so we can inflict Hashem's vengeance on Midian."[34]

According to one opinion, the truly righteous were too humble to declare themselves as such, and instead, they were identified by others.[35]

"What did Midian do against Hashem?" someone called out.

"They acted against the Jewish people," Moshe answered, "which is the same as acting against Hashem."[36]

There was a murmur of comprehension.

"We need a thousand men from each tribe," Moshe said, "including the tribe of Levi,[37] for a total of twelve thousand men.[38] We also need an additional twelve thousand men to look after the arsenal and another twelve thousand men to join Pinchas, the Kohen anointed for war, in prayer[39] on the battlefield."[40]

---

32. *Ohr haChaim, Midrash haGadol* on *Bamidbar* 31:3; *Sifrei* 157.

33. Rashi, *Midrash haGadol*, Rokeach on *Bamidbar* 31:3.

34. Rashi, Rav Saadiah Gaon on ibid.; *Bamidbar Rabbah* 22:2.

35. See Rav Saadiah Gaon, *Bamidbar* 31:5; *Sifrei* 157.

36. Rashi, *Bamidbar* 31:3; *Bamidbar Rabbah* 22:2; *Sifrei* 157; *Pesikta d'Rav Kehana* 29:187.

37. Rashi, *Bamidbar* 31:3; *Bamidbar Rabbah* 22:2; *Sifrei* 157. Including Levi, the total would be thirteen thousand. Some therefore suggest that twelve thousand refers to those who were forced into service, whereas Levi went willingly (*Rav Ovadiah Bartenura al haTorah; Imrei Shefer*). Others group the tribes of Menashe and Ephraim together. Alternatively, Pinchas was the only Levi who participated. As mentioned below, he was sent to finish what he started (*Yalkut haEizovi*). Some maintain that Levi wasn't included, for that tribe never went to battle (Ralbag; Gra).

38. Rashi, *Bamidbar* 31:4; *Sifrei* 157; *Bamidbar Rabbah* 22:3. In actuality there were far more than one thousand righteous men in each tribe. However, this cap allowed the less righteous to blend in among the righteous on the home front without being stigmatized by their exclusion from battle.

39. War needs a Kohen's prayer, as well as the Kohen to lead them into battle.

40. See *Bamidbar Rabbah* 22:3; *Sifrei* 157; *Midrash Aggadah, Bamidbar* 31:4. According to one opinion, there were only two thousand men available for each

Many people did not share Moshe's alacrity and enthusiasm for the mission. They knew that its successful completion would bring Moshe's death that much closer, and they wanted to do everything to delay that inevitable event as long as possible.

For years, Moshe had struggled with the belligerence and contentiousness of the Exodus generation. He had heard them say that their patience was about to run out and that they would stone him.[41] But now, a new generation exhibited a different attitude. They were prepared to delay the attack on Midian and their own subsequent entry into the land, if only that would give them a little more time with Moshe.

But Moshe refused to consider even the slightest delay. "We must attack immediately," he told the people.[42] "Remember that you are avenging Hashem's honor, which was sullied by your sins, and not only your twenty-four thousand brethren who perished in the plague."

Knowing that they would be fighting to defend Hashem's honor rather than for just vengeance or booty, the Jewish people were mollified.[43]

According to another view, when the Jewish people refused to go into battle, divine lots were cast, and based on the results, the people were persuaded to go and fight without delay.[44]

The Midianites were led by their five powerful kings: Evi, Rekem, Tzur, Chur and Reva, all of whom had been involved in the conspiracy against the Jewish people. They fielded a

---

tribe. This figure dovetails with the fact that twenty-four thousand men participated, corresponding to the number who died under Midian's influence (Tur). See *Malei Omer*.

41. See *Shemos* 17:4. Yet the Jewish people never meant that. On the contrary, now that Moshe was to die, the Jews wanted him to live longer (*Emek haNetziv*; *Sifrei* 157).

42. Rashi, *Bamidbar* 31:5; *Sifrei* 157; *Bamidbar Rabbah* 22:3.

43. See *Ohr haChaim*, Alshich, *Sifsei Kohen*, Malbim on *Bamidbar* 31:3, 7.

44. *Bamidbar Rabbah* 22:3.

multitudinous army to defend against the Jewish attack, vastly outnumbering the twelve thousand Jewish fighters. Nonetheless, the Jewish fighters more than made up for the difference in fearlessness, morale and inspiration. They were confident in Hashem's assistance, for they were fighting His war. The weapons they carried were insignificant; the fortunes of battle would not revolve around their martial skills[45] but rather on their righteousness and merits.

"Let Pinchas, the Kohen anointed for war, lead the fighters into battle," Hashem told Moshe.[46] "He initiated this mitzvah by killing Kosbi the daughter of Tzur, who is Balak, and he should finish what he began with the same high level of zeal by killing her father and annihilating the Midianite military forces.[47] Furthermore, he has a special mission to avenge the honor of his ancestor Yosef, who was sold into slavery by the Midianites.[48] Pinchas will also have the Sanhedrin join him on the battlefield."[49]

As per Moshe's instructions, Pinchas prepared the sacred utensils needed for the battle — the holy ark of the Torah,[50] the golden *tzitz* engraved with Hashem's holy Name that the Kohen Gadol wore on his forehead,[51] and the rest of the priestly vestments[52] and the ceremonial trumpets used in battle.[53]

---

45. Ramban, Tur, *Midrash haGadol*, Alshich, *Sifsei Kohen*, Malbim on *Bamidbar* 31:2, 5–6. As we will see later, Bilam himself mocked the small army.

46. Seforno, *Rav Ovadiah Bartenura al haTorah* on *Bamidbar* 31:6; *Sotah* 43a.

47. *Targum Yonasan*, Rashi, *Toldos Yitzchak*, Ibn Ezra, *Lekach Tov*, *Ohr haChaim* on *Bamidbar* 31:6–8; *Bamidbar Rabbah* 22:4.

48. Rashi, *Bamidbar* 31:6; *Sifrei* 157 with *Emek haNetziv*; *Sotah* 43a. See *Bereishis* 37:36. Pinchas was related to Yosef from his mother's side. In addition, Yosef had resisted adultery, so now his descendant Pinchas would wipe out the adulterers (Maharal).

49. *Sotah* 43a.

50. Rashi, *Bamidbar* 31:6; *Sifrei* 157; *Bamidbar Rabbah* 22:4.

51. *Midrash Aggadah*, *Bamidbar* 31:6.

52. *Targum Yonasan*, ibid.; *Bamidbar Rabbah* 22:4; *Tanchuma*, *Mattos* 3.

53. Rashi, Rokeach on *Bamidbar* 31:6; *Sifrei* 157. Yehoshua meanwhile joined

Why did Moshe single out the *tzitz* from among all the other priestly vestments for special mention? He was concerned that Bilam would attempt to use witchcraft against the Jewish fighters. The holy *tzitz* would nullify the occult powers and allow the Jewish people to overcome Bilam and kill him.[54]

The War Begins

Pinchas and the Jewish fighters marched fearlessly into battle and gained the upper hand immediately.[55] They surrounded the Midianites on three sides, leaving only one avenue of escape.[56] The Midianites' numerical advantage was quickly negated. Pinchas pointed the *tzitz* at the enemy, and the power emanating from the holy Name struck them down instantly.[57]

But the battle was not easily won. Bilam had come to Midian to collect his reward for causing the deaths of twenty-four thousand Jews.[58] Although the incident at Shittim had been staged to protect Moav, Midian was also a beneficiary,[59] and furthermore Balak, the Moabite king who had commissioned Bilam, was himself from Midian, and the responsibility for recompensing Bilam fell on the Midianites.[60]

As Bilam watched the battle unfold before his eyes, he knew that if he didn't intervene all would be lost. Using his powers

---

Moshe in prayer, just as Aharon had done previously in wartime (cited in *Torah Sheleimah, Bamidbar* 31:35).

54. *Bamidbar Rabbah* 22:5.

55. Alshich, *Bamidbar* 31:6.

56. *Targum Yonasan, Midrash haGadol* on *Bamidbar* 31:7, *Sifrei* 157. See Rambam, *Melachim* 6:7.

57. *Sifsei Kohen, Bamidbar* 31:7.

58. Rashi, *Bamidbar* 31:8; *Sifrei* 157; *Sanhedrin* 106a; *Bamidbar Rabbah* 20:20; Zohar, *Balak* 193b. According to *Derashos Rav Yehoshua ibn Shu'eib*, Bilam also wanted to see how things had turned out for Kosbi. Alternatively, he made one last-ditch effort to curse the Jews now that they had sinned (*Chizkuni*).

59. *Gur Aryeh, Bamidbar* 31:8.

60. *Maskil l'David, Bamidbar* 31:6. See Mizrachi.

of sorcery, he levitated the five Midianite kings high into the air with him alongside them. Having escaped the battlefield safely, they could plan a counterattack. They had not, however, gone far enough. Pinchas looked up at the sky and saw the Midianite kings high overhead. He pointed the *tzitz* at them, and they instantly plummeted to the ground and fell, dazed but still alive, atop the piles of slain Midianites.[61] They were immediately taken prisoner.[62]

Bilam descended to the ground and stood face-to-face with Pinchas.

"Do you really expect to be victorious?" he taunted. "When you had every one of your six hundred thousand male adults available to you as fighters you could not vanquish the Midianites. Have you forgotten that you suffered twenty-four thousand casualties because they induced you to sin? Well, how do you expect to be victorious with only twelve thousand fighters? So I'm going to offer you some advice: Leave while the leaving is good. Flee for your lives. And don't forget to pay me for my advice before you go."

"You'll soon receive your payment in full," said Pinchas, "but not exactly in the way you meant it. Believe me, you'll get everything you deserve."[63]

Bilam was unconcerned. Again using his powers of sorcery, he spread his arms wide until they became hardened like stone, and pronouncing the ineffable Name of Hashem, he flew into the heavens until he reached as high as the heavenly Throne.

Pinchas tried to bring him down with the *tzitz*, but clouds obscured his vision. Pinchas prayed and uttered the holy Name, and suddenly, the clouds parted. Pinchas caught a glimpse of Bilam and pointed the *tzitz* at him. The emanations from the holy Name struck Bilam and flung him to the ground. Bilam looked around in desperation and realized there would be no escape.

---

61. Rashi, *Bamidbar* 31:6.
62. *Ohr haChaim*, *Bamidbar* 31:8.
63. Rashi with *Sefer Zikaron*, ibid.; *Sifrei* 157 with *Emek haNetziv*.

"Wait a minute, Pinchas," he said. "I repent. Believe me, I've seen the error of my ways, and I truly repent. Spare me, and I give you my word of honor that I will never curse your people again."

"Don't even bother," said Pinchas. "You and I both know that you are incorrigible. Back in the days of Yaakov, you took on the guise of Lavan and sought to harm our forefather. Later, you advised Pharaoh in Egypt to kill the Jews. After they left Egypt, you urged Amalek to attack the Jewish people. You failed again and again, but you never wavered from your resolve. In your latest encounter with my people, you disobeyed Hashem and you even defied Balak, your own employer. Your intentions have always been evil, and now that you're trapped, you expect to declare your repentance and escape the consequences of everything you've done? Have you lost your mind?"

"So is that a No?" said Bilam. "Can we at least have a maybe?"

"Don't waste your breath. I'm going to turn you over to the Sanhedrin, who are here on the battlefield."[64]

Bilam was brought before the Sanhedrin. He tried to defend his actions, but his arguments were unconvincing. The Sanhedrin withdrew to deliberate.

"This man caused the death of twenty-four thousand men," said one of judges of the Sanhedrin. "I suggest we sentence him to death."[65]

"This man practiced all sorts of sorcery and witchcraft," said another judge. "That alone is punishable by death."[66]

"The inappropriate behavior with his she-donkey," said a third judge, "is in itself sufficient cause to execute him."[67]

---

64. See *Tanchuma, Balak* 14, *Mattos* 4; *Bamidbar Rabbah* 20:20; Zohar, *Balak* 193b; *Targum Yonasan, Yalkut Reuveni*, Rokeach on *Bamidbar* 31:8; *Yerushalmi Sanhedrin* 10:2. See *Sotah* 43a; *Yalkut Shimoni* 785.

65. *Sanhedrin* 106a.

66. *Emek haNetziv.*

67. *Yalkut Ma'yan Ganim, Bamidbar* 31:8. See *Sanhedrin* 105b.

Bilam's fate was sealed. The Sanhedrin ruled that Bilam should be executed by all four forms of capital punishment. They strangled Bilam almost to the point of death, fulfilling *chenek*. Then they poured molten lead down his throat, fulfilling *sereifah*. Following that, they stoned him until his life hung by a thread, fulfilling *sekilah*, and then they beheaded him with a sword, fulfilling *hereg*.[68]

So ended the story of Bilam. "The camel went to demand horns for himself," people said about him in an analogy, "and returned with his ears cut off." He came for money and left a dead man.[69]

The Torah makes special mention of Bilam's being killed with the sword. Why? Because Bilam tried to turn the strength of the Jewish people against them. The Jewish people seek to triumph through their power of speech in prayer and supplication, while the nations seek to succeed through their proficiency with weapons, as it says concerning Eisav, "And you shall live by your sword." Bilam tried to use the power of speech to curse the Jewish people. Therefore, the tables were turned on him as well, and the Jewish people killed him with the sword.[70]

After the execution of Bilam, the five Midianite Kings, stripped of power and status, were beheaded on the battlefield.[71] The entire Midianite army had been annihilated. The Jewish fighters had not suffered a single casualty.[72] They took the Midianite women

---

68. See *Sanhedrin* 106a with Rashi, Maharsha. See also *Yad Ramah* there. According to *Iyun Yaakov*, Bilam's witchcraft kept him alive until he was beheaded.

Rosh suggests that Bilam (Lavan) was killed by the very sword that was driven into the mound of stones representing Lavan's peace treaty with Yaakov, which Bilam had violated. See Chapter 9, note 39.

69. *Sanhedrin* 106a with Rashi.

70. Rashi, *Bamidbar* 31:8; *Sifrei* 157. See *Bereishis* 27:40. See also *Sifsei Kohen, Bamidbar* 31:8.

71. *Ohr haChaim, Bamidbar* 31:8.

72. *Sifsei Kohen*, ibid.

and their small children captive and plundered all their livestock, as well as clothing, ornaments, gold, silver and precious metals.[73] Then they set fire to all their cities,[74] houses of worship, castles and palaces.[75]

The Aftermath

The righteous among the fighters did not tamper with any of the booty they had plundered from the land of Midian. Instead, they turned everything over intact to Moshe, Elazar the Kohen and the entire Jewish community.[76] But a number of youths could not resist the temptation.[77]

Moshe and all the tribal princes went out to meet the returning fighters with honor and blessings[78] outside the encampment, because they were impure from coming into contact with the Midianite corpses.[79] They also wanted to confront the youths who had taken some of the booty without permission.

Moshe turned to the generals. "You were responsible for the conduct of your soldiers," he said to them.[80] "You should not have left a single female alive. Yet you've left so many alive.[81] Why did you do this? These women were the ones who led our men into sin and caused so many thousands of deaths.[82] Even if they were

---

73. Ibn Ezra, *Midrash haGadol* on *Bamidbar* 31:9, 11.

74. Rav Saadiah Gaon, *Bamidbar* 31:10.

75. Rashi, ibid.; *Sifrei* 157.

76. Ibid.; *Bamidbar Rabbah* 22:4. See *Emek haNetziv.*

77. Rashi, Bamidbar 31:11; Sifrei 157. *Sifsei Kohen* explains that they too intended to give the spoils to Moshe. See *Maskil l'David;* Malbim. According to *Sanhedrin* 43b, based on *Yehoshua* 7, Achan was among the plunderers.

78. Moshe thus showed that he didn't suspect them of taking the spoils for themselves (*Sifsei Kohen*).

79. *Chizkuni*, Rashbam, *Midrash haBeiur*, Abarbanel, *Lekach Tov* on *Bamidbar* 31:13.

80. Rashi, *Bamidbar* 31:14; *Sifrei* 157. See Malbim.

81. Ibn Ezra, *Bamidbar* 31:15.

82. *Bamidbar* 31:16; Rambam, *Issurei Biah* 12:10.

coerced into doing it, it was certainly of their own volition that they caused the men to worship the idol Pe'or.[83] If you are forbidden to spare even one person when you invade Canaan, certainly you should understand that you spare no one from the nation that caused our people to sin."[84] He pointed at one of the women. "Look! Don't you recognize her? She is the one that led so-and-so astray. Why is she still alive?"[85]

Pinchas understood that, although Moshe was addressing the generals, his reprimand was directed principally at him. He was only delivering it in an oblique manner out of respect for him.[86]

"Your point is well-taken, Moshe," said Pinchas, "but you never told us to kill non-combatant Midianites.[87] You did not make such a demand in previous wars, so how could we know what you wanted? We decided it was better to leave them alive and do nothing until you gave us guidance. We knew we could kill them later, but what could we do if we killed them wrongfully?"

"Why did you bring them here?" asked Moshe.

"We brought them here as spoils of war," answered Pinchas, "and also to sanctify Hashem's holy Name by showing off our victory. There were no immoral intentions here whatsoever."[88]

"How can you or I know what took place behind closed doors when the soldiers captured these women?" asked Moshe. "Perhaps that's the very reason the soldiers left them alive. After all, as the anointed Kohen of war, you weren't entering homes to take the

---

83. *Ohr haChaim, Bamidbar* 31:16; *Anaf Yosef, Sanhedrin* 106a. See *Bamidbar Rabbah* 9:45.

84. *Yalkut Reuveni, Bamidbar* 31:15.

85. Rashi, *Bamidbar* 31:16; *Yalkut Shimoni* 785; *Sifrei Zuta.*

86. Ramban, *Akeidas Yitzchak* on *Bamidbar* 31:6, 14.

87. Moshe had nonetheless expected them to know enough to kill the women, because they had caused the men to sin (*Shelah*).

88. Ramban, *Bamidbar* 31:6; Seforno, *Akeidas Yitzchak, Sifsei Kohen* on *Bamidbar* 31:15; *Emek haNetziv, Sifrei* 157. See *Devarim* 20:14.

spoils. How can you know for sure that nothing inappropriate took place?"[89]

"May I have permission to speak?" said one of the generals. "I can shed some light on what occurred in Midian."

"Speak," said Moshe.

"I can vouch for the behavior of the righteous fighters," said the general. "We maintained a very high standard of morality. No fighter entered a Midianite home alone. Everyone made sure to go about in pairs as a safeguard against the possibility of immoral behavior. Also, when jewelry was removed from a captive or taken from her home, we obscured her face with soot.[90] The fighters behaved with proper fear of Heaven."[91]

"I am pleased to hear your words," responded Moshe. "They are reassuring. And I accept the statements of Pinchas, our esteemed Kohen anointed for war. I pardon you all for any inadvertent missteps you may have taken.[92] Now, I want all male children of any age[93] killed immediately, so that they don't grow up with grudges against us and perhaps become our sworn enemies.[94] As for the women, that will require one more step.[95] Any female who is old enough to have relations with a man, even if she

---

89. *Emek haNetziv, Sifrei* 157.

90. As an act of modesty, in order to protect themselves from their evil inclination.

91. See *Shir haShirim Rabbah* 4:3; *Targum Yonasan*, Alshich on *Bamidbar* 31:50. Another reason the fighters traveled in pairs was so that if someone perished, his partner could provide definitive testimony to his family regarding the death (Rokeach, *Bamidbar* 31:54).

92. Fourteen years later, when the tribes of Reuven, Gad and Menashe were ready to leave Eretz Yisrael and settle on their land, they built an altar signifying their union with the Jewish people despite their geographical separation. Pinchas then wrongfully accused them of building this altar for illegal sacrifices or, worse, idol worship. Only after he learned of their motives did he support their actions. See *Yehoshua* 22.

93. Rokeach, *Bamidbar* 31:17.

94. *Minchah Belulah*, Ralbag on ibid.

95. Maharik, *Moshav Zekeinim* on ibid.

hasn't done so, shall be put to death. Those who are younger can be spared. You may keep them for yourselves, either to marry or as maidservants."[96]

"How will we know if a girl is of the proper age?" one man asked.

"Place all the female captives in front of the *tzitz,*" Moshe replied. "The faces of those old enough to have relations will miraculously take on a greenish or yellowish tinge."[97]

The Laws of Purification

"Now let us turn to other matters," said Moshe. "Whoever killed a person or touched a corpse shall cleanse himself outside the encampment. He shall not enter the courtyard of the Mishkan for seven days."

"What about those who didn't touch a corpse," asked one man, "but touched swords that touched a corpse?"

"Those people too are ritually impure," said Moshe, "as if they had actually touched the corpse itself."[98]

"Are non-Jewish captives considered ritually impure? Do our laws in this matter apply to them as well?"

"No. They aren't susceptible to ritual impurity unless they convert to Judaism. If they do, the laws apply to them."[99]

"How shall we cleanse ourselves to remove the ritual impurity?"

"You must be sprinkled with water mixed with the ashes of the *parah adumah,* the red heifer."

"Only our bodies?"

---

96. *Ohr haChaim,* Rokeach, *Sifsei Kohen, HaKesav vehaKabbalah* on *Bamidbar* 31:18. See Rambam, *Issurei Biah* 12:10; *Yevamos* 60b. See *Ben Yehoyada* regarding why even those females who didn't participate but were capable deserved death.

97. *Yevamos* 60b with Maharsha; Rashi, *Kli Yakar* on *Bamidbar* 31:17; *Sifrei* 157.

98. Rashi, *Bamidbar* 31:19; *Sifrei* 147.

99. Rashi, *Bamidbar* 31:19; *Sifrei* 157. Compare *Midrash Aggadah.*

"No. All your garments must undergo purification, be they leather articles, goat products such as articles made from horns, hooves and bones, and every wooden article."[100]

"How is this done?

Moshe was at a loss for a reply, because he had momentarily forgotten the laws of purging and purifying vessels that had become ritually impure. He had recently spoken to the Jewish people in anger, and as a consequence, he could not recall the laws.[101] But he took advantage of the situation to enhance the prestige of Elazar, the Kohen Gadol, who would assume greater authority for halachic matters after Moshe's death. He stepped aside and referred these questions to Elazar. The people saw that he had accorded Elazar the same respect that he had to Yehoshua, and they were duly impressed.[102]

Division of the Spoils

Miraculously, not a single captive or animal died on the seven-day trek back from Midian.[103] Hashem now instructed Moshe to take inventory[104] of the captives[105] and livestock and divide these spoils into two equal parts, one of which was to be given to the fighters and the rest to the Jewish people.[106]

A tax of one five-hundredth—one-fifth of 1 percent—of the spoils designated for the fighters was to be given to Elazar.[107] A larger tax of one-fiftieth—2 percent—of the spoils designated for the rest of the Jewish people who had not risked their lives on the

100. Rashi, *Bamidbar* 31:20; *Sifrei* 157; *Chullin* 25b.

101. See Rashi, *Bamidbar* 31:21; *Pesachim* 66b.

102. *Emek haNetziv, Sifrei* 157; *Bamidbar* 31:21–24.

103. Ramban, *Bamidbar* 31:49; Malbim, *Bamidbar* 31:32.

104. Rashi, *Bamidbar* 31:26.

105. Captives included non-Midianites living in Midian, both male and female (*Tosefos Rav Ephraim al haTorah*).

106. Rashi with *Sefer Zikaron, Bamidbar* 31:27.

107. *Bamidbar* 31:29.

battlefield, was to be given to the Levi'im entrusted with the care of the Mishkan.[108]

This tax was levied only on the captives and livestock. The rest of the spoils were not taxed, and were allowed to remain in possession of those who had taken them or were allotted them.[109]

"As you already know," the generals now said to Moshe, "we miraculously suffered no casualties in Midian, and no man was led astray by any Midianite woman during the war. We believe that there is a clear connection between the two. Because we behaved righteously, we merited to have everyone return safely.[110] Nonetheless, some of us may have entertained inappropriate thoughts in some provocative situations, and therefore, we wish to bring both an offering of thanks for the miraculous victory and an atonement sacrifice for the inappropriate thoughts. And we want to turn over all gold articles, including bracelets, anklets, rings, earrings and any other bodily ornaments."[111]

Moshe and Elazar accepted these gold articles and brought them to the Ohel Mo'ed.[112] The gold was melted down and formed into sacred vessels as a lasting remembrance of the miracle of the war and the saintliness of the Jewish fighters who had waged it.[113]

---

108. *Bamidbar* 31:30. This was a fitting percentage, since the twelve thousand fighters constituted one-fiftieth of the Jewish population of six hundred thousand (Abarbanel; Malbim). Furthermore, the Kohanim and Levi'im had earned these tithes by praying and bringing merit to the soldiers (Malbim; *Ha'amek Davar*; *Sifsei Kohen*).

109. Rashi, *Bamidbar* 31:32.

110. Rabbeinu Bachya, Rokeach on *Bamidbar* 31:49.

111. Rashi, Ramban on *Bamidbar* 31:49–50; *Shabbos* 64a. This donation also atoned for the debauchery of Pe'or.

112. Seforno, *Bamidbar* 31:54.

113. See Ramban, Rabbeinu Bachya, *Minchah Belulah, Ha'amek Davar* on *Bamidbar* 31:51–54.

16 The Land of Gad and Reuven

The tribes of Gad and Reuven were more than neighbors sharing the same banner. Both tribes were made up of mighty warriors who fought on the front lines against the enemies of the Jewish people. As such, they accumulated disproportionately large amounts of the spoils of war, including numerous livestock,[1] especially in the wars against Sichon and Og[2] and against Midian.[3] The members of both tribes were also accomplished herdsmen, and in time, their livestock grew beyond that of the other tribes.[4]

1. See *Lekach Tov*, *Ohr haChaim*, Alshich on *Bamidbar* 32:1.
2. *Midrash haCheifetz*, *Yalkut Me'or haAfeilah* on ibid.
3. *Lekach Tov*, Rokeach on ibid.
4. Abarbanel, ibid.

With their vast flocks and herds of livestock, the tribes of Gad and Reuven needed abundant pastureland, and the lands of Ya'azer and Gil'ad, captured from Sichon and Og, suited their purposes perfectly.[5] They lay in a pleasant shady valley,[6] and the rich and fertile land was covered with grassy meadows.[7] But it was on the eastern side of the Jordan River, and for them to stay there they would have to separate from the other tribes crossing into Canaan. In order to do that, they would need permission.[8]

The leaders of these two tribes made their way to the Ohel Mo'ed to meet with Moshe, Elazar and the rest of the Jewish princes.[9] The tribe of Gad was the mightier of the two,[10] and it was they who had initiated the idea of settling on the other side of the Jordan River.[11] Therefore, the representatives of Gad spoke for both tribes.

"Honored leaders," they began, "the territories of Ataros, Divon, Ya'azer, Nimrah, Cheshbon, Elaleh, Svam, Nevo and Beon are all parts of the land of Sichon and Og which we captured some time ago.[12] Because this land is eminently suitable for our abundant livestock,[13] we would like to establish our inheritance there. Moreover, we are especially scrupulous in respecting the property of others, and we do not want our livestock to stray onto the lands of others and graze there. Therefore, it would be best if we have

---

5. Alshich, Malbim on *Bamidbar* 32:2.

6. *Bechor Shor*, Devarim 3:19.

7. See Rav Saadiah Gaon, Ibn Ezra on *Bamidbar* 32:1, 4.

8. *Ohr haChaim*, *Bamidbar* 32:1.

9. *Ha'amek Davar*, *Bamidbar* 32:2.

10. Ramban, Rabbeinu Bachya on ibid. Gad also had more livestock than Reuven (Alshich).

11. *Chizkuni*, Rabbeinu Bachya on ibid.

12. Rashi, *Bamidbar* 32:3. See Malbim regarding why the land of Gil'ad isn't mentioned here.

13. Seforno, *Midrash Aggadah*, Malbim on *Bamidbar* 32:1, 3.

spacious pastures separated from the pastures of others."[14]

"You have no special rights to these lands," Moshe replied. "This territory was conquered by all the Jews, not just by your tribe and the tribe of Reuven."

"This land was conquered miraculously," they replied, "and it belongs to Hashem more than to any tribe in particular. We just feel that considering the circumstances of our relative needs, we should have first claim to it."[15]

"How do you know," challenged Moshe, "that Hashem wants any of the tribes to inherit this land?"

"If He allowed us to conquer it," they replied, "it was most probably because He wants our people to inherit it."[16]

"So you want to stay here," said Moshe. "All the tribes participated in its conquest. Do you now expect the other tribes to conquer Canaan by themselves without your help?"

"We don't see why we are needed," they said. "The conquest is all miraculous anyway, so what difference does it make if we are there or not?"[17]

"Indeed?" said Moshe. "Or are you perhaps afraid to fight the Canaanites?"

"We are not afraid of anyone," they said. "You see that we are willing to remain here by ourselves without the protection of the entire nation. This should certainly confirm that we are fearless."[18]

---

14. See *Midrash haGadol, Chemdas Yamim* on *Bamidbar* 32:1; *Koheles Rabbah* 1:13.

15. *Ohr haChaim, Bamidbar* 32:3. In truth, the tribesmen of Gad chose that land because they knew, either through tradition or through prophecy, that Moshe would secretly be buried there (Rashi with *Sifsei Chachamim, Devarim* 33:21). However, presumably out of respect for his "privacy," they said they wanted to settle east of the Jordan for its large pasturing land. Gad also felt it improper for Moshe to be alone while his people were in Eretz Yisrael. See *Sha'arei Aharon*.

16. Alshich, Malbim on *Bamidbar* 32:4.

17. *Ohr haChaim*, Alshich on *Bamidbar* 32:3–4.

18. See Ramban, *Ohr haChaim*, Alshich on *Bamidbar* 32:1–5.

"But don't you want a share in the land promised to Avraham instead of this foreign land?"

"It seems to us that if Hashem's hand led us to conquer this land, it must have the same status as the Holy Land itself."[19]

"I have heard your responses," Moshe said, "but they are not satisfactory. You say that you are not needed to conquer Canaan, because Hashem is orchestrating the conquest. The second part is correct but not the first. A great effort is still required on the battlefield. Do you expect the rest of the tribes to struggle and fight again while you sit comfortably in your pastures?[20] When the people see that you remained behind, they will think you are indifferent to the Holy Land or that you are afraid. It will undermine their morale."[21]

"But that is simply not true," they answered.

"Perhaps, but that would be the impression.[22] Look, the tribe of Gad has the heart and might of a lion. Yaakov blessed you with great might and prowess. You are the tribe that should be leading the conquest of Canaan. When the other tribes see that the mightiest tribe has stayed behind, they will all lose heart.[23] They will be dispirited and frightened, and they will refuse to invade the land and fight for our inheritance.[24] You will be no different from your fathers in the previous generation."[25]

"Why do you say that?"

"Think about what the spies did and what they caused," said Moshe. "Because they lacked faith, they devised a plan to frighten

---

19. *Ohr haChaim*, Malbim on *Bamidbar* 32:3. Additionally, because Moshe would be buried there, they wanted to live on land that carried his merit (Rashi, *Devarim* 33:31).

20. *Ohr haChaim*, Alshich, *Ha'amek Davar*, Malbim on *Bamidbar* 32:6.

21. Abarbanel, *Ha'amek Davar*, Malbim on ibid.

22. *Tzeror haMor*, Alshich on ibid.

23. *Sifsei Kohen*, Alshich, Malbim on ibid.

24. Rav Saadiah Gaon, Rashi, Abarbanel on *Bamidbar* 32:7.

25. Alshich, ibid.

the Jewish people until they refused to enter the Holy Land. Now again, the people will follow your lead and refuse to go, and you will have caused them to defy Hashem."[26]

"What are you saying?"

"Your remaining here would have terrible consequences. The last time something like this happened, Hashem decreed that all males between the ages of twenty and sixty of that entire generation had to die without seeing the land, and that the people should wander in the wilderness for almost forty years.[27] Those forty years are not quite over yet. We are still in the wilderness, for all intents and purposes. Hashem's anger has almost been extinguished, but any further delay in entering the land could quickly reignite it.[28] And what would happen then? We might remain outside the land for another generation.[29] So tell me, do you want to be like Korach and the spies, who also separated themselves from the Jewish people and faced a bitter end?"[30]

A Solution Is Offered

The men from Gad and Reuven saw how they had upset Moshe. They decided to withdraw and confer with each other before continuing the conversation. There had to be a solution that would satisfy his concerns.[31]

"He is not really bothered by our desire to stay here," one of them said. "His argument is that we will destroy the morale of the other tribes by staying behind. We should offer to join the other tribes in their conquest of Canaan."[32]

---

26. Seforno, *Midrash haGadol*, Alshich on *Bamidbar* 32:6–7.
27. Rashi, *Bamidbar* 32:13.
28. Alshich, *Bamidbar* 32:14.
29. Alshich, *Ha'amek Davar*, Malbim on *Bamidbar* 32:15.
30. *Tzeror haMor*, *Bamidbar* 32:14. See Malbim, Abarbanel on *Shofetim* 5:14–15 regarding Devorah's criticism of Reuven for not joining in the war against Sisera.
31. See *Minchah Belulah*, *Tzeror haMor*, *Ohr haChaim* on *Bamidbar* 32:16.
32. Abarbanel, *Bamidbar* 32:16.

They discussed the matter, and the proposal carried the day. The men returned to Moshe.

"You should not think that we are afraid," they said.[33] "We are prepared to cross the Jordan River and fight alongside the rest of the tribes. But first we have a request to make."

"Make your request," said Moshe.

"As a former shepherd," they said, "you are known to be compassionate to animals.[34] So before we begin the conquest of Canaan, we need a little time to build corrals, stables and stockades for our livestock in these territories.[35] When those are complete, we will build fortified towns for our families and young children within these stockades. This will make our families doubly secure, as any invaders would have to penetrate the structures we built for our animals first. The animals themselves would form a secondary buffer before the invaders could even approach the towns."[36]

"Go on."

"With our livestock and families secure, and no baggage or duties like those of the other tribes to slow us down,[37] we can mobilize quickly for battle.[38] We will lead the charge into battle at the head of the fighters[39] and remain with them until we have conquered the entire land and apportioned it among the people.[40]

"You might be wondering why we are willing to stay for so long. Don't be concerned that we are looking to take additional land on the western side of the Jordan River.[41] We assure you that we do not intend to take full possession of our lands until the

---

33. *Ha'amek Davar, Bamidbar* 32:17.
34. Alshich, ibid. See *Shemos Rabbah* 2:3.
35. Radak on *Bamidbar* 32:16; *Kli Yakar, Bamidbar* 32:1.
36. *Tosefos Rav Ephraim al haTorah, Kli Yakar* on *Bamidbar* 32:1, 24.
37. *Chizkuni*, Alshich, *Bechor Shor* on *Bamidbar* 32:17.
38. Rav Saadiah Gaon, Rashi, Ibn Ezra on ibid.
39. Rashi, ibid. See *Devarim* 33:20.
40. *Ohr haChaim*, Alshich, *Minchah Belulah* on *Bamidbar* 32:17–18.
41. Rashi, *Bamidbar* 32:18.

rest of the tribes have taken possession of theirs.[42] When these conditions will be met, only then will we return to the eastern side of the Jordan.[43]

"This will be the best of all worlds for the other tribes. With our taking our shares here, they will all receive larger shares. And still, we will lead them into battle and fight until the finish.[44] We will show that we are not afraid to fight or to leave our families alone while we help conquer Canaan.[45] The people will realize that the only reason we have to take our share here is to accommodate our exceedingly abundant livestock."[46]

"First, I must express my dismay at your priorities," said Moshe. "Why this foolish haste to stake your claims? Are you worried someone will take them from you? And why do you mention your livestock before your children? You seem to be more concerned about your animals than about your sons and daughters. You need to get your priorities straight. You must first build towns for your children, and only afterward corrals for your sheep."[47]

"Yes, those are indeed our priorities," the men from both tribes answered. "We simply wanted to build the animal enclosures to provide additional protection for our families, as we explained."

"If you really had faith in Hashem's protection," countered Moshe, "you would build the towns for your families and trust in Hashem to watch over them.[48] Not once in your remarks have I heard you mention the Almighty."[49]

Looking back on history, we see that the clever Bilam and

---

42. *Ha'amek Davar*, Ralbag on *Bamidbar* 32:17, 21.
43. Rashi with Mizrachi, *Bamidbar* 32:19.
44. Abarbanel, Alshich on *Bamidbar* 32:16.
45. *Midrash haGadol*, *Minchah Belulah*, Alshich, *Ha'amek Davar* on *Bamidbar* 32:16–17.
46. Alshich, *Bamidbar* 32:16.
47. Rashi, ibid.; *Bamidbar Rabbah* 22:9. See Rashi, *Mishlei* 20:21.
48. *Kli Yakar*, *Bamidbar* 32:1.
49. *Ohr haChaim*, *Minchah Belulah* on *Bamidbar* 32:21.

Achitophel, the mighty Shimshon and Golias, and the wealthy Korach and Haman all ruined their lives because they reached for something that wasn't meant for them. The tribes of Gad and Reuven were so involved with their possessions that they separated themselves from the rest of the Jewish people and declined to live in the Holy Land. Ultimately, they would suffer the consequences of their decision when they were the first of the tribes to be exiled by Sancheriv,[50] eight years before he exiled the rest of the ten tribes.[51]

"Now regarding your offer," Moshe continued, "I'm not sure whether it's serious and genuine, or whether you are trying to deceive us in order to take possession of this land. But this I do know for sure:[52] your success in battle will depend on the extent to which you keep Hashem in mind. Let your thoughts turn away for a moment from the land you desire and the might you possess, and realize that your primary concern should be to sanctify Hashem's Name by defeating His enemies. Don't go into battle with your thoughts on your property. Don't go into battle with your faith in your strength. Concentrate with all your might on fighting Hashem's war. If you do that, everything will fall into place."[53]

"So does that mean that you agree to our request?" they asked.

"It depends on your intentions. Will all of you march into battle, or will it be just your mightiest warriors? Your request that we wait while you build towns and corrals indicates to me that you all intend to go. Otherwise, why would we need to wait? The men left behind can build the fortifications.[54] Although the

---

50. *Bamidbar Rabbah* 22:7.

51. *Tosefos Rav Ephraim al haTorah, Bamidbar* 32:1.

52. Abarbanel, *Bamidbar* 32:20.

53. See *Ohr haChaim, HaKesav vehaKabbalah, Minchah Belulah*, Malbim on ibid.; Rambam, *Melachim* 7:15.

54. See Alshich, *HaKesav vehaKabbalah* on *Bamidbar* 32:20–22.

conquest of Canaan will require a lot of effort, we all know that Hashem will bring us victory.[55] Your presence is not needed for your strength, but to support the morale of the people, as I explained before.[56] As far as I'm concerned, it would be enough for you to stay until the conquest is complete. But since you offer to stay until the land is apportioned, I must hold you to that commitment.[57] The people will be pleased that you didn't take full possession of your lands before they could take possession of theirs.[58] In brief, your responsibility to the people is to fight the war, and your responsibility to Hashem is to stay for the apportionment, as you promised."[59]

"We accept," they said.

"If you meet these conditions," Moshe continued, "your children will be safe and you will all return unharmed,[60] richer than you already are.[61] Most of all, you will have proven that your wish to inherit this land is honorable. If, however, you fail to meet these conditions or fight in the Name of Hashem,[62] you will have transgressed against both Hashem and the people, and as punishment you are liable to suffer casualties while in battle.[63] It will also prove that all along your intentions were dishonorable.[64] Finally, if you return to find your families unharmed, that will be

55. *Ohr haChaim, Bamidbar* 32:21.

56. *Me'am Lo'ez, Yehoshua* 1.

57. Rashi with Mizrachi, *Ohr haChaim* on *Bamidbar* 32:20. This pledge would amount to an additional seven years west of the Jordan.

58. Ralbag, *Bamidbar* 32:21.

59. *Ha'amek Davar, HaKesav vehaKabbalah* on *Bamidbar* 32:23.

60. See *Ohr haChaim, Ha'amek Davar* on *Bamidbar* 32:21–24.

61. *Midrash haGadol, Bamidbar* 32:20. Although Reuven and Gad said they would not take any spoils back from conquering Canaan, Moshe nevertheless blessed them with wealth.

62. *HaKesav vehaKabbalah*, ibid.

63. See Rav Saadiah Gaon, *Ohr haChaim, Ha'amek Davar* on *Bamidbar* 32:21–24.

64. Seforno, *Bamidbar* 32:23.

the ultimate vindication that you have met all the conditions and that you fought for Hashem's sake."[65]

An Agreement Is Reached

The men of Gad and Reuven conferred once again to formulate a response.[66]

"Moshe, we agree to the terms you have set forth," they said. "We'll build towns for our children before building enclosures for our livestock. And we'll send forth our warriors to fight in the Name of Hashem."[67]

Satisfied, Moshe now informed Yehoshua, Elazar and the tribal princes of the agreement he had made with the tribes of Gad and Reuven.

"To avoid future disagreements," he told them, "I charge you all with insuring that the tribes of Gad and Reuven meet the conditions regarding their inheriting the land east of the Jordan.[68] If they send their warriors and join you in the conquest of Canaan, only then shall you give them the land of Gil'ad[69] as well as the lands of Sichon and Og.[70] If they don't, however, they won't receive this land. They'll receive their portions spread out in the land of Canaan."[71]

The men of Gad and Reuven, however, had concerns about Moshe's instructions.

"Moshe, we are completely sincere," they said. "But we would

---

65. *Chasam Sofer*, *Bamidbar* 32:24.

66. See *Ha'amek Davar*, Rokeach, Tur on *Bamidbar* 32:25. See Rashi; Alshich.

67. *Ohr haChaim*, Alshich on *Bamidbar* 32:25–26. Alshich adds that to hasten their departure, the men of Gad and Reuven only rebuilt cities in ruins, which was quicker than building cities from scratch.

68. Rashi, Abarbanel, Alshich, *Kli Chemdah* on *Bamidbar* 32:28.

69. See Ramban, *Bamidbar* 32:29.

70. Seforno, *Bamidbar* 32:28.

71. See Ramban, Alshich on the subject of receiving a portion in Canaan if they didn't fulfill their duty.

really like to take possession of our land now, because we need to clear our minds of our possessions and concentrate on fighting for the sake of Hashem. You can always take away our portion if we don't meet our commitments."[72]

"You are right," said Moshe, and he gave them the land right away.[73]

When the men of Gad and Reuven surveyed the land they had been given, they realized that they had much more than they needed. They reported this discovery to Moshe, and he offered this surplus land to any tribe that wanted to join the tribes of Gad and Reuven.[74] Among the descendants of Menashe, the families of Machir and Yair[75] also raised livestock and had an appreciation for good grazing land.[76] They agreed to join Gad and Reuven.

The tribe of Menashe was thus split into two parts—one on the eastern side of the Jordan River, and one on the western side with the rest of the tribes. There was a certain justice in this development. Menashe, as the close assistant to his father Yosef in the royal government of Egypt, had engineered the arrest of Binyamin and caused the brothers to rend their garments, and now the portion of his descendants would be split as well.[77]

---

72. Malbim, *Bamidbar* 32:28–31.

73. Seforno, *Ohr haChaim*, Malbim on *Bamidbar* 32:28–33. According to Ramban, Moshe gave them only the cities within the territory of Gil'ad. Alshich notes that the non-fighting men who stayed behind rebuilt and improved the cities while their army joined the rest of the Jews.

74. Ramban, Ralbag on *Bamidbar* 32:33.

75. Yair was actually from the tribe of Yehudah. Only his mother came from Menashe. See Ramban.

76. Ramban, *Bamidbar* 32:33.

77. *Chizkuni*, ibid.; *Bereishis Rabbah* 84:20. See *Let My Nation Descend*, p. 319. According to *Tzeror haMor*, the tribesmen of Menashe had always been included in this settlement, but the Torah didn't mention them until now because of their insignificant number. *Ha'amek Davar* theorizes that many within this tribe were scholars, so their purpose on the eastern side of the Jordan was to heighten the spirituality of the other tribes settling there.

Unlike Gad and Reuven, Menashe received their territory from Moshe

The tribe of Gad built the fortified towns of Divon, Ataros and Aroer.[78] The tribe of Reuven rebuilt the lands of Cheshbon, which included Nevo, the place where Moshe was to die.[79] Moshe distributed the lands that once belonged to Sichon and Og. He gave the land of Gil'ad to Menashe's firstborn son Machir, a land filled with fortified towns and thus perfect for the elderly Machir.[80] The men from both Machir and Yair drove out any remaining inhabitants in their lands and renamed the towns which had once borne the names of idols.[81]

The tribes of Gad and Reuven and the half-tribe of Menashe would follow through on their promise. They would spend seven years conquering Eretz Yisrael and remain an additional seven years until it was divided and apportioned for the settlement of all the Jewish people. When these tribes saw how fertile and productive the Holy Land was, they cringed and commented, "Better one spoonful of pleasure in this land than a palmful of toil on the eastern side of the Jordan River."[82]

---

unconditionally, regardless of their participation in the conquest of Eretz Yisrael (*Me'am Lo'ez, Yehoshua* 13, 22).

78. Rashi with *Sifsei Chachamim, Bamidbar* 32:36.

79. See *Sotah* 13b.

80. *Chizkuni, Bamidbar* 32:40.

81. See Rashi with *Targum Unkelos, Bamidbar* 32:38–41. Yair would eventually die in the tragic defeat of Ai, after Achan had taken spoils from Yericho. See Radak, *Yehoshua* 7:5.

82. *Vayikra Rabbah* 3:1 with *Yefeh To'ar; Yalkut Shimoni* 786. See *Me'am Lo'ez, Yehoshua* 22.

17 Final Instructions

Nearly forty years had passed since the Jewish people had come forth from Egypt. Their encampment had relocated in the wilderness forty-two times. They had fought wars and gained victories. They had received instruction on the apportionment of the land. And now, as this momentous era was finally drawing to a close, Hashem instructed Moshe to inscribe in the Torah all the travels and events that took place during that time.[1]

This is comparable to a king whose son fell ill, and in order to find a doctor who could cure him, he had to cross the wilderness

1. See Ramban, *Bamidbar* 33:1.

to a distant land. The doctor cured the ailing prince, and father and son embarked on the journey homeward. Along the way, the king and his son reminisced about the different events that took place at each station of their journey. "Here you were ill," the king would remark. "Here you felt cold." "Here you had a headache."

The Jewish people coming out of Egypt, despite all their glory, were quite an ill nation spiritually. Their spirit and resolve were tested numerous times, and all too often they failed to pass the test. But after forty years of trials and travails, they were finally spiritually healed and purified to the point that they were worthy of entering the Holy Land.

By recounting the locations of the forty-two successive encampments, Moshe reminded the people where they had been ill, where they had rebelled and so on. These reminiscences were a cathartic experience, a form of closure that came face-to-face with what had transpired and awakened in their hearts a determination that they would never become spiritually ill again.[2]

Moreover, Hashem wanted their travels recounted so that there would be an eternal record of the glorious miracles He had performed for them, from the exodus from Egypt to their encounter with Edom, from the Well of Miriam to the victories over Sichon and Og.[3]

The miracles that took place during this era were also a harbinger of events that would take place during the final redemption. In the End of Days, the Jewish people will find themselves once again in the wilderness, and they will once again be the beneficiaries of Hashem's salvation and miracles, just as they had been when they left Egypt and wandered into the wilderness.[4]

---

2. See Rashi with *Gur Aryeh*, *Me'am Lo'ez* on ibid.

3. *Bamidbar Rabbah* 23:1; *Tanchuma*, *Mas'ei* 1. In addition, during all this time, no snake or scorpion ever harmed them.

4. Rabbeinu Bachya, Abarbanel on *Bamidbar* 33:1. See *Yechezkel* 20:35–36; *Michah* 7:15.

This very wilderness that hosted the Jewish people during their forty-year sojourn will one day be transformed from the arid and parched land it once was, into populous cities. It will blossom into a flourishing oasis of human habitation. In contrast, the empires of Edom and the other nations of the world that had oppressed the Jewish people will in turn be transformed into barren wastelands and desert.[5]

Another reason it was important to document the journeys of the Jewish people in the wilderness was because otherwise, history would concoct a different scenario about this nation that had somehow survived a forty-year journey through the wilderness. "That's impossible," the nations of the world would say. "No full-fledged nation with millions of people could survive under such inhospitable conditions. Like desert nomads, they surely found oases with plentiful water and vegetation that allowed them to live without divine intervention."[6] Or else they would surmise that the Jewish people were lost in the wilderness for forty years and managed to survive purely by blind chance.[7] But with their travels documented in the Torah, everyone would be able to recognize the deliberate path of their journey and learn about the miracles that sustained them.[8]

This entire sojourn could have been avoided, of course, had the Jews remained faithful to and trusting in Hashem and not transgressed. They were but an eleven-day journey away from entering the Holy Land when everything came apart. The record of their seemingly interminable travels would thus be a painful but necessary reminder to the Jewish people of the effects of sin.[9]

---

5. If an insensate wilderness can be rewarded for hosting the Jewish people, how much more so will be the reward for someone who hosts a *talmid chacham*. See *Bamidbar Rabbah* 23:4; *Yeshayahu* 35:1–2.

6. Ramban, *Bamidbar* 33:1, quoting *Moreh Nevuchim* 3:50.

7. *Midrash haGadol, Bamidbar* 33:1.

8. *Midrash haGadol*, Ramban on ibid., quoting *Moreh Nevuchim* 3:50.

9. *Sifsei Kohen, Bamidbar* 33:2. The initials of the words *Eileh mas'ei Bnei*

Moshe had been keeping a running journal of the Jewish people's travels, and following Hashem's instructions, he recorded all of them in *parashas Mas'ei* of *Sefer Bamidbar*.[10]

Eradicating the Inhabitants

Hashem instructed Moshe that upon entering Eretz Yisrael the Jewish people would be responsible for carrying out five tasks. They were to conquer and apportion the land, establish the national borders, set aside special cities for the Levi'im and create cities of refuge for those guilty of accidental murder.

Although Moshe would not be able to carry these out personally, Hashem consoled him that it would be done according to the instructions he himself would give Yehoshua.[11]

"Upon conquering the land," Hashem commanded Moshe to instruct the Jews, "you shall drive out all the inhabitants. Demolish and destroy their idols, temples and other houses of worship.[12] Heed this warning: have no mercy on them,[13] for if you fail to do what I have commanded, your stay in the land will not be permanent.[14] The people you allow to remain will betray you and cause you harm. They will be as needles in your eyes and thorns in your sides. They will surround and constrict you, giving you neither the means of escape nor the ability to be rescued.[15]

Yisrael, "These are the journeys of the Children of Israel" (*Bamidbar* 33:1), allude to the four exiles of the Jewish people: Edom, Medea, Babylonia and Yavan (Greece). The travels through the wilderness symbolize all these exiles, which the Jews brought upon themselves by worshiping the golden calf (*Yalkut Reuveni*).

10. See *Ohr haChaim*, Rokeach on *Bamidbar* 33:2.
11. See Abarbanel, *Bamidbar* 33:50.
12. *Midrash haGadol*, *Bamidbar* 33:52.
13. *Devarim Zuta* 17.
14. Rashi, *Bamidbar* 33:53.
15. Rashi, *Bamidbar* 33:55.

"Your hearts will be blinded to the truth and will lead you to assimilate with the nations and follow their evil ways of idolatry.[16] But this will not stop them from hating you, for they will cause you much suffering and will take pleasure in it.[17] And so I will eventually do to you as I sought to do to them. I will exile you from your land—the very thing you were to do to them—leaving it depopulated.[18]

"These commands shall be on your mind when you walk across the riverbed of the Jordan, which will part before you. Should you cross the Jordan and not intend to rid the land of its inhabitants and their idols, I will inundate you with the river waters and you will be swept away."[19]

The outcome Hashem warned the Jews against can be compared to a man who took pity on a baby wolf and used one of his sheep to nurse it. The man lamented that this compassion eventually came back to haunt him when the grown wolf killed the very sheep that had nurtured it. Hashem warned the Jews that should they allow any of the seven nations to remain in the land with them, these very people would ultimately harm them.[20]

Most notably, King Shaul compassionately spared the Amalekite king Agag, and eventually Haman, Agag's descendant, sought to annihilate the Jewish people from the face of the earth.[21]

In His instructions regarding the destruction of the idols, Hashem insisted that not even the slightest trace be allowed to remain. The evil influence of idolatry is so strong that even a negligible remnant could lead a person astray.[22]

---

16. Tur, Ramban on *Bamidbar* 33:55–56.
17. *Midrash haGadol, Bamidbar* 33:55.
18. *Minchah Belulah,* ibid.
19. Rashi, *Bamidbar* 33:51–52.
20. *Devarim Zuta* 17.
21. See *Megillah* 10b; *Midrash haGadol, Bamidbar* 33:56.
22. Ralbag, *Bamidbar* 33:52.

After Moshe's death, when the Jewish people crossed the Jordan River into the land, Yehoshua would repeat these words of warning to them in the name of Moshe to insure that they were heeded.[23]

The Boundaries of Eretz Yisrael

Hashem now showed Moshe the exact boundaries of the future Eretz Yisrael. It was essential to know precisely what was considered part of the Land and what was not, because certain mitzvos can be performed only in Eretz Yisrael.[24]

Hashem also showed Moshe important events that would occur in the future of the Jewish people; their struggles, their leaders, their righteous men and women, and their sinners. He showed him Shimshon from the tribe of Dan and his assault on the Pelishtim. He also showed him the victory of Barak from the tribe of Naftali over Sisera, the Canaanite general.[25]

The Cities of Refuge

As mentioned earlier, the tribe of Levi would not inherit a portion of the land. Instead, its members would be dedicated to the service of Hashem, concerned with spiritual matters rather than business and finance. Nonetheless, Hashem in His kindness instructed the other tribes to set aside forty-eight towns from their own portions as places of residence for the tribe of Levi.[26] Each town was to include a one-thousand-*amah*-wide swath of land encircling it that was to remain clear of any crops

---

23. See *Sotah* 34a; *Yehoshua* 4, 23.

24. Rashi, *Bamidbar* 34:2.

25. *Bereishis Rabbah* 23:5.

26. See *Ohr haChaim, Bamidbar* 35:2; Rambam, *Shemittah* 13:1; *Sefer haChinuch* 408. These cities must have been already built and ready for occupancy (*Sifsei Kohen*).

or construction, so that the towns would have beautiful views on all sides and plenty of fresh air. Another one-thousand-*amah*-wide swath of land was to be set aside for fields and vineyards.[27]

These forty-eight Levite towns also served as cities of refuge, places to which inadvertent murderers could seek asylum from the vengeance of their victims' families.[28] Hashem wanted these to be where the Levi'im lived, because the Levi'im's holiness and their land would help atone for the sins of those who sought refuge there.[29]

Of these forty-eight, six were to serve as the principal cities of refuge. These six would provide protection even if the murderer was not aware that he was in such a city, while the other forty-two would provide protection only to those who consciously sought asylum in them.[30] Moshe would designate the three principal cities of refuge that would serve the eastern side of the Jordan River, and fourteen years later Yehoshua would designate the three that would serve the rest of the land.

Hashem further told Moshe that although he would designate the three cities of refuge east of the Jordan, they would not become

---

27. *Midrash haGadol*, Rashi on *Bamidbar* 35:2–4 and *Sotah* 27b. Another opinion has two thousand *amos* outside the city limits designated for fields and vineyards (Rambam, *Shemittah* 13:2).

28. See Rashi, *Bamidbar* 35:6; *Bamidbar Rabbah* 23:14; *Makkos* 9b; Rambam, *Shemittah* 13:1. There were forty-five Levite cities west of the Jordan (forty-two belonging to the Levi'im plus three cities of refuge), and three cities of refuge on the east side of the river. On the west side of the Jordan, they were not divided equally among the nine tribes. They were distributed according to the proportionate size of each tribe and its land (*Midrash haGadol*). See *Yehoshua* 21. See also *Yehoshua* 21:27, *I Divrei haYamim* 6:46.

29. *Sefer haChinuch* 408. Additionally, both the Levi and the fleeing murderer were considered foreigners in their respective lands. As such, they were fit for each other. *Kli Yakar* explains it thus: The forty-eight cities were divided into forty-two and six (see below in the text), and the number forty-two parallels the Jewish people's journeys. The Levi'im and accidental murderers remained foreign dwellers in these towns, just as the Jews were foreigners in the wilderness.

30. *Makkos* 10a with Rashi.

operational until the other three in Eretz Yisrael were also established.[31] Otherwise, people would be motivated to leave Eretz Yisrael and seek asylum in the three cities east of the Jordan.[32]

Considering that there were far more people living west of the Jordan River than east of it, why was there an equal number of cities of refuge on both sides of the river? This was because there would be a much higher incidence of bloodshed in the territory of Gil'ad—which is east of the Jordan River—than in Eretz Yisrael.[33] The inhabitants of Gil'ad would be guilty of sins such as murder and fraud, and their footsteps would be covered with blood.[34] Although premeditated murderers could not seek refuge in these cities, the inhabitants of Gil'ad would kill covertly without witnesses, making their murders impossible to prosecute. The murderer would then seek refuge in one of the cities in order to escape the avenging families of their victims.[35]

Thus concluded Hashem's final instructions to Moshe regarding the various issues that needed to be addressed before the Jewish people entered the land. All that remained now was Moshe's final address to the people.

---

31. *Makkos* 9b with Rashi.

32. *Meshech Chochmah, Bamidbar* 35:13.

33. *Makkos* 9b–10a with Rashi. Ramban explains that the Holy Land naturally cultivates fewer murderers than other lands.

34. See *Hoshea* 6:8.

35. See Rashi with Mizrachi, *Imrei Shefer*, Ramban on *Bamidbar* 35:14.

18

Forty Years in Review

Hashem had told Moshe again and again, ten times in all, that he would not live to enter the Holy Land together with the Jewish people, and in the end, Moshe resigned himself to his fate.[1] On Rosh Chodesh Shevat, thirty-six days[2] before he was to die, he asked Hashem for one last opportunity to review the Torah with the Jewish people.

Hashem approved of the idea,[3] but He

---

1. See *Midrash Petiras Moshe*, in *Otzar Midrashim* 364.
2. *Sefer Devarim* begins with the word *eileh* (these), whose numerical value is thirty-six, symbolizing that the events in this book this took place thirty-six days before Moshe's death (Rabbi Yehudah heChasid). Furthermore, for thirty-six years Yehoshua had served Moshe, and now, for the final thirty-six days of his life, Moshe would serve Yehoshua (*Midrash Petiras Moshe*, cited in *Otzar Midrashim* 365).
3. See Rashi, *Midrash haGadol*, Rokeach, Malbim on *Devarim* 1:1–5.

also wanted Moshe to include a final rebuke and admonition to the people and thereby reinforce their faith and loyalty. In later years, there would be no one like Moshe to intercede for them when they erred, and therefore Moshe's last words to them needed to fortify them against sin.[4]

"But I hesitate to rebuke the Jewish people," Moshe said. "The last time I rebuked them at Mei Merivah for rebelliousness, I was punished with not being allowed to enter the Land of Israel."

"Do not worry," Hashem told him. "It is appropriate now."

This is comparable to a master and his disciple who encountered a glowing hot coal. The disciple mistook it for a precious jewel and reached for it, but his fingers were scorched by the fire. A few days later, the master and his disciple came across another glittering stone. The disciple thought that it looked valuable, but he hesitated to touch it, afraid that it too would burn his fingers. "Do not worry," his master told him. "This one really is a precious jewel. It is safe to touch it."

It had been inappropriate for Moshe to rebuke the people when they thirsted for water. But with his death imminent, it was indeed appropriate to leave them with a message of rebuke that would stay with them long after he was gone.[5] Yaakov had also waited until he was on his deathbed to rebuke his children, because they would be more receptive to his words at that time. With Yaakov's time running out, they knew that they would not have to face him repeatedly in shame for their shortcomings, and they also knew that the rebuke would be limited in its duration. This opened up their hearts to acknowledge that it was for their own good and to listen without reservation. In the future, Yehoshua would learn from his predecessors and wait until shortly before his death to rebuke the people.[6]

---

4. *Yalkut Shimoni* 785. See *Devarim Rabbah* 3:11.
5. *Devarim Rabbah* 1:8.
6. *Sifrei*, Rashi on *Devarim* 1:1–2.

A Time for Rebuke

Moshe assembled all the Jewish people without exception for his rebuke. Everyone would have the opportunity to challenge anything he said, and no one would ever be able to say, "I wasn't there when Moshe spoke, but had I been there I would have voiced my dissent."[7]

Moshe spoke to the people with gentleness, love and devotion,[8] revisiting some of his earlier themes in order to implant them deep in the consciousness of the people.[9] His voice carried miraculously through the entire encampment so that everyone heard him clearly.[10]

He spoke about the reluctance of the people to enter Yam Suf and their complaints before they received the *mahn*. He spoke about the terrible sin of the golden calf and the dreadful consequences of the spies' slander.

"The journey from Mount Sinai to the Holy Land," he said, "should have taken eleven days. But Hashem showed His love for you by shortening the journey to three days. You were so close, so close. Your arrival in the Land was imminent. You could have easily overcome the thirty-one Canaanite kings. Look how easily you vanquished Sichon and Og. But the spies lacked faith in Hashem, and they slandered it. They perished, and you were doomed to wander through the wilderness for thirty-eight more years.[11]

Moshe then rebuked them regarding Korach's rebellion[12] and their disputatious behavior at Mei Merivah. They should have learned a lesson from what happened to Miriam when she spoke out

---

7. Rashi, Rokeach on ibid. See *Yalkut Reuveni*. See also Ramban on *Devarim* 4:41.

8. Zohar, *Ha'azinu* 286a.

9. *Tzeror haMor, Devarim* 1:1. Many heard these admonitions for the first time, as they hadn't yet been born at the time of these sins.

10. *Yalkut Reuveni, Minchah Belulah* on *Devarim* 1:1.

11. See *Bechor Shor, Devarim* 1:4.

12. Rather than mentioning Korach, Moshe alluded to Dasan and Aviram's role in the rebellion. See Ramban; *Minchah Belulah*; Abarbanel.

against Moshe and was then afflicted with *tzara'as*, but they didn't. And then he rebuked them regarding the incident at Shittim.[13]

"It is because of you that I cannot enter the land," Moshe told them. "When I called you rebels at Mei Merivah, Hashem was angry with me and decreed that neither I nor my remains could enter the land.[14] I prayed 515 prayers before Hashem finally told me to stop. Yehoshua had been designated as my replacement, and nothing I could do would change that.[15]

"Consider yourselves fortunate that Hashem forgave you for the grievous transgression of the incident with Pe'or, after I prayed for you. As for me, I was not that fortunate.[16] If you listen to His decrees and follow in His ways, Hashem will continue to forgive you for the sins of the past. But what about the future? I will no longer be with you to pray for you and intercede on your behalf as I have done in the past. You must therefore be more vigilant in avoiding sin and adhering to Hashem's path."[17]

The Jewish people remained silent throughout the lengthy rebuke. No one protested that most of the sins Moshe had mentioned had been committed by the previous generation. They could have argued that they could not be held accountable for the sins of their fathers, but they accepted Moshe's words with silence and humility, and they would be blessed because of it.[18]

---

13. *Midrash haGadol*, Rashi on *Devarim* 1:1–2.

14. *Sifrei*, Rashi on *Devarim* 3:26, 4:21–22. See *Devarim Rabbah* 2:2. Had Moshe entered Eretz Yisrael, the Beis haMikdash would never have been destroyed. For rather than venting His anger on stone and wood, leaving the Jewish people to survive, Hashem would have punished the Jews themselves, which would have been a far greater tragedy than the destruction of the Temple. See *Eichah Rabbah* 4:14; Rashi, Tosafos on *Kiddushin* 31b; Malbim, *Aderes Eliyahu*, *Me'am Lo'ez* on *Devarim* 3:26.

15. *Sotah* 13b.

16. Rashi, *Devarim* 3:29.

17. See *Chizkuni*, *Devarim* 4:22.

18. *Devarim Rabbah* 1:13; *Devarim* 1:10–11. In fact, this was in and of itself a test for the Jews: Would they protest the rebuke? (*Sifsei Kohen*).

Ironically, it was Bilam, the enemy of the Jewish people, who blessed them, and it was Moshe, their devoted leader, who rebuked them. Had the reverse happened, however, people might have thought that the blessings and rebukes were merely expressions of the emotional dispositions of the ones who delivered them. Now, however, they saw clearly that both the blessings and the rebuke came directly from Hashem.[19]

Moshe Repeats the Torah

Moshe went on to review the entire Torah[20] in seventy languages,[21] as he had done during the giving of the Torah. In this way, the Torah would exist in all the language groups and would thereby always be accessible to the Jewish people no matter where they lived and which language they spoke.[22] These translations would also prevent non-Jews from saying that had they understood the Torah they would have converted. Now anyone who wanted to convert and learn the Torah would find it accessible.[23]

For thirty-six days, Moshe vigorously expounded all the laws previously given at Mount Sinai and in the wilderness.[24] He taught them the Oral Torah and all that it encompassed.[25] He taught them

---

19. *Devarim Rabbah* 1:4.

20. Because many of this generation were not present when the Torah was given at Sinai, Moshe repeated the Ten Commandments as well as the rest of the Torah (Rabbeinu Bachya, *Chizkuni* on *Devarim* 5:1). Thus, *Sefer Devarim* is also called *Mishneh Torah*, "a repetition of the Torah."

21. See below in more detail.

22. *Shabbos* 88b; *Tanchuma, Yisro* 11, *Devarim* 2; Rashi, *Devarim* 1:5; Zohar, *Devarim* 146a; *Sifsei Kohen, Shemos* 20:1; *Tiferes Yisrael* 31. See *Let My Nation Serve Me*, p. 218.

23. *Sotah* 35b; *Me'am Lo'ez, Devarim* 1:5.

24. *Midrash haGadol, Devarim* 1:1; *Seder Olam* 10; *Yalkut Shimoni* 797. The latter laws are those given in *parashiyos Mishpatim* through *Devarim*.

25. *Me'am Lo'ez, Devarim* 1:5.

everything right then and there, for there would be no tomorrow.[26]

"Don't forget what I've taught you now and what you've been taught at Mount Sinai," he said.[27] "Anyone who has a question or has forgotten something, this is your last chance to ask me to enlighten you, for I'll be gone soon.[28] Remember, I have brought down the entire Torah. There is nothing left in Heaven for you to receive from someone else at a later time. What I give you now is the Torah in its entirety. Take advantage of this opportunity, and learn all the Torah you can from me."[29]

Instruction about the Land

At this time, when all the Jews assembled in one place, Moshe identified the locations of the cities of refuge.[30] This was the last administrative task that was still his responsibility, and with it accomplished, the people could be sure that before long Yehoshua would lead them into the land.[31] But there were conditions. The conquest would be successful only if they followed the laws of the Torah,[32] cleansed the land of its idols and places of worship, and absolutely avoided assimilation with its inhabitants.[33]

During all this time, Moshe had referred again and again to his imminent death and how it would impact on the fortunes of the people. By doing so, he had hoped that the people would be

26. *Imrei Noam, Pa'aneiach Raza* on *Devarim* 1:1.

27. Ramban, *Devarim* 4:21.

28. *Midrash haGadol, Devarim* 1:5; *Yalkut Shimoni* 801; Rambam's introduction to his commentary on Mishnah.

29. See *Devarim Rabbah* 8:6. See also *Ha'amek Davar, Devarim* 1:3.

30. Ramban, *Devarim* 4:41. See also Ibn Ezra; Seforno. Because Moshe couldn't enter Eretz Yisrael, he delineated these cities now, so he could be rewarded as though he'd done so at the right time, which was after the Jews conquered and inherited Eretz Yisrael. See Malbim, *Devarim* 4:21.

31. Abarbanel, *Akeidas Yitzchak* on *Devarim* 4:41.

32. See *Chizkuni, Devarim* 4:1.

33. See *Devarim* 7:1–9; Rashbam, *Devarim* 7:9; *Midrash haGadol, Devarim* 19:1.

inspired to pray for a reprieve so that he could enter the land with them and continue to be their advocate and protector. But to his dismay, this wasn't happening.

"My dear people," Moshe said, "I was willing to die so that six hundred thousand of you would survive the incident of the Eigel. Is it too much to ask that the six hundred thousand should beseech Hashem to pardon just one man? Have you forgotten all I've done for you during these forty years in the wilderness? Why haven't you prayed for my entrance into the land?[34]

"You haven't, and my fate is sealed. So remember my last words to you: keep laws and mitzvos of the Torah, and you will surely be blessed. If you don't, you may likely suffer a curse from Hashem.[35]

"You will soon cross the Jordan River into the land.[36] Do not fear the thirty-one Canaanite kings. You triumphed over Pharaoh and the Egyptians, and you will prevail against the Canaanites. Accept Hashem's sovereignty, love Him and fear Him, and He will support you and protect you from all harm. Keep the laws of *bris milah* and Shabbos, and you'll remain on the land. Remember that the land belongs to Hashem. If you abide by His laws, you will flourish there."[37]

Having completed his review of the general laws and mitzvos pertaining to fearing and serving Hashem in all places, Moshe now turned to the laws that applied specifically to the land. The Jewish people's first obligation after they crossed into Eretz Yisrael would be to assemble at Mount Gerizim and Mount Eival and make a public declaration of the blessings for those who obey the

---

34. See *Devarim Rabbah* 3:11, 7:10; *Yalkut Shimoni* 785.

35. See Rabbeinu Bachya, *Minchah Belulah*, *Bechor Shor*, Rokeach on *Devarim* 11:26.

36. *Midrash haGadol*, Devarim 9:1.

37. See Rabbeinu Bachya, *Tzeror haMor* on *Devarim* 11:22–25; Abarbanel, *Devarim* 7:17; *Bereishis Rabbah* 46:9; *Shemos* 19:5. See also *Ha'amek Davar*, Malbim on *Devarim* 11:31.

Torah and the curses for those who don't.[38] Moshe then explained the laws of sacrificial offerings, the tithing of fruits, the laws of charity[39] and the laws of bringing *bikurim*—the first fruit to ripen after they would settle into the land.[40]

Critical to their continued stay in Eretz Yisrael was the appointment of righteous and conscientious judges to implement the laws.[41] If there would be true justice in the land, Hashem would fight their wars for them and insure that they would prevail over their enemies.[42]

Moshe established priorities for the Jewish people. They were to eradicate Amalek, appoint a king and build the Beis haMikdash.[43] He then reminded the people about the leaders' responsibilities, including the establishment of the cities of refuge and the rules of war, along with the king's responsibilities in conducting them.[44]

Twelve Monoliths

Moshe now informed the Jewish people that the Jordan River would split open to allow them to cross into the land. Once they were across, they were to erect twelve monoliths in the river, representing the twelve tribes, to memorialize this great miracle.[45] They were then to bring twelve more monoliths,

38. See Seforno, *Emek haNetziv,* Maharil Diskin on *Devarim* 11:27. Moshe merely mentioned this mitzvah now and would elaborate later (Ramban, *Devarim* 11:29).

39. See *Devarim* 12:6, 14:22, 15:8.

40. Rashi, *Devarim* 26:1; *Kiddushin* 37b.

41. See Rashi, *Devarim* 16:20.

42. *Midrash haCheifetz, Devarim* 16:18.

43. *Devarim Rabbah* 5:10; *Sanhedrin* 20b. See Seforno, *Devarim* 19:2.

44. See Seforno, *Devarim* 19:2.

45. Rabbeinu Bachya, *Devarim* 27:1; *Yehoshua* 4:9. These monoliths would be set up in two rows of six each.

identical to each other, each measuring forty *se'ah* in volume.[46] They were to transport these immediately to Mount Gerizim and Mount Eival,[47] sixty *mil* distant, adjacent to the land of Shechem in the land that would fall to Ephraim.[48]

They did not need to be concerned about the difficulty of transporting such huge stones such a long distance. Miraculously, they would make the journey in an instant.[49]

Once the stones were at the designated mountains, they were to coat them with plaster and inscribe on them the Torah translated into all seventy language groups, so that it would be accessible to any of the seventy nations who chose to study it.[50] Although this was a massive undertaking, miraculously it would be accomplished almost instantaneously. Hashem wanted the Torah inscribed at the same location where the blessings and curses would be intoned. In this way, the very mountains would bear witness that the Jewish people had entered this new covenant

---

46. All twelve stones were to be equal in weight, symbolizing that in order to inherit Eretz Yisrael, all twelve tribes had to be equal in piety and righteousness.

47. Seforno, *Emek haNetziv* on *Devarim* 11:29–30. See *Sotah* 35b; Rashi, *Sifsei Chachamim* on *Devarim* 27:2, regarding three sets of stones that would be established. These three sets of stones would teach the Jews the three fundamentals of Judaism: Moshe's Torah taught belief in the Torah, the stones in the Jordan affirmed Hashem's existence, and the stones on Mount Eival inculcated belief in reward and punishment.

48. See *Sotah* 32a; Rashi, *Devarim* 11:30.

49. *Sotah* 36a; *Chizkuni*, *Devarim* 11:29; *Me'am Lo'ez*, *Yehoshua* 4.

50. *Sotah* 32a; Rashi, *Devarim* 27:8; Rabbeinu Bachya, *Devarim* 27:1. These stones contained either the entire Torah (Ramban, *Devarim* 27:3), the 613 mitzvos (Ibn Ezra, quoting Rav Saadiah Gaon), *Sefer Devarim*, the Ten Commandments or the blessings and curses. See Radak, *Metzudos* on *Yehoshua* 4; Rabbeinu Bachya, *Devarim* 27:3; *Me'am Lo'ez*, *Yehoshua* 8:32.

According to *Sotah* 35b, the Torah was written on the stone, then covered with plaster. Eventually, the nations would send their scribes to peel off the plaster and record the Torah for themselves. According to *Ha'amek Davar*, *Devarim* 27:8, the Torah was written in *lashon hakodesh* at Mount Eival and in the rest of the seventy languages at Gilgal. See Maharsha, *Sotah* 35b; *Me'am Lo'ez*, *Yehoshua* 8:32.

to keep the Torah. The gift of the Land was dependent on this covenant. Without the Torah, there would be no Jewish land.[51]

Once the Torah was properly inscribed, the people were then to assemble at these two mountains to intone the blessings and the curses, after which they were to combine the twelve monoliths into a single altar and bring peace offerings and other sacrifices upon it. Then there was to be a great feast celebrating a renewed pledge of allegiance to the Torah. Later, when this feast took place, Yehoshua used the occasion to establish the blessing for Eretz Yisrael in the Grace after Meals.[52] Upon leaving Mount Gerizim and Mount Eival, they were to dismantle the altar and reassemble it when they settled in Gilgal.[53]

The Jewish people's first mitzvah upon entrance into the land was to make a renewed commitment to Hashem and the Torah. Inscribing the Torah on the great stones and bringing the offerings would be a strong expression of that commitment. The expressions of Hashem's reciprocal commitment would be manifest in their miraculous crossing of the Jordan River, their instantaneous arrival at the distant mountains and the miraculous achievement of inscribing the entire Torah in seventy languages in no time at all.[54]

---

51. The Torah's inscription at Mount Eival would show that the Jews accepted the curses they were about to proclaim for those who failed to uphold the Torah (*Bechor Shor, Devarim* 27:4).

Yehoshua also brought stones, but they were brought only two and a half months after Moshe's stones.

52. See *Sotah* 36a with Tosafos; *Aderes Eliyahu, Re'eh.*

53. See *Sotah* 32a, 35b–36a; *Yerushalmi Sotah* 7:3; Rashi, Rabbeinu Bachya on *Devarim* 27:1; *Yehoshua* 4:9. See *Chizkuni, Sefer Zikaron* and *Gur Aryeh*, which resolve an apparent contradiction between Rashi on *Devarim* 27:1 and *Sotah* 35b.

The stones on which Moshe explained the Torah aren't addressed here. See *Sotah* 35b.

54. See Alshich, *Kli Chemdah* on *Devarim* 27. See also *Sotah* 36a; Seforno, *Devarim* 29:8.

Mount Gerizim and Mount Eival

Earlier, Moshe had delivered a stern and lengthy warning to the Jewish people regarding the future. If they would keep the Torah and fulfill the mitzvos, he assured them, they would receive bountiful blessings. But if they would not, a torrent of curses would rain down on them.[55] This promise of blessings and curses was to be formalized by the people at the two mountains, and would reinforce their covenantal commitment to the Torah.[56]

There had never been any idol worship on Mount Gerizim,[57] and not surprisingly, it was resplendent with lush greenery.[58] Mount Eival, on the other hand, had often been the scene of idol worship, and although it was right next to the verdant Mount Gerizim, it was a desolate, rocky crag.[59] The blessings were, therefore, to be intoned on Mount Gerizim and the curses on Mount Eival, graphically showing the people the benefits of righteousness and the consequences of iniquity even to inanimate mountains—and all the more so, to human beings.[60]

Six tribes[61]—Shimon, Levi,[62] Yehudah, Yissachar, Yosef and Binyamin—were to take up positions on Mount Gerizim,[63] and the

---

55. See Rashi, *Devarim* 11:26–30. See also Ramban, *Devarim* 11:29.

56. See *Me'am Lo'ez, Yehoshua* 8:33.

57. *Midrash haCheifetz, Devarim* 11:29.

58. Rav Samson Raphael Hirsch, ibid.

59. *Midrash haCheifetz,* Rav Samson Raphael Hirsch on ibid.; *Me'am Lo'ez, Yehoshua* 8:33.

60. See *Me'am Lo'ez, Yehoshua* 8:33.

61. Compare Radak, ibid.

62. See *Sotah* 37a; Mizrachi, *Mesiach Ilmim* on *Devarim* 11:29, 27:12. The Levi'im unfit for carrying the Mishkan, i.e., those under age thirty and over age fifty, joined their fellow Jews on the mountain, while those fit for such service stood below to utter the blessings and curses.

63. Why these six? Shimon was chosen first because, unlike his brothers, he wasn't blessed by Yaakov (or Moshe, for that matter). Yehudah is the king, Yissachar represents Torah, Yosef was considered the firstborn, and the Beis

other six — Reuven, Gad, Asher, Zevulun, Dan and Naftali — were to stand on Mount Eival.[64] The holy ark containing the Torah was to remain on the low ground between the two mountains. The Kohanim were to form a circle around the ark, and the Levi'im were to form an outer circle around the Kohanim.[65]

The Levi'im were to turn toward Mount Gerizim and call out,[66] "Blessed is the man who will not make a molten image,"[67] and the tribes assembled on both mountains would cry out, "Amen!"[68] Then they would turn toward Mount Eival and declare, "Cursed is the man who makes a molten image," and the tribes assembled on both mountains would cry out, "Amen!"[69]

Then they would repeat the process again and again. Facing Mount Gerizim, the Levi'im would say, "Blessed is he who does not degrade[70] his father and mother," and the people would say, "Amen!" "Cursed is he who degrades his father and mother," and the people would say, "Amen!"[71]

"Blessed is he who does not encroach on the boundary[72] of his

---

haMikdash would be built in Binyamin's portion of Eretz Yisrael (*Tosefos Rav Ephraim al haTorah*).

64. This group contained the maidservants' four children plus Leah's eldest and youngest sons (*Chizkuni, Mesiach Ilmim* on *Devarim* 27:11). See Abarbanel.

65. *Sotah* 32a.

66. *Sotah* 37b; *Yerushalmi Sotah* 7:4. See Seforno, *Kli Yakar*, Malbim, *Me'am Lo'ez* on *Devarim* 27:12–15 regarding why the Torah doesn't mention the blessings. The Tur notes that the numerical value of "Gerizim" (270) equals that of the words *haberachah yiyeh bo*, "the blessing shall be on it."

67. Having boycotted the golden calf, Levi is subtly blessed here (*Maskil l'David*).

68. Most commentaries aver that these sins were chosen because they are usually committed in secrecy. Compare Rabbeinu Bachya; Abarbanel.

69. Rashi, *Devarim* 11:29, 27:12. This curse refers to the idol of Michah (*Midrash haBeiur*).

70. Rashi, *Devarim* 27:16.

71. This curse alludes to the children of Eli the Kohen (*Midrash haBeiur*). It also refers to Yehudah, who fooled his father, Yaakov, with the bloody tunic (*Maskil l'David*).

72. Rashi, *Devarim* 27:17.

neighbor." "Amen!" "Cursed is he who does." "Amen!"[73]

"Blessed is he who does not mislead a blind man." "Amen!" "Cursed is he who does." "Amen!"[74]

"Blessed is he who does not subvert the judgment of a convert, orphan or widow." "Amen!" "Cursed is he who does." "Amen!"[75]

"Blessed is he who does not lie with the wife of his father, his father's or mother's daughter, his mother-in-law or an animal." "Amen!" "Cursed is he who does." "Amen!"[76]

"Blessed is he who does not attack his fellow in secret[77] by slandering him." "Amen!" "Cursed is he who does ." "Amen!"[78]

"Blessed is he who does not take a bribe to kill an innocent person." "Amen!" "Cursed is he who does." "Amen!"[79]

"Blessed is he who upholds the words of the Torah to perform them." "Amen!" "Cursed is he who does not." "Amen!"[80]

---

73. This curse alludes to Achav and the vineyard of Navos (*Midrash haBeiur*) and to Yissachar, who preceded Reuven in the inauguration offerings (*Maskil l'David*).

74. The blessing is an allusion to Yosef, who soundly advised Pharaoh regarding his dreams (*Maskil l'David*), and the curse to Chananyah ben Azor, who was a false prophet (*Midrash haBeiur*).

75. The blessing alludes to Binyamin, who allowed Yisro's children to dwell in his portion in Eretz Yisrael temporarily (*Maskil l'David*), and the curse to the children of Shemuel, who were corrupt judges (*Midrash haBeiur*).

76. A reference to Avshalom, Shimshon and Amnon regarding their lewd actions (*Midrash haBeiur*); to Reuven, who moved his father's bed; and to Gad, Asher and Zevulun, later tempted by promiscuity (*Maskil l'David*).

77. This refers to the sin of *lashon hara* (Rashi, *Devarim* 27:24), i.e., derogatory speech about another person.

78. *Targum Yonasan*, Rashi on *Devarim* 27:24; *Pirkei d'Rabbi Eliezer* 53. This curse alludes to Doeg's gossip about David (*Midrash haBeiur*) and to Dan, who slandered the children of Leah to Yosef (*Maskil l'David*).

79. The blessing is an allusion to Naftali, who refused to help Yehudah annihilate Egypt (*Maskil l'David*), and the curse refers to Geichazi and the money he took from Na'aman (*Midrash haBeiur*).

80. This curse alludes to Achaz, who closed the houses of study (*Midrash haBeiur*). Ramban explains that "upholding" here means accepting the Torah in full, deeming no part of it irrelevant.

In all, there were eleven curses,[81] corresponding to eleven of the tribes. There was no curse corresponding to the tribe of Shimon. Moshe would not bless Shimon before his death when he blessed the other tribes, but out of respect for the tribe, he did not want to have a curse correspond to it.[82]

Blessings and Reproof

"Great blessings will come upon you if you heed the laws of the Torah and do Hashem's mitzvos," Moshe told the Jewish people. "Even if you neither want nor need these blessings, they will pursue you nonetheless. But just as fulfilling the Torah brings blessings, failure to do so will have tragic consequences."[83]

As Moshe began to speak about these terrible consequences, the heavens and the earth began to shudder, the sun and the moon grew dark, the stars lost their sparkle, the trees stopped swaying, and all was silent.

"Woe to our children who must endure such calamity," the patriarchs cried out from their graves. "They face annihilation!"

"Do not worry," a heavenly voice called out. "The oath I swore to you that your children will prevail is still in effect. Despite the tragedies and suffering they may endure, they will always survive as a nation."[84]

When Moshe completed his lengthy description of the numerous consequences that awaited them should they stumble,[85] the Jewish people were paralyzed with fear, and the blood drained from their faces.

---

81. Excluding the final one, which encompassed the entire Torah (*Sifsei Chachamim*). See Tosafos, *Sotah* 37b.

82. Rashi, *Devarim* 27:24.

83. See Rabbeinu Meyuchas, Rabbeinu Bachya on *Devarim* 28:2. Despite any blessings received in this world, the Jews' main reward comes in the next one (Rashi, Seforno on *Devarim* 7:11).

84. *Targum Yonasan*, *Devarim* 28:15.

85. As enumerated in *parashas Ki Savo*.

"Ninety-eight consequences!" they wailed. "Who could withstand such suffering?'

"Don't be afraid," Moshe reassured them. "You've angered Hashem many times in the past, and you still endure. Despite any suffering that may befall you, you will thrive as a nation.[86] You are like the day, with darkness displaced by daylight. As a nation, the darkness of your travails will atone for your sins and hence bring you light and success.[87]

"You're all familiar with Hashem's miracles, beginning with the exodus from Egypt and continuing through the wondrous victories over Sichon and Og. Never forget that your garments and shoes never wore out or got soiled during your forty years in the wilderness.[88] Remember that the *mahn* came to you without any effort.[89]

"Why has Hashem done all this for you? In order to remove all distractions so that you can concentrate on the Torah and on reaching the highest levels of faith and spirituality.[90] Embrace the Torah, as I have advised you to do, and Hashem will always take care of you and destroy your enemies."[91]

---

86. Rashi, *Devarim* 29:12; *Tanchuma, Nitzavim* 1. According to *Sha'arei Aharon*, this *midrash* disagrees with the view that the covenant with the Jews was sealed on the day of Moshe's death, for he rebuked them all on one day—thirty-six days beforehand. Other commentaries posit that this reproof was given over a thirty-six-day period, culminating on Moshe's last day.

87. Rashi, *Devarim* 29:12.

88. *Tzeror haMor*, ibid.

89. Malbim, *Devarim* 29:4–5.

90. Ibid.

91. *Tzeror haMor, Sifsei Kohen* on *Devarim* 29:1, 6. Before his death, Yehoshua, too, reviewed the miracles Hashem had performed for the Jewish people. See *Yehoshua* 24.

19

Moshe's Last Day

Although no other person had ever been told the exact time of his death, Hashem wanted Moshe to know his because he had many tasks to complete before his time on earth expired. He had to anoint Yehoshua as his successor, he had to caution the Jewish people to remain faithful to the Torah, he had to complete the writing of the Torah and he had to deliver his final blessing to the Children of Israel. Furthermore, since no one would actually see Moshe's final resting place, people might think he had not died but had simply vanished. Therefore, it was important that the time of his impending death be public knowledge.[1]

1. *Me'am Lo'ez, Devarim* 34:1.

A Renewed Covenant

On his final day,[2] Moshe assembled all[3] the Jewish people one last time to forge a renewed covenant under his direction. They came without exception: Yehoshua and Elazar, the tribal princes, the Sanhedrin, the elders, the officers, the judges, men, women and children, and all the converts.[4]

"You are all standing here today," Moshe began, "to endorse the covenant you will soon be making at the mountains of Gerizim and Eival.[5] It is not just those of you here who are entering this covenant with Hashem but also all the souls of past and future generations.[6]

"Many of you were not present at Mount Sinai forty years ago,[7] except for the older people among you. At that time, the people entered a covenant with Hashem to be His chosen people,[8] but that covenant was abrogated when they made the Eigel[9] and

---

2. Rashi with Mizrachi, *Devarim* 29:9. *Sha'arei Aharon* comments that when Moshe tells the Jewish people at the start of *parashas Nitzavim*, "You stand *this day* all of you before the Eternal, your God.... That you should enter into the covenant of the Eternal, your God" (*Devarim* 29:9–11), he means the day of his death, which "began" several verses earlier, in *Ki Savo*, where he also refers to "this day" (29:3) and to "this covenant" (29:9).

According to *Midrash haBeiur*, Devarim 29:9, Moshe delivered this speech up to thirty-seven days prior to his death. See Rashbam; *Ohr haChaim*. See also Rabbeinu Bachya, *Devarim* 31:2; *Tzeror haMor* 29:1.

3. Rabbeinu Meyuchas, *Devarim* 29:11.

4. See Rashi, Seforno, *Aderes Eliyahu* on *Devarim* 29:9.

5. See Ralbag, Abarbanel on *Devarim* 29:11.

6. *Devarim* 29:14. These generations included future converts as well (Rokeach). See Rabbeinu Bachya; Malbim; *Aderes Eliyahu* for an in-depth explanation on how one man's acceptance affects his offspring hundreds and thousands of years later.

7. See *Me'am Lo'ez*, *Devarim* 29:12. See also Rashi, *Yechezkel* 16:59.

8. Right after leaving Egypt, the Jews had entered into a covenant in Marah as well. See *Shemos* 15:26, 24:8. The covenant they are now about to establish, then, is their third.

9. Rabbeinu Bachya, *Devarim* 29:11.

when I broke the Luchos.[10] Therefore, you must all accept upon yourselves with an oath, enforced by dire consequences for its violation, that you will forever be Hashem's nation.

"You are all bound together as one nation, and Hashem has already bound Himself to you in that He will never turn away from you. Look at all the effort He put forth to show you that you are His chosen nation. This covenant we are forging here today confirms that just as Hashem has obligated Himself not to turn away from you, you will not turn away from Him.[11]

"But beware! Perhaps there are some among you who would forsake this covenant and wander off to serve the idols of the neighboring nations.[12] Perhaps those people will say, 'I bless myself with peace and serenity.[13] I am an individual who is part of the greater Jewish community, and I will be protected from Hashem through the community's merit. Indeed, Hashem's admonishment is for an entire people, not for each individual.[14] I will thus be immune to the curses and admonitions Hashem has planned for sinners.'[15]

"I, therefore, warn you not to think that way. Hashem will single you out and punish you—and not just for the deliberate sin. Even your errors and mistakes will be coupled with your sins of negligence.[16] Hashem's anger will rise with fury to punish you with all the curses and admonitions until you are wiped off the face of the earth.[17]

"In future times, when the world sees massive destruction

---

10. *Me'am Lo'ez,* ibid.
11. Rashi with Mizrachi, *Devarim* 29:12.
12. With every Jew present, no one could later claim he'd never accepted this covenant (*Chizkuni, Devarim* 29:11).
13. Rashi with Mizrachi, *Devarim* 29:17–18.
14. *Aderes Eliyahu.*
15. Rashi, *Devarim* 29:17–18.
16. Ibid.
17. Rashi, *Devarim* 29:19.

visited upon the Jewish people, even the foreign nations will recognize that it is because they forsook Hashem and His covenant and turned to idol worship.[18]

"But know this: despite the evil ways some of you may choose, all is not lost. Hashem has given you the mitzvah of *teshuvah*, the ability to repent and wipe your slates clean. Just as there is punishment for sins, there are blessings for those who repent. And when you repent, Hashem will one day deflect all the curses and admonitions onto your enemies.[19]

"As I conclude the words of this covenant, let the heavens and the earth that exist until eternity bear witness that I have told you both the reward and the punishment that derive from your actions."[20]

Encouragement and Consolation

Once the covenant was concluded, the people dispersed and returned home.[21] As his last hours slipped by, Moshe wanted to bid farewell to all the people. He could have sounded trumpets or sent messengers to call them together for a new assembly,[22] but he decided to humble himself and go to their homes and speak to their hearts with words of consolation and encouragement.[23]

"Today is 7 Adar," he told them.[24] "I am exactly 120 years old today.[25] Do not let my impending death upset you, for I could not have taken you into the Land anyway.[26] It is not because I am too

18. *Devarim* 29:24.

19. See *Devarim* 30:7 with *Ha'amek Davar*.

20. Rashi, *Devarim* 30:19. See Ramban, *Devarim* 30:15.

21. Ramban, *Devarim* 31:1.

22. *Bereishis Rabbah* 96:3; *Koheles* 8:8; Rashi, *Devarim* 31:28; Rabbi Yehudah heChasid, *Chizkuni* on *Devarim* 31:1.

23. See Ibn Ezra, *Tzeror haMor*, Abarbanel, *Sifsei Kohen* on *Devarim* 31:1–2.Moshe now blessed each tribe (Ibn Ezra). See Ramban, *Devarim* 31:24.

24. *Kiddushin* 38a.

25. Rashi, *Devarim* 31:2; *Sotah* 13b.

26. Seforno, *Devarim* 31:1.

weak or decrepit to do so.[27] You can see for yourselves that I am still full of vigor, and indeed, I've made the effort to visit each of your homes.[28] Rather, my inability to enter Eretz Yisrael is because Hashem does not allow me to enter.[29] Had I been allowed, my age would not have been a factor."[30]

"This is so sad, Moshe," the people responded. "All the Torah you've taught us and would have continued to teach us will now be lost. How will Yehoshua be able to make up for such a loss?"[31]

"Don't worry," Moshe answered. "The loss is not as great as it seems.[32] The wellsprings of Torah and the gates of wisdom have closed to me today,[33] and I can no longer attain any additional knowledge even if I were to live.[34] Moreover, I am no longer able to transmit the Torah effectively.[35] Yehoshua, on the other hand, will be able to do so.[36] He is a prophet,[37] and the knowledge I've transferred to him will serve him in good stead.[38] Treat him well. Revere him as you revered me, and regard his leadership as the embodiment of my own, as if I were still alive."[39]

---

27. Rashi, *Devarim* 31:2; *Sotah* 13b.

28. *Kli Yakar, Devarim* 31:1. Compare Ramban; Seforno.

29. Rashi, *Devarim* 31:2.

30. See *Anaf Yosef, Sotah* 13b. See also Radvaz, *Sheilos v'Teshuvos* 2:782. Moshe's punishment was not that he died when he did, but that he couldn't enter Eretz Yisrael. Had Moshe not sinned, he could have lived to 120 and entered the land earlier. According to *Maskil l'David, Bamidbar* 27:12, he would have lived another 120 years in Eretz Yisrael. See *Yevamos* 49b–50a with Maharsha; *Shabbos* 55b with Maharsha, *Iyun Yaakov*.

31. See *Tzeror haMor, Devarim* 31:1.

32. See Ramban, Rabbeinu Bachya, Mizrachi on *Devarim* 31:2.

33. Rashi with Mizrachi, ibid.; *Sotah* 13b.

34. See *Sifsei Kohen, Devarim* 31:2; *Iyun Yaakov, Sotah* 13b.

35. See *Anaf Yosef, Sotah* 13b. For an in-depth view, see the introduction to *Sefer Hafla'ah*, note 29.

36. Rashi, Ramban, *Lekach Tov* on *Devarim* 31:2; *Sotah* 13b.

37. *Chizkuni, Devarim* 31:3.

38. *Tosefos Rav Avigdor, Minchah Belulah, Sifsei Kohen* on *Devarim* 31:1–3.

39. *Sifsei Kohen, Devarim* 31:2.

"But wouldn't you recover your wisdom in the Land of Israel?" the people persisted. "It is known that the air of the Holy Land makes one wise."[40]

"It is all moot, because Hashem does not allow me to enter."[41]

"But what about our safety? Who will protect us?"[42]

"You needn't worry about that either. With the Shechinah going before you and after you[43] and Yehoshua leading the way, you will destroy the nations just as Hashem destroyed Sichon and Og, the Emorite kings. Hashem will deliver the Canaanites into your hands, and you will inherit the land. Just strengthen yourselves in Torah and good deeds. Be strong and courageous. Don't be afraid or fainthearted in battle. Fear only Hashem. Have faith that He will not forsake you or abandon you."[44]

As Moshe spoke to the people, reassuring them that Yehoshua would be a worthy successor, he concealed his own sadness that the overflowing wellsprings of Torah that had once filled his being had now been temporarily obstructed.[45] The transfer of his mantle of leadership to Yehoshua was almost complete. Very soon, it would no longer be shared at all.

Moshe Writes Sifrei Torah

On this final day of his life, Moshe wrote thirteen *sifrei Torah*, one for each of the tribes and an additional one to be placed inside the *Aron Kodesh*.[46] Deep inside his heart, Moshe still nurtured a faint spark of hope

---

40. Maharsha, *Bava Basra* 158b.

41. Maharsha, *Sotah* 13b.

42. *Tzeror haMor, Devarim* 31:1.

43. *Targum Yonasan, Minchah Belulah,* Tur on *Devarim* 31:3. The verse begins and ends with the word "Hashem" to show that He was watching the Jews in front and in back.

44. Rashi, *Lekach Tov* on *Devarim* 31:6.

45. *Devarim Rabbah* 9:2.

46. The thirteenth *sefer Torah* represented the tribe of Levi. From it, all others would be copied (*Minchah Belulah*).

that there would be a last-minute reprieve during the time it took him to write the *sifrei Torah*; that the sun would set, the day would pass and he would still be alive.

The sun had lost some of its power when Moshe had once stopped it from setting, and it assumed that it would recover its full power when Moshe passed away. On that day, it did indeed recover its power when Hashem commanded it to remain aloft and extend the length of that day so that Moshe could complete his writing.[47] He completed a *sefer Torah* and gave it to the tribe of Levi.[48]

How exactly was this task accomplished? Some suggest that all along, while Moshe was receiving installments of the Torah from Hashem, he wrote them down immediately, and on this last day all he had to do was add the finishing touches and bind them into scrolls. Others say he wrote nothing during all those years, and on that last day he wrote everything from beginning to end.[49]

When Moshe delivered a completed Torah to the tribe of Levi first, the rest of the people protested. "What is this, Moshe?" they said. "Is the Torah only for the members of your own tribe? What about us? Will we be told later that it was never given to us?"

Moshe was pleased to see that each and every Jew wanted the Torah and its laws for himself. "Indeed, today you have received the Torah as if you were standing at Mount Sinai forty years ago," he proclaimed. "I have also written twelve more *sifrei Torah*, one for each of the tribes."[50]

With the Torah in hand, Moshe went on to explain the mitzvah

---

47. *Devarim Rabbah* 9:2; *Devarim* 31:5; Rambam's introduction to his commentary on Mishnah.

48. See Ramban, *Midrash haBeiur* on *Devarim* 26:16–18; Rashi, *Devarim* 29:3. See also Rashi with *Imrei Shefer, Devarim* 31:9.

49. See *Gittin* 60a with Tosafos, Rashba. See also Ramban, introduction to *Sefer Bereishis; Chazon Ish, Orach Chaim* 125.

50. See Rashi with *Imrei Shefer, Devarim* 31:9; Rashi, *Devarim* 29:3; Alshich, *Devarim* 27:16. Based on Rashi and *Devarim Rabbah* 9:2, it would appear that the tribes didn't know they were to each receive a Torah scroll.

of *hakhel*, which calls for the assembly of all the Jewish people once every seven years, on Chol haMo'ed Sukkos following the end of the Sabbatical year.

At this assembly, the entire Jewish people[51]—men, women and children of all ages—were to come hear their king read the Torah and encourage Torah study among all of them.[52] This assembly would reinforce Jewish identity and the conviction that the Torah is the mainstay and lifeblood of the Jewish people. It would bring them to proper reverence for Hashem and love for the Torah.[53]

This assembly would strengthen the people's fear of Hashem and leave a profound impression on all of them, especially the children. For the rest of their lives, they would remember the exciting childhood experiences of this joyous assembly on Yom Tov in Yerushalayim.[54]

Yehoshua Is Anointed

"The time of your death draws near,"[55] Hashem said to Moshe. "It is time for you to call Yehoshua to the Ohel Mo'ed[56] and officially transfer your leadership upon him and crown him with prestige.[57] His presence at the Ohel Mo'ed will signify the end of your rule and the beginning of his.[58] You shall transfer this power in front of the Jewish people so that they see that Yehoshua's knowledge comes from you. He is the moon

---

51. See Tur, *Devarim* 31:11.

52. See Ramban, Seforno, Abarbanel on *Devarim* 31:9.

53. See Rashi, *Devarim* 31:10, 12; Rambam, *Chagigah* 3:3; *Sefer haChinuch* 612; *Sotah* 41a. See also Rashi with *Sifsei Chachamim*, *Vayikra* 19:1.

54. *Minchah Belulah*, *Devarim* 31:13. See also Ramban.

55. Hashem said this five days before Moshe's death (*Mo'ed Katan* 28; *Me'am Lo'ez*, *Devarim* 31:14), giving him time to prepare Yehoshua's transition (Rashi).

56. *Ha'amek Davar*, *Devarim* 31:14.

57. See Ramban, Seforno, *Ohr haChaim*, *Moshav Zekeinim*, *Tzeror haMor* on *Devarim* 31:14, 23.

58. *Tzeror haMor*, *Devarim* 31:14.

that is illuminated by the rays of your sun."[59]

Moshe was happy to transfer the mantle of leadership to Yehoshua,[60] but even on his final day, he was not quite ready to give up the last vestiges of hope for being allowed into the land. He had begun a seven-day prayer regimen on Rosh Chodesh Adar, and he was now in its last phase.[61]

"Hashem, after all that I have witnessed," Moshe prayed, "the great miracles and wonders I've seen and in which I participated—is it possible that I can just simply die?"

"Moshe, I do not want you to die," said Hashem, "but the time has come. What still troubles you?"

"I fear the Angel of Death."

"Do not be afraid. I will not deliver you into his hands. Your death will be unlike any other. There will be no debility, sickness or breakdown in your body. You will simply die when you are told to die. Other people have friends and family to make the final arrangements, but My entourage and I will attend to you.[62]

"Do you know why? When the Jewish people were leaving Egypt, the people were occupied with accumulating gold and silver from the Egyptians; but you occupied yourself for three days, with much toil and exertion, to find Yosef's coffin and bring it along. Whereas the other people loaded Egyptian treasures onto their shoulders, you bore Yosef's coffin on yours. This was a great act of kindness, and as a result, you will merit that I will arrange your burial."[63]

"I don't want to be buried here," said Moshe. "I beg You to let me live."

"Enough, Moshe," said Hashem. "I have considered this, and

---

59. See Ramban, *Panim Yafos* with *Sha'arei Aharon* on ibid.

60. *Midrash haGadol*, ibid.

61. *Devarim Rabbah* 9:2; *Vayikra Rabbah* 11:6. See *Matnos Kehunah*. Regarding Moshe's continued prayers, see *Devarim Rabbah* 2:5, 11:10. It isn't clear if these prayers were included in the 515 attributed to him.

62. *Devarim Rabbah* 9:5.

63. *Devarim Rabbah* 11:7; *Yalkut Shimoni* 865.

this is the way of the world. Each generation has people who guide it, lead it and rule it. Your time to serve Me has expired, and the time for your disciple Yehoshua to succeed you has arrived.[64] The light of your sun must now set, and the moon, which represents Yehoshua, must rise and illuminate the Jewish people. The sun and the moon cannot coexist in one sky.[65] If the sun is shining, the moon is completely obscured. The sun must set. Then the moon can reflect its light and shine. Turn your attention to giving Yehoshua encouragement for the responsibilities that await him.[66] Remember, his moon is a reflection of your light, and when it shines, it will perpetuate the legacy of your greatness."[67]

"Hashem, with the gates of wisdom closed to me and open to Yehoshua, it is obvious that I'm no longer equipped to lead the Jewish people in the proper manner. But perhaps I can still be allowed to live. If I cannot take the Jewish people into Eretz Yisrael as their leader, may I at least go in as a private citizen, a common member of the Jewish community, under Yehoshua's leadership? Let Yehoshua be the leader, and I will be his disciple."[68]

"Very well, if that is what you wish. But you will not find it satisfactory. Bring him here so that I can speak with him."[69]

Moshe made his way to Yehoshua's tent and found him sitting and teaching. Stooping because of his height, Moshe quietly entered the tent, and remained standing unobtrusively while he listened to Yehoshua teach.

---

64. *Tanchuma, Va'eschanan* 6.

65. Zohar, *Va'eschanan* 260b, 283a, 284a; *Sotah* 13b with Rif. Yehoshua would now be radiant as a sunset (*Ha'amek Davar*).

66. Zohar, *Va'eschanan* 260b, 284a.

67. *Sotah* 13b with *Ben Yehoyada*.

68. *Devarim Rabbah* 9:9; *Tanchuma, Va'eschanan* 6. See *Midrash haGadol*, Abarbanel, Alshich, Malbim on *Devarim* 3:23–25.

69. *Devarim* 31:14. As noted below, Hashem didn't actually lift the ban on Moshe's entering Eretz Yisrael. Rather, He allowed this dialogue to play itself out, so Moshe could see that he couldn't enter Eretz Yisrael even on his own terms.

While he was in Yehoshua's tent, a few people came looking for him in his own tent with questions about Torah points.

"Where is Moshe?" they asked when they saw he wasn't there.

"He went to Yehoshua's tent," they were told.

They went off to Yehoshua's tent and were startled to see Moshe standing while his student Yehoshua was sitting.

"Yehoshua, what are you thinking?" they said. "How can you sit and teach while Moshe, your *rebbe*, stands here?"

Yehoshua looked up and saw Moshe standing there. He immediately rent his garments. "*Rebbe, rebbe*, father and master!" he cried out. "What have I done?"

Moshe said to the newcomers, "Why have you come here?"

"We've come to learn Torah from you," they replied.

"I'm sorry," said Moshe, "but I can no longer teach you."

"We will not leave until you do."

"Learn from Yehoshua," a heavenly voice called out to the people, "and accept upon yourselves to be taught by him."

Accordingly, Yehoshua took his position at the head, with Moshe on his right and Aharon's sons on his left. As Yehoshua taught, Moshe couldn't understand what Yehoshua was saying, because the wellsprings of his Torah had been closed off to him.

When Yehoshua finished teaching, the people said to Moshe, "Explain to us the Torah that Yehoshua just taught. We want to hear it from you."

"I don't know what to say," Moshe replied despondently. "I cannot explain what Yehoshua taught you."[70]

After the others had left, Moshe said to Yehoshua, "I've come here by Hashem's command. He has summoned you to the Ohel Mo'ed, and I've come to escort you."

They walked back together with Moshe on Yehoshua's left as is the custom with a disciple and his *rebbe*. As they entered the

---

70. *Tanchuma, Va'eschanan* 6. See *Midrash Petiras Moshe*, cited in *Otzar Midrashim* 362. As noted earlier, Moshe lost his teaching ability but not his knowledge.

Ohel Mo'ed, a cloud of glory inserted itself between Moshe and Yehoshua, leaving Yehoshua in the inner part of the Tent and Moshe in the outer part.[71] This cloud was a signal that a revelation was about to take place,[72] and now, for the first time, Yehoshua would hear it with Moshe, a clear sanctification of Yehoshua as the next leader.[73]

The revelation began.[74]

"Moshe, after you die," said Hashem, "after the Jewish people will rise up and conquer the land, there will come a time when they will stray into idol worship and turn their backs on My covenant. My anger will rise against them, and I will abandon them. Many evils and troubles will befall them.[75] Therefore, you shall write down this song that I will dictate to you. Teach it to the Jewish people until they know it fluently.[76]

"This song will bear witness that I warned the Jewish people about the consequences of abandoning Me and the Torah. It will remind them that all the suffering in exile is justified because they ignored My warnings and violated their oaths.[77] At the same time, it will also bear witness that despite the hardships and suffering they will endure, the Jewish people will never forget the Torah; it

---

71. *Devarim Rabbah* 9:9; *Midrash haGadol, Devarim* 33:5; *Midrash Petiras Moshe,* cited in *Otzar Midrashim* 362.

72. *Tzeror haMor, Devarim* 31:15.

73. *Lekach Tov,* Ramban with *Sha'arei Aharon* on ibid.; *Sotah* 13b with Rashi.

74. Ramban, *Ha'amek Davar* with *Sha'arei Aharon* on *Devarim* 31:15.

75. *Me'am Lo'ez, Devarim* 31:16–18.

76. *Bechor Shor,* Malbim on *Devarim* 31:9, 22. The first verse of the song, *Devarim* 32:1, begins with a *hei* and ends with a *yud,* the first two letters of Hashem's Name. The last verse, *Devarim* 32:43, begins with a *hei* and ends with a *vav,* the last two letters of the Name. Thus, Hashem embedded His seal of approval within this song (*Pa'aneiach Raza*).

77. See Rashi, *Chizkuni, Bechor Shor,* Abarbanel, Malbim on *Devarim* 31:9, 21; Zohar, *Va'eschanan* 284b. See Zohar, *Ha'azinu* 287a, for why this *parashah,* filled with rebuke and reprimand, is called a song.

will continue to be studied even in the most difficult times."[78]

The revelation came to an end, but it was immediately followed by another. This time Hashem spoke only to Yehoshua.[79]

"Yehoshua, your time to lead the Jewish people has begun," said Hashem. "I command you[80] to strengthen yourself in Torah, mitzvos and good deeds.[81] Be strong and courageous. Don't be afraid of or intimidated by your enemies. Fear only Me.[82] When you bring the Jewish people across the Jordan, do not give them any choice. If they don't want to go, force them to go anyway. Hit them on the head if you must.[83] And finally, if Moshe asks what I just told you, do not tell him."

When the revelation came to an end, Moshe looked at Yehoshua and said, "What did the Shechinah tell you?"

Yehoshua was in a quandary. Hashem had forbidden him to relay the revelation to Moshe, yet Yehoshua was thoroughly devoted and loyal to Moshe. He could not conceive turning a deaf ear to his requests.

"With the greatest respect to my *rebbe*," he said, his voice filled with sadness and grief, "didn't you once tell me that you were not allowed to disclose the contents of any revelation unless you received specific permission?"

"Yes," said Moshe.

"How then can I reveal to you what Hashem has said to me without first getting His permission?"

Moshe bowed his head in great sorrow. "Better one hundred deaths to Moshe," he said, "than for him to be jealous even once."

---

78. Rashi, *Minchah Belulah* on *Devarim* 31:21.

79. According to *Ha'amek Davar* with *Sha'arei Aharon*, *Devarim* 31:22, Moshe immediately left the tent to write the song into the *sefer Torah*, while Hashem spoke to Yehoshua alone.

80. Ramban, *Devarim* 31:14.

81. *Midrash haGadol*, Ralbag on *Devarim* 31:14, 23.

82. *Lekach Tov*, *Devarim* 31:6. See Rashi with Mizrachi, *Devarim* 31:14.

83. Rashi, *Devarim* 31:7; *Sanhedrin* 8a. See *Kli Yakar*, *Devarim* 32:1.

Hashem had warned Moshe that he would not be satisfied with an arrangement in which he was subservient to Yehoshua, and now Moshe finally understood what Hashem had meant.[84] Moshe was the humblest of men, as seen from his reaction to the prophecies of Eldad and Meidad, and the elevation of Yehoshua to his high position did not awaken the slightest feeling of jealousy in his heart. On the contrary, he was boundlessly happy for his disciple, whom he loved with all his heart. Nevertheless, he could not bear the thought of being excluded from the divine revelations to which he had become so accustomed. Nor could he bear the thought of no longer being able to teach Torah to the Jewish people. And he certainly didn't want to risk developing unwanted feelings of jealousy over time. He finally realized that he would be best off leaving this world and continuing on to the next.[85]

High up in Heaven, Hashem was addressing the complexities of the transition that was under way. "Who will rise up for Me against evildoers?" He said. "Who will stand up for Me against the iniquitous?[86] Who will come to the defense of the Jewish people when I am angry? Who will defend them when they sin?"

The ministering angel Matatron bowed and said, "Master of the universe, Moshe is Yours both in his lifetime and in death. He will live even in death."

"Moshe may live on," said Hashem, "but the difficulty lies with the future of the Jewish people. With Moshe gone, who will defend them when they arouse My anger?" [87]

Meanwhile, the completed *sefer Torah* was placed by the Kohanim in or attached to the holy ark in the *Kodesh haKodashim*,

---

84. *Devarim Rabbah* 9:9; *Tanchuma, Va'eschanan* 6; *Midrash haGadol, Devarim* 33:5. See also *Tiferes Tzion, Devarim Rabbah* 11:5.

85. *Chasam Sofer*, citing Gra; *Be'er Moshe*, found in *Midrash Rabbah haMev'uar*.

86. *Tehillim* 94:16.

87. *Tanchuma, Va'eschanan* 6.

the Holy of Holies.[88] In the innermost sanctum, where only the Kohen Gadol was allowed to enter once a year, the Torah would be protected from heretical hands who might want to corrupt the text to suit their purposes. And for all future generations, no matter how far the Jewish people might stray, the integrity of the Torah would be assured, as all *sifrei Torah* would originate from the master copy, to be disseminated throughout the Jewish people and handed down from generation to generation.[89]

Moshe Introduces Yehoshua

Moshe's vigor had not diminished even on his last day on this earth. His voice still rang out with its full power as he addressed Yehoshua in front of all the people regarding the transfer of leadership to his disciple.[90]

"Yehoshua," Moshe began, "Hashem has assured you that the burdens of leadership will not fall on your shoulders alone. The elders give you guidance and counsel. Follow their advice and recommendation.[91] Just strengthen yourself in your Torah and mitzvos.[92] Be strong and courageous, for you will lead the Jewish people and conquer the land Hashem has promised to your forefathers. Don't be afraid or intimidated. Hashem will be with you."[93]

---

88. See *Bava Basra* 14a; Rashi, *Devarim* 31:26. The Torah was placed either in the *Aron Kodesh* with the Luchos or on a shelf attached to the *Aron Kodesh* on the outside. Placement alongside the Luchos would symbolize that the Torah was just as holy as this divine handiwork brought down from the heavens.

89. Seforno, Malbim on ibid.

90. Alshich, *Devarim* 31:30.

91. Rashi, *Devarim* 31:7.

92. *Midrash haGadol*, ibid.

93. *Yalkut Shimoni* 941.

Moshe and the Song

Hashem then dictated the song, which He had previously mentioned, to Moshe, who wrote it down with Yehoshua's assistance.[94] When it was complete, he left the Ohel Mo'ed[95] and called together all the Jewish people to teach it to them,[96] but since he was no longer at the apex of his authority, he did not use a sounding of the trumpets to summon the people.[97] While all the people would learn the song, it would also reveal esoteric knowledge of the Torah to a select few.[98]

"Fall silent, O heavens and earth," he began, "from the praise you offer up to Hashem.[99] Do not rouse yourselves, for I have words to speak."

A great commotion immediately arose in the upper worlds.

"Moshe, Moshe," a heavenly voice called out, "who is this human being that dares to silence the world?"

"I am here to call out Hashem's Name," Moshe replied, "and ascribe greatness to Him."[100]

The upper worlds allowed Moshe to continue. Moshe, who "listened to" and heeded the words of the Torah, now merited having the heavens and the earth listen to him.

"Listen, O heavens, for I will speak," Moshe continued. "Lend an ear, O earth, to the words of my mouth.[101] O heavens and earth,

---

94. See Ramban, *Ohr haChaim, Tzeror haMor,* Abarbanel on *Devarim* 31:19, 22; *Bechor Shor, Devarim* 32:44. This assistance may have included only proofreading and making copies to distribute to the Jewish people.

95. *Targum Yonasan, Devarim* 32:44.

96. *Devarim* 31:28.

97. Rashi, ibid.; Rabbi Yehudah heChasid, *Chizkuni* on *Devarim* 31:1.

98. Zohar, *Ha'azinu* 287a; *Tzeror haMor, Devarim* 32:44. See *Shitah Mekubetzes, Nedarim* 38a. The entire Torah and its laws are represented and implicit in the song (*Aderes Eliyahu, Ha'azinu*).

99. *Devarim Rabbah* 10:2; *Tehillim* 19:2.

100. See Zohar, *Ha'azinu* 287a; *Tanchuma, Ha'azinu* 1; *Devarim Rabbah* 10:1.

101. *Devarim* 32:1. See *Yeshayahu* 1:2.

you who were Hashem's first creations,[102] I call on the two of you to bear witness to what has transpired here.[103] Tomorrow I will be gone, and should the Jewish people transgress the Torah and claim they never accepted Hashem's covenant, who will contradict them? Only you, O heavens and earth, who will last forever. You will attest that the Jewish people entered a covenant and then violated it. You will testify that Hashem's ways are just, and that all suffering that befalls the Jewish people was rightly deserved.[104]

"My flock, O Jewish people, let the heavens bear witness. Having no conscience, no intellect, no free will, the heavens never deviated from their role. In all your years, have you ever seen the sun rise in the west or set in the east? Look at the earth and let it too bear witness. In all your years, have you ever seen barley seeds produce wheat?[105] These same heavens and earth will bear witness that, if you follow Hashem's path, the heavens will bring you rain and dew and the earth will yield fruit for you. But if you don't, the rain will cease and the earth will remain barren.[106]

"Lend an ear and listen to the 613 mitzvos you've been given.[107] Obey the laws of the Torah[108] that Hashem sent down from Heaven in a blaze of fire atop Mount Sinai.[109] Observe the mitzvos that relate to the heavens, such as sanctifying the new moon and the seasonal holidays that derive from it. Observe the mitzvos that

---

102. Ramban, *Devarim* 32:1.

103. *Sifrei, Ha'azinu*. See *Avodah Zarah* 3a and Tosafos.

104. Rashi, *Devarim* 32:1; *Sifrei, Ha'azinu*.

105. Rashi, *Devarim* 30:19; *Sifrei, Ha'azinu*. According to *Sanhedrin* 108b, during the Mabul the constellations were out of order, so the sun rose in the west and set in the east. In addition, the sun stood still for Moshe, Yehoshua and King Chizkiyahu. See the introduction to Maharal's *Gevuros Hashem* regarding the significance of and differences between miracles and nature and how they coexist.

106. See Rashi, *Devarim* 30:19; *Sifrei, Ha'azinu*; *Chizkuni, Devarim* 30:19.

107. Tur, *Devarim* 32:1.

108. *Aderes Eliyahu*.

109. *Devarim Rabbah* 10:4; *Sifrei, Ha'azinu*.

relate to the earth, such as the agricultural laws.[110] The heavens and the earth were created on condition that you keep the Torah. If you forsake it, everything will return to the primordial chaos.[111]

"You are all a composite of Heaven and earth, your souls being from Heaven and your bodies from the earth. If you keep the Torah, no earthly creature will have power over you; you will be untouchable. But if you forsake the Torah, you will be vulnerable to the predators of the world.[112]

"The heavens and the earth follow Hashem's commands through no choice of their own. But you can choose right from wrong, and therefore you can earn great reward for obedience and incur great punishment for disobedience.[113] But this I can assure you: if you live a righteous life in this world, you will enjoy a rich afterlife in the next world."[114]

Moshe then spoke to the people about their beginnings in the wilderness, and he warned them about their destiny until the End of Days.[115] He reminded them about the unlimited kindness with which Hashem sustained them in the wilderness and how He would continue to sustain them in the Holy Land.[116] He told them that sadly, they were likely to go astray[117] eventually and

---

110. *Sifrei, Ha'azinu.*

111. *Kli Yakar, Devarim* 32:1.

112. *Midrash haGadol,* ibid.

113. Rashi, *Devarim* 30:19.

114. *HaKesav vehaKabbalah,* ibid.

115. Rabbeinu Bachya, *Devarim* 32:1.

116. *Bechor Shor, Devarim* 31:30; Rabbeinu Bachya, *Devarim* 32:1.

117. *Devarim* 31:28. Moshe didn't say this in Hashem's Name, for if Hashem told them they would sin, they would have no free will. Tragically, though, they did indeed sin, enduring multiple exiles and horrific suffering as a result (*Tzeror haMor*; Abarbanel). See *Shemos Rabbah* 9:1.

Nonetheless, the Jews remained fully observant during Yehoshua's lifetime and for two years afterward. Thus, not until thirty years after Moshe's speech here did they begin worshiping idols. For while Yehoshua was alive, it was as though Moshe himself lived on (Rashi; Tur).

show their ingratitude, and that this would anger Hashem. These transgressions would lead to expulsion from the land, bitter exiles and great suffering.[118] But Hashem's actions would be just and His judgment righteous, because the Jewish people had been warned.[119] The heavens and the earth would bear witness.[120]

Words of Consolation

The song was mostly about rebuke and warning, but it concluded with words of consolation. Despite all the travails that the Jewish people would face through their long history, they would ultimately merit the coming of Mashiach, and they would be redeemed.[121] At that time, Hashem would avenge their suffering and destroy their enemies.[122]

Moshe taught the song he had written to all the people and explained it to them[123] until they understood it and could repeat it perfectly.[124] He then expressed his pride in the Jewish people, who had shown so much character by accepting Moshe's warnings and

118. Rabbeinu Bachya, *Devarim* 32:1.

119. *Bechor Shor*, *Devarim* 31:26, 32:4.

120. *Devarim* 31:29. Having told the Jews that the heavens and earth would testify about them, Moshe here told the witnesses themselves (Rashi).

121. Abarbanel, *Devarim* 31:30.

122. *Bechor Shor*, ibid.; Rabbeinu Bachya, *Devarim* 32:1.

123. See Ramban, *Lekach Tov*, *Panim Yafos* on *Devarim* 31:26–30. Opinions abound regarding how and how many times Moshe taught the Jews the song, since verses 22, 28, 30 and 44 all refer to his teaching it and warning the people. As with Moshe's prayer and Yehoshua's ascension to leadership, I have endeavored to reconstruct events simply and clearly.

124. *Bechor Shor*, Malbim on *Devarim* 31:9, 22. Abarbanel contends that Moshe taught the song three times to three groups of Jews. Malbim writes that Moshe taught the entire song, then reviewed it piecemeal to deepen the Jews' understanding, just as he had taught the entire Torah. See *Shitah Mekubetzes*, *Nedarim* 38a; Rambam's introduction to his commentary on Mishnah. See also *Ha'amek Davar*, *Devarim* 1:3.

Regarding when this teaching took place, see *Tzeror haMor*, *Ohr haChaim* on *Devarim* 31:22.

rebuke without complaint or protest. For this they deserved to be blessed. And as he continued to speak in the same conciliatory tones, he did indeed bless them.[125]

During this last of Moshe's teaching sessions, Yehoshua served as his *meturgman*, repeating the teachings to the broader crowd.[126] Yehoshua also had his own *meturgman* to assist him in disseminating his own teachings to the masses.[127] The people thereby saw Yehoshua elevated to the highest level of teaching alongside his master Moshe; even before the leader departed, his successor was already emerging.[128] That Shabbos would become known as the "Shabbos of the Two Partners."[129]

Despite this great honor, Yehoshua never lost his humility. He conducted himself as he had when he was a mere disciple.[130]

"Pay heed to all I have said to you today," Moshe said as his address drew to a close. "Direct your own eyes and ears toward the Torah[131] and instruct your children to do so as well. Put all your efforts into the Torah, for doing so will benefit your life in both this world and the next: it will bring you wisdom and understanding in this world, and bounteous reward in the World to Come."[132]

---

125. *Midrash haGadol, Devarim* 31:28.

126. *Aderes Eliyahu, Ha'azinu; Midrash Petiras Moshe,* cited in *Otzar Midrashim* 366.

127. *Sifrei,* Rashi on *Devarim* 32:44.

128. Ibid.

129. *Sotah* 13b; *Sifrei,* Rashi on *Devarim* 32:44.

130. *Sifrei,* Rashi on *Devarim* 32:44. Yehoshua behaved just as he had when still called Hoshea.

131. Rashi, *Devarim* 32:46.

132. Rashi, *Devarim* 32:47. See *Yerushalmi Pe'ah* 1:1.

20 Moshe's Blessings

The last day of Moshe's life had thus far been a whirlwind of activity. He had written thirteen *sifrei Torah*, summoned the heavens and the earth to bear witness, and written and taught the people a complex song of rebuke, encouragement and promise—and amazingly, it was still only noon.[1]

---

1. *Tzeror haMor, Devarim* 32:48. Who wrote the last eight verses of the Torah, including the statement that Moshe died? Some say Moshe; others, Yehoshua. Some suggest that Moshe wrote the final verses with his tears, and Yehoshua filled them in with ink. See *HaKesav vehaKabbalah, Devarim* 34:5. See also *Bava Basra* 15a with *Iyun Yaakov*; *Menachos* 30a with Rashi; *Sifrei*, Rashi on *Devarim* 34:5; Ibn Ezra, Rabbeinu Bachya on *Devarim* 34:1; *Yalkut Shimoni* 965. Compare Abarbanel. See *Yehoshua* 24:26. And see Rambam's introduction to his commentary on Mishnah.

According to *Yalkut Reuveni*, Moshe himself wrote that he died, because he had already begun dying, a process that lasted a day. See Maharal, *Chiddushei Aggados, Bava Basra* 15a.

He completed the task of teaching the Jewish people the rest of the Torah and spoke his final words to the people. His time of death had arrived.[2]

"What will become of me without you?" Yehoshua asked Moshe. "What will I do when the tribes squabble over the portions they receive? What if this one wants mountainous terrain and this one insists on a valley?"

"You need not worry," Moshe replied. "The land has already been apportioned by divine lots. I assure you that there will be no squabbles when the actual apportionment takes place.[3] Now, listen to me. We have very little time left together. If you have any questions, ask them right now."

"It is written about me," said Yehoshua, "that I never stepped out of the tent of Torah study. Should a person like me still have questions?" These words were chosen carefully enough, lest they could have been mistaken for the expression of an arrogant person, but still they upset Moshe. For this failing, Yehoshua would forget three hundred laws of the Torah during the mourning following Moshe's death. The people would also forget these laws and come to Yehoshua for enlightenment, but he would be unable to give it.

"I've also forgotten these laws," he would say to them.

"Then can you retrieve them from Heaven?" they asked.

"I'm afraid not. Now that Moshe is gone, Heaven will no longer restore the forgotten parts of the Torah."

"Then these laws are forgotten forever?" the people would ask.

"Absolutely not," he would reply. "These laws can be recovered by diligent study but not by a gift from Heaven."

Eventually, Osniel ben Kenaz would mend the gaps in the Torah through his analysis and expositions—with the help of divine assistance, of course.[4]

---

2. Abarbanel, *Devarim* 32:50.

3. *Midrash Petiras Moshe*, cited in *Otzar Midrashim* 366. See Ralbag, *Devarim* 34:1.

4. *Temurah* 16b; *Yalkut Shimoni, Devarim* 940; *Me'am Lo'ez, Devarim* 1:5, *Yehoshua* 1; *Midrash Petiras Moshe*, cited in *Otzar Midrashim* 362.

Final Task

Moshe was left with one final task. Most of what he had said to the Jewish people in the last phase of his life had been rebukes and admonitions, but he did not want to leave them on such an austere note. He wanted his parting words to express consolation and comfort. It was important that the last words they heard from him would be blessings.[5]

As Moshe had reminded them earlier, the people had been the very cause of his inability to enter the land, but that did not prevent him from blessing them with all his heart.[6] And so he prepared to bless each of the tribes separately, and then all the people together. The blessings were delivered through his powers of prophecy,[7] and he began with words of praise to Hashem.[8]

"How worthy are the Jewish people," he said, "that they are the chosen of Hashem, and how worthy they are to receive this blessing.[9] Indeed, while the Jewish people proudly accepted the offer of the Torah, Eisav and the rest of the nations of the world rejected it.[10]

"And when the Children of Israel received the Torah, they gladly shouldered its yoke despite the restrictions it entailed.[11] They clung to You, Hashem, in difficult times, as when they were in the wilderness without food and water,[12] and they will continue to cling to you in the future when they will fall into the hands of the foreign nations. Even in times of divine anger, the righteous

---

5. *Sifrei*, Abarbanel on *Devarim* 33:1. See also Rashi ad loc. Some say Moshe blessed the Jews before ascending the mountain. Alternatively, he ascended first, and then, moments before expiring, he blessed the people. I have followed the first approach and have therefore placed the blessing here. See Rashi, *Rav Ovadiah Bartenura al haTorah*, Rashbam on *Devarim* 33:1; *Chizkuni*, *Devarim* 34:1.

6. *Tzeror haMor*, *Ohr haChaim* on *Devarim* 33:1.

7. Ibn Ezra, ibid. See *Devarim Rabbah* 11:3.

8. *Sifrei*, *Lekach Tov* on *Devarim* 33:1.

9. Rashi, *Devarim* 33:2.

10. *Sifrei*, Rashi on ibid.

11. *Sifrei*, Rashi on *Devarim* 33:3.

12. Ramban, ibid.

among them will seek refuge in Your shadow, confident that You will protect them.[13]

"Hashem, You have shown an intense love for each tribe, giving them the respect and recognition deserving of a full-fledged nation.[14] And even if they stumble, You will always consider them Your people.[15] You also demonstrate Your intense love to the converts, who recognized the singularity of the Jewish people, and graciously accept them into the fold."[16]

With this introduction complete, Moshe was now ready to bless the individual tribes. He would pick up the thread where Yaakov had left off in blessing his children over two hundred years earlier.[17] There would be no hint of rebuke in Moshe's blessings, as there had indeed been in the blessings Noach, Yitzchak and Yaakov delivered to their children, since rebuke can sometimes elicit negative reactions. Moshe's words to the Jewish people would be only blessings.[18] He would not speak directly to the people he blessed. Instead, he would speak to Hashem in their presence.[19]

Reuven's Blessing

"Hashem, Yaakov excluded Reuven from the blessings he gave his children," Moshe began. "I now implore You, Hashem, O King of the Jewish people, to let a blessing rest upon Reuven. Should this tribe be excluded there would not be the full

---

13. See *Sifrei*, Rashi, *Tosefos Rav Ephraim* on ibid.

14. Rashi, ibid.

15. *Minchah Belulah*, *Lekach Tov* on ibid.

16. See Rosh, Rashbam, *Ohr haChaim* on ibid.

17. *Sifrei*, *Devarim* 33:1; *Devarim Rabbah* 11:1. Yaakov's blessing was followed with the word *zos*, "this" (*Bereishis* 49:28), and Moshe began his with *Vezos haberachah* (*Devarim* 33:1).

18. *Tanchuma*, *Vezos haBerachah* 1.

19. Rashi with *Imrei Shefer*, *Minchah Belulah* on *Devarim* 33:8. Moshe then prayed that his blessing would indeed rest upon the Jewish people (Seforno, *Devarim* 33:2).

complement of twelve tribes, and as a consequence, Your royal Throne would be incomplete.[20]

"Let the tribe of Reuven live in this world, and let him not be barred from the World to Come. Let the incident of his moving Bilhah's bed be forgotten, since he has fully repented.[21]

"May they live and take their position in the vanguard of the Jewish people, leading them, with Gad, into war ahead of the other Jews. Their wives and children will remain on the other side of the Jordan River during the conquest of Canaan. May they survive in their absence and welcome their husbands and fathers upon their return."[22]

Shimon's (non) Blessing

The spirit of Yaakov came to Moshe along with the spirits of his children Shimon and Levi. In age order, Shimon and Levi were the next in line, and Yaakov wanted Moshe to bless them. "I couldn't bless these children," he said to Moshe, "because of the harsh judgment the Shechinah would have brought upon them. You, however, are the 'master of your household' and can bless anyone you wish."[23]

Moshe agreed to bless Levi, but he would follow rather than precede Yehudah (see below). As for the tribe of Shimon, Moshe declined to bless them because of the incident at Shittim, but he did include an allusion to Shimon's blessing in the blessing of Yehudah when he said, "Hashem should *hear* the voice of Yehudah." (The name Shimon comes from the word *shema*, hear.) Yehudah's blessing would therefore extend to Shimon in some respects, especially since Shimon's portion in the land was subsumed into Yehudah's portion. Moshe hoped that the tribe

20. See Rashi, Ramban, *Tzeror haMor* on *Devarim* 33:5–6.
21. *Sanhedrin* 92a with Maharsha; Rashi, *Devarim* 33:6.
22. Ramban, Abarbanel on *Devarim* 33:6. See *Bechor Shor*.
23. Zohar, *Vayechi* 236a. See Rabbeinu Bachya, *Devarim* 33:1.

of Yehudah's close association with the tribe of Shimon would have a positive effect on the latter. Yehudah, the lion, would thus pacify Shimon, the angry ox, and hold the tribe back from violence.[24]

Yehudah's Blessing

Although Levi was older, Yehudah was blessed next, since his confession of guilt in the incident of Tamar persuaded Reuven to confess his guilt in the incident with Bilhah.[25]

"Hashem, for forty years," Moshe prayed, "Yehudah's remains have found no rest in his coffin, a consequence of the banishment he accepted upon himself if he didn't return Binyamin to Yaakov. While it is true that he returned Binyamin safely, his words took effect nevertheless. But now it is time for his bones to come to rest in the merit of his setting a good example and inspiring Reuven to confess his sin. Reuven's remains are intact; so should Yehudah's be the same." Moshe's prayer was answered, and Yehudah's bones ceased to rattle.[26]

Originally, only Yehudah's remains found rest, but not his soul. As a result, he was banned from the heavenly academy, which nourishes the soul. Only through Moshe's prayers did Yehudah's soul reach a level rivaling that of the other righteous

---

24. Rashi, Ramban, *Tzeror haMor* on *Devarim* 33:7; *Midrash haGadol, Devarim* 33:1; *Midrash Tehillim* 90.

This *midrash* is consistent with *Tzeror haMor*, which states that Moshe prayed that all twelve tribes be represented. Additionally, even if Moshe didn't bless Shimon, since Yaakov already had (he only cursed his anger), the inclusion of Reuven meant that all the tribes were blessed by either Yaakov or Moshe.

25. Rashi, *Devarim* 33:7; *Bava Kamma* 92a; *Makkos* 11b with Rashi, Maharsha. *Lekach Tov* writes that since Yehudah was royalty, he was second only to the firstborn, Reuven. Additionally, with Shimon joining Yehudah, who led the Jews in war, it made sense to place Yehudah next to Reuven, as all three were on the front lines in conquering Canaan. See *Chizkuni*; Abarbanel.

26. See *Makkos* 11b and Tosafos ad loc. Rashi with *Sefer Zikaron, Devarim* 33:7. See also *Let My Nation Descend*, p. 361.

sages in the academy. Thus, he finally arrived at his proper station in Heaven.[27]

"Hashem, listen to the voice of Yehudah," Moshe prayed. "Listen to the prayers of Yehudah's royal descendants King David and King Shlomo. Listen to King Asa when he will pray for protection against the Cushites. Protect King Yehoshafat from the Amonites and King Chizkiyahu from Sancheriv.[28] Hashem, may You bring peace to his people. Fight his battle and take vengeance on his behalf."[29]

Levi's Blessing

Moshe then blessed Levi, who would perform the holy service in the territory of Yehudah.[30]

"Your Urim v'Tumim,[31] which are integral to guiding the people," Moshe said, "deserve to be given to Your devout ones.[32] Hashem tested the tribe of Levi at Masah and contended with them at Mei Merivah, yet they did not join the complainers. They remained faithful to You[33] and protected me against those who threatened to stone me.[34]

"At the Eigel, when I said, 'Whoever is for Hashem, rally around me,' the entire tribe of Levi answered my call. They stood ready to disregard family ties completely if I commanded them to kill sinners from other tribes who might be related to them, such as a mother's father or brother, or perhaps a daughter's son. Their

---

27. *Makkos* 11b; *Sotah* 7b; *Bava Kamma* 92a. See Maharsha.

28. Rashi, *Lekach Tov* on *Devarim* 33:7.

29. Rashi, ibid. Both Yaakov and Moshe praised Yehudah as a lion. Yet Yaakov emphasized Yehudah's leadership within the Jewish people, while Moshe stressed his military prowess.

30. See Rashi, Ramban, Rabbeinu Meyuchas on *Devarim* 33:8, 12. See also *Megillah* 26a.

31. In actuality, Moshe mentioned the Tumim before the Urim. See *Minchah Belulah, Shelah* on why.

32. *Pa'aneiach Raza*, Rabbeinu Meyuchas on *Devarim* 33:8.

33. Rashi with Mizrachi, ibid.

34. *Yalkut Pisron Torah*, ibid.

family ties were as nothing in the face of the need to combat the worship of false gods.[35] And they distinguished themselves not only regarding *avodah zarah*, but also regarding *milah*. Only the tribe of Levi circumcised their children in the wilderness despite the circumstances.[36]

"Because of the above mentioned virtues,[37] and because the tribe of Levi are impervious to flattery,[38] they should be deemed fit and worthy to teach Your laws, guide the people and perform the holy service in Your sanctuary.[39] They deserve to burn incense before Your Presence and bring burnt-offerings upon Your Altar.[40]

"Hashem, bless their meager possessions, such as *terumah* and *ma'aser*,[41] so that they can concentrate on the Torah and adjudicating its laws.[42] Bless their small army, the army of the Chashmonaim, so that they should strike down the myriad Greeks who will challenge them.[43] Strike down the opponents of the priesthood, and prevent its enemies from ascending."[44]

---

35. Rashi, Ibn Ezra on *Devarim* 33:9; *Yoma* 62b with Rashi.

36. Rashi, Seforno on *Devarim* 33:9. See *Yevamos* 72a for further explanation why the Jews refrained from circumcising themselves.

37. Rashi with *Sifsei Chachamim*, *Sefer Zikaron* on *Devarim* 33:10.

38. *Tzeror haMor*, *Devarim* 33:9.

39. Rashi with *Sifsei Chachamim*, *Sefer Zikaron* on *Devarim* 33:10. See *Malachi* 2:7 with Rashi. See also *Yoma* 26a.

40. Rashi, *Devarim* 33:10.

41. Ibn Ezra, Rabbeinu Bachya on *Devarim* 33:11.

42. Seforno, ibid.

43. Rashi, ibid.; *Bereishis Rabbah* 99:2. Dedicated to Temple service, not warfare, Levi needed Moshe's blessing in fighting the Greeks (Rav Yosef Ya'avetz).

44. Rashi, *Devarim* 33:11. Moshe here is referring to Korach and Uziyahu, king of Yehudah (Seforno).

Yaakov had cursed Levi's (and Shimon's) anger. Since then, however, Levi had earned Moshe's highest blessing: dedication to serving Hashem and teaching the Jewish people.

Binyamin's Blessing

Following Levi, Moshe blessed Binyamin, in whose portion the Beis haMikdash would stand.[45]

"As the youngest of the tribes," Moshe said, "they are Hashem's beloved.[46] May His beloved, who never bowed down to Eisav and who didn't participate in the sale of Yosef,[47] dwell securely by the Shechinah. Unlike in the Mishkan that traveled from place to place, the Shechinah will remain in one place when the Beis haMikdash is built.[48] It will remain in the portion of Binyamin—that is, Yerushalayim—and protect Binyamin forever.[49] The Beis haMikdash shall rest between his shoulders; it will be built twenty-three *amos* below the highest point of his portion."[50]

Yosef's Blessing

Following Binyamin, who would have the Beis haMikdash in their portion, Moshe blessed the tribe of Yosef, in whose portion the Mishkan of Shiloh would be established.[51] Like Binyamin, they would have the Shechinah in their territory, but unlike Binyamin, it would be only temporary.[52]

---

45. See *Chizkuni, Devarim* 33:12.

46. *Tzeror haMor*, Riva on ibid.

47. *Sifrei*, ibid.

48. Abarbanel, ibid.

49. Rashi with Mizrachi, ibid.

50. Rashi, ibid. Eretz Yisrael is the highest land, and the Beis haMikdash is its highest point. However, the Temple was built just short of Binyamin's peak.

Yaakov blessed the leadership of Binyamin's descendants, while Moshe addressed his association with the Beis haMikdash.

51. Because Yosef averted his gaze from Potiphar's wife, he was privileged to partake of sacrifices even in his territory, since from there the Mishkan could be *seen*. See *Zevachim* 118b; *Moshav Zekeinim*.

52. Rashi with *Sifsei Chachamim, Tzeror haMor, Rav Ovadiah Bartenura al haTorah* on *Devarim* 33:12.

"Hashem has blessed the land of Yosef," Moshe said, "for there is no land better in the entire Holy Land than his.[53] Its sweet[54] dew falls steadily[55] from the heavens above and gently waters the fruits, and its wells and subterranean waters below rise to moisten and irrigate the land.[56]

"Their land is exposed to the sun, which will sweeten their crops,[57] and they will enjoy the fruits that ripen to sweetness through the workings of the moon. Crops such as cucumbers and pumpkins, which blossom and ripen from month to month, are ripened by their exposure to the moon.[58]

"Adam listened to his wife, and the earth was thereby cursed. Yosef didn't listen to Potiphar's wife, and therefore the earth of his land was blessed.[59]

"Hashem supervises Yosef's land more closely than He does others', for indeed, the mountains on his land were created before the mountains on the others'.[60] His mountain ranges are first to ripen their fruits,[61] and his hills produce fruit perpetually even when there is hardly any rainfall.[62]

"May their land be blessed with sweetness and fullness, by the goodwill of Hashem, Who revealed Himself to me at the thorn bush.[63] May this blessing come onto Yosef's head, and onto

---

53. *Sifrei*, Rashi on *Devarim* 33:13.

54. Rashi, Ramban on ibid.

55. *Me'am Lo'ez*, ibid.

56. *Sifrei*, Rashi, *Bechor Shor* on ibid.

57. *Sifrei*, Rashi on *Devarim* 33:14.

58. *Targum Unkelos*, Rashi, Radak on ibid. This "solar/lunar" blessing harks back to Yosef's dream about the sun and the moon (*Kli Yakar*).

59. *Me'am Lo'ez*, *Devarim* 33:13.

60. Rashi with *Sifsei Chachamim*, *Devarim* 33:15.

61. *Sifrei*, Rashi on ibid.

62. Rashi, ibid.

63. *Targum Unkelos*, Rashi on *Devarim* 33:16. Just as Moshe refrained from looking at the burning bush when the Shechinah revealed Itself to him, Yosef refrained from looking at Potiphar's wife. Thus, Moshe was blessed

the crown of the one separated from his brothers when he was sold.[64]

"Yosef, the firstborn,[65] is a great[66] ox,[67] a tough and mighty ox,[68] which is the king of domesticated animals.[69] He will merit such a warrior in his descendant Yehoshua, who will vanquish many kings.[70] Glory has been given to Yehoshua:[71] he has the strength of an ox and the beauty of a *re'eim*'s horns. He will first gain fame in his victory over the five kings in Giv'on and will continue with the eventual conquest of the thirty-one kings of nations who acquired some residence or land in Canaan.[72] With his right horn, Yehoshua from Ephraim shall gore myriad people from the ends of the earth, and with the left horn, Gid'on from Menashe shall kill thousands of Midianites."[73]

---

with a radiant countenance, and Yosef with immunity to the evil eye (*Divrei David*).

64. Rashi, ibid.

65. *Bechor Shor, Devarim* 33:17. Yosef was Rachel's firstborn and acquired Reuven's firstborn status as well.

66. Rashi, *Devarim* 33:17.

67. Rashi, *Bereishis* 49:6.

68. Rashi, *Devarim* 33:17.

69. *Chizkuni*, ibid.

70. Rashi, ibid. According to Ralbag, this blessing refers to Mashiach ben Yosef.

71. Rashi, ibid.

72. *Sifrei*, Rashi on ibid.

73. Rashi, Ramban on ibid. See *Me'am Lo'ez, Yehoshua* 10:12–14. By placing Ephraim before Menashe, Moshe concurs with Yaakov's decision to favor Ephraim over Menashe in leadership (*Tosefos Rav Ephraim al haTorah*).

Yosef merited multiple blessings over his brothers due to his suffering while incarcerated, and because he remained humble even as viceroy of Egypt (*Tzeror haMor*).

Both Yaakov and Moshe blessed Yosef's portion of Eretz Yisrael. Yet Yaakov addressed some of the history leading up to this blessing, while Moshe addressed the leadership of Yosef's future descendants.

Zevulun's and Yissachar's Blessings

"Zevulun, you shall rejoice in your leaving," Moshe continued, "by succeeding when you sail the seas for trade and commerce.[74] Yissachar will succeed in learning Torah in your tents, and through this learning, you, Yissachar, will be able to set leap years and calculate the calendars.[75]

"You will enjoy a partnership in which Zevulun joyfully departs in ships to engage in commerce, the profits from which sustain Yissachar, who engages in the study of Torah. Zevulun, you are the younger one and yet you are mentioned first, because Yissachar's Torah depends on your support.[76]

"Yissachar will suckle from the wealthy bounty of the sea with which Zevulun returns, and he will be freed to learn Torah.[77]

"As a result of calculating the calendars, Yissachar will summon the tribes to gather at the Beis haMikdash for the festival pilgrimages to bring offerings.[78] Zevulun and Yissachar will proudly join them and bring their offerings in gratitude for their success.[79]

"Zevulun, the seashore is your portion. On those shores you will find valuable *tiryas*,[80] and the *chilazon* sea creature, whose blood will be used to dye *tzitzis* fringes. On the sands of these shores, you will find the most precious white glass, while gems and jewels from capsized ships come ashore and are left buried under the sand. These are all part of the great riches with which your territory will be blessed.[81] So great will your wealth be that

---

74. Rashi, *Bechor Shor*, Abarbanel, *Me'am Lo'ez* on *Devarim* 33:18.
75. Rashi, ibid.
76. Ibid. See *Bereishis Rabbah* 72:5, 99:9.
77. Rashi, *Devarim* 33:19. Yissachar was blessed with fertile farmland (*Chizkuni*).
78. Rashi, Abarbanel on ibid.
79. Abarbanel, ibid.
80. One interpretation of the *Targumim* defines *tiryas* as the tuna fish.
81. *Sifrei*, Rashi with *Sefer Zikaron*, *Minchah Belulah*, *Da'as Zekeinim* on *Devarim* 33:19. See *Megillah* 6a; *Menachos* 44a.

you will have to hide some of your bounty in the sand.[82]

"Zevulun will also rejoice in the knowledge that Yissachar's learning will protect him when he goes out to war.[83]

"Zevulun's commercial concerns will draw merchants from foreign lands to the Mediterranean coast of his northern shores. They will admire his business ethics and seek to discover the source of his tribe's morality. Already on the borders of the land, they will head south and tour Yerushalayim to observe the customs and practices of the Jewish people. The foreigners will see that the Jews live united, that they worship one God, that they eat the same foods—unlike the non-Jewish nations, who don't serve the same gods and whose foods differ from one another. So impressed will they be with the Jewish people that they will admit the futility of their religion and say, 'There is no nation like the Jewish nation.' As a result of initially seeking commerce with Zevulun, they will convert to Judaism."[84]

Gad's Blessing[85]

"Blessed is the territory of Gad," said Moshe, "whose pastureland will continue to expand toward the east[86] until his portion exceeds all the other portions in size.[87]

"As their territory is on the border, the tribe of Gad needs might and strength, and indeed, they are compared to a lioness

---

82. Rabbeinu Bachya, *Devarim* 33:19.

83. *Targum Unkelos*, *Chomas Anach* on *Devarim* 33:18.

84. *Sifrei*, Rashi on *Devarim* 33:19. Both Yaakov and Moshe blessed the partnership of Zevulun and Yissachar. Yaakov blessed them separately, emphasizing the strength of each tribe, while Moshe addressed them together.

85. Dan and Naftali should have been blessed next, but Moshe wanted to contrast Gad with the righteous Yissachar and Zevulun, for they settled in Eretz Yisrael while he rejected it (*Tzeror haMor*, *Devarim* 33:20).

86. *Sifrei*, Rashi, Bechor Shor on *Devarim* 33:20.

87. Seforno, ibid.

that lives with confidence in the face of her enemy.[88] Their might will only continue to expand their land as their enemies withdraw from before them.[89]

"The killing strokes of their swords are easily recognized, for they sever the head and the arm of their enemy with one single blow.[90]

"The conquest of the Holy Land commenced with the conquest of Sichon. The tribe of Gad saw fit to be first to take a portion of the conquered land east of the Jordan River.[91] They chose it knowing, through either tradition or prophecy, that Moshe's burial site, hidden and concealed from any creature, would be located in those lands.[92] They wanted Moshe to be buried in their portion, because he was their beloved leader who had guided them, taught them and carried out Hashem's righteous commands,[93] and who would eventually lead them into the World to Come.[94]

"Because of Gad's might, the tribe will march at the head of the people, leading the fighters in the conquest of the Holy Land.[95] In this way, they will fulfill their righteous promise to remain across the Jordan River until they have conquered and apportioned the land."[96]

---

88. Rashi with *Gur Aryeh, Rabbeinu Meyuchas* on ibid.

89. See Ibn Ezra, Seforno on ibid.

90. *Targum Yonasan,* Rashi on ibid. When Gad lifted his sword, the enemy would cover his head with his handheld shield. Thus, one blow from Gad cut off both head and hand (*Da'as Zekeinim;* Rav Chaim Paltiel).

91. *Sifrei,* Rashi on *Devarim* 33:21.

92. Rashi with *Sifsei Chachamim,* ibid. Gad felt that Moshe shouldn't be alone while his people were in Eretz Yisrael. See *Sha'arei Aharon.* Alternatively, the name "Gad" means "fortune," for this tribe was simply fortunate to have Moshe buried in its territory (*Me'am Lo'ez, Yehoshua* 13).

93. *Bechor Shor,* Seforno on *Devarim* 33:21.

94. *Sifrei,* Rashi on ibid.; *Bamidbar Rabbah* 19:13; *Devarim Rabbah* 2:17.

95. *Sifrei,* Rashi on *Devarim* 33:21.

96. In different ways, both Yaakov and Moshe blessed Gad's mighty defense of the Jewish people.

Dan's Blessing

"Dan is blessed with the title of a young lion," said Moshe,[97] "for he also resides on border territory, where he must be strong to protect the Jewish people from invaders.[98] He will tear apart the dwelling places of those living in the neighboring Bashan mountains.[99] He too was on the front line in the conquest of the land.[100]

"Dan's land drinks from the streams of Bashan, and the Jordan River goes forth from his portion, irrigating his land in the process.[101]

"The tribe of Dan will spring forth in two places. Given a territory in the center of the land, they will soon outgrow it and conquer new lands in the northeast."[102]

Naftali's Blessing

"Naftali's territory, the valley of Ginnosar," Moshe said, "is filled with Hashem's blessings so that it satisfies and fulfills the desires of its inhabitants.[103] Despite their riches, they will be satisfied with what they possess.[104] Their fruits will ripen early, and they'll eat their fill of their harvests before others even taste their own

---

97. Yehudah traveled first, and Dan last, so the Jews were protected front and back by "lions" (*Me'am Lo'ez*). This blessing also alludes to Shimshon, from the tribe of Dan, who tore apart his enemies like a lion (*Ohr haChaim*).

98. *Sifrei*, Rashi, *Da'as Zekeinim* on *Devarim* 33:22. See *Tzeror haMor* for why Moshe skipped Asher, Gad's full brother, and blessed Dan and Naftali next.

99. Rokeach, Ralbag on ibid.

100. Abarbanel, ibid.

101. *Targum Unkelos*, Rashi on ibid.; *Bechoros* 55a.

Thus, the Jordan's Hebrew name, Yarden, is a contraction of *yered Dan*, "descending from Dan" (*Da'as Zekeinim*).

102. Rashi, *Devarim* 33:22. While Yaakov likened Dan to a viper, toppling its enemies, Moshe compared this tribe to a young lion protecting the Jewish people. He also praised Dan's territory.

103. *Sifrei*, Rashi on *Devarim* 33:23.

104. *Sifrei*, *Toldos Yitzchak*, *Minchah Belulah* on ibid. Often, wealthy people are not satisfied with their wealth (*Koheles* 5:9). Naftali received a blessing that despite their wealth, they would not feel anxious to acquire more.

harvests. People who visit the territory of Naftali and see its bounty will bless Hashem.[105]

"Naftali will also be blessed with much wisdom, attained in the houses of study in the land of Teveriah.[106] They will take possession of Lake Kinneret and its southern shoreline, wide enough to spread out their fishing nets and retrieve them."[107]

Asher's Blessing

"Asher is blessed with sons like no one else," Moshe said.[108] "No tribe increased its population in the wilderness after the original census to the extent that Asher did.[109] It is said of the tribe of Asher that its householders are the elite of mighty men of valor, chiefs and princes. No other tribe is so broadly distinguished with such titles.[110]

"The tribe of Asher is blessed with wealth.[111] Their land flows with oil like a fountain, and if they chose to, they could bathe in oil. One day, the people of Ludkia will need 140,000 gallons of oil. They will send an emissary to the territory of Asher, and their entire requirement will be fulfilled.[112]

"All their land is pleasing to their brothers," Moshe continued.[113] "They too shall be pleasing to their brothers and be pleased by

---

105. *Chizkuni, Bechor Shor, Da'as Zekeinim* on ibid.

106. *Sifrei, Me'am Lo'ez* on ibid. The initials of the first three words of Naftali's blessing, *Naftali seva ratzon*, spell the word *nesher*, eagle, for this tribe is swift as an eagle in doing the will of Hashem (Tur).

107. Rashi with *Sifsei Chachamim*, ibid.; *Bava Kamma* 81b. While both Yaakov and Moshe praised the land of Naftali and its swift yielding of fruit, Yaakov also blessed this tribe with fleet-footedness and the benefits thereof.

108. *Sifrei*, Rashi on *Devarim* 33:24.

109. *Da'as Zekeinim*, ibid. See *Bamidbar* 1:41, 26:47 for census figures.

110. Ramban, ibid.; *I Divrei haYamim* 7:40.

111. *Divrei David, Devarim* 33:24.

112. *Sifrei*, Rashi on ibid.; *Menachos* 85b.

113. *Lekach Tov, Devarim* 33:24.

them. They will exchange oil for the produce of their brothers.[114] And the daughters of Asher are so appealing that their hands in marriage are sought by the Kohen Gadol and anointed kings."[115]

Moshe also took this opportunity to remove a ban placed on Asher during the days of Yaakov. Serach, the daughter of Asher, was the first to inform Yaakov that Yosef was still alive, but the brothers thought that she had acted prematurely and without proper planning. They accused Asher of betrayal for allowing the secret of Yosef's survival to be divulged, and therefore, they ostracized him. Now, so many years later, Moshe lifted the ban during his blessing to Asher.[116]

Asher's land was blessed with a good climate, which made it agriculturally rich.[117] There were also mineral riches in the form of iron and copper in the mountains that surrounded its territory.[118] The metals symbolized Hashem's protection of Asher's wealth.[119] The rich bounty of oil also assured that the people of Asher would be healthy, robust, strong-boned[120] and with good blood circulation, and would live long in good comfort.[121] The people of Asher would, therefore, guard the northern borders well, like a barrier of iron and copper.[122]

---

114. *Sifrei*, Rashi on ibid.

115. Ibid. See *Bereishis Rabbah* 71:10, which alludes to Asher's daughters' applying the abundant local oil to their skin, which kept them youthful and appealing. See also *Pesachim* 43a.

116. Tur, *Devarim* 33:24. See *Sukkah* 56b; Tosafos, *Bereishis* 45:26. See also *Let My Nation Descend*, p. 368. Alternatively, Asher was banned for divulging Reuven's sin (*Chizkuni; Me'am Lo'ez*).

117. *Minchah Belulah, Devarim* 33:25.

118. *Targum Yonasan, Minchah Belulah* on ibid.

119. Ramban, ibid.

120. These Jews were blessed with retaining their strength despite the hard labor of mining metal (*Midrash haGadol; Me'am Lo'ez*).

121. *Targum Yonasan, Sifrei*, Rashi, *Da'as Zekeinim*, Ramban on *Devarim* 33:25. See *Chullin* 24b.

122. *Sifrei*, Ramban on *Devarim* 33:25. Rashi writes that this blessing pertains

A Blessing to the People

"To the Jewish people as a whole," said Moshe, "I bless you[123] that as long as you adhere to Hashem's will, silver and gold will flow into your land; foreigners will pay gold and silver for its blessed fruits.[124] Hashem will help you succeed in physical, material and spiritual matters.[125]

"The heavens are the abode Hashem has chosen. Beneath Him dwell the mighty ones like Sichon and Og. Looking up at Him, they tremble and perspire in their vulnerability, their strength ebbing away in His presence. Hashem came to your assistance and helped you drive away your enemies.[126]

"There is none like Hashem among all the deities in the world. There is no rock like Hashem, Who straddles the heavens to assist you, Whose majesty extends over the clouds. He rules the heavens and the earth, the upper and lower spheres. He rules the constellations and all their pathways and all that lies beyond them. He protects you thoroughly.[127]

"You are dear to Hashem. He created the world on account of the Jewish people, and you are His abode.[128] Because He is with you,[129] each and every one of you will dwell securely by himself

---

to the entire Jewish people. The warriors of each tribe would live in the border towns, thereby "locking out" the nation's enemies.

Both Yaakov and Moshe blessed the land of Asher with abundant oil. Moshe further blessed this tribe with protecting the Jewish people and mining valuable metals from its mountains.

123. Ibn Ezra, *Devarim* 33:26.

124. *Sifrei*, Rashi on *Devarim* 33:25.

125. *Me'am Lo'ez*, *Devarim* 33:26.

126. *Targum Yonasan*, Rashi with Mizrachi on *Devarim* 33:27. These enemies include Amalek (*Chizkuni*) and Golias (*Me'am Lo'ez*).

127. See Rashi with *Sifsei Chachamim*, *Sefer Zikaron*, *Da'as Zekeinim*, Ralbag, *Me'am Lo'ez* on *Devarim* 33:26.

128. Abarbanel, *Devarim* 33:27; *Shemos Rabbah* 38:4.

129. Rashi with *Sifsei Chachamim*, *Devarim* 33:28.

when you cross the Jordan River and drive out the enemy.[130] Each of you shall live in tranquility under his vine and fig tree, even if you are remote from one other, for you will have no need to band together against attacks by enemies or wild animals.[131]

"As Yaakov blessed you when he said that Hashem would be with you and return you to the land of your fathers, your choice to live isolated and apart from the other nations will do you no harm. It will not resemble the forced isolation Yirmeyahu will endure when he foretells the destruction of the Beis haMikdash.[132] You will also benefit from Yitzchak's blessing, 'May Hashem grant you the dew of the heavens and the fat of the earth.'[133] You will have much grain and wine, and the heavens shall drip with dew. And finally, you will all share in each other's blessings to a certain degree, for all the blessings I have given to each individual tribe are also collectively for you all.

"My dear people, who among the peoples of the world are like you? Your salvation comes from Hashem, your strength from His being your shield and triumphant sword. It does not derive from your swords alone.[134]

"Your enemies will try to delude you into forming an alliance with them," continued Moshe, referring to the Giv'onim, "but they will become your slaves instead.[135] As long as you are at peace among yourselves, other nations will also seek stratagems

---

130. *Lekach Tov*, ibid.

131. Rashi, ibid. See Rashi, *Tehillim* 3:9; *Sanhedrin* 104a. This security is based strictly on the Jewish people's dwelling alone, apart from the non-Jewish nations. Should the Jews mingle and assimilate, Hashem will no longer protect them (*Me'am Lo'ez*).

132. *Sifrei*, Rashi on *Devarim* 33:28.

133. *Bereishis* 27:28. *Sifrei*, Rashi with *Sifsei Chachamim* on *Devarim* 33:28.

134. See *Sifrei*, Rashi, *Me'am Lo'ez* on *Devarim* 33:29.

135. *Sifrei*, Rashi on ibid.

to be in your good graces, for they will recognize how singularly fortunate you are.[136]

"You will be wildly successful. You will plant your feet on the necks of the mighty, and you will vanquish and destroy the kings of Canaan.[137] In fact, you will also be impervious to the power and control of angels and constellations. Only Hashem will have any effect on your standing in this world.[138]

"But aside from the delight you will enjoy in this world, Hashem will be your salvation in the next world. Who is like you, who merits in both this world and the next? You are indeed a fortunate nation!"[139]

As Moshe completed his words of blessing, the people anxiously scrutinized his face.

"Moshe, what will become of us if you leave us?" they said. "How will we survive without you?"

"Do not worry," Moshe replied. "All the miracles you witnessed were performed for your sake, not mine. Hashem's love and compassion for you has sustained you and protected you until now. Be faithful to Him, and He will take care of you."

The people heard these words with relief. "*Hashem Hu haElokim!*" they all cried out together. "Hashem is the Lord!"[140]

---

136. *Lekach Tov, Me'am Lo'ez* on ibid.

137. *Sifrei*, Rashi on ibid. See *Me'am Lo'ez, Yehoshua* 10:12–25.

138. *Minchah Belulah*, Ralbag on *Devarim* 33:29.

139. Rabbeinu Bachya, *Me'am Lo'ez* on ibid.

140. *Midrash Petiras Moshe*, cited in *Otzar Midrashim* 367.

Boundaries of the Twelve Tribes

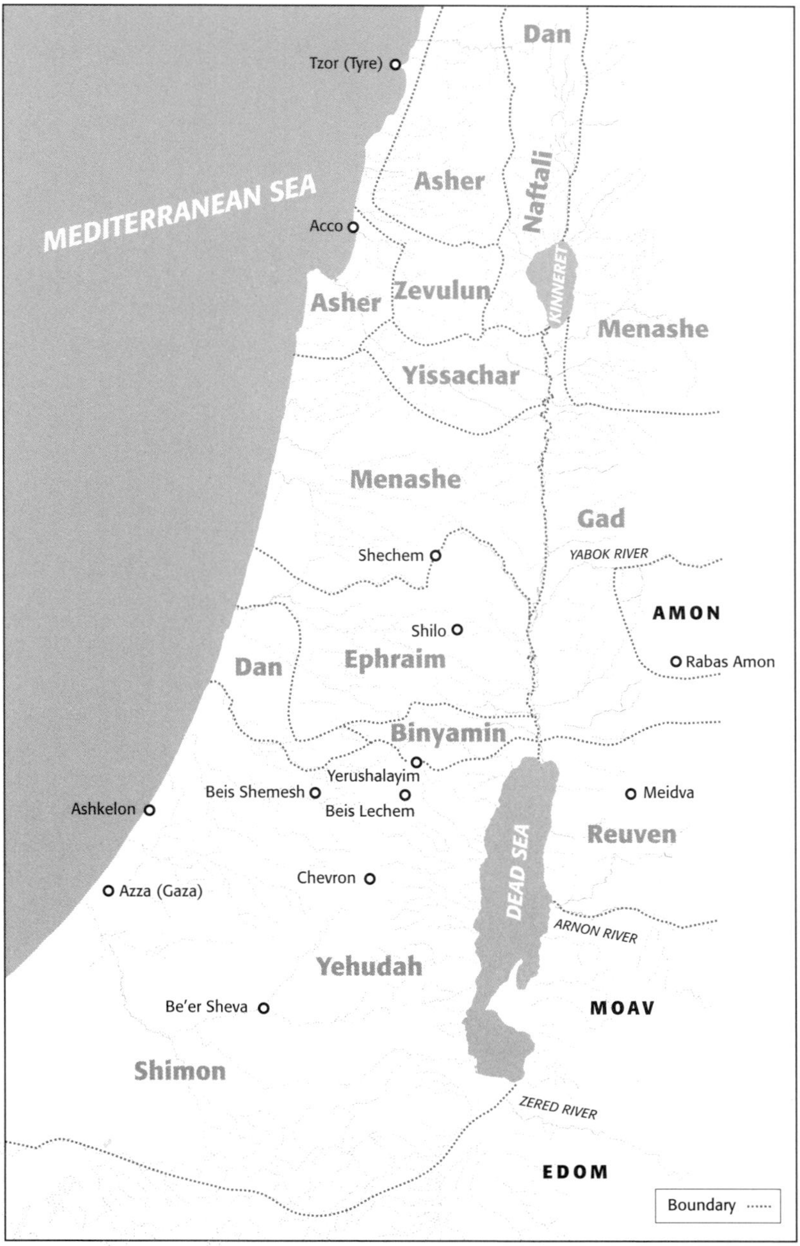

21 Struggles with Death

On the seventh day of the month of Adar, at the height of the day, with the Jewish people encamped near Mount Nevo in the land of Moav opposite the city of Yericho in Canaan across the Jordan River,[1] Moshe's life finally reached its conclusion.[2]

"Moshe, it is time," Hashem began. "You must prepare yourself for burial. But first, go up onto Mount Ha'avarim, because from there you will be able to see the Holy Land from afar. The land is dear to you, so I am giving you, in your last moments, the opportunity to see it with your own eyes.[3]

1. See *Devarim* 32:50; *Aderes Eliyahu*; Rashi, *Iyov* 2:9.
2. Ibn Ezra, *Devarim* 32:50.
3. Rashi with *Gur Aryeh*, *Devarim* 32:50, 52.

Afterward, you will die on this mountain by a divine kiss in the manner you found so desirable when you saw Aharon pass away. The light of the Shechinah will touch your body, and your soul will depart.[4]

"You will die here and not cross into the land, because you failed to sanctify My Name before the Jewish people at Mei Merivah.[5] Your death will atone for that sin.[6]

"You will go up onto the mountain in full view of all the people, and everyone will know you will not be coming back down. Should anyone make an attempt to prevent Me from carrying out My decree, it will not succeed. If they try to do so through prayers, I will immobilize their thoughts."[7]

Many people were indeed entertaining such thoughts. They could not accept that their beloved leader was about to pass away. He had taken them out of Egypt, he had erected the Mishkan, he had brought them quail and *mahn*, he had slaked their thirst with water from Miriam's Well, and he had taught them Torah. How could they allow him to leave them?

"Let us block his way so that he cannot ascend the mountain," they said to each other. "Let us pray with all our might that Hashem leave him with us."

But no one could thwart Hashem's will.[8] With one great leap, Moshe ascended the mountain,[9] which was twelve step-levels

---

4. *Mo'ed Katan* 28a; Rashi, *Sifrei* on *Devarim* 32:50; Rashi, *Devarim* 34:5.

5. See Rashi, *Devarim* 32:51–52.

6. Seforno, *Devarim* 32:50.

7. Rashi with *Be'er baSadeh*, *Sifrei* on *Devarim* 32:48.

8. Rashi, *Sifrei* on ibid. See *Targum Yonasan*, *Devarim* 32:50.

9. This was the last of Moshe's several ascents before he died. As noted earlier, he cherished the opportunity to see the Land of Israel and consequently frequented the mountain (Abarbanel, *Devarim* 32:50). From Moshe's longing for Eretz Yisrael, the Jews learned to appreciate the gift of entering it (*Derashos haRan* 9).

high[10]—demonstrating his still-youthful vigor—and prepared himself for his own burial.[11]

Moshe looked longingly at the Holy Land spread out before him in the distance. Hashem granted him the supernatural ability to see beyond the range of human vision.[12] With his powers of prophecy, he also saw all that would happen throughout the world. He saw the present and the future events, even the eventual resurrection of the dead. He saw the Holy Land in all its glory and also in all its suffering. He saw it in its tranquility and in its oppression and destruction.[13] He saw it inhabited by the twelve tribes and he saw the delineated portions in which they would reside.[14]

He looked toward the northern, western, eastern and southern portions of the land and saw its entire future. He saw the tribe of Ephraim participate in Yehoshua's victory over the Canaanites, and he saw the long Davidic royal dynasty of the tribe of Yehudah. He saw the tribe of Dan descend into idol worship and Shimshon, their judge-leader, emerge to save them. He saw Barak of Kedesh Naftali gain a glorious victory over Sisera.[15] He saw Me'aras haMachpeilah and the graves of the patriarchs. He saw Shlomo and the Beis haMikdash, and he saw the eventual battle of Gog and Magog.

Moshe's visions went beyond the terrestrial world, and he saw

---

10. *Sotah* 13b; Rashi, *Devarim* 34:1. Some say these twelve steps symbolize the twelve tribes, showing that Moshe was greater than the entire nation. Others write that each step represented ten years of Moshe's life. Additionally, with eleven stages of prophecy, Moshe jumped to twelve, surpassing all other prophets. In any event, Moshe leapt to great heights both physically and spiritually in his final moments on earth. See *Akeidas Yitzchak* 105; *Megaleh Amukos, Va'eschanan*.

11. Ibn Ezra, *Devarim* 32:50.

12. Rashi, *I Divrei haYamim* 25:5; *Midrash haCheifetz, Devarim* 34:1.

13. *Sifrei*, Rashi on *Devarim* 34:1–2.

14. *Midrash haGadol, Devarim* 34:1.

15. *Sifrei, Targum Yonasan*, Rashi on *Devarim* 34:1–2.

the gloom of Gehinnom and the splendor of Gan Eden.[16] The sight of Gehinnom frightened him, but Hashem assured him that he would never step foot there.[17]

"Thank you," said Moshe. "I have seen so much, and now I have one more request. I have asked You at other times to show me the secrets of how You manage the world, and You have denied my request. Perhaps I can see them now."

"I will grant this to you," said Hashem, "for your death is imminent. I will grant you what no one has ever attained and that no one will ever attain again."

Hashem granted Moshe the fiftieth level of wisdom, and at long last, he gained a full understanding of the world.[18]

"Moshe, now you have seen the land and its eventual settlement," said Hashem, "and you will soon meet the patriarchs in the next world. Tell them that the conditions of the exile have been fulfilled. Tell them I have kept My oath and that the Jewish people are indeed taking possession of the land. They will thank you for the knowledge and for all your efforts to bring their children, of whom you are one, to the Promised Land."[19]

Moshe's Soul Departs

Moshe purified himself in the manner of seraphic angels.[20] The angel Michael came to prepare his bier, the angel Gavriel spread a fine linen over it and the angel Zagzagel placed another around it. Michael and Gavriel then took

16. Ibid., *Devarim* 34:2–3.
17. *Bamidbar Rabbah* 23:5.
18. *Yalkut Shimoni* 966.
19. *Sifrei, Midrash haGadol,* Rashi, *Ohr haChaim* on *Devarim* 34:4; *Yalkut Shimoni* 965. Though the Jewish people hadn't yet entered the Promised Land, Hashem's oath had indeed been fulfilled, since the land of Sichon and Og was to some degree considered Eretz Yisrael and Moshe prophetically envisioned Eretz Yisrael already inhabited by Jews (Maharsha).
20. *Devarim Rabbah* 11:10.

their positions on opposite sides of the casket.

"Moshe, touch your eyelids, so that your eyes are closed," Hashem said.

Moshe did so.

"Place your hands on your chest."

He did.

"Place one foot over the other."

Again, he complied.[21]

"My daughter," Hashem called out to Moshe's soul, "I have placed you in the body of Moshe for 120 years. Now it is time for you to come back to Me. Come now, and don't delay."

"Master of the universe," responded the soul, "I know that You are the Lord of all spirits and souls. The souls of the living and the dead are in Your hands. You created me, formed me and inserted me into Moshe's body for 120 years. Is there a body as pure as Moshe's, a body that has never experienced a foul smell, a body that has never been touched by any kind of vermin? I don't want to leave."[22]

"Do not worry," said Hashem. "I will not place you into another person ever again. I will place you in the upper spheres under the Throne of Glory near the closest angels."

"The angels don't impress me," said the soul, "for when they descended to earth they became corrupted.[23] Moshe, on the other hand, parted from his wife from the time You began to reveal Yourself to him regularly. His holiness is even greater than that of the angels of Heaven. I want to remain in his holy body."[24]

At that moment, the light of the Shechinah touched Moshe's

---

21. Ibid.; *Tanchuma, Va'eschanan* 6; *Da'as Zekeinim, Devarim* 34:5.

22. Some say the soul worried that it would have to be reincarnated in another body in order to fulfill the mitzvos associated with Eretz Yisrael. Yet Moshe's desire to enter the Holy Land was equivalent to fulfillment of those mitzvos, so the soul was appeased (*Ya'aros Devash* 2:6). See *Arvei Nachal, Behar*.

23. See *Bereishis* 6:4; *Bereishis Rabbah* 26:7.

24. *Devarim Rabbah* 11:5, 10.

body. The soul experienced the overwhelming pleasure of the Divine Presence, a pleasure much greater than that of being in Moshe's body. Moshe had been given a divine kiss, and his soul willingly departed from his body.[25]

Even after Moshe's life expired, the brilliant radiance of his face was not diminished.[26] His body remained supple and full of moisture. His eyes were still sharp and glowing.[27] His entire body remained as fresh as if it were full of life, because he had used his body only for spiritual ends.[28]

Moshe, the servant of Hashem, passed away exactly at the age of 120 years. He was born on 7 Adar, and he passed away on 7 Adar in the year 2488 after creation. Hashem completes the years of the righteous, allowing them to live out their final year until the exact date on which they were born.[29]

---

25. *Tanchuma, Va'eschanan* 6; *Devarim Rabbah* 11:10 with *Tiferes Tzion*. Regarding the "kiss of death," see *Ohr haChaim, Vayikra* 16:1.

26. See *Chizkuni*, Rabbeinu Bachya, *Lekach Tov* on *Devarim* 34:7.

27. Rashi, *Ha'amek Davar* on ibid. See Ibn Ezra, *Shemos* 34:33.

28. *Me'am Lo'ez, Devarim* 34:7.

29. *Kiddushin* 38a; *Sotah* 12b, 13b; *Tanchuma, Va'eschanan* 6. Much commentary has been written regarding when exactly Moshe died and how old he was. The Gemara writes that Moshe died on Shabbos. (Rokeach, *Devarim* 34:4, notes that the second letters of the words *Moshe avdi meis*, "Moshe My servant died," spell the word Shabbos.) Chazal also tell us that he wrote thirteen Torah scrolls on his day of death. Yet how could he have written on Shabbos? And how could he himself have written that he died?

Furthermore, the Torah states that Moshe died at the age of 120. Yet if he was born and died on 7 Adar, he actually lived 120 years and a day. According to *Sifrei* 357, however, Moshe died in the Hebrew month of Nisan, and an opinion in *Yalkut Shimoni* places his death in Shevat. Additionally, if Moshe passed away during a leap year, in which of the two Adars did he die? The *mahn* continued for forty days after his death, until 16 Nisan. Therefore, he died in the second Adar.

For the purposes of this book, either Moshe's death continued into Shabbos, or he was buried on Shabbos, at Minchah time, when *Tziduk haDin* is addressed. Yosef and David were also laid to rest at Minchah time on Shabbos. In honor of these three righteous men, we say three verses of *Tzidkascha* at Minchah, representing *Tziduk haDin*. See Zohar, *Yisro* 88b; Tosafos, Maharsha on *Kiddushin* 38a;

Moshe Is Mourned

A heavenly voice called out to the entire encampment of the Jewish people, which measured twelve *mil* by twelve *mil*. "Moshe has died," the voice announced with sorrow.[30] "Who will now rise up against evildoers? Who will now rise up against the iniquitous? Who other than someone as humble as Moshe can lead a people and be heeded? Who like Moshe can lead a people away from sin? Who else can seek forgiveness when they transgress?[31] Never again will there arise from Yisrael a prophet like Moshe. Never again will the Shechinah rest upon a person as it rested on Moshe."

"A pious one has been lost to the world," said the heavens.

"And the one who was upright among men is no more," said the land. "There is no one who lived on this earth as humble as Moshe, whose prayers were answered in Heaven above."[32]

"He carried out Hashem's justice," said the angels.

"He carried out Hashem's laws with Yisrael," said the Jewish people.

"He who walks in his integrity will come in peace and to them who rest in their resting places," said the angels and the people together.[33]

"Who is so wise," said Hashem, "that he can mediate between Me and My children?[34] Where can one find such wisdom?"[35]

Tosafos, *Menachos* 30a; Rosh, *Pesachim* 10:13; *Bach, Mishnah Berurah, Orach Chaim* 292; *Shibolei haLeket, Shabbos* 126; Maharil 31, 231; *Chasam Sofer* 6:29; *Ya'aros Devash* 2:11; *Sefas Emes, Rosh Hashanah* 11a; *Seder HaDoros* 368; *Yalkut Shimoni, Beshalach* 16, *Yehoshua* 15; *Me'am Lo'ez, Devarim* 34:5. See also *Yerushalmi Rosh Hashanah* 3:8 (*Let My Nation Serve Me*, p. 79).

30. *Sifrei, Devarim* 34:5.

31. *Tehillim* 94:16.

32. *Michah* 7:2; *Devarim Rabbah* 11:10; *Sotah* 13b; *Me'am Lo'ez, Devarim* 34:5.

33. *Yeshayahu* 57:2.

34. *Koheles* 8:1.

35. *Devarim Rabbah* 11:10; *Sotah* 13b with Rashi; *Da'as Zekeinim, Devarim* 34:5.

A heavenly voice could be heard to say, "Moshe, who wrote the thirteen *sifrei Torah*, has passed away."[36]

Yehoshua had been searching for Moshe and couldn't find him. When he heard that his master had passed away, he wept. "Help me, Hashem," he said, "for the devout one is no more."[37]

Yehoshua would continue to cry and mourn for days until Hashem would tell him to stop.[38]

Among the people, the men mourned the passing of Moshe with a special intensity. Of course, the women mourned as well, but they were not personally stricken by his passing to the extent that the men were. When Aharon passed away, however, the intensity of the mourning was equal among the men and the women. Aharon had always pursued peace, and had often entered the homes of the people to mediate disputes between husbands and wives. Thus, all the people saw his passing as a personal loss. But Moshe ruled with an iron hand, teaching the laws of the Torah without compromise or concession, and therefore the men who learned from him directly felt a greater personal loss than did the women.[39]

Moshe's Burial

No one attended Moshe's funeral: not the Jewish people, not the angels; only Hashem.[40] In this way, his body and soul remained attached and connected to the sanctity of the Shechinah.[41]

Moshe's burial east of the Jordan River would bring merit to the generation of the wilderness that died here. They would be

36. *Sotah* 13b with Maharsha.

37. *Tehillim* 12:2.

38. *Yalkut Shimoni* 940; *Da'as Zekeinim, Devarim* 34:5.

39. See Rashi, *Devarim* 34:8; *Sanhedrin* 6b with Tosafos; *Pirkei d'Rabbi Eliezer* 17; *Avos d'Rabbi Nasan* 12 with *Binyan Yehoshua*. See also *Shemos Rabbah* 5:10.

40. *Tanchuma, Va'eschanan* 6; *Sotah* 13b.

41. *Minchah Belulah, Devarim* 34:6.

worthy of resurrection, and Moshe would personally escort them into the Holy Land.[42]

Moshe was buried in the land of Moav in a place called Beis Pe'or—close to where the sin of Pe'or had occurred. His burial place had already been prepared during the final twilight of the six days of Creation. His interment near a place of sin would serve as atonement for the transgression of the Jewish people who worshiped the idol of Pe'or under the influence of the Moabite women.[43]

Moav, the place of Moshe's death, was in the territory of Reuven, but he wasn't buried there. Hashem transported his body a distance of about three miles to the site in the portion of Gad where he would be buried.[44] Reuven was the symbol of repentance, and the knowledge that Moshe had died in his portion reminded the people that, with Moshe gone, their only protection was through righteousness and repentance.[45]

The details of Moshe's death and burial remain mysterious to a large extent. In fact, according to one opinion, Moshe attended to his own burial, entering the subterranean chamber that would house his remains at the exact moment of his death.[46] The Gemara also cites an opinion that Moshe, like Yaakov, didn't actually die. As he served Hashem in his lifetime, he continues to serve

---

42. *Tzeror haMor, Devarim* 32:49. Had Moshe been buried in Eretz Yisrael, the Beis haMikdash would not have been destroyed. Yehoshua knew that, so he mourned Moshe's passing all the more (*Me'am Lo'ez, Devarim* 34:5).

43. *Sotah* 14a; *Tzeror haMor, Devarim* 32:49; Rashi, *Devarim* 34:6. See *Avos* 5:6. For this reason too (in addition to the one cited in the previous note), Moshe couldn't be buried in Eretz Yisrael.

44. *Sotah* 13b. See *Yalkut Reuveni* regarding Gavriel's role in Moshe's burial.

A tunnel or cave connected Moshe's grave to the tomb of the patriarchs (*Sifrei, Devarim* 34:5). In this sense, Moshe too was buried along with them in Me'aras haMachpeilah (*Yalkut Reuveni*).

45. Maharsha, *Sotah* 13b.

46. See *Bamidbar Rabbah* 10:17; Rashi, Ibn Ezra, Rabbeinu Nissim on *Devarim* 34:6. According to *Me'am Lo'ez, Devarim* 34:7, Tziporah was buried with Moshe.

Hashem to this day. Some take this to mean that Moshe and the Torah he gave from Sinai live on forever.[47]

Despite the common knowledge that he was buried in the land of Moav in the valley at Beis Pe'or, Moshe's actual grave would never be found.[48] Hashem didn't want the Jewish people to pray at Moshe's grave to get his assistance in abolishing the decree of the destruction of the Beis haMikdash. Hashem wanted the Jewish people to rather exert themselves to harness the power of His Thirteen Attributes to uproot His decrees.[49]

Moreover, Hashem did not want Moshe's burial place to become a place of religious adulation and ultimately a form of idol worship. The Egyptians had contemplated deifying Yaakov had his remains been buried in Egypt. Others might deify Moshe if the place of his burial was known.[50]

Centuries later, Roman emperors would ask the governors of the district of Pe'or to be shown the location of Moshe's grave. They would be taken high atop the mountain, where a mirage of Moshe's grave was visible below. When attempting to descend to the grave, however, that same mirage would move to the top of the mountain. Frustrated, the search party would separate into two groups, one going down and one going up. But this was also futile, for the searchers on the top imagined that they saw the grave below and those below imagined that they saw it above them.[51]

Why did the Romans want to know the location of Moshe's grave? Their motives were not pure. Pe'or was well known for

---

47. See *Sotah* 13b with *Iyun Yaakov, Nachalas Yaakov;* Zohar, *Terumah* 174a; *Me'am Lo'ez, Devarim* 34:5. Compare *Ohr haChaim*. See also *Bereishis Rabbah* 96; Rambam's introduction to his commentary on Mishnah.

48. *Sotah* 14a; *Tzeror haMor, Devarim* 34:5–6. Moshe himself didn't know where he would be buried. Maharsha explains that because Moshe was entirely spiritual, no earthly burial ground can be designated as his "resting place."

49. See *Sotah* 14a with *Ben Yehoyada; Yismach Moshe, VeZos haBerachah* 153.

50. See Abarbanel, *Devarim* 34:6.

51. *Sotah* 14a with *Ben Yehoyada; Sifrei, Devarim* 34:6.

its illicit pleasures, and some of the Romans wanted to experience them while being protected by Moshe's spiritual presence.[52] Others wanted to post guards all around the gravesite to prevent the Jewish people from praying there for protection against the Romans.[53]

Others contend that Moshe's burial place remains unknown as a punishment of sorts for his failure to kill Zimri at Shittim and then forgetting the law on how to treat the matter of Pe'or. As a result, his unmarked burial site at Pe'or would atone for his transgression.[54]

---

52. *Sotah* 14a with *Iyun Yaakov*.
53. *Sotah* 14a with *Ben Yehoyada*.
54. *Bamidbar Rabbah* 20:24.

22

Moshe's Legacy

Until the very end, Moshe had been Hashem's loyal and devoted servant, privileged to enter the innermost sanctums of Heaven. The Torah acknowledges this status by referring to him as "Moshe, the servant of Hashem."[1] He had no desires or motivation other than to fulfill the will of Hashem and the welfare of His people.[2] Through his efforts, he endowed the Jewish people with four crowns — the crown of Torah, the crown of *kehunah*, the crown of royalty and the crown of a good name — the last one surpassing all the others.[3] And even during the last moments of his life, he sought to bless the Jewish people.[4]

---

1. See *Minchah Belulah*, Rabbeinu Bachya, Gra on *Devarim* 34:5. Avraham and David also received this title.
2. See Radak, *Yehoshua* 1:1. See also *Kovetz Ma'amarim*, p. 48.
3. *Targum Yonasan, Devarim* 34:5.
4. *Tzeror haMor, Devarim* 33:1.

"I am greater than you," Adam could conceivably say, "because I was created in the image of Hashem by His own hands."

But Moshe could respond, "Perhaps, but you fell from your stature when you ate from forbidden fruit. I, however, kept the radiance of Hashem's glory even in the last moments of my life.[5] While the serpent brought you death in your lifetime, I used the serpent to bring life to people in the wilderness."

"I am greater than you," Noach could conceivably say, "because I survived the Mabul."

But Moshe could respond, "Perhaps, but while you saved yourself from the flood, you couldn't save the rest of your generation. I, however, saved not only myself but my entire generation from annihilation after they worshiped the Eigel. And while Hashem enjoyed your sacrifice, He did not demand that you bring more. In my days, Hashem commanded us to bring two sacrifices daily.

"I am greater than you," Avraham could conceivably say, "because I sustained and fed travelers and taught them to bless Hashem."

But Moshe could respond, "Perhaps, but you sustained uncircumcised people both in the wilderness and in inhabited areas. I, however, sustained the circumcised Jewish people only in a wilderness—a far more difficult task. Moreover, when you questioned the inheritance of the land, you brought about the exile to Egypt.[6] I, however, redeemed the people from Egypt."

"I am greater than you," Yitzchak could conceivably say, "because I extended my neck at the Akeidah and saw an image of the Shechinah."

But Moshe could respond, "Perhaps, but your vision was dimmed toward the end of your life. I, however, saw the Shechinah face-to-face and never lost the fullness of my eyesight."

"I am greater than you," Yaakov could conceivably say, "because

---

5. *Devarim* 34:7.
6. See Ramban, *Bereishis* 15:8; *Nedarim* 32a.

I fought with ministering angels and prevailed."

But Moshe could respond, "You fought them on this earth, in your own surroundings, and you were slightly injured. I, however, fought them at the time of the giving of the Torah in Heaven, in their surroundings, and prevailed without injury."

"I am greater than you," Yosef could conceivably say, "because I overcame the temptation of my master's wife."

But Moshe could respond, "Perhaps, but I separated from my permissible wife for forty years."[7]

Moshe was greater than all of Creation.

On the first day, light was created, and yet Moshe was able to capture the light emanating from the Torah.

On the second day, the heavens were created, and yet, while the heavens can never descend to the earth, Moshe was able to ascend from the earth to the heavens.

On the third day, the waters were created and fixed in their designated place, and yet Moshe was able to overpower the waters and split the sea.

On the fourth day, the heavenly bodies of illumination were created, and yet, through Moshe's merit, the clouds of glory brought illumination to the Jewish people in the wilderness without the benefit of the sun and moon.

On the fifth day, animals were created, and in Moshe's time, animals were allowed to be eaten.

On the sixth day, humankind was created, and Moshe, the ultimate human being, was comparable to all the Jewish people combined.[8]

Once a human infant adrift in Egyptian waters, Moshe became a man of Hashem and turned those very waters into blood. Once

---

7. *Devarim Rabbah* 11:3; *Midrash Petiras Moshe*, cited in *Otzar Midrashim* 362, 383.

8. *Midrash Petiras Moshe*, cited in *Otzar Midrashim* 384. Regarding this comparison, see Rashi, *Shemos* 18:1; *Da'as Zekeinim, Bamidbar* 7:13; *Devarim Rabbah* 11:10; *Tanchuma, Beshalach* 10.

a human fugitive running from Pharaoh, he became a man of Hashem and drowned that very Pharaoh. He went up to Heaven as a man and came down as a man of Hashem, someone whose face was so radiant it could not be viewed. In a sense, Moshe was both angel and man, because he was able to dwell in this world and ascend to Heaven as well.[9]

There had never been a prophet as great as Moshe nor would there ever be another like him. Only Bilam, among the foreign nations, would rival Moshe is some aspects of prophecy, but even he was no match for Moshe. And after the incident at Shittim, Moshe prayed that the foreign nations would never again have another man even remotely capable of prophecy.[10]

The Jewish people, however, would have many more prophets, yet not one of them could rival Moshe in the quality or the sheer volume of his prophecy. Moshe never had to pray for a revelation or wait to receive one. He spoke with Hashem in the familiar manner of friends who speak to each other whenever they so choose. The clarity of his prophecy was also far superior to that of any prophet before or after him. He spoke with Hashem face-to-face, so to speak—a relationship beyond all levels of prophecy. No one could even begin to comprehend what Moshe comprehended.

Moshe is known as the father of all prophets. Because of the singular nature of his prophecy, his would always be the final word regarding what Hashem wants from the Jewish people. The revelation at Mount Sinai, with all those assembled hearing Hashem speak to Moshe, authenticated him and his prophecies for all eternity. Sinai alone gave him his credibility with the people and mitigated his having to prove himself as a prophet via the miracles he performed. All future prophecies would be extensions of Moshe's prophecy, and all future prophets would have to prove that they were indeed prophets.

---

9. *Devarim Rabbah* 11:4. See *HaKesav vehaKabbalah, Devarim* 33:1.

10. See *Lekach Tov*, Abarbanel on *Devarim* 34:10. See also Rashi, *Shemos* 33:16.

Moshe was also in a class by himself regarding his powers and the wonders and miracles he performed. From the miracles in Egypt to the splitting of the sea, from the *mahn* to the Well of Miriam, from the miraculous wonders in the time of Korach to the victorious wars, no one could ever surpass Moshe's achievements. Until his last day, capable of writing thirteen *sifrei Torah*, teaching the song and blessing the Jewish people collectively, Moshe didn't lose one drop of his endurance or resiliency. Others, such as the prophets Eliyahu and Elisha, performed miracles, but they were isolated incidents in secluded environments. Moshe, however, stood alone in terms of the duration of his miracles, their magnitude and their frequency. No one could rival him or ever will.[11]

After Moshe's Death

The Jewish people cried and mourned for thirty days, until 7 Nisan, as is the custom for the death of a Talmudic scholar.[12]

Moshe's death was an irreplaceable loss. For one, everyone who had previously merited *ruach hakodesh* suddenly lost it when Moshe died,[13] because divine inspiration requires a joyous state of mind. Even Yehoshua lost his prophetic spirit during this time, as he became despondent, his heart turning to stone.[14]

---

11. See Zohar, *Vayishlach* 170b; Rambam, *Yesodei haTorah*, chs. 7:6 and 8, and *Moreh Nevuchim* 2:35; *Sifrei*, *Chizkuni*, Rav Saadiah Gaon, Rashi, Ramban, Rabbeinu Bachya, *Tosefos Rabbeinu Nissim*, *Minchah Belulah*, Rabbi Samson Raphael Hirsch on *Devarim* 34:10–12. See also Ibn Ezra, *Devarim* 5:3; Rabbeinu Bachya, *Vayikra* 1:1; *Shemos Rabbah* 2:6, 21:2. And see *Let My Nation Wander*, p. 126 ff.

Shemuel and Moshe are considered equal (see *Tehillim* 99:6; *Berachos* 31b), but only in greatness and leadership, not in prophecy (*Minchah Belulah*). Certain outstanding people, such as Hillel, were worthy of Moshe's level (*Rosh Hashanah* 21b; *Sanhedrin* 11a), but only in specific attributes. No one ever rivaled Moshe in totality (*Me'am Lo'ez*, *Devarim* 34:10).

12. See Rambam, *Eivel* 13:10.

13. *Devarim Rabbah* 11:10 with *Tiferes Tzion*.

14. *Tzeror haMor*, *Devarim* 34:8.

But after thirty days, Hashem spoke to Yehoshua.

"How long will you go on mourning?" He said. "Do you think only you lost Moshe? I also lost Moshe. Let it be a consolation to you to know that he is destined for eternal life in the next world."[15]

On the morning of 7 Nisan, Hashem informed Yehoshua that it was time to cross the Jordan River and enter the Holy Land. For the Jewish people, the transition from Moshe to Yehoshua was difficult. As great as Yehoshua was, he was not Moshe, but the people knew that he brought continuity as Moshe's disciple. He was not the greatest scholar of the generation. Others, such as Osniel ben Kenaz, were greater.[16] But Yehoshua was Hashem's messenger, and therefore, he commanded the respect and complete obedience of the people.

Yehoshua now commanded that the period of mourning come to an end and everyone prepare for the final journey into the Holy Land. The people followed his lead, and preparation immediately began.[17]

An era had come to an end. No longer would the Jewish people be escorted by the cloud of glory. No longer would they drink water from a miraculous well or eat *mahn* that fell from Heaven.[18] But in the merit of Yehoshua, the *mahn* continued for two more weeks after the period of mourning so that the people would have food as they began the invasion, until they brought the *omer*-offering on 16 Nisan. Nonetheless, the residual *mahn* did

---

15. *Yalkut Shimoni* 940; *Da'as Zekeinim, Devarim* 34:5.

16. See *Temurah* 16a.

17. *Tzeror haMor, Bechor Shor*, Abarbanel, *Me'am Lo'ez* on *Devarim* 34:9, *Yehoshua* 1. Outwardly the people complied, but internally that generation never ceased to mourn their great loss (Abarbanel; *HaKesav vehaKabbalah*).

18. *Kiddushin* 38a; *Midrash haGadol, Devarim* 33:8. According to Rosh, *Devarim* 32:13, Hashem stopped the *mahn* in order to motivate the Jews to conquer Eretz Yisrael and reap its produce. See *Me'am Lo'ez, Yehoshua* 5:11–12.

not provide its original wide range of tastes.[19]

On this very day—7 Nisan—Yehoshua sent scouts into the land for three days to gather information on Yericho, the first objective of the invasion. On 10 Nisan, the Jordan River miraculously split for the Jewish people, and they crossed into Eretz Yisrael.[20]

The Completion of the Torah

The Book of Devarim completes the first third of the Written Torah, known as the Chumash—the Five Books of Moses. It is followed by *Nach,* an acronym for *"Nevi'im* and *Kesuvim"*—Prophets and Writings.[21]

The last word of the Torah is *Yisrael,* which begins with a *yud,* the smallest letter of the Hebrew alphabet, and ends with a *lamed,* its tallest letter. This teaches us that the great should associate with the small. No one among the Jewish people is so great that he can ignore those of lesser greatness.[22] The first letter of the Torah is the *beis* of *bereishis.* Together with the Torah's final letter, the *lamed,* it spells the word *lev,* heart. This teaches us that one who puts his entire heart into his Torah study, and whose heart is full of faith in Hashem, will merit miracles that will sustain him, such as those performed by Moshe.

The Torah ends by lauding Moshe's greatness. According to Rashi's commentary, the last verse reminds us that Hashem thanked Moshe for breaking the Luchos. The breaking of the Luchos inspired the Jewish people to repent over the Eigel, giving them a fresh start toward acceptance of the Torah. It taught the Jewish people the power and efficacy of repentance. In fact, none of creation would have come into existence if there had not been the possibility of repentance.

---

19. *Kiddushin* 38a with *Iyun Yaakov; Midrash haGadol, Bereishis* 6.
20. *Meshech Chochmah, Shemos* 16:10; *Me'am Lo'ez, Yehoshua* 3.
21. See *Me'am Lo'ez, Devarim* 34:12; *Menachos* 30a with commentaries.
22. *Me'am Lo'ez, Devarim* 34:12.

The Torah begins with Hashem's creation of the heavens and the earth, and it concludes by mentioning the miracles Moshe performed. This is to remind the Jewish people that all those miracles derived from Hashem, the Creator of the universe, and that everyone is worthy of miracles if he has faith in Hashem's ability to perform them.

The first word of the Torah is *bereishis*, and the last word is *Yisrael*. This tells us that Hashem created the world for the sake of Yisrael, the holy Jewish people, the first of His produce. The Jewish people are worthy of Hashem's miracles even today, just as they had been in the days of Moshe. If the Jewish people have faith in Hashem, they will merit the *beis* from the word *bereishis*, which alludes to the word *berachah*, blessing.

Furthermore, the first and last words of the Torah also tell us that the world was created for the sake of Torah and for the sake of the Jewish people, who will accept the Torah. Otherwise, there is no basis for the world's existence. The survival of the Jewish people, therefore—and indeed, of the entire world—depends on the Jewish people studying Torah, living by its laws and guidelines, and having unshakable faith in Hashem. This is the message of the broken Luchos, and the Torah concludes with it as well: Without Torah, there is nothing.[23]

23. See *Me'am Lo'ez, Devarim* 34:12; *Avodah Zarah* 3a; Rabbi Yehudah heChasid, *Devarim* 34:12. See also *Yirmeyahu* 2:3.

AFTERWORD

A Proper Perspective

(Based on a discourse given by
Rabbi Avigdor Miller *zt"l*)

The story of the generation of the wilderness cannot justifiably be concluded without discussing the overall scope of this forty-year journey. From tragedy to eventual triumph, this generation experienced a multitude of events, some of which reflected and were the result of their sins but most of which testified to their righteousness.

There is a dispute in the Mishnah (see *Sanhedrin* 108a) whether the generation of the Midbar, the wilderness, will receive a portion in the World to Come. Irrespective of this dispute, it must be made clear that a majority of these people were among the most righteous the world has ever known. While there were six hundred thousand males between the ages of 20 and 60, the Jewish nation's total population was in the millions.

Despite these numbers, the Torah documents only two instances in forty years where Shabbos was desecrated. The first one involved one individual — the wood gatherer — and the second involved the men who followed Dasan and Aviram's guidance. One has to consider how great a feat of righteousness this was: millions of Jews celebrating over two thousand Sabbaths and festivals, and yet only twice was there a desecration. An amazing feat indeed!

Added to this were some legitimate complaints and rare instances of rebellion that could easily be justified. Who wouldn't complain if he didn't have water for three days? Out of millions of Jews, is it inconceivable that a few would complain if all they had to eat was an oil-and-honey-flavored, wafer-like substance for forty years? When we look at the big picture, these rebellions were quite mild compared with events in subsequent generations: heresy, conversion and idol worship, to name a few. No generation in the history of the Jewish people can compare to the holy generation of the Midbar. This indeed must be the lasting lesson of this book.